A SHEARWATER BOOK

# One *with* Nineveh

Paul R. Ehrlich
and Anne H. Ehrlich

# One
*with*
# Nineveh

*Politics, Consumption, and the Human Future*

ISLANDPRESS / SHEARWATER BOOKS

*Washington · Covelo · London*

A *Shearwater Book*
*Published by Island Press*

Copyright © 2004, 2005 Paul R. Ehrlich and Anne H. Ehrlich

First Island Press cloth edition, March 2004
First Island Press paperback edition, August 2005

SHEARWATER BOOKS is a trademark of The Center for Resource Economics.

*Library of Congress Cataloging-in-Publication data.*
Ehrlich, Paul R.
One with Nineveh : politics, consumption, and the human future /
Paul R. Ehrlich and Anne H. Ehrlich.
p. cm.
Includes bibliographical references and index.
ISBN 1-59726-031-2 (pbk: alk. paper)
1. Sustainable development.  2. Consumption (Economics)
3. Overpopulation.  4. Social justice.  I. Ehrlich, Anne H.  II. Title
HC79.E5E354  2004
338.9′27—dc22      2003024789

*British Cataloguing-in-Publication data available.*

Printed on recycled, acid-free paper ⊛

Design by David Bullen

Manufactured in the United States of America

10  9  8  7  6  5  4  3  2  1

For Luke, Carmen, Lena, Travis, Lucy, Anton, Jack, Sophie, Anna, Matthew, Tor, Kalea, Henry, and their generation—in the hope the big black coal will be on its way out when they can read this.

And to the late Loy Bilderback, friend and intellectual companion to us for half a century.

# Contents

God of our fathers, known of old—
Lord of our far-flung battle-line—
Beneath whose awful Hand we hold
Dominion over palm and pine—
Lord God of Hosts, be with us yet,
Lest we forget, lest we forget!

The tumult and the shouting dies—
The captains and the kings depart—
Still stands Thine ancient sacrifice,
An humble and a contrite heart.
Lord God of Hosts, be with us yet,
Lest we forget, lest we forget!

Far-call'd our navies melt away—
On dune and headland sinks the fire—
Lo, all our pomp of yesterday
Is one with Nineveh and Tyre!
Judge of the Nations, spare us yet,
Lest we forget, lest we forget!

RUDYARD KIPLING, "Recessional," 1897

# Preface to the Paperback Edition

It's been an eventful year plus since *One with Nineveh* was first published, and we think the issues that concerned us while we were writing it have been all too dramatically illuminated by recent events. What frightens us is that we detect a sea change in cultural evolution, especially in attitudes and the political atmosphere in the United States. There is no reason to alter the book's basic themes in this paperback edition, but there are plenty of reasons to add an afterword, bringing the world situation up to date and probing this sea change and its implications. Humanity's peril has deepened at a rate even we did not expect, and the need for action has accordingly escalated. There are some bright spots, however, and everything possible must be done to expand them.

We are grateful to Gretchen Daily, Lisa and Tim Daniel, John Holdren, Sally Mallam, Bob Ornstein, Terry Root, and Steve Schneider for their constructive comments on the afterword. We are sad to report that our good friend and colleague Loy Bilderback, one of those to whom we dedicated *One with Nineveh,* passed away last summer. He was discussing these issues with us until the very end. Loy would have been tough on our ideas and exposition as usual, and he is sadly missed.

*Stanford, California*
*15 June 2005*

# One
## *with*
# Nineveh

# Introduction

## HOSTAGES TO HUBRIS

"Lo, all our pomp of yesterday
Is one with Nineveh and Tyre!"
RUDYARD KIPLING, "Recessional," 1897[1]

The great capital city of the Assyrian Empire was Nineveh, located on the Tigris River in ancient Mesopotamia. At the height of its glory, more than six centuries before the birth of Christ, it was surrounded by rich irrigated farmlands, covered some nine square miles,[2] and had an estimated population of 120,000 people, an enormous concentration for the time.[3] Nineveh was a city of huge palaces and temples and gorgeous sculpture.[4] It is thought by some experts to have been the actual site of the combination of fancy gardens and waterworks known as the Hanging Gardens of Babylon,[5] one of the so-called Seven Wonders of the Ancient World.

When pioneering British archaeologist Austen Henry Layard discovered the remains of Nineveh and its fantastic ancient palaces in the 1840s, he found a landscape dramatically different. Of the Mesopotamian environment in which the ruins lay, he wrote, "Desolation meets desolation; a feeling of awe succeeds to wonder; for there is nothing to relieve the mind; to lead to hope, or to tell of what has gone by."[6] The fabled biblical cities such as Nineveh and Babylon were represented by mere dirt mounds in the desert, and the human population of the area was a small fraction of what archaeologists believe was supported in ancient Mesopotamia's heyday.

For millennia before Nineveh became the Assyrian capital, Gardens of Eden created by irrigation had dotted the Mesopotamian desert, which was the first region of the world to become urbanized, some 6,000 years ago.[7] Hilly areas adjacent to that desert five millennia earlier were among the first places where human beings invented farming,[8] which ultimately made possible the rise of cities. Civilizations in Mesopotamia, as elsewhere, came and went over the centuries. The once thriving Sumerian civilization in the southern area between the Tigris and Euphrates rivers (*Mesopotamia* means "between the rivers") disappeared almost 4,000 years ago.[9] The more northerly Mesopotamian civilizations that replaced the Sumerians gradually repeated their fate and passed out of history. The Assyrian Empire crumbled when Nineveh itself was sacked in 612 BC by the Chaldaeans under King Nabopolassar, the father of Nebuchadnezzar.[10]

What caused the thriving Edens of Mesopotamia eventually to be replaced by the barren landscape that Layard found? Successive sweeps of conquering armies certainly played a role, but archaeologists have discovered that the Assyrians and their successors were slowly weakened, up through the fifth and sixth centuries AD, by a decline in their natural resource base. One underlying cause of the gradual deterioration of the entire region was deforestation in the hills and mountains, the source of the area's water supply.[11] Another was environmentally unsustainable irrigation. Indeed, cuneiform tablets from more than 4,000 years ago, before the time of the Assyrian Empire, tell us that irrigation was already causing salts to build up in the soil, and the Mesopotamians lacked the artificial drainage technology that could counter that process. Growers switched from wheat to more salt-tolerant barley, and the area in which any crops could be cultivated was steadily reduced. Those processes weakened the cities and made them more vulnerable to capture. They fell victim to a series of invaders,[12] culminating in the Middle Ages with the Mongols.[13]

During the long decline,[14] strife made it difficult to maintain the irrigation canals, which filled with silt. Salinization, soil degradation, and desertification gradually turned a land that once produced abundant food and supported numerous rich cities with an artistic culture[15] into the sweltering, dusty desert the Europeans found in the early nineteenth century. As Jared Diamond recently put it, the region committed "ecological suicide."[16] Even today, food must be imported to feed the region's population.[17]

"Recessional," Rudyard Kipling's famous 1897 poem that refers to Nineveh's fall, is a cautionary tale about pride and arrogance, itself written during the high tide of the British Empire.[18] Early civilizations, not just in Mesopotamia and Egypt but also elsewhere in the Middle East, Mesoamerica, and East Asia, were notoriously hierarchical, ruled over by people with enormous presumption. This is attested by the abundant remains of pyramids and palaces created by the labor of thousands over decades for the use of a tiny elite. So it certainly would not be surprising if those in the upper crust of Mesopotamian societies were focused on maintaining their social positions, fighting their frequent wars of conquest and defense, and pursuing other immediate concerns, but paying little attention to the gradual environmental decay that was undermining the foundations of their civilization. The Assyrians were aggressively expanding their territory in the three centuries before Nineveh fell, creating one of the first empires anywhere with a truly imperial administration in which local governors and garrisons were employed to control subject territories.[19]

The highly professional army of Assyria, with armored cavalry, well-drilled infantry, war chariots, and giant siege engines, was much feared and produced a flow of spoils to enrich Nineveh's ruling classes.[20] As bas-reliefs and royal annals record, Assyrian kings as a matter of state policy used terror in dealing with powerful foes. Sargon II put down an insurrection in the Northern Kingdom of Israel; sacked Samaria, its capital; and bragged of deporting 27,280 of its citizens, as well as "their chariots and gods, in which they had trusted."[21] One of Assyria's last monarchs, Ashurbanipal, who ruled from 668 BC to 627 BC, wrote as follows about his treatment of a conquered people: "I destroyed them, tore down the walls and burned the towns with fire; I caught the survivors and impaled them on stakes in front of their towns."[22] The

Assyrian Empire for a time was enormously successful, spurred trade in the area, amassed substantial wealth, and spread the hegemony of its sun god, Ashur. But even in the relatively slow-paced past, the fully developed Assyrian Empire lasted only a little more than a century, from 744 BC to 612 BC.

The Greek word *hubris* best describes the kind of overweening pride, arrogance, and presumption memorialized in those Assyrian royal annals and the extensive bas-reliefs of Nineveh (nearly two miles of them in one palace). Of course, displays of hubris are not confined to ancient times, or to the region between the Tigris and the Euphrates, or even to the glory days of the British Empire. In our time, notions of the United States' inevitable hegemony, its moral correctness, and its nation-building ability, along with its urge to spread the religion of unconstrained capitalism, seem demonstrations of hubris to rival those of Nineveh's ancient kings. In this context, the region of Nineveh is now very much in the news: the ruins of the Assyrian capital lie in the suburbs of the Iraqi city of Mosul, and the site of ancient Babylon is about fifty miles south of today's Baghdad.

If the military attacks on Iraq and their sorry aftermath have been the stuff of extensive media coverage, what *hasn't* been in the headlines is attention to the modern worldwide version of salinization of fields and siltation of irrigation canals. The evening news and morning headlines have virtually ignored the increasing strain on humanity's life-support systems—the physical and biological systems that make an area habitable—let alone its causes, its increasingly important role in world politics, and its consequences for the future of human well-being. More specifically in the case of Iraq, the relationship between the United States' invasion of the oil-rich Mesopotamian region and the environmentally destructive dependence of Western societies on fossil fuels as their primary energy source is almost never explored.

No one knows whether the leaders of early Mesopotamian empires even realized the long-term threat they faced. For them, ignorance may have played as great a role as hubris. Unlike us, they had no historical precedents to alert them, and the ecological decline of their region stretched over millennia. In contrast to the situation in Mesopotamia, the warning symptoms for us have appeared over a few decades, suddenly enough to attract some attention and to be analyzed by specialists. And they are not concentrated in a particular geographic area but trace to humanity's domination of the entire planet and the clash between our ways of life and Earth's ability to support those lifestyles. The dire environmental dangers our civilization faces are certainly no secret, even if they are more ignored than acknowledged in the halls of government and offices of the mass media. For decades, environmental scientists have warned of interconnected environmental trends, such as losses of plant and animal diversity, rapid climate change, and the spread of toxic chemicals over Earth, that, unless reversed, could ultimately bring down our civilization. Unlike regional ecological collapses experienced in the past (such as Mesopotamia's), this time the collapse would be *global*.

Consider the following statement: "Human beings and the natural world are on a collision course. Human activities inflict harsh and often irreversible damage on the environment and on critical resources. If not checked, many of our current practices put at serious risk the future that we wish for human society and the plant and animal kingdoms, and may so alter the living world that it will be unable to sustain life in the manner that we know. Fundamental changes are urgent if we are to avoid the collision our present course will bring about."[23]

A collision course with the natural world? Are these the ravings of a fringe group? Hardly. The quotation is from the 1993 *World Scientists' Warning to Humanity*, endorsed by more than 1,500 leading scientists, including more than half of the living Nobel laureates in science. The modern scientific community long ago reached a consensus that growing numbers of people, together with rising levels of consumption, especially among the world's rich, are threatening the natural underpinnings of human life.

Another report in 1993, this one issued by fifty-eight of the world's academies of science (including the National Academy of Sciences in the United States, the Royal Society in the United Kingdom, the Chinese Academy of Sciences, the Indian National Science Academy, the Brazilian Academy of Sciences, and the Third World Academy of

Sciences), stated: "The magnitude of the threat . . . is linked to human population size and resource use per person. Resource use, waste production and environmental degradation are accelerated by population growth. They are further exacerbated by consumption habits. . . . With current technologies, present levels of consumption by the developed world are likely to lead to serious negative consequences for all countries. . . . As human numbers further increase, the potential for irreversible changes of far-reaching magnitude also increases."[24]

Despite great efforts to get newspaper and television coverage for these vital statements by the world scientists and the academies of science, both 1993 statements disappeared virtually without a trace. In the world in general and the United States in particular, very few political leaders or members of the general public have been discussing the implications of continued growth of the global population, which is expected to be almost 40 percent larger by 2050, or expansion of current consumption patterns, which threaten to outstrip Earth's resources in coming decades. There is also little recognition that increases in population and consumption underlie a plethora of today's most serious problems, from air and water pollution and land degradation to declining fishery yields, increasing risks of epidemics and famines, and climate change. Nor is concern expressed about the dangerous erosion of human life-support systems through extinction of populations and species of other organisms. Even fewer people seem to realize how interconnected these problems frequently are with social and political challenges such as poverty, inequity, crime, and international conflict.

One reason for the collective failure to address the collision course scientists speak of and the complex of environmental, health, social, and security problems related to it—the "human predicament"[25]—presumably is denial. Most individuals see themselves and their nations as having more than enough immediate problems. Why get excited about longer-term ones that they little understand and feel powerless to deal with? Better just to refuse to accept their importance or to rationalize their postponement.

Another reason, we believe, is that the United States, perhaps more than other contemporary nations, is afflicted by a collective pride, based partly in ignorance, that we call "social hubris." The prevalence of that hubris is demonstrated weekly by the pundits who infest the Sunday morning television talk shows—the "public intellectuals" representing America. Important environmental trends are almost never mentioned. When something like global warming is discussed, it is always as one more political issue rather than something well established by abundant scientific evidence and potentially much more threatening to civilization than Saddam Hussein could ever have been. Indeed, the hubris of our society is perhaps best demonstrated by a widespread misapprehension of its power. It is assumed that the forces of nature can be ignored and that instances of environmental deterioration amount to a simple, temporary loss of amenities instead of a pressing problem that eventually may threaten the lives of millions of people and the future well-being of all of humanity. Social hubris induces people to believe that the environment can somehow be put on hold and be repaired later if society deems it necessary and decides to throw enough money and new technology at it.

The triumphs of science and technology are themselves, of course, one source of social hubris. People, especially the world's affluent, are surrounded by technological miracles. The work of science harnessed by technology brings us color pictures of events faraway in space and time. We can travel from coast to coast in much less time than it took George Washington to go from his home in Mount Vernon, Virginia, to the temporary capital in Philadelphia when he was president. Via e-mail and telephone, we can instantly communicate with friends across the world. We live in climate-controlled comfort and eat human-modified foods brought from the far corners of Earth. We can determine with the flick of a switch whether to be in bright light or darkness regardless of the position of the sun. If our car breaks down, we can plug in a new computer module to fix it, or we can easily replace the car itself with another mass-produced version. Should we personally be unlucky enough to break, science often can fix us. It can supply us with a heart substitute in some cases or even install a new heart if a donor is available. An admittedly cranky and inequitable medical system still gives us the kind of care Louis XIV—or even Franklin Roosevelt—couldn't even have dreamed of. Humanity collectively understands so much more about how the world works than it did when we, the authors, were born in the early 1930s, that we find it mind-boggling. Yet such marvels are taken for granted by everyone now. From that perspective, it's an all-too-easy step to believe that damage done to natural systems can always be repaired or replaced, like broken cars or weakened hearts—that technological fixes can clean up all our messes.

Humanity's hubris is not entirely misplaced. Advances in technology have allowed *Homo sapiens* to dominate Earth, and they could play an important role in helping our civilization change course and avoid the collision with nature that scientists predict. Indeed, most scenarios for that avoidance entail our making tremendous technological progress.

But history and scientific analysis show that humanity cannot count on technological fixes alone being sufficient. The claim that "technology will fix the problems" has been around for decades[26]—decades in which the putative advantages of claimed technological "fixes" have often failed to appear or proved to be offset by unforeseen nasty side effects. We're not feeding the world's poor people on leaf protein or algae grown on sewage sludge, as was once proposed.[27] Nuclear-powered agro-industrial complexes are not solving human energy and food problems.[28] Having more freeways doesn't get us to work faster; instead, it tends to increase traffic congestion and slow commute times.[29] A major exception to date has been the "green revolution," the transfer of the technology of modern high-yield agriculture from rich to poor countries. So far, this has generally been adjudged a triumph, although the final verdict is not yet in.[30]

Most scientists recognize that new technologies ordinarily produce not only benefits but also costs, so careful cost-benefit analyses should always be done before deploying them. Indeed, blind faith in technology as a panacea often seems most intense among the people with the least understanding of science, people who are not trained to consider systematically the uncertainties that always accompany proposed solutions. Technological advances are critical to achieving a sustainable society—that is, one not destroying its environmental underpinnings and resource base.[31] But technological advances alone won't save us. And they seldom address important quality-of-life issues. Science and technology might eventually permit 12 billion people to live sustainably on Earth, but in the style of factory chickens. Is that a desirable goal?

We don't think that hubris and accompanying denial are the only reasons that growing human population and increasing consumption are largely ignored. Human beings did not evolve nervous systems that can easily detect the gradual changes, taking place over decades, that characterize environmental problems.[32] Our senses and brains are great at detecting, and getting us to react appropriately to, charging lions or baseballs whizzing toward the plate. But our nervous systems don't easily detect smog getting worse during a lifetime or register the slow accumulation of nuclear weapons in India and Pakistan as threats to survival. We can't detect greenhouse gases that are building up in the atmosphere without using special instruments or learning to interpret the data scientists garner from those instruments. If the triumphs of science and technology that fill our homes are easily seen all around us, the signs of population-consumption problems—with some exceptions, such as hideous traffic jams—require some additional attention and study to appreciate. They don't easily motivate people to action.

The claim that humanity is on a collision course with the natural world is a frightening one, and hard to digest. What actually is the evidence behind the claims of scientists and others that society is on such a course? And if trends in population size and consumption patterns are big problems, what can be done about them? After describing the rise to dominance of our species and how that *has* put us on a collision course obscured by our hubris, in the chapters that follow we'll turn to the first major theme of the book: that global population growth and overconsumption by the rich are indeed two key but neglected factors. Both are intimately intertwined with current politics and keeping us on that collision course the scientists warned about more than a decade ago.[33]

How maldistribution of power impedes the great progress that we *could* be making toward a humane and sustainable society is the second major theme of *One with Nineveh*. Power is the ability of individuals and organizations to get others to act as the power-holders wish, not as those others would choose on their own. Most power is possessed by governments, corporations, other social institutions, and, ultimately, wealthy individuals, who often have disproportionate influence in the first three categories. Wealthy societies today use their power to give themselves a way of life that would be unsustainable if adopted by even half of the human population; they manage that trick by usurping disproportionate shares of the world's resources. In so doing, and by persuading other human beings that they too might attain such unsustainable affluence, they leave all of us and our descendants hostages to hubris—not only theirs but also ours as a society.

Hubris-based misuse of power, in our view, is a major reason why increasing overpopulation and runaway consumption—driving forces in environmental deterioration—are not being adequately assessed or addressed. It is also a basic reason for the failure of the scientists' statements to get public attention: those in power have created a milieu in which analyses that question the basic course of society are not defined as "news." That milieu similarly dismisses from the conventional media information that might motivate people to take action. People in positions of power usually have what they consider higher, more immediate priorities than dealing with little-understood medium- and long-term problems that they believe can easily be solved if necessary. When individuals have the power to influence or even control the flow of information—as politicians, corporations with huge advertising budgets, and media moguls do—there is little inclination to broadcast news that might interfere with their short-term gains. Indeed, when politicians can enrich their friends or increase their chances of re-election by lying or papering over serious problems, the temptation may become irresistible, especially if they don't believe that the price to be paid by their contemporaries or by future generations will be very high.

Today, the political right uses its power to make further enrichment of the wealthy the primary goal of social policy, blithely confident that decay of the human environment, even if serious, will not be a grave problem for those with the financial means to keep their personal surroundings safe and pleasant. Those on the right believe that their end of the lifeboat is unsinkable. People on the political left try to use their power to lessen economic and political inequity, but they often assume that in a more equitable world environmental problems could and would be dealt with easily. Those on the left think that if the lifeboat's load were appropriately redistributed and properly balanced, its capacity would be essentially infinite.

The leaders of the United States (and to a lesser degree those of other rich countries) are now acting like the political right of the world, believing that America can maintain its affluence while the gap between the rich and the poor widens. Despite the obvious demonstration of vulnerability provided by the terrorist attacks of September 11, 2001, the assumption seems to be that the rich nations can somehow become the global equivalent of a gated community.

We think that all these assumptions show a lack of contact with reality. Collective hubris reinforces the desires of many of the most powerful segments of civilization, and it helps create collective denial. It prevents people from seeing what society's environmental choices mean for our children and grandchildren. Will they live in a world of continual resource wars, fearful of plagues and terrorism and lacking the freedoms and comforts still available to many in the West today? Will they be mystified yet horrified witnesses, via television, to the hunger and suffering of ever larger portions of humanity? Or will they be able to live fulfilling lives relatively free of fear for themselves and their own descendants in a more equitable and sustainable world?

The *World Scientists' Warning to Humanity* is quite explicit about what will be required to steer and brake wisely in order to avoid the collision and achieve the happier result:

Five inextricably linked areas must be addressed simultaneously:

1. We must bring environmentally damaging activities under control to restore and protect the integrity of the earth's systems we depend on. We must, for example, move away from fossil fuels to more benign,

inexhaustible energy sources to cut greenhouse gas emissions and the
pollution of our air and water. . . . We must halt deforestation, injury to
and loss of agricultural land, and the loss of terrestrial and marine plant
and animal species.

2. We must manage resources crucial to human welfare more effectively.
3. We must stabilize population. This will be possible only if all nations
   recognize that it requires improved social and economic conditions,
   and the adoption of effective, voluntary family planning.
4. We must reduce and eventually eliminate poverty.
5. We must ensure sexual equality, and guarantee women control over
   their reproductive decisions.[34]

Sadly, almost no progress has been made on these issues in the
decade since the warning was issued in 1993. President Bill Clinton's
administration did surprisingly little to address those issues, and the
George W. Bush administration has been determinedly moving in the
opposite direction. It is not just the United States that is now held
hostage by this political hubris. Even as the Bush administration rapidly dismantles hard-won national environmental protections and
subverts civil liberties at home, it is blocking international efforts to
protect humanity's life-support systems (for instance, repudiating the
Kyoto Protocol on climate change) and shredding the embryonic system of global governance painstakingly created (in large part under
American leadership) in the years since World War II. America's current leaders are absolutely certain they are doing the right thing. We,
to say the very least, are not so sure. About the only thing we *are* sure of
is that issues rooted in environmental concerns, such as population
size, patterns of consumption, control of resources, and deployment
of related technologies, will increasingly underlie the politics of the
future.

The failure of humanity as a whole, and the United States in particular, in recent decades to come to grips with fundamental environmental issues and their often obscured but already gigantic economic
costs calls for a fresh examination of potential solutions. How can we
escape being hostages to hubris and move toward a society that will put
us on a more promising course?

Much of *One with Nineveh* is an examination of possible solutions to the problems created by too many people for the planet to sustain, too much consumption by the well-off, and maldistribution of power. So, having defined the human predicament, we'll crawl out on some shaky limbs. We'll suggest measures, some of them radical, that might allow humanity in general, and the world's sole remaining superpower in particular, to alter course and work toward achieving a sustainable world. Our globalizing civilization urgently needs to explore ways of reorganizing societies, even without assurance that the steps taken will be successful.

Dealing with population, consumption, and power will not be easy. But each day that we do nothing forecloses options for creating a better future, for avoiding Nineveh-like ecological suicide in our time. We see no choice but to attempt the possible rather than accept the unacceptable.

# Chapter 1

## THE HUMAN PREDICAMENT

"We hold dominion over palm and pine"
RUDYARD KIPLING, "Recessional," 1897[1]

Is HUMANITY REALLY on a collision course with the natural world, which supports us all? Are we really in a predicament? It seems hard to believe. Most readers of this book, including us, lead quite nice lives; we are not poor. We are well housed and well clothed and have access to an incredibly rich variety of food and material things to make life comfortable and convenient, even luxurious. Our kids and grandchildren are well educated, and many electronic diversions are piped directly into our homes. Predicament? Most people in the world would give anything to share *our* predicament— and more than a few would like to see us not enjoy so much luxury (and that's part of the human predicament).

We suspect that you share our natural ambivalence here. By the world's standards, you're probably leading a rather comfortable life, with no obvious, immediate threats in sight—and yet you know that humanity is in trouble. In coming to grips with this evident paradox, with our troubled thoughts for future well-being, we've found it helpful to deliberately expand our perspective. By adopting an ecologist's view of time and space, one can consider stretches of time hundreds of generations long and view all of Earth as a neighborhood. Doing so reveals a picture of great triumph in the rise of our species to planetary dominance—but also of the increasingly troubling side effects of that triumph.

## An Ecological View

Most of the universe is lonely, harsh, and often violent—inhospitable beyond anything humanity has ever experienced. The other planets in our solar system offer none of the comforts of Earth—not even such essentials as breathable air, abundant water, or a level of gravity suitable for human beings. Planets associated with distant star systems have been observed, but with no assurance that they can or do support any life—still less life that we might find recognizable. Earth is humanity's only home and the only one we are ever likely to have. It is uniquely suited to life, including human life, and we are utterly dependent on its characteristics and capacities, especially its sumptuous panoply of life, which evolved over more than 4.5 billion years.

Just suppose, through a quirk of space-time, we could look through a telescope at Earth as it was some 16,000 years ago, when there were perhaps two or three million people. Would we recognize it? Some aspects would seem essentially unchanged: the arrangement of the continents, the oceans, and many major rivers and lakes would look very much as it does today. But other aspects might seem quite strange: a much greater extent of ice on northern continents and polar seas, for instance, and coastlines somewhat different, thanks to a lower sea level then. We might notice much broader expanses of forest both in ice-free temperate regions, such as North America, Europe, Asia, and southern South America, and in tropical regions of Central and South America, Asia, and Africa. But, most remarkable, there would be no obvious signs of human activity—no large cities or towns, no Great Wall of China, no farm fields, pastures, or clear-cut swaths in forests, no big dams or reservoirs, no open-pit mines or quarries, no highways or railways traced across continents.

At higher magnification, we would see a very different array of large animals inhabiting the continents: huge woolly mammoths, giant ground sloths and beavers, saber-toothed cats, and numerous other unfamiliar creatures, as well as more familiar ones such as deer, antelopes, horses, and bears. And, if we looked very carefully, we might notice a few small groups of human beings living in temporary camps scattered across Africa, Europe, Asia, and Australia and subsisting by hunting large and small herbivorous animals and gathering edible plants from their surroundings. At night, we might be able to spot a few campfires and an occasional wildfire in grassland or forest—a great contrast to the brilliant clusters of artificial lights visible over much of the land in contemporary satellite photos.

Suppose now our space-time shift fast-forwarded to 200 years ago—just after 1800, as the industrial revolution was gaining momentum in Europe and a billion or so people inhabited Earth. How much change would we notice from nearly 16,000 years earlier? Perhaps not as much as you might expect. Of course, the glaciers would have retreated, and continental outlines and sea levels would be virtually identical with those of today. Most tropical regions would still be heavily forested, as would most of eastern North America and northern Eurasia. The Mediterranean basin and the Middle East, however, would appear to be semi-desert, and many of the large animals of the Pleistocene would have disappeared entirely, while others, such as lions and elephants, would have had their ice-age distributions greatly restricted.

Signs of human occupation would be considerably more obvious and widespread; villages, towns, and some quite large cities, such as London, Paris, and Shanghai, would be visible, as would many areas of farmland, mainly centered in European and Asian areas of high production today. Development in North and South America would be largely confined to coastal areas; Africa would appear rather spottily settled and cultivated, but with no large cities south of the Sahara. In Europe and North America, where industry was gaining a foothold, there would be as yet no electric power or motorized transport. Fuel for heat and metalworking would be wood or coal (making cities quite smoky); power would come from water mills or windmills, lighting from candles or oil lamps. A nighttime view from space would reveal only a little more light than that produced by the campfires of ice-age hunter-gatherers. Thus, even as recently as 200 years ago, the adverse environmental effects of the human population of roughly a billion people were significant but still very small by comparison with today's.

## Building the Human Enterprise

A nighttime view from space today, however, brings home just how massively and rapidly humanity has transformed its earthly home in the process of becoming the dominant animal on the planet. Most of Earth's land areas are now ablaze with light from cities, towns, highways, oil-well flares, and agricultural burning. In 16,000 years (an eye-blink in geologic time), the human population has expanded more than a thousandfold in number, from a few million to more than 6 *billion* by the turn of the twenty-first century. By comparing tonight's view with one from two centuries in the past, one begins to grasp how much of that transformation has occurred in just 1 or 2 percent of the time since glaciers stood a mile thick over the present site of New York City. In daylight, it also would be strikingly evident that the sixfold increase in population size and some thirtyfold increase in industrial activity since 1800 have resulted in the nearly complete occupation and transformation of Earth's land surface for human habitation.

During the sixteen millennia since the height of the ice age, human beings have domesticated animals and learned to plant and harvest crops; they have found ways to extract raw materials, process them, and manufacture products on a massive scale. People have devised means that allow them to travel a thousand times more rapidly and have created enormous cities and astonishingly complex social systems. When we look at Earth's surface from a jet airplane today, obvious signs of that activity are almost everywhere except in polar regions, deserts, the tops of mountain ranges, tropical forests, and the oceans. Some 28 percent of the world's ice-free land area is now dedicated (as cropland or pasture) to producing food for human beings, and much of the rest is used for less intensive grazing or for extraction of forest products and other resources.[2]

*Homo sapiens* has now become a truly global geological force. Among other things, it has changed the amount and patterns of light reflected back into space from Earth's surface, altered vast biogeochemical cycles that circulate the elements upon which our lives depend, freed many minerals from Earth's crust at rates comparable to or even exceeding those of natural processes such as wind and water erosion, and withdrawn so much water from large rivers that they sometimes no longer reach the sea.[3] The scale of the human enterprise[4] is now so gigantic that people are significantly altering even the gaseous composition of the atmosphere and changing the climate.[5]

The principal driving forces of those environmental impacts, which multiply together to batter the global systems that provide us with food, fresh water, and an equitable climate, are population growth, overconsumption, and the use of wasteful and often damaging technologies, combined with the particular social, political, and economic arrangements that facilitate or even promote high levels of consumption.[6] Everyone contributes to the collision course, but some far more than others. The most damaging and far-reaching assaults on the natural world are caused by the wealthy few, with their enormous affluence and collective power, rather than by the much more numerous poor. Those in the rich and powerful minority draw resources and goods from the entire planet, and they have been responsible for most of the environmental degradation over the past half-century because their average consumption per person is so high. These inequalities have great implications not only for the differing effects on the environment but also for the different strategies that will be needed in building a sustainable future.

## Unequal Dominators

The newly industrialized nations of Europe and North America led a surge of population growth in the nineteenth and early twentieth centuries. All the advances and accomplishments entrained by the industrial revolution enabled humanity to support an ever larger population by channeling Earth's natural productivity more and more into systems modified for human use[7] and by exploiting new mineral and energy sources, especially stored energy from long-vanished life: fossil fuels. It also stimulated trade between continents and nations, and it dramatically changed power relationships among them in ways that persist today. Some regions prospered and gained power, and others did not—for reasons that are not entirely understood. Important factors historically, as explained by Jared Diamond, have been regional differences in the quality and quantity of productive land and in the availability of environmental resources (e.g., the lack of animals suitable for domestication in Africa).[8]

Other key factors may include such historical accidents as locations where market economies first thrived; cultural traits that allowed industrialization to take hold and the sorts of institutions that developed to support it;[9] who carried what disease where; which nations managed to build empires; whether colonized nations were originally rich or poor; and how colonizers behaved.[10] Whatever the details of causation, human domination of the world in the twentieth century had the unfortunate side effect of creating a division between prospering industrialized nations and poor traditional societies (or "developed" and "developing" nations).

The divergence is seen as well in the different demographic paths the two groups have followed: the industrialized nations eventually lowered their birthrates, while the non-industrial regions of Latin America, Asia, and Africa did not. When modern medical technology was introduced in industrially less developed countries after World War II, the result was a dramatic drop in mortality rates and a population explosion.

The best news today is that populations in most industrialized countries (notably excepting the United States) are no longer expanding, and some have even begun to shrink slightly. Rapid population growth still prevails in many developing countries, however.[11] More than 95 percent of the population growth in the next half-century is projected to be in developing regions, which unfortunately are the least able to cope with billions more people.

The divergence between population growth rates in industrialized and developing regions has been more than matched by the still widening disparity in wealth and power,[12] even as the extent of affluence and the amount of resource consumption *on average* worldwide have both multiplied. While building their industrial systems throughout much of the nineteenth and twentieth centuries, western Europe, North America, and, later, Japan grew ever richer. By the end of the twentieth century, these nations had achieved economic dominance over most of the world. People in industrialized nations have secured the lion's share of the gains, while those in the poorest regions have gained little or nothing.[13] Human dominance of the planet, in effect, has been a function more of temperate-zone "pine" than of tropical "palm."

In the process, life for millions of human beings has been made safer, more secure, culturally richer and more comfortable, and relatively free of diseases and environmental risks. Yet these remarkable accomplishments have mostly benefited only the inhabitants of wealthy industrialized countries and the affluent classes of the developing world. Along with the colossal expansion of the human enterprise and unprecedented affluence achieved by some hundreds of millions of people, perhaps 2 to 3 billion others have attained modest levels of comfort and security. While this is truly a major achievement, it too has an underside: more and more people are increasingly (and mostly unknowingly) joining in the escalating assault on the global environment, complicating the prospects for escaping the human predicament. Billions more are still struggling in marginal conditions, ensnared in poverty and hopelessness. Almost 3 billion people live on less than two dollars a day;[14] the poorest among them in many ways are probably worse off materially and culturally than many of our ice-age ancestors were thousands of years ago.[15]

The bright lights visible from space today show not only where people are but also, and even more vividly, where the wealth is. Suppose instead we could see a time-lapse view of Earth that showed trends not in nighttime light but in income over recent decades; average per capita GDP (gross domestic product—which one can think of as roughly per capita annual income)[16] in North America and Europe more than tripled between 1950 and 1999 (in constant U.S. dollars),

while people in Africa south of the Sahara gained only slightly until the
mid-1970s and then lost ground.[17] Many African countries, indeed,
are saddled with huge debts and mired in poverty, and that failure of
economic development has had severe consequences for Africa's environment as well as its people. Of course, the poor cause significant
environmental damage locally and regionally, but it is often because
they don't have the resources to prevent it: for instance, local devege-
tation caused by the need for fuelwood, or the deterioration of farmland because poor farmers lack access to adequate fertilizers or means
of protecting the land.

Other developing regions in the world range from being as poor as
much of Africa to having middle-range incomes and even to being
essentially fully developed.[18] Here, also, poverty often leads to poor
husbandry of the land and other environmental problems, but growing affluence in other quarters portends not only improved circumstances for millions of people but also greatly increased contributions
to global problems such as climate change.

The former Soviet Union, although industrialized, made slow gains
in per capita income until 1991, when the union was dissolved. The
entire Soviet bloc suffered a severe economic setback from which the
now-independent eastern European and central Asian nations have
only begun to recover. Thanks to development policies in a USSR that
paid scant attention to pollution prevention or mitigation, environmental problems are legendary in the region.[19]

Today the rich nations,[20] with less than 15 percent of the world's
population, account for nearly 80 percent of the world's income.[21] The
United States alone, with 4.6 percent of the world's people, accounts
for nearly 29 percent. The 2.6 billion people in middle-income countries share 17 percent, but the low-income countries, with 2.4 billion
people, have access to less than 3.5 percent of the world's income. To
compare to the poorest subset of those poor nations, the per capita
GDP of the United States in 2000 was roughly seventy-five times
those with the lowest incomes. Even when large differences in purchasing power are taken into account, the average American has about
seventeen times the income as a person in a low-income nation.

That huge and growing disparity in income levels translates into an enormous differential in economic and political power between Americans and the citizens of the poorest countries. Between 1870 and 1990, the per capita income gap between richest and poorest countries *widened* some fivefold, and the gap in average income between all other nations combined and the richest one—the United States—multiplied about tenfold.[22] To compare extreme examples, the average annual purchasing power of a person living in sub-Saharan Africa (excluding South Africa) is roughly $1,000 (U.S. dollars); the average in North America (United States and Canada) is $33,510.[23]

Such inequities are a major feature of the human predicament. Furthermore, they translate into enormously greater impact on global life-support systems—especially since the power differential has allowed an environmentally careless rape of the resources of the powerless. The inequalities thus determine a great deal of the magnitude and geographical details of environmental destruction, and they are a substantial barrier to our changing course and avoiding the collision with the natural world that the world scientists warned us about more than a decade ago. If global sustainability is to be achieved, it will require greatly enhanced cooperation among all peoples—and enormous differences in wealth, requiring very different approaches to achieving sustainability, will not be conducive to such cooperation.

## More Food, Less Security

Agriculture is clearly humanity's most important activity—we all have to eat. It is also inevitably a major, probably the principal, cause of environmental disruption. The vast differences in purchasing power further compound civilization's most fundamental challenge: making it possible for everyone in a growing population to have an adequate diet while reducing human impacts on the global environment. One of humanity's most important accomplishments in the past half-century has been a substantial increase in the availability of food supplies worldwide. While the global population grew from 2.5 billion in 1950 to 6.1 billion in 2000, food production, as measured by production of cereal grains, which form the basis of the human diet,[24] approximately tripled.[25]

In discussions of human population and basic sustenance, two questions always arise. First, is malnourishment a function of maldistribution of food? And second, even if there would be enough food to feed everyone adequately today with more equal distribution, can enough be produced to go around in the future? And a third question should also be asked: what will be the environmental impact of supplying the growing human population with food, especially given current means of food production?

In the 1960s, when the population growth rate had accelerated to 2 percent per year, the outlook for increasing food production rapidly enough to ensure an adequate diet for the entire population was not encouraging. More than one-quarter of the population—nearly a billion people, almost all in less developed countries—was deemed significantly undernourished then, and famines were major threats in many poor countries. Creating a secure global food system, given the prevalence of hunger and the rapid rate of population growth in the less developed world, became an urgent task that would require a doubling of harvests in roughly twenty-five years.

Partly in response to rising concern about the prospects of feeding the growing population in the 1970s, however, the effort was made, and food production rose well ahead of population growth in the next two decades. Thanks to the rapid spread in developing regions of the so-called green revolution—the creation by geneticists of high-yield strains of the major grains that, with generous applications of water and fertilizers, greatly increased harvests—grain production in many regions, especially South Asia, East Asia, and Mexico, rose spectacularly. Whether a shift to focusing the human feeding base on a few strains of a handful of crops was the best long-term strategy from a biological or social viewpoint remains to be seen, but it was an enormous medium-term technological success.[26]

By the late twentieth century, 50 percent more grains were being produced than would have been required to provide sufficient calories to feed everyone in the world—assuming distribution were equitable and none were fed to livestock. Thanks to the expanded harvests, a significant slowdown in global population growth, and an ability to provide emergency food supplies in cases of dire need, the proportion of the world's people who are seriously underfed has declined to a level substantially lower than it was in 1970, although the absolute numbers remain about the same. Like other resources, food is far from equitably distributed, and chronic hunger continues to be widespread among the world's poorest people, who cannot afford to buy food on the market and are unable to grow enough food for themselves. Some 800 million people, mostly in the lowest-income countries, are undernourished or suffering from specific nutritional deficiencies, the Food and Agriculture Organization of the United Nations estimates.[27]

Despite some progress in alleviating chronic hunger, the problem persists, and the economics of development and the global agricultural system are largely responsible. Generous subsidies to the farm sectors in industrialized nations and low prices on the world market for staple foods undermine the livelihoods of poor farmers in developing nations.[28] Development policies in many poor nations for decades have favored urban populations while neglecting the agricultural sector. The result is that rural populations are often trapped in poverty, unable to sell their crops and earn more income or to avail themselves of modern technologies to increase their production.

A central issue for the nutritional portion of the human predicament is finding ways to increase food consumption among the poor, and that means finding ways to enable the poor to lift themselves out of poverty. A Stanford University colleague of ours, agricultural economist Walter Falcon, points out, "The world food *economy* is driven primarily by income growth, not mainly by population growth, and certainly not by hunger."[29] One of humanity's major tasks thus is to increase rural incomes, either by creating jobs or by increasing farm productivity and providing markets, so that the rural poor can afford to buy the food they need.

Gross differences in power maintaining gross differences in economic status are the overlooked elephant at the picnic—the most neglected aspect of human control of Earth's bounty. Power determines

what people can choose to eat and whether they can obtain enough to
eat. More than half the cereals produced worldwide are consumed
directly by people. They supply most of the calories consumed by the
poor; in medium-income societies, they still account for an important
portion of diets.[30] In the most affluent societies and among elites in
developing nations, diets are rich in meat and other animal products
(from livestock generously fattened with feed grains) and myriad other
foods often grown in faraway places and shipped to markets. Feed
grains account for more than 40 percent of cereals grown worldwide;
they are consumed by livestock and, increasingly, by farmed fish.
Directly or indirectly (through livestock feeding), the wealthiest 20
percent of the world's people have access to and consume nearly half of
the world's output of food crops and an even greater proportion of
animal products, few of which the poor can afford.[31]

Beyond such inequities, the second and third fundamental questions of human population and basic sustenance remain. How far into
the future can food production continue to be increased, not only to
keep up with continuing population growth but also eventually to feed
everyone in the world adequately, without causing unacceptable environmental damage? The world population, 6.4 billion people in 2004,
is still increasing rapidly and is projected to be near 9 billion in 2050.
Humanity is adding about 77 million people per year (almost the population of Germany) to those Earth must feed. Despite a significant
drop in the growth *rate,* that annual increment (absolute number of
people added per year) is still slightly larger than it was in 1974[32]
because the base population is so much bigger now. Fortunately, if
demographic projections are correct, the annual increment, which
peaked around 1990 at 95 million people, should continue to fall in the
future. But the natural life-support systems underpinning agriculture
must deal with actual numbers of people, not percentages, and the
global population is projected to grow by another 1.5 to 3 billion people
in the next several decades.

To feed a substantially larger population by the late twenty-first
century and improve diets among the poorest third of the population,
global food production will have to rise by as much as 65 to 100 per-

cent. Exactly how large an increase is needed will depend mainly on how much population growth is ahead. To some extent, it will also depend on whether today's substantial post-harvest losses to rodents, insects, and spoilage can be significantly reduced. Conservative estimates of those losses range from more than 10 percent for cereals to more than twice that for fruits, vegetables, and seafoods.[33] In the poorest nations, losses are often considerably greater, possibly ranging as high as 30 percent in some areas. And some of the greatest opportunities for increasing available food supplies locally exist in places that most need improvement of storage and distribution facilities.

The green revolution has now mostly run its course for the major cereals; it has been adopted in nearly all areas where soils and climate are suitable, although there are areas where yields are still well below those achievable under the best husbandry.[34] Less widely used crops, especially the root and tuber crops that are staples in poor areas of South America and Africa, have not been given the crop improvement attention they deserve. The funding of international agricultural research stations that could do the required research is pathetic, and heavily promoted new agricultural technologies now available are unlikely to repeat the green revolution's achievements.

With the maturing of the green revolution, raising food production further is becoming increasingly difficult, especially in developing regions where populations are still rapidly expanding. In most of these regions, the amount of undeveloped arable land remaining is limited at best. High-quality agricultural land, like other natural resources, is unevenly distributed around the world, and people in the great majority of countries are more or less dependent on imported food. Only a handful of countries are dependable major producers and exporters of surplus grains.[35] The biggest by far is the United States, yet the U.S. population is still growing fast enough that the size of future grain production surpluses available for export is open to question.

The modern high-yield technologies, while brilliantly productive, have an inherent set of environmental drawbacks that may undercut their success over the long term. These crop strains are built on a narrow genetic base and generally are planted in large-scale monocultures year after year in the same fields; both of these circumstances make them more vulnerable than traditional varieties to pests and diseases.[36] Ironically, the international Convention on Biological Diversity, adopted by 187 nations, has had the unintended consequence of restricting the ability of agricultural researchers to add desperately needed strains to the gene banks upon which high-yield agriculture depends.[37] Novel genetic material is crucial to maintaining genetic diversity in crops and thus is a key resource for breeding new lines of crops to meet attacks of ever-changing pests and to adapt strains to changing climatic regimes.

Modern biotechnology, often touted as the "new" green revolution, is not likely to triple yields[38] of basic crops as the green revolution did, although it can offer improvements in some crops, new weapons against old problems such as pests and crop diseases, or increased tolerance for arid climates or saline soils.

Finally, monoculture planting and constant tillage often increase rates of soil erosion, and the heavy inputs of farm chemicals contribute to pollution problems. The deterioration of many productive lands and competing uses for both land and water are already undercutting the remarkable agricultural achievements of the past fifty years. Indeed, global grain production per capita has not increased since the mid-1980s,[39] and no breakthrough is in sight for boosting food production on the scale of the green revolution. The cumulative effects of all these factors, along with the potential negative consequences of rapid climate change on food production, may be leading us toward absolute food shortages in the not-too-distant future.

To paraphrase an "encouragingly Malthusian" summary of the world food situation by geographer Vaclav Smil, one of the most knowledgeable analysts (and one who has generally been more optimistic than we have), there do not seem to be any insurmountable *biophysical* reasons why the world should not be able to continue to feed itself for the next two generations. He believes that, in that half-century, "a combination of well-proven economic and technical fixes, environmental protection measures, and dietary adjustments"[40] can produce enough food to feed everyone without further undermining the environmental systems that support agriculture. Throw in sensible management of global fisheries and good luck with climate change, and in principle we might agree.

But we are far from sanguine that those steps will be taken effectively everywhere. Problems on the social and economic side may well prove much more limiting than any biophysical ones. Among the difficulties are the control of some agricultural technologies by a few giant corporations and problems with the transfer of crop seed technologies introduced by new international agreements on intellectual property rights, including attempts to patent and control the use of specific crop strains.[41] Some of the more egregious of the latter cases have been described by scientist and activist Vandana Shiva as "biopiracy."[42] Other problems include aversions in some rich countries to genetically modified foods, which are leading developing countries to reject them, despite their needs for improved food sources.

Severe problems arising from such maldistributed power are layered on top of the interaction between population growth and mounting consumption. Consequently, there is reason for concern about both the biophysical and the socioeconomic prospects for feeding a population that might well still be expanding after 2050. Dominance does not necessarily imply control.

## Undermining the Enterprise: Depleting Natural Capital

Natural capital, like human-created capital such as factories and computers (durable goods employed in production), generates a flow of benefits for humanity. Resources such as agricultural lands, forests, sources of fresh water, fishery stocks, and wetlands—elements of natural capital that, as opposed to petroleum and metal ores, are normally considered renewable—are now being lost or degraded at an alarming rate. They are, in essence, being turned into non-renewable resources. Indeed, it is clear that, in gaining its dominant position on the planet, humanity has already consumed a large portion of its vast inheritance of natural capital. Many consequences of environmental deterioration, including possibly faltering food security, can be ascribed to losses of natural capital. And, ironically, much of the loss of capital is caused directly or indirectly by agriculture itself, the endeavor most vulnerable to environmental damage.

Expansion of the human enterprise has generated a history of changing land use, especially since the invention of agriculture 10,000 years ago. Forests, wetlands, and grasslands alike have been converted for food production around the world, a process that has greatly accelerated in the past century or two. In ancient Greece more than 2,000 years ago, it was noticed that unwelcome changes often followed the removal of forests from mountain watersheds: more frequent droughts, floods, and losses of topsoil to erosion. In a famous line, Plato described deterioration in Attica: "What now remains compared with what then existed is like the skeleton of a sick man, all the fat and soft earth having wasted away, and only the bare framework of the land being left."[43] The philosophers' observations and warnings went unheeded, as did those of many other observers through the centuries, as forests disappeared in much of the Mediterranean region, and western and southern Asia—all areas that had hosted the rise and fall of the earliest civilizations. Eventually, the widespread deforestation probably contributed to a gradual and substantial change in the climates of those regions to warmer, drier, and generally less productive regimes as they did around Nineveh.

Deforestation has spread throughout the world's temperate regions since the Middle Ages, although forests have regenerated in many of the cutover areas in Europe and eastern North America.[44] Deforestation continues throughout the world as ancient forests are removed for timber or fuelwood or to create agricultural land, or some combination. But now it is happening on much larger scales and far faster than in earlier centuries. Of Earth's original forest cover, only about half remains today, and about 30 percent of that has been fragmented or degraded by selective removal of valuable trees.[45] Worldwide deforestation has escalated recently; more than 4 percent of the forest area that remained in 1990 was lost by 2000.[46] More than 90 percent of the losses in that decade were in tropical forests, which contain an estimated half or more of the planet's biodiversity—populations and species of non-human organisms. Of the small amount of forest worldwide that was replanted or allowed to regenerate, barely a fourth was in the tropics. All too often, tropical forest losses, especially if replanting is delayed, are for practical purposes permanent.

As the human enterprise has expanded, the local and regional changes due to large-scale deforestation have tended to coalesce to produce effects that are nearly global. Predictably, as tropical forests have been depleted and fragmented across wide areas, changes in regional climate have followed. Thus, unprecedented droughts and even huge fires have occurred both in the Amazon basin of South America and in Southeast Asia. Massive fires in Borneo in 1997–1998 destroyed some 5 million hectares (almost 20,000 square miles) of forest and decimated many species of wildlife already threatened with extinction, including our cousins the orangutans. The fires also generated huge clouds of smoke that spread throughout Southeast Asia, polluting the air for many weeks.[47] In Brazil's Amazon basin in the late 1990s, enormous fires spread from agricultural areas into moist forests that had never been known to burn, but which forest fragmentation, depleted water tables, and local climate change had made vulnerable.[48]

Even in developed countries such as the United States, poor forest management has led to large-scale forest fires. In the summer of 2002, record forest fires burned more than 7 million acres in the United States.[49] Those fires, ironically, may have been amplified by changes in climate (to warmer and drier), resulting directly from deforestation; global warming, to which deforestation contributes; or a combination of both. The huge fires in southern California in October 2003 may have had similar links to climate change, compounded by diseased stands of trees and poor urban planning.

The world's grasslands and savannas have also been subjected to massive transformation by humanity. By the second half of the twentieth century, Earth's temperate grasslands and tropical savannas had virtually all been converted for crops or grazing, many of them had been degraded by invasive species, and less and less "virgin" land suitable for crop production remained available. This no doubt has been a factor behind the trend toward greater agricultural intensification, led by the green revolution, with its dependence on abundant water and chemical inputs (fertilizers and pesticides) to support the high-yield varieties of staple crops. The downside of green revolution technology is that it can accelerate soil erosion and encourage overuse of fertilizers and pesticides, which can degrade the productive capacity of agricultural land and create serious pollution problems in water bodies.

These drawbacks have been problems in industrialized countries for decades, and now the same problems from accelerated erosion and overuse of farm chemicals are being seen increasingly in developing countries as a consequence of the green revolution. There, they often appear in more serious forms because soils tend to be more fragile in the tropics, and sun and rainfall regimes are harsher. Losses of farmland quality, due largely to erosion, may have depressed total worldwide crop production by as much as 13 percent over the past half-century,[50] but sound estimates are difficult to come by.

In developing regions, degradation often occurs when marginal lands are cultivated or grazed by poor farmers who cannot afford industrial inputs and good management practices. Subsistence farmers are commonly relegated to steep hillsides and other marginal are as because wealthier landowners have the power to take over more productive floodplains to raise cash crops, often for export. Such hilly and arid areas are especially susceptible to degradation. Many tropical lands are exposed to more severe weather than are temperate agricultural regions. It is important to remember that soils, if not carefully tended, can be a non-renewable resource on a time scale of significance to society. They are normally generated at rates of inches per millennium, but in some areas they are being eroded at rates of inches per decade.[51] Unfortunately, there are no reliable estimates of whether or how long current rates of erosion can be sustained without loss of productivity. Although degradation could be reduced by effective, relatively inexpensive steps to husband and increase soil fertility, incentives and resources to use them are often lacking. For very poor farmers in developing regions, even simple measures may be quite beyond reach.

Finally, agricultural land everywhere is also being lost to urbanization. The suburbs and housing developments resulting from growing populations and rising consumption swallow millions of acres of prime farmland around the world every year.[52] In the United States, more than 8,000 square miles of land have been disappearing each year under suburban sprawl, most often land of superior quality for agriculture.[53] The expansion of urban land use in the past few decades has significantly outstripped population growth in many parts of the country.[54] The sprawl results from population growth and poor land-use and transport planning, and it contributes seriously to traffic congestion, air pollution, and other urban problems. Such trends are problems not only in the United States but also increasingly in the developing world, as seen dramatically in China. The way these trends unfold, and their consequences for food production, will depend upon factors such as population growth, changes in average household size, and town and city planning policies—all of which are subject to substantial uncertainties.

Considering agriculture's central place in humanity's rise to dominance and its crucial importance in supporting civilization, it is tragic that most people in the richest nations, including their political leaders, are largely unaware of how agricultural systems work or of the constraints on them—especially their dependence on natural capital. Indeed, it is possible to get through urban educational systems and major universities in the United States without learning even the basics of agriculture.

## Water: Overdrawn and Underappreciated

Besides the Great Wall of China, the most massive structures ever built by human beings have been dams. The first one we know of was built by the Egyptians about the time of the great pyramids at El Lahun,[55] allowing that early society to fill and empty the lake in a 700-square-mile depression known as the Fayoum to help regulate the flow of the Nile. Thousands of years later, in the 1960s, one of the world's largest dams was built by joint Egyptian and Russian efforts on the Nile at Aswan. The Aswan High Dam is two miles long, three-fifths of a mile wide, and 364 feet high and contains an amount of material equivalent to seventeen great pyramids.[56] More than 90,000 people and several ancient monuments had to be relocated as Lake Nasser filled behind the dam—nothing compared with the million or so people currently being displaced by China's Three Gorges Dam project on the Yangtze River.[57] Dams, and the lengths to which societies will go to construct them, are monuments to the importance of water to civilizations. Originally, dams were used to control floods and provide irrigation water, but in the early industrial revolution they were employed to drive water wheels to run machinery in factories, and most recently, of course, they have been used to generate hydroelectric power.

It is no surprise, then, that the most salient element of humanity's renewable natural capital destined to be in short supply in the twenty-first century may well be fresh water.[58] As populations grow and economies modernize, demand for water increases substantially and competition for scarce supplies intensifies. In developing regions, more than 2 billion people are surviving with inadequate supplies of water for household use—lacking even a minimal amount for drinking, cooking, and washing.[59] In some water-short cities such as Amman, Jordan, running water is provided to households for only a few hours a day.

Adequate water supplies are essential not only directly for human well-being but also for food production. On average, about 70 percent of freshwater withdrawals for human use are for agriculture. Some 18 percent of the world's cropland is under irrigation to provide the abundant water on which the high crop yields of modern agriculture depend, especially cereals, about 60 percent of which are produced on irrigated land.[60]

The amount of land under irrigation worldwide expanded rapidly after 1950, but the expansion has slowed in the past two decades to less than the rate of population growth. Irrigation often proves to be a temporary measure. Even deserts can be made to produce crops, but irrigation water must be provided by diversion from nearby rivers or from groundwater.[61] Many deposits of "fossil" groundwater, supplies that accumulated during the ice ages, are now being drained, and other aquifers are being drawn down faster than they can be replenished by natural recharge. Land heavily irrigated from surface sources is often subject to degradation as salts build up in the soil. If the water table rises too near the surface, crops become waterlogged. These problems, which eventually contributed to the downfall of Mesopotamia and some other early civilizations, still beset irrigated lands and are causing increasing amounts of irrigated land to be withdrawn from production.[62]

The three largest grain-producing countries, China, India, and the United States, are the biggest users of irrigation water, and all three have experienced serious water shortage problems.[63] India, China, and another large country, Pakistan, all previously mostly self-sufficient regarding food, may soon be importing grain as do other water-stressed nations. More than 70 percent of China's grain production depends on irrigation, but rising urban demand for water and depletion of aquifers are constraining food production. Meanwhile, Beijing and other cities are facing critical shortages of water for their populations, and the problem is growing worse.[64] In 1975, for the first time, the Yellow River was so dry it failed to reach the sea for fifteen days, disappearing short of the coastline. Beginning in 1985, it has run dry each year—for 133 days in 1996; for 226 days in 1997, a drought year. In the summer of 2003 it dropped to its lowest level in fifty years. India, an important green-revolution success story in the 1970s, like China, relies on irrigation for its increased grain production. That country too is now experiencing serious groundwater depletion and water shortages, especially in its northern wheat belt.

In the United States, most rice and much wheat are irrigated; irrigation of the latter is rapidly depleting the Ogallala Aquifer, which underlies the high plains from eastern Wyoming and southern South Dakota to northern Texas. The presence of that aquifer, the largest in the United States, is "like having the waters of Lake Ontario nearby, ready to be tapped at will to water fields of corn, milo, wheat, and alfalfa," as historian John Opie put it.[65] For a decade or two, shrinkage of underground water supplies has been contributing to farm abandonment in the northern plains.[66] Now rice farmers even in rainfall-rich Arkansas are seeing an end to their profligate water use.[67]

In California, aquifers are less important than the water stored in the snowpack of the Sierra Nevada and the Rocky Mountains, transported from the moist, sparsely settled north or from the lower Colorado River to the populous south and the agriculturally important Central Valley. A population growing significantly more rapidly than the national average has swelled the state's cities, pushed urban sprawl over prime farmland, and increased urban demand for water. That demand has led to clashes with farmers who view access to cheap, abundant water as their sacred right—a view confirmed by the heavy subsidies they enjoy. Efforts to rationalize California's water regime have been frustrated by a maze of conflicting interests and legal precedents,[68] and the whole system will be threatened if global warming significantly reduces the storage capacity of mountain snows. Similar problems plague most of the American West.

Increasing pressures on limited sources of irrigation water will inevitably translate into tightening constraints on food production. In arid regions of the world, as populations have grown beyond the ability of local water supplies to support sufficient domestic food production, more and more countries have turned to food imports to fill the nutritional gap. By 2002, more than a quarter of global grain exports were to water-stressed countries in Asia, Africa, and the Middle East.[69] Although considerable scope remains in most regions for more efficient and rational use of water in agriculture (as well as in other uses), economic and political barriers often impede the adoption of appropriate measures. Some gains in efficient use have been made, mainly in industrialized countries thus far, often by the use of water-saving technologies pioneered in water-short Israel.[70] Matching supply more closely to demand and shifting to less water-intensive crops could also reduce pressures on limited supplies.

While industrialized nations need further improvement in the efficiency of their water use, many developing regions lack the infrastructure to provide both farms and cities with reliable water supplies,[71] and agricultural productivity lags as a result. Misuse of power also plays a big role. Rather than sensibly allocating water efficiently, many governments and corporations are mounting ever more costly and short-sighted water megaprojects in which they often see short-term gains.

They are "replumbing" the planet with huge dam projects and water diversions, such as the Three Gorges Dam in central China, in a search for supply-side solutions to what is basically a demand-side problem.[72] In ecological time, dams are short-term solutions—usually temporary structures. The reservoirs behind them fill with silt in decades or centuries, depending on the vegetative cover and soil erosion conditions in their watersheds. It is rarely economic to dredge behind them, so they eventually become waterfalls.

As competition for scarce water resources has grown, large corporations have seen opportunities for profit. Privatization of water supplies has become a contentious issue in both developed and developing countries. Local governments traditionally have been responsible for allocating water resources but have sometimes found it an impossible job. Yet privatization of water, despite promises of lower cost and more dependable supplies, too often has resulted in the opposite. In places as disparate as San Diego, California, and Lima, Peru, the consequences have been higher prices and less dependability.[73]

Abundant clean water is also required by the plants, animals, and microbes of many natural ecosystems—that is, of natural combinations of organisms and their non-living surroundings. It is also critical to the maintenance of wildlife and fisheries. Yet rivers and streams have long been subject to diversion for human purposes, siltation from soil erosion, and pollution by farm chemicals, industry, and partially treated or, in many developing regions, untreated sewage. Wetlands, which provide valuable environmental services in regulating and purifying water supplies, have been drained and converted to farmlands and subdivisions everywhere. Dams, siltation from injudicious logging in watersheds, and pollution have been blamed for the precipitous shrinkage of salmon populations on the West Coast of the United States, abetted by overfishing. In 2002, during a serious drought, the federal government allowed farmers on the California-Oregon border area to divert so much water from the Klamath River that 30,000 or more salmon were killed.[74]

More immediately, the lack of clean, safe water for people to drink is a growing problem in many regions.[75] Unsafe drinking water causes serious health problems, especially for vulnerable children and infants in poor countries. The World Health Organization ranks waterborne disease among its top ten global health risks.[76] It is estimated that as many as 1.2 billion people—one in every five worldwide, nearly all of them in developing regions—have no access to safe drinking water. Some 2.4 billion lack adequate sanitation.[77] Peter Gleick of the Pacific Institute for Studies in Development, Environment, and Security estimated in 2002 that by 2020 more than 100 million people would die from water-related diseases as a consequence of lack of clean water, unless much more is done to improve the situation.[78]

What of the idea of desalinizing seawater to cope with water shortages? It can help, at high cost, in augmenting urban supplies in the coastal cities of rich countries or in irrigating very high-value crops such as strawberries grown near seashores. But, unfortunately, for staple crops inland, the cost of removing the salt and pumping the water to fields is prohibitive and will remain so for the foreseeable future.

The quality of water is also important, from the standpoint of both human health and environmental security. While industrialized countries have been relatively successful in recent decades in curbing the flow of human wastes and industrial pollutants into surface waterways (though, in the United States, wastes from confined animal-feeding operations are "point sources" that still lack adequate regulation),[79] control of substances from "non-point" sources, mainly farms, has not been achieved. Perhaps the most dramatic manifestation of farm chemical overuse has been the huge and growing "dead zone" in the Gulf of Mexico, some 7,000 square miles in extent (almost the size of Massachusetts),[80] which has been blamed on a massive influx of fertilizer runoff from farms and lawns, along with sewage, delivered every summer from the central United States by the Mississippi River.

Another concern is the increasing contamination of groundwater sources with various pollutants, including heavy metals, farm chemicals, and industrial chemicals of various stripes. In the United States, about half of the population depends on wells for drinking water, and thus many people are, unknowingly, directly exposed to these contaminants. Others may be exposed through food when crops have been irrigated with contaminated groundwater. Such groundwater contamination problems have plagued parts of Europe and are increasingly seen in developing countries as they industrialize.

While it is widely agreed that problems of both supply and quality of water are increasingly serious elements in the collision course, for agriculture or for human health, accurately assessing them and their consequences has proven both difficult and contentious. Even more difficult is resolving local conflicts among competing users, especially when traditions and older laws enforce irrational allocations under changed circumstances. Such dilemmas are becoming more and more common in both industrialized and developing nations.[81] Acting sooner rather than later to implement appropriate water management policies, however, could alleviate the current domestic and industrial shortages, help prevent worse problems, and allow greater increases in food production, among other benefits. The gap between what societies could do about such problems and what they *are* doing, however, remains very wide.

## Oceanic Resources

Humanity's dominance of the planet is dramatically illustrated by its ability for the past decade or so to vacuum the oceans of some 100 million tons of fish every year, utterly changing marine ecosystems in the process. The recent history of ocean fisheries has consistently been one of overexploitation followed by a collapse and then a shift to another fish stock. But the number of remaining "underfished" stocks is diminishing. Fish and shellfish, important human food sources though they are, have not benefited from much protective attention. Overall, the oceans have increasingly been exploited, and even though fish harvests have continued to increase, fishery after fishery has collapsed.[82]

Even though people cannot occupy oceans in the same way they do land, the human-caused environmental impacts on marine environments have been substantial and too often ignored; out of sight, out of mind seems to be the ruling philosophy. For millennia, people have availed themselves of the ocean's rich bounty of food sources; until the late 1960s, however, the possibility of overexploitation was scarcely considered. Then, shooting wars erupted over cod fisheries in the North Atlantic, and public awareness grew that several species of the ocean's great whales were seriously endangered.[83] In 1971, the first great fishery crash, that of Peruvian anchoveta, stirred questions about the sustainability of the previously rapidly rising global fish harvests.

By 1994, about three-fifths of all important oceanic fish stocks were considered seriously depleted or in danger of being so.[84] Yields of more than a third of those fisheries were falling, and the rest had reached the limit of sustainable yield and were vulnerable to declines if pressure increased. It now appears that the global oceans have lost more than 90 percent of their large predatory fishes. Many, such as tuna, sharks, cod, and swordfish, are important sources of human nutrition, and all of them play important roles in maintaining the structure of the ocean ecosystem. Perhaps worse yet, large areas of the complex ecosystem on the ocean floor, a critical fish habitat, are being destroyed by bottom trawling.[85] In the famous Georges Bank fishing grounds off Nova Scotia, according to fisheries expert Daniel Pauly, "trawlers trailing dredges the size of football fields have literally scraped the bottom clean, harvesting an entire ecosystem—including supporting substrates such as sponges—along with the catch of the day."[86]

The situation seems bound to get worse because the oceans are increasingly besieged at their margins.[87] Roughly half of humanity already lives in coastal areas, and more people are moving in. As a result, silt, waste oil, and other contaminants are entering nearshore waters. The flow of pollution that causes the dead zone in the Gulf of Mexico damages shrimp and other fisheries; similar effects are seen elsewhere, if less dramatically. Construction of onshore housing and other development projects produces silt that harms coral reefs, and coastal development destroys huge areas of salt marshes and mangroves every year, ecosystems that serve as nurseries for many oceanic fish species.[88] In the United States, the equivalent in oil of the *Exxon Valdez* spill[89] washes off the country's streets and driveways and into the oceans every eight months.[90]

Before the 1990s, the global harvest of wild fish was already shrinking.[91] Rapid growth in aquaculture (fish farming) has been taking up the slack and has helped to fill the demand for seafood[92] while disguising the growing problems of the wild fish stocks. But aquaculture is subject to many of the economic and environmental drawbacks of high-yield agriculture.[93] It is even directly connected to those problems by the rising quantity of cereals being produced to feed farmed fish. It also contributes to oceanic overexploitation by utilizing "trash fish"—fish species not usually marketed for human consumption but essential components of the oceanic food web—as fish meal for feed.[94] Questions have been raised as well about the healthfulness of grain-fed farmed fish, about the hybridization of farmed species with wild ones when the former escape their pens, and especially about releases of genetically modified fish that can hybridize with wild stocks.

Finally, disparities in power show up in the fisheries area too. Aquaculture was first promoted as a way to improve food supplies in poor countries. But farmed fish is marketed mainly to affluent customers who can pay premium prices. In addition, fish farms often have been established in areas that previously provided wild-caught fish or shellfish for subsistence coastal populations in developing countries (those that require the seafood to eat, producing no surplus for sale), thus creating one more wedge between rich and poor. Poor nations also can ill afford the patrolling necessary to protect their marine resources, leaving them vulnerable to exploitation by industrialized fishing interests. High prices paid in the rich world for saltwater aquarium fishes and for exotic dishes such as "grouper lips" (about $1,000 a plate in Hong Kong; a single grouper can bring as much as $200)[95] lead to dynamiting and cyanide poisoning of coral reefs and the destruction of artisanal fisheries, upon which poor people often depend for small but vital protein components of their diets.

## A Big Question

So, will civilization be able to provide sufficient food and meet basic needs for every human being in the future? We have our doubts, based on historical experience, awareness of growing threats to that ability, and predictions that the human population may increase by 2050 by almost half again the number of people who exist now. Agricultural systems seem slated to endure increasing stresses from population pressures, declining land quality, water shortages, and mismanagement of inputs. Societies may not take full advantage of the potential gains from improved post-harvest storage and distribution systems. Critical supplies of fresh water for agriculture are not superabundant; future increases in food production will depend on much better management of water supplies. Maintaining food harvests from the oceans is becoming a substantial challenge as well.[96] And soils, forests, and wetlands, so important in many dimensions of the human predicament, are under broad assault.

Clearly, our dominating civilization has yet to come to terms with the limits of Earth's life-support capacity. Losses and depletion of natural capital, from which humanity receives a steady flow of interest in the form of natural services, are ubiquitous and largely ignored.[97] Like the profligate son of the biblical parable, many societies are spending their capital—depleting their resources—rather than living on the interest that it could provide as annual harvests of crops, constantly replenished soils, sustainably exploited fish stocks, and forests cut no faster than they can regenerate themselves. Standard economic systems give far too little value to natural capital, and losses or reductions in productivity are not customarily recorded in national accounts.[98] And the possibilities of substituting manufactured, human, or social capital for lost natural capital are slim, to say the least. Many nations are thus unwittingly impoverishing themselves, and all the while standard economic measures indicate that wealth is increasing. So the human triumph of dominance over Earth is a partial triumph and a mixed blessing—as will be made clearer in the next chapter.

# Chapter 2

## THE COSTS OF SUCCESS

"We are already living on an overloaded world. [Recent efforts to increase Earth's carrying capacity have been drawing down] finite reservoirs of materials that do not replace themselves within any human time frame. Thus [the] results *cannot be permanent*. This fact puts mankind out on a limb which the activities of modern life are busily sawing off."

WILLIAM R. CATTON JR., 1980[1]

HUMANITY HAS ACHIEVED its unprecedented dominance over the natural world by clever technological strategies that have allowed it to exploit its inheritance of natural capital to the utmost and to transform into resources substances such as petroleum, uranium, and aluminum that once were of little or no use. But this success and the consequent hubris have come at a mounting price. It's time to consider the costs of our species' triumph beyond the most basic ones involved with providing us with food and shelter before first uncovering the underlying factors that exact those costs and then seeking ways to reduce their impacts.

## The Downside of Dominance

A brave lady was responsible almost single-handedly for alerting people to some of the costs of success. Biologist Rachel Carson in 1962 published the book *Silent Spring,* which served as a catalyst for the modern environmental movement.[2] Carson was a brilliant writer, and her image of springtime with no birdsong, a prospect resulting from lavish overuse of pesticides, caught the public's imagination as had no previous environmental metaphor. Rather than an unquestioned boon to humanity, the use of substances such as DDT was portrayed as a practice that extracted a price, sometimes a high one, for the benefits produced. Carson was attacked mercilessly by those in the pesticide industry and by scientists in their pay.[3] But gradually most of the scientific community got into the fray on her side, and her basic concerns were found to be more than justified.[4] Sadly, she died of cancer in 1964, before she could see any of the advances in environmental safety her work stimulated, such as the banning of DDT for most uses in the United States in 1972.

Carson's influence went far beyond the institution of better controls over the use of pesticides. It alerted the public to a basic fact: that along with an array of unquestioned benefits, the industrial revolution had given rise to a new set of subtle but dangerous adverse environmental effects, many of them stemming from the adoption of fossil fuels as energy sources and as a feedstock for industrial chemicals. By the last third of the twentieth century, the "side effects" on human health and the environment of the use of modern synthetic chemicals as pesticides and in other applications had become subjects of mounting concern in developed countries, alongside the more obvious problems of air and water pollution. That concern helped to fuel increasing efforts to address these problems. The decade of 1969–1979 saw passage of a series of landmark laws in the United States, including the National Environmental Policy Act of 1969 (NEPA), the Clean Air Act and the Clean Water Act, the Endangered Species Act of 1973, and the Superfund legislation of 1980 to clean up toxic waste sites. Parallel efforts were under way in Europe, Canada, and Japan, where regulations were put in place that were often patterned on the American laws. By the 1980s and 1990s, as the industrialized nations were gaining some control over pollution, similar difficulties started to mount in developing regions, which were beginning to industrialize but lacked laws and technologies to control emissions and toxic releases. Air pollution, once a notorious health hazard in London, Los Angeles, Tokyo, Pittsburgh, and Paris, now plagues Mexico City, São Paulo, New Delhi, Beijing, Jakarta, and Cairo.

Serious though they can be (as we'll see later), pollution problems nonetheless are only a part of the damage humanity is causing to the world's environment. One doesn't have to be a rocket scientist to recognize that we have followed the biblical injunction—we have gone forth, multiplied, and subdued Earth.[5] But it's hard to comprehend how thorough and costly that subjugation has become, still less what it means for future human well-being.

No place on Earth remains untouched today by human activities, however pristine a few places may still appear. Most of our planet's original ecosystems have been modified over the centuries, sometimes to extremes, in order to serve the production of food, as we saw in chapter 1, and to fulfill other human needs and demands. As the rapidly expanding human enterprise has asserted control over natural capital and diverted more and more of its productivity to human uses, the result has been a progressive loss or disruption of natural ecosystems and mounting symptoms of interference with the basic geochemical processes that make Earth habitable. Every time an automobile is added to the world's fleet, every time a new patch of forest is cleared to plant crops or build a vacation home, every time another person is added to the world's population, every time an oil company buys another politician, the chances of achieving a sustainable world are reduced, because the natural systems we all depend on will be a bit further diminished. Each change seems a small one and frequently is believed to be an "improvement"; in terms of enhancing the lives or well-being of people locally, it may well be so. But in aggregate, these changes pose grave risks to our civilization. The often irreversible character and cumulative effects of myriad small alterations escape notice. But they lead to the kinds of consequences international groups of scientists have been warning about: degradation and loss of habitats, decline in the ecological bases for human life through extinctions of populations and species, redirection of the course of evolution, alteration of Earth's climates, dispersal of poisons, redistributions of plant and animal species, and reduction in human defenses against plagues.

## Nature's Services and Ecosystem Loss

In addition to the blaze of artificial light visible from space at night and multitudinous human structures visible by day, profound changes in land cover are apparent in satellite images—often highlighted by sharp boundaries between deforested and forested areas or desertified landscapes and those irrigated or protected from overgrazing. When the National Oceanic and Atmospheric Administration's satellite passes over Borneo and Sumatra, it records the gigantic forest fires started by smallholders or international timber companies and perpetuated by coal seams ignited secondarily. The wonderful forests of those islands, composed primarily of a mixture of species of the family Dipterocarpaceae, are rapidly being cut and replaced with huge oil palm monocultures to produce oil for export. The forests, long the world's main source of tropical hardwood timber, appear doomed.

We count ourselves lucky to have visited Malaysia and Indonesia in 1996; we even unexpectedly encountered an orangutan in Borneo, looking as if she somehow were aware of her likely fate. If current trends continue, the destruction of the dipterocarp forest may foreshadow the disappearance of most of the world's other tropical forests. Other forms of natural capital, such as wetlands and old-growth forests in temperate regions, are being eaten up as well.

We tend to take for granted Earth's natural ecosystems, such as forests, grasslands and savannas, marshes and wetlands, river systems, and deserts. But they are all part of Earth's unique life-support system and provide critical services[6] to society. The indispensable services provided by ecosystems include the creation and maintenance of the qualities of Earth's atmosphere that are essential for life; modulation of climate and weather; stabilization of the hydrological cycle (the cycle that brings us supplies of fresh water) and moderation of floods and droughts; recycling of critical nutrients, detoxification and disposal of wastes, and generation and replenishment of soils so essential for agriculture and forest growth; plant pollination (including pollination of crops); control of pests and organisms that carry human diseases—and much more. Ecosystems also provide humanity with goods: medicines and industrial materials from wild plants, fungi, and animals; forest products and non-agricultural foods (game and wild plants) from land; and food from the sea.[7]

Technological substitutes, of course, have been developed for some of nature's services in certain circumstances. For instance, dams are constructed and reservoirs filled to regulate an area's water supply and to help prevent floods and relieve droughts. Sewage treatment plants are built to decontaminate water, though to do so they harness the same bacteria that perform that service in nature. The use of synthetic fertilizers in agriculture is another example, as is the synthesis of medicinal drugs. Even these accomplishments, though, depend on the use of natural substances as the basis or as templates for the processes and often have negative environmental effects, as when dams disrupt salmon spawning runs.

Humanity thus is not as independent of nature as people sometimes like to believe. Indeed, for most ecosystem services, such as regulation of the hydrological cycle or the global climate or cycling of essential nutrients, we have too little knowledge of how substitutions might be made and near certainty that the job couldn't be done at the scale required. In the early 1980s, Paul and his colleague Hal Mooney examined attempts to maintain services by substituting different organisms for ones that had gone extinct, and concluded: "Satisfactory substitutes are unlikely to be found at anything like the rate that ecosystems are now being degraded."[8] Since then, the tide of losses has surged ever higher; satisfactory substitutes have relatively rarely been found, even at local levels, and the rate of ecosystem degradation has accelerated.

Despite humanity's dependence on nature's services, their value remains unappreciated by most people, a failure of perception that is heightened in our increasingly urbanized civilization. Too few of us realize that major portions of our fruits and vegetables come to us courtesy of natural pollinators, that we would have no harvests to speak of but for the constant replenishment of soils and nutrients by natural processes and the activities of natural enemies of crop pests, or that distant forests help slake our thirst, water our crops, and protect us from floods. Seldom do we reflect that all our foods and most medicines were originally derived from nature, or that the very air we breathe is a product of the interaction of organisms with the atmosphere over eons. As ecosystem services falter, however, people may begin to appreciate their value more fully; unfortunately, such valuation may come too late for us to preserve the stability of the systems we all depend upon.

One reason for the continued disregard for the services nature provides is that their benefits to society are not accounted for in markets. Consequently, market prices of activities that disrupt nature's services are below the social cost of these activities. For example, the price at which a wetland is sold for conversion to agricultural land is below the full social cost of losing the wetland, since the costs from the lost ecosystem services from the wetland—for example, loss of flood control, water filtration, and habitat—are not captured in the wetland's sale price. Social costs include the external costs borne by society, beyond the internal costs paid by people or firms that are producing a product or carrying out an activity. Most of the benefits we get from the organisms of natural ecosystems are "positive externalities" to society; correspondingly, the costs society incurs when those benefits are reduced are "negative externalities."

As another example of this important point of ecological economics, positive externalities provided by natural forests include the sequestration of carbon, which otherwise would remain in the atmosphere as carbon dioxide ($CO_2$), a process that thus reduces the risks of adverse climate change for all of us. More immediate benefits include moderation of local climate (protection from floods and drought) and maintenance of soil and water quality. Such functions are rarely given a value in markets today.[9] If Sara sells the right to harvest the trees on her woodlot to Sam, for a variety of reasons, the market price of that right will not reflect the fact that Sara's grandchildren (and Sam's, and ours) may have to live in a slightly worse climate because of it. The market price for trees does not include that social cost. Nor does the government put a tax on the transaction (as it could) to try to ameliorate the failure of the market price for trees to reflect their true social value. Put another way, calculations of, say, the market costs of clearcutting a forest usually do not capture many of the negative externalities associated with forest loss, such as increased flooding, biodiversity decline, and release of $CO_2$. Sam pays less for the trees than their true social value both because the market does not consider these costs and because the government doesn't apply a tax to "internalize" those externalities. Thus, instead of Sam paying the true costs of clearcutting the trees, we all end up paying the social costs.[10]

## Loss of Biodiversity

The ecosystem modification that should be of greatest concern is the accelerating loss of biodiversity. The plants, animals, and microorganisms that share Earth with us are the most irreplaceable form of natural capital.[11] Many environmental scientists and most environmentalists feel ethically bound to try to conserve biodiversity for its own sake.[12] Biodiversity must be conserved not just for its own sake, however, but also for the sake of civilization because of its crucial role in providing that indispensable array of ecosystem services and goods.

A recent study by conservation biologist Andrew Balmford and his colleagues estimated that the benefits to society of conserving the "wild nature"[13] still existing in 2002 would be at least 100 times greater than the costs. The authors say, "Our relentless conversion and degradation of natural habitats is eroding human welfare for short-term private gain. In these circumstances, retaining as much as possible of what remains of wild nature through a judicious combination of sustainable use, conservation, and, where necessary, compensation for resulting opportunity costs makes overwhelming economic as well as moral sense."[14] Yet, compared with the need, only a pathetic level of funding is available for the attempt to preserve humanity's natural capital, perpetuate those positive externalities, and internalize the negative ones.

Whether the Balmford group's estimate of benefits is accurate may be open to question, but two things are indisputable. Clearly, the social benefits of preservation enormously exceed the costs even if the 100:1 ratio estimate is high, although there are good reasons, presented in the study, to believe that estimate is a *lower* bound. Second, despite this lack of balance between benefits and costs, bit by bit wild nature will continue to be destroyed, eventually increasing the public's perception of the value of whatever remains.

A few decades ago, concern for preservation was focused on the slowing of a frightening acceleration in the extinction of species.[15] It was then that scientists realized that humanity had entrained a catastrophic round of species extinctions globally, comparable to the one that exterminated the dinosaurs and many other organisms 65 million years ago.[16] British ecologist Norman Myers, who has been one of the foremost scientists calling attention to major environmental problems, was a key player not only in pointing out the extinction crisis but also in suggesting that much of *species* diversity could be preserved by protecting relatively small portions of Earth's surface that had high concentrations of diversity—"hotspots," Myers called them.[17] As a result, many organizations have concentrated their efforts on the task of preserving biodiversity hot spots, even though preservation of such small areas may be quite temporary because many of the species there may already be doomed.[18]

Later it was recognized that loss of *population* diversity was a closely related and equally important extinction problem.[19] Populations are groups of individuals of the same species that inhabit a given area, usually to one degree or another isolated from other populations of the same species and often genetically distinct.[20] First estimates of the diversity of populations were made by Jennifer Hughes, now of Brown University, and her colleagues, and a frightening rate of population extinction was calculated.[21] Population extinctions, of course, precede species extinctions—many populations of passenger pigeons were wiped out long before the last population was destroyed, causing the extinction of the species. Population extinctions also lead to the loss of ecosystem services. If the population of spruce trees in the canyon upstream from your house in Colorado is cut down, its flood protection service will be lost. That the same species of spruce has abundant populations elsewhere will be of little consolation as you struggle to keep your head above water while riding your house downstream.

Indeed, it would theoretically be possible to lose no more *species* diversity at all and yet, because of declines in *population* diversity, suffer such a steep decline in ecosystem services that humanity itself would go extinct. If every species were somehow reduced to just one minimum-sized sustainable population, the human population could not feed itself (think of there being only one small plot each of rice, wheat, and corn; a vegetable patch; a flock of chickens; two hives of honeybees; all watersheds denuded except for a few patches of plants, etc.). In this thought experiment, species diversity would have been maintained, but people would soon disappear.[22]

Fortunately, many dedicated people around the globe are struggling to preserve nature. But without a major transformation of thinking about the environment, and especially about the drivers of its deterioration, the destruction of wild nature will most likely continue. A major reason is the influence of what political scientists call "mobilization bias." That means that some relatively small groups of people who have a huge stake in taking or preventing an action will hold sway over a much larger collective in which each individual has a relatively small stake. A coastal real estate developer can make a fortune by destroying an intact coastal marsh in Florida and replacing it with a marina. But all the fishers in the area and all the consumers of fish each have only a very small stake in the loss of the fish nursery function of that particular marsh and will not be inclined to organize and offer a bigger bribe than the developer has given to the Florida politician who will back the development.[23]

Connected to this is that old bugaboo of standard economics— imperfect information. For the economic system to work properly, consumers and policy makers must be well informed about the choices they are making. Do you suppose the president of the United States, the prime minister of Great Britain, or the president of Russia has ever so much as heard of an ecosystem service?

Some ecosystem services indeed are so far out of sight or mind that no one appreciates them until they disappear. Recently, a mysterious disease or widespread poisoning has been wiping out vulture populations in India. These scavengers are important in supplying the ecosystem service of decomposition, the breakdown of organic wastes into chemical forms that can serve as nutrients in plant growth. Vultures also play a central role in the burial rituals of India's Parsi community. The Parsi people leave their dead out for the vultures, which provide a "sky burial." And when sacred cows die in India, their carcasses are traditionally left where they fall. But the decline of vultures has greatly increased the amount of carrion available to other scavengers, which has caused an explosion in populations of pariah dogs, which compete with vultures. One result seems to have been a great increase in the risk of rabies (proportionately more Indians die of rabies each year than citizens of any other nation—29 deaths per million people).[24] The carrion bonanza is also likely to increase the populations of disease-carrying rats.[25] Vulture populations had already been greatly depressed in Southeast Asia as a result of food shortages caused by uncontrolled hunting of large hoofed mammals and, perhaps, also because of poisoning by agrochemicals and persecution.[26] We are reminded of the comment made a quarter-century ago by nature and travel writer Ken Brower, in reference to the near extinction of the California condor: "When the vultures watching your civilization begin dropping dead . . . it is time to pause and wonder."[27]

## Redirecting Evolution

Besides having become the dominant ecological force on the planet, humanity has become the foremost evolutionary force. Human redirection of evolution is not merely a recent phenomenon. When people first invaded the Western Hemisphere 12,000 to 15,000 years ago, they wiped out the sloths, giant beavers, mammoths, and other large plant-eating animals. In the process, they changed the selection pressures on the hemisphere's flora, permanently altering the evolutionary future of many plants in the Western Hemisphere.[28] Through those changes, they greatly modified the environment for other animals as well, altering their evolutionary trajectories. Nevertheless, compared with us, our distant ancestors were pikers when it comes to influencing the future of evolution.[29]

Humanity's role in deliberately changing evolutionary pressures to alter the character of desired species has been especially obvious in the use of artificial selection to produce domesticated plants and animals, including wheat, rice, corn, numerous fruits and vegetables, dogs, horses, chickens, pigs, sheep, and cattle, all to our benefit. The animals we have reshaped are now the only animals in the same league as people in terms of the total weight of their species; cattle, for example, now number about 1.3 billion individuals, thus roughly equaling *Homo sapiens* in total weight.[30]

The genetic tools with which we have created our domesticates have evolved as well, changing from the simple and largely inadvertent selection practiced by the first agriculturalists to the highly sophisticated technologies of molecular biology that provide us with the controversial genetically modified organisms (GMOs) of today. We'll dodge the controversy surrounding such genetic modification except to say that, like all new technologies, its effects for good or evil will depend on how it is used, and great care must be taken to watch out for possible hidden biophysical (especially ecological) and social risks.

While a triumphant humanity has been lavishing scientific attention on a handful of domesticates, countless other species of organisms have been heedlessly displaced or pushed to extinction, to our great risk.[31] Among many other things, those organisms represent raw material for the geneticists who are striving to keep us in the business of high-yield agriculture, geneticists who must often modify crop strains to keep them ahead of the ever-evolving pests and pathogens that attack them. Even more crucially, of course, all those organisms are components of the complex web of life without which humanity could not long survive.

Over the entire globe, human beings for centuries have been redirecting evolution in another way as well—by moving plants and animals out of their natural habitats and introducing them into new ecosystems. The undesirable alien species range from nasty weeds to voracious insect pests and crop pathogens. The effects of such introductions are often very destructive because the newcomers normally have not coevolved[32] with the living elements of the recipient system, and thus few or no natural enemies of the new arrivals may be present in the invaded environment. Goats, mongooses, kudzu vines, house cats, cane toads, opuntia cactus, brown tree snakes, Nile perch, starlings, cheatgrass, mosquito fishes, Mediterranean fruit flies, zebra mussels, feral pigs, and numerous other biological invaders have wreaked havoc in one place or another around the world, changing selection pressures in local communities and often causing extinctions of native species through competition for resources or through predation.[33] Even rabbits, innocuous creatures in their original habitats, became serious pests by competing with sheep and native mammals for grass after their introduction into Australia. Farmers are increasingly faced with serious costs related to dealing with such newcomers. As a single example, in Australia most weeds are exotic, and the cost of trying to control them is estimated at $1.7 billion annually. The overall problem of dealing with exotics, which so often tend to degrade natural capital, is wonderfully covered in science writer Yvonne Baskin's recent book, *A Plague of Rats and Rubbervines*.[34]

Human beings as an evolutionary force have also generated resistance among targeted organisms to various drugs and pesticides. We have altered the evolutionary trajectory of organisms ranging from the AIDS virus, the dangerous bacterium *Staphylococcus aureus,* the spirochaete that causes syphilis, and the protozoans that give us malaria to the many disease-transmitting mosquitoes, the corn earworm, and the brown rat,[35] often at substantial costs to ourselves. Indeed, in the course of altering the land surface of Earth and changing the characteristics of the global ecological system, translocating myriad organisms between countries and continents, dispersing toxic substances globally, and influencing climates, *Homo sapiens* has unwittingly changed the selective regime for many, if not most, organisms.

In sum, human beings destroy entire populations of other organisms (as when we pave over or plow under their habitats or hunt them

to extinction), compete with them (as when we decimated the aba-
lones that once were a rich source of food for sea otters), and move
them around and alter their evolutionary futures. The irony is that by
doing so we are changing our own evolutionary futures, both impoverishing and competing ultimately with *ourselves,* since other organisms
are working parts of our life-support system and coevolve with us.

## Climate Change

Among the longer-term trends that cast a shadow over civilization's
future are, of course, changes in climate. Some changes will be natural,
but others are related to human modifications of the planet's natural
systems and processes, and they will occur regardless of whether policy
makers (in their hubris) choose to recognize their causes. Changes in
climate are increasingly traceable to human-caused alterations in the
gaseous composition of the atmosphere and to land-use changes that
alter the amount of solar energy reflected from Earth's surface and
change the circulation patterns in the lower atmosphere. The scientific consensus is clear that climates around the world have begun to
change significantly and that human activities are largely responsible.[36]
It is within our collective power, however, to do something about those
changes.

Over the twentieth century, the global average temperature on
Earth's surface rose by about 1 degree Fahrenheit (0.6 degree Celsius),
and the average sea level rose some 4 to 7 inches (0.1 to 0.2 meter).
The 1990s apparently were the warmest decade since weather records
have been kept, and probably the warmest in two thousand years or
more.[37] Extreme weather events, such as heat waves and fierce storms,
have become more common and are appearing in places where they
have never been seen before. The 2003 summer heat wave in Europe
that killed upward of 15,000 people in France and fueled forest fires in
France, Spain, and Portugal is a case in point. Although no single event
can be blamed on global warming, the apparent increase in frequency
and intensity of such occurrences indicates that climate change is under
way.[38] In addition, scientists have observed changes in the distribu-

tions of birds, butterflies, and many other organisms that are consistent with adaptation to changing climates.[39] Glaciers from Alaska to Patagonia, Switzerland, and East Africa are melting faster than they have in recent history; sea ice is retreating apace in both the Arctic and Antarctic,[40] with serious results for wildlife in both regions. Yet, disturbing as they may seem, the changes that became increasingly evident in the late twentieth century are likely to be dwarfed by those in prospect for the twenty-first and beyond.

Humanity is nudging Earth's long-evolved climate system by emitting rising amounts of greenhouse gases into the atmosphere. Greenhouse gases—$CO_2$, methane, nitrous oxide, and water vapor—are natural constituents of the atmosphere that help to make the planet habitable by acting as insulators and keeping average surface temperatures well above freezing. Without those gases, most of Earth's surface would be too cold to support more than limited microbial life and would be whipsawed by hot and cold extremes between day and night, summer and winter.[41] But there can be too much of a good thing—especially if it arrives too fast—and humanity's additions of surplus amounts of these natural greenhouse gases, plus some human-made ones, are threatening to destabilize our present benign climatic system by causing a buildup of heat in the planet's lower atmosphere.[42] That heating warms both the land surface and the upper layers of the ocean. The latter causes the seawater to expand, which is one reason for the rising sea level. Atmospheric heating also speeds evaporation of water from oceans and land, thus causing a buildup of water vapor in the atmosphere. This in turn magnifies the effects of the other greenhouse gases in a positive feedback.[43]

The burning of fossil fuels is the principal cause of rising greenhouse gas emissions, although other human activities contribute, especially deforestation (which is responsible for an estimated one-fourth of emissions), other land-use changes, agriculture, and some industrial activities. $CO_2$, added to the atmosphere mainly by the burning of coal, oil, natural gas, and vegetation, is the leading culprit in human-induced global warming, but methane ($CH_4$), nitrous oxide ($N_2O$), chlorofluorocarbons (CFCs), and some other chemicals are also involved.[44] In combination, they roughly double the greenhouse effect caused by $CO_2$. Methane is produced by a variety of sources, including natural emissions from wetlands. Human-caused emission sources include rice paddies, flatulence of cattle, landfills, and leaky gas mains and equipment. Nitrogen oxide is emitted in land clearing, deforestation, and use of nitrogen fertilizers. CFCs and some other fluorine-based chemicals, used mainly as refrigerants, become especially long-lived greenhouse gases in addition to their adverse effects as depleters of the stratospheric ozone layer.[45]

Because greenhouse warming is likely to accelerate the movement of water from Earth's surface to the atmosphere by evaporation and by the activities of plants,[46] and to alter atmospheric circulation and cloud cover in ways that are hard to predict in detail, there is considerable uncertainty about the precise ways that climate will change in any given locality. Will it be warmer or locally cooler at times? Will there be more rain or snow, or less overall, and how might the timing of rainfall or snowfall change? Will storms become more frequent and (quite likely) more fierce? And how will these changes vary as time goes on and the greenhouse gas buildup proceeds?

Complex computer models designed to assess the likely changes under a variety of assumptions about shifts in energy use and changes in other activities can offer a broad-brush description of likely trends. But these generally assume no changes of other kinds that may affect climates locally. Even without greenhouse gas emissions, changes in climate would continue to occur as the population grows and development proceeds, for example. And there is no question that local and regional climates have been altered over the centuries by anthropogenic (human-caused) changes in land use, especially by deforestation—as the present hot, dry climates of the once-forested Fertile Crescent hills and Mediterranean basin demonstrate. The question of how those continuing ecological changes will play into changes caused by global warming makes prediction of local effects even more problematic. The climate models all do agree, however, on two things: if there were an immediate halt to *all* anthropogenic greenhouse gas emissions, the gases already emitted would continue to warm the atmosphere for many decades, and the warming would keep raising the sea level for centuries.[47]

Possible consequences of global warming for the human population include more frequent deadly heat waves (like that in Europe in 2003), more frequent and more severe hurricanes and tornadoes, an increase in floods and droughts (causing more frequent crop failures and giant wildfires), and the spread of tropical diseases such as malaria and dengue fever into formerly cooler climes. Rising sea levels and increased coastal flooding are virtually certain. Among the most important consequences to be concerned about are the potential effects of climate changes on agricultural production worldwide, especially in the tropics, where every calorie counts and populations are still expanding. The consequences are largely unpredictable except for the not surprising conclusion that poor farmers, especially in developing regions, will have more difficulty adapting to the changes than will affluent ones, who have more mobility and access to modern technologies. Uncertainty about climatic consequences is no reason for complacency, however. We are not talking about trivial changes. Note that a temperature rise of 9 degrees Fahrenheit (5 degrees Celsius), which is far from impossible during this century, is roughly the temperature difference between that time when there was a mile of ice over New York and today.

The effects of rapid climate change on biodiversity, that key element of humanity's natural capital, may be even more crucial—and signs of change there are already manifest.[48] When climates changed significantly in the distant past (as at the end of the ice age), plant and animal species, along with their microbial associates, had time to adapt or change their distributions to fit new weather conditions. Today, climates are likely to change too fast for some organisms to adapt, and movements to new locations with newly appropriate climates will be critically hindered by vast stretches of human-altered landscapes— farms and pastures, cities, wide freeways, and the like. Birds and flying insects may migrate easily, but ground-bound reptiles and mammals will have a tougher time, while trees and other plants, which change distributions slowly by means of seed dispersal, may be seriously blocked. With their various components being subjected to different pressures and responding in different ways, ecosystems will in essence be torn apart, and many species and populations may not survive. The implications for the ability of such fragmented ecosystems to continue providing adequate levels of natural services are not encouraging.

Perhaps most serious of all is the possibility of climatic surprises as human activities warm the planet. Sudden, drastic shifts have occurred in the past.[49] For example, the gradual warming after the last ice age was interrupted by an abrupt return to glacial conditions in northeastern Canada and most of Europe some 13,000 years ago. Most of the trees and much of the other flora and fauna that had reinvaded Europe in the warmer period were killed off during a half-millennium-long "mini" ice age, named the Younger Dryas after the pollen of an arctic plant that became common in marsh sediments at that time. The reversal to glacial conditions appears to have occurred in less than a century, perhaps much less. It possibly was triggered by a pulse of fresh water flooding into the North Atlantic when a glacial dam broke and released the waters of a gigantic lake into the Saint Lawrence drainage. That flood may have suppressed the Gulf Stream flow that warms Europe.[50] Little is understood about what might set off such a radical shift in apparently stable processes, but the Younger Dryas event was the sort of surprise that today could have devastating consequences for much of industrial civilization.

## Planet-wide Poisons

Sudden climate change is not the only potential source of unwelcome surprises on a global scale. In many ways, the story of technology and the modern industrial enterprise has been one of frequent revelations of unexpected side effects of some technological miracle. Humanity's genius can get the best of it—and one of the places this shows clearly is in the manipulation of organic molecules and other industrial chemical processes. Synthetic organic compounds and other substances, many of them toxic, that are emitted by human activities may now have created a serious global problem. While most petroleum is used as fuel, a portion serves as a feedstock for a gigantic industry to shape carbon-containing molecules into ever more diverse forms. Plastics are doubtless the most familiar of those. They are now so ubiquitous that even those of us born before the plastic age can hardly remember what it was like before plastics seemingly constituted half of our packages and gizmos, carpeted much of the land surface of Earth as trash, and filled the oceans with floating debris. Although plastic trash is an eyesore and is occasionally responsible for the deaths of marine birds and other animals, plastics generally don't present the threat that many other human-made chemical products do.

Tens of thousands of synthetic organic compounds have been released into the global environment in the past six or seven decades, and new ones are constantly being introduced. Since the 1960s, there has been growing concern about possible subtle or long-term effects of such widespread releases and about potential adverse interactions among them. These substances include pesticides and a great diversity of chemicals such as polychlorinated biphenyls (PCBs) that have been used in industry, as well as a variety of others that are added to the environment when they leach out of plastics. In some cases, especially that of pesticides, millions of tons have been produced each year. PCBs were banned from use a few decades ago, but they remain widely dispersed in the environment. Used extensively as insulators and coolants in electrical equipment, as plasticizers, and in numerous other applications,[51] they are known cancer-causing substances (carcinogens) and can be very toxic in high concentrations.

Pesticides have often been overused, and the residues of persistent ones such as DDT have been dispersed far and wide by wind and water, even reaching the polar regions.[52] Both DDT and PCBs, along with many other chlorinated hydrocarbons, persist in the environment and bioaccumulate—that is, they build up in food chains—and can reach lethal concentrations in top predators such as eagles and hawks. Before it was banned in the United States and other developed countries in the 1970s, DDT was causing increasing havoc among wildlife, especially birds. While human beings seem to be relatively insensitive to direct toxic effects of compounds such as DDT, indirect effects resulting from their chemical similarity to natural hormones have raised new questions about their consequences for human health.[53]

Since DDT was banned, there has been gradual recovery among the most severely affected wildlife species in the United States, but DDT and its equally toxic and persistent breakdown products are still found almost everywhere. Even in recent years, they have been found in the air of California cities[54] and in the rain over the Midwest.[55] DDT is still being produced and used in some developing regions, especially in the tropics to control mosquito-borne diseases, although efforts are being made by the international community to replace it with less disruptive pesticides.

Pesticides and their chemical relatives are by no means the only important toxic materials that have created environmental problems. Heavy metals such as lead, cadmium, and mercury also can bioaccumulate in food chains and are toxic to human beings. Lead from gasoline was a significant component of air pollution in the United States until leaded gas was banned in the 1970s. Since then, blood levels of lead have fallen precipitously in American children; as they fell, it became possible to measure effects on mental function even at very low levels.[56] Another heavy metal, cadmium, is used in some industrial processes and emitted in the burning of fossil fuels. Exposure to even very small amounts over a period of time can cause decalcification of bones and kidney damage. A serious cadmium poisoning occurred in a Japanese village in the 1960s, caused by a contaminated well.[57] Mercury, released in iron smelting and coal burning, is a major problem in the Great Lakes region, where consumption of mercury-laden fish poses a health hazard, especially for children and pregnant women. Mercury, the flow of which into the oceans has been increased severalfold by human activities,[58] also has built up to dangerous levels in long-lived oceanic fish such as tuna, king mackerel, and swordfish.[59] Mercury's dark side was dramatically revealed in Japan in the 1960s in the form of an outbreak of Minamata disease, in which hundreds of people suffered madness and loss of control of bodily functions and dozens died horrific deaths.[60] The cause was poisoning by methyl mercury from the effluents of chemical plants owned by the Chisso Corporation.

Some ubiquitous toxic substances in air and water may adversely affect food production, although data are sparse. Common air pollutants emitted by cars and power plants, especially oxides of nitrogen and sulfur, are known to inhibit plant growth and reduce forest and crop productivity. In the air, either can be converted to forms that cause acid precipitation, which is damaging to sensitive aquatic and forest ecosystems. Air and water pollution in China are estimated to reduce the value of farm products in that heavily contaminated nation by 2 to 3 percent.[61] Adverse effects of air pollution on human health, including asthma and other lung diseases, have been well documented and are rising nearly everywhere, including in the United States,[62] but most alarmingly in cities in developing regions.[63]

Unsettled questions about the long-term, even intergenerational, effects of some widespread chemicals, especially those synthetic organic compounds that have structures similar to natural hormones,[64] make it difficult to evaluate the public health consequences of exposure to toxic substances. Disruptive effects of these hormone-mimicking compounds on development processes in many species of wildlife have been observed in which animals develop with extra or missing limbs or abnormal reproductive organs, and there is increasing evidence that they may cause subtle problems in human beings exposed to even tiny amounts in utero or in infancy. Among observed aberrations in children that may be results of such exposure are abnormal sexual development, behavioral problems, and possibly some mental retardation. These endocrine-disrupting compounds include such ubiquitous and persistent substances as PCBs, DDT, and dioxin.

Even less is known about potential synergistic interactions among compounds; many chemicals may be harmless alone but produce toxic effects when combined with others. Even so, some observers claim that there is nothing to worry about, since over much of Earth life expectancies are gradually increasing. But the question is, would they have increased even more, and would the quality of life have been better, had society been more careful in its deployment of synthetic organic compounds? Has a widespread and gradual poisoning been a major downside of human success?

## The Epidemiological Environment

One of the most frightening (and, until recently, least appreciated) aspects of our condition is the deterioration of our epidemiological environment—the growing chances of succumbing to an infectious disease.[65] Scientists have long recognized that the ability of pathogenic microorganisms to perpetuate themselves in a human population depends in part on the size and density of that population. While our huge population size is one sign of the success of *Homo sapiens,* it simultaneously carries a cost of greater vulnerability to epidemics. Infected people usually either get well and become at least temporarily immune to the disease, or die. If there are few people in a population, or they are widely dispersed, the pathogen that invades that segment of humanity from an animal reservoir runs out of individuals to infect and leaves that society free of the disease. Human beings got rid of smallpox globally by using vaccination to produce so many immune individuals that the virus died out.

Smallpox couldn't have been a serious problem for our hunter-gatherer ancestors because their populations were small and scattered. As the global human population grew, though, so did the opportunities for pathogenic organisms, and many of them transferred from other animals, especially domestic ones, and established themselves in the human population. Thus, smallpox itself is thought to have been derived from cowpox, and influenza seems to mutate frequently into new forms as it passes repeatedly between pigs, ducks, and people. Lassa fever, Ebola hemorrhagic fever, hantavirus pulmonary syndrome, and Marburg hemorrhagic fever are all deadly diseases originating in mice, other rodents, and (in the case of Marburg virus) monkeys. Plague is also endemic in many wild mammals, from rats to squirrels, and is transmitted to human victims by fleas; rabies is transmitted directly by a bite from the animal victim. And, of course, the expansion of cities created wonderful conditions for pathogens, once they infested *Homo sapiens*.

The most recent addition to the list of emerging viral diseases, severe acute respiratory syndrome (SARS), may be thought of as a form of revenge from the realm of species humanity has endangered. The disease may have first appeared in Foshan, China, about ninety miles from Hong Kong, among people who were preparing rare animals for the cooking pot. A virus very similar to the SARS virus has been isolated from masked palm civet cats, once common but increasingly rare, and from a raccoon dog, both food items in China.[66] It is possible, but in our view unlikely, that people had infected the animals that were tested. Only time will tell, but the possibility that domestic cats might represent a potential SARS reservoir is not a cheering one.

The hazardous state of our epidemiological environment is best exemplified by the HIV/AIDS epidemic, which is causing havoc in many parts of the world. HIV (human immunodeficiency virus) is believed to have been transferred to people from other primates in Africa and thence transmitted between individuals through sexual contact, contaminated blood, or needles used by drug addicts.[67] In 2002, an estimated 38.6 million human beings had HIV or AIDS.[68] Thus, about the number of people who live in Italy are infected worldwide with a fatal, rapidly spreading disease, and the epidemic appears to be still in its early stages, with vast disasters potentially lying in wait for populous countries such as China, India, and Indonesia. It is the first modern disease with the potential to devastate human societies in the way bubonic plague devastated Europe in the fourteenth century.

Today, rapidly expanding human populations are pressing close to natural reservoirs of a variety of pathogens. Among the deadliest known threats are Ebola, Lassa, and Marburg viruses, various hantaviruses, and the viruses responsible for killer influenza outbreaks.[69] The more people there are living in close proximity to animal reservoirs of pathogens, the higher are the chances of a disease successfully transferring into, and becoming established in, the human population. Even more threatening may be unknown viruses, as HIV and the coronavirus causing SARS were a few decades ago. HIV/AIDS may be only the first of the serious new global epidemics long predicted by biologists and epidemiologists.[70] The risks are exacerbated by the swiftness of modern transportation systems. If a ship carrying bubonic plague had left Shanghai for Bombay in 1700, by the time the ship reached its destination, everyone would have been either dead or recovered. In very stark contrast, HIV was carried to four continents by a single airline purser on a 747 within a matter of days.

Rapid transport systems are disseminating vectors (disease-carrying organisms) as well as animal reservoirs and infectious human beings. West Nile virus arrived in North America in 1999, one suspects in an infected traveling human being (it was first discovered in New York City). Since it infects birds and is transmitted by mosquitoes, it had a natural method of rapid spread, and it occupied essentially the entire United States by 2003. In 2002 there were an estimated 400,000 human infections,[71] mostly mild, with about 80,000 infections presumably producing cases of West Nile fever. There were 2,700 confirmed cases of the serious meningoencephalitis caused by the virus. The virus is similar to the poliovirus, which can produce the serious post-polio syndrome (PPS)—including cognitive problems and muscle weakness or paralysis decades after the initial polio infection. If there are late-onset symptoms of West Nile sequelae similar to PPS, as one observer commented, "North America is sitting on a time bomb."[72]

A more recent known import to the United States has been monkeypox, a less lethal relative of smallpox. It presumably arrived via Gambian pouched rats brought in as pets and subsequently invaded prairie dogs in pet stores and then people.[73] It normally carries a death rate of about 10 percent, but as of this writing no case in the United States has been fatal. Nonetheless, the incident underlines the serious problems that can be created by moving animals (and plants) speedily around the globe—a problem exacerbated by the disproportionate power of corporations that desire to serve global markets without barriers created to protect the long-term health of humanity.

In addition to rapid transport, gigantic cities, many containing huge slums filled with poorly nourished (and thus immune-compromised) people, make the situation even more threatening. Furthermore, with a general warming of climate, diseases such as malaria, dengue fever, yellow fever, various encephalitides (inflammations of the brain), and leishmaniasis (various nasty illnesses caused by protozoans of a group different from those that give you malaria) may become threats to temperate-zone countries, such as the United States and Italy, or temperate regions in tropical countries, such as Mexico and Peru, which have been largely free of tropical scourges for more than a century.[74]

Aside from a possible containment of SARS, about the only "good" news on the epidemiological front is that the anthrax attack in the United States in 2001, the threat of more bioterrorism, the still expanding AIDS epidemic, and the surfacing of SARS, at first seemingly from nowhere,[75] have reawakened the U.S. government's and public's interest in the problem of infectious diseases in general and the dangers posed by emerging diseases.

## Overshoot

While gaining its position of dominance over the natural world, *Homo sapiens,* especially in the past several decades, has achieved and exercised so much power over the planet's resources and rich panoply of life as to compromise the capacity of Earth to sustain the human enterprise, thus putting us on that collision course with nature that the world's scientists warned us about. Indeed, there is considerable evidence that the enormous expansion of the human enterprise has already caused *Homo sapiens* to overshoot the long-term carrying capacity of Earth—the number of people that could be sustained for many generations without reducing the resources necessary to similarly maintain an equal population size in the future.[76]

In 2002, a large and diverse team of scientists used existing data to determine how much of the biosphere would be required to support today's human population sustainably—that is, "to translate the human demand on the environment into the area required for the production of food and other goods, together with the absorption of wastes."[77] The scientists considered the needs for croplands and grazing lands, forests for timber, productive fishing grounds, infrastructure (housing, transport, industry, hydroelectric power, etc.), and carbon sequestration (to prevent an atmospheric buildup of $CO_2$) to support the population. The study, while preliminary, conservatively[78] estimated that humanity's "load" was equal to about 70 percent of the biosphere's regenerative capacity in 1961, that it had exceeded that capacity since the 1980s, and that, at the time of the study, it had reached more than 120 percent of capacity.

Much can be learned about the human overshoot of Earth's carrying capacity through the useful tool of ecological footprint analysis. This work was begun decades ago by economist Georg Borgstrom[79] and brought to fruition by William Rees and Mathis Wackernagel.[80] The eco-footprint of a designated population is "the total area of land and water ecosystems required to produce the resources that the population consumes, and to assimilate the wastes that the population produces, wherever on earth the land/water are located."[81] Eco-footprint analysis indicates that *Homo sapiens* has already exceeded the long-term carrying capacity of our planet by as much as 40 percent.[82] Such estimates are, to say the least, heavily dependent on the assumptions that go into them. But this, other analyses, and even common sense suggest the human enterprise is already unsustainable—human demand is outstripping what nature can supply—even though the great majority of human beings have not even approached the extraordinary American level of resource consumption. The eco-footprint of an average American is roughly four times the human average, and as much as ten times larger than those of the citizens of very poor countries such as Bangladesh and Chad. That difference does not just reflect different consumptive desires and incomes; it reflects the great disparity in power between the United States and the poorest nations.

Today's poor people endure a different kind of poverty from what people did a hundred years ago, in large part because of the escalating consumption by the rich.[83] Previously, the poor often found ways to sustain themselves and lead satisfactory lives, enriched with cultural and religious practices. Now they aspire to the American lifestyle, but they have been given a model of "development" that too often increases the misery of the majority, even though an elite minority in poor countries may enjoy Western-style affluence. The continued failure to ask what human beings really want, and to ensure for the poor a better level of well-being by their own standards, could easily endanger the well-being of Americans through increased social and political instability and the debilitating costs of continuous wars of empire.

## Tying It All Together

The various trends in the human predicament that are generating overshoot are, as one might expect, not independent. For instance, it is commonplace to believe that hunger in the world is caused by poverty and a malevolent economic system, and that population growth is not connected to the problem. In a recent article about genetically modified foods in an important anthropological journal, any mention of population size in connection with malnourishment was repeatedly called "playing the Malthus card."[84] Certainly, factors such as agricultural subsidies in rich countries and pressures to produce cash crops for export in poor ones have greatly contributed to problems of hunger and famine. So have the gross inequities in income and power that plague humanity; poverty is one of the worst environmental problems. If everyone were willing and able to share more equitably, for example, if the rich were willing to modify their current diets and greatly reduce their consumption of beef and other animal products, then hunger could be done away with. Ample food is produced today to feed more than 6 billion people a reasonable diet, but a disproportionate share goes to the already overfed.[85]

Nevertheless, hunger *is* connected to population size and growth, and it may well be more so in the future. The need to feed ever more people has led to an expansion of areas supporting crops (especially in poor countries) and an intensification of agriculture (especially in rich countries). Further intensification, especially in developing regions, will be necessary in order to keep increasing food production at least until the world population has passed its peak size and a basic level of nutrition for all societies has been achieved. If the human population were not already huge and still growing, providing that basic diet would be much easier and would carry fewer environmental risks.

Of all human activities, as we've noted, agriculture arguably has the greatest environmental impact, especially in the destruction of biodiversity—the plants, animals, and microbes that share Earth with us and upon which our lives depend.[86] Farmland often offers little habitat for organisms not directly producing crops or animal products for people; land under intensive agriculture, least of all. The escape of farm chemicals from intensive agriculture can have devastating effects on adjacent biological communities and sometimes affects distant ones.[87] That in turn is already having negative effects on agriculture through a decline in the ecosystem service of natural pollination of crops, by the poisoning of insect pollinators.[88] Thus, agriculture itself can destabilize the very processes it depends upon for success.

Climatic stability also is essential to maintaining, let alone increasing, the high levels of agricultural production required to feed our enormous population. Yet agriculture itself contributes to climate change, both by adding greenhouse gases to the atmosphere and by changing the rate at which energy from the sun is reflected back to space locally (technically, Earth's "albedo").[89] Darker areas, such as forests, reflect less sunlight than do most farm fields, ocean surfaces, and ice caps, as well as most clouds. The overall directions of change in albedo are uncertain because it depends in each case on the system that existed previously and the amount of cloud cover. Most reflected light returns to space, but the sunlight absorbed by dark surfaces is re-radiated as heat and adds to global warming. Deforestation significantly changes albedo, both directly and indirectly, by changing cloud cover as well as devastating local biodiversity and adding $CO_2$ to the atmosphere. Destabilization of the climate assails biodiversity as well, exterminating populations and species that cannot adapt or move fast enough to keep up with changing habitats, species that may have played important roles in support of agricultural systems.

Population, consumption, and power can also interact to worsen the consequences of "natural" disasters. Too many people and economic inequality in Honduras, combined with overharvesting of forests and planting of crops on steep slopes, turned a nasty hurricane into a catastrophe in 1998. Many of the poor in that country had no alternative to living in precarious situations. Hurricane Mitch dealt them a devastating blow, triggering floods and mudslides that would not have occurred if there had been fewer people, land had not been overexploited, and the distribution of land had been more equitable so that the poor were not crowded into vulnerable areas. Mitch killed thousands of people and made tens of thousands homeless in Honduras and Nicaragua. Most of the victims were squatters who lived on riverbanks or in villages on steep mountainsides.[90]

In India, much of the coastal mangroves in the Bay of Bengal have been destroyed to make way for shrimp farms designed to supply global trade with the rich countries. In 2000, a giant cyclone (its unprecedented wind speeds possibly related to global warming) struck the coast, devastating communities never before affected by a cyclone because the coastal buffering of the mangrove swamps was gone. As a result, 30,000 people and about 100,000 cattle were killed.[91]

Interactions such as those between poverty and vulnerability to storms, along with the underlying factors of population growth, demand for tropical timber and high-priced seafood in rich countries, persisting economic inequities, and other elements of the human predicament, are too seldom appreciated. So too are characteristics of some of those interactions—problems of scale, threshold effects, nonlinearities, lag times, complexity, and the like—which plague analysis of environmental and social issues as well as sometimes having devastating consequences. As an example of the difference scale can make, 10,000 people scattered along the Mississippi River could defecate into it and biodiversity's natural waste-disposal service would keep the water flowing into the Gulf of Mexico pure enough to drink. Increase the scale a thousandfold or so and the sewage from the many millions living along the Mississippi and its tributaries today must be treated (or water withdrawn must be purified) if there are not to be serious public health problems. In the San Francisco Bay Area of the 1860s, the atmosphere could be used as a convenient garbage dump—cooking fires and belching cattle didn't pose much of a problem. By the 1960s, the need for controls on fires, power plants, and automobile exhaust had become all too evident to choking residents.

*Problems of scale* are nearly ubiquitous in environmental matters. A town of 2,000 people cannot sustain a measles epidemic; a city of 500,000 easily can.[92] If the ancient Greeks ruined Attica, the Greeks suffered. There were perhaps only 200 million people in the whole world in those days, with little or no contact between sizable population centers. But if the rich keep dumping record amounts of $CO_2$ into the atmosphere, everyone in the world is likely to suffer. There are some thirty times as many people in the world now as there were 2,500 years ago; all are tightly linked in a globalized society and using the atmosphere as a garbage dump.

All the problems connected to the scale of the human population also may contain *threshold* factors—sudden transitions from one environmental state to another. River water may remain potable as more and more people are added, up to a point, and then suddenly the density of some pathogenic microorganism may cross a threshold so that there are enough of the organisms in a drink of water to make an average person seriously ill. Excess fertilizer can flow into the Gulf of Mexico with relatively little effect until a threshold is crossed and a dead zone appears. Similarly, thresholds are common in processes of land degradation; soil erosion can proceed unnoticed for a long time, and then suddenly the land's productivity may drop disastrously.

Climate is an example of a *nonlinear* system, one in which a steady rise in an input does not necessarily result in a steady rate of change, but instead may cause a slow response at first, which then accelerates as the input rises. Through recent human history, Earth's climate seemed to be in a rather stable equilibrium. For instance, changes in solar input produced in each hemisphere by Earth's travel around the sun result in what we call seasons. Stability is indicated by the failure of summer to spiral away to a heat death for the planet, or of winter to keep getting colder until everything freezes. The perturbation caused by increased solar heating in summer causes not a permanent change but one that returns to the previous state as the solar flux begins to diminish after the summer solstice.

But what is known about the history of Earth's climate suggests that there have been other, quite different stable states. If we push hard on the system (for example, by continuing to inject greenhouse gases into the atmosphere), a threshold might be passed that would thrust the climate into a very different stable state—one that could be disastrous for human society. Development of today's civilization occurred during a long period (roughly 11,000 years) of unusually stable and favorable climate, but there is no guarantee that the climate will remain that way. Remember the Younger Dryas! Humanity is now gambling that we won't run into a similar nonlinearity as Earth is warmed by anthropogenic activities. Such a nonlinearity would have a devastating effect on biodiversity and ecosystem services—especially because human modification of Earth's ecosystems has already made them much more vulnerable and less likely to be resilient.

Many of the problems we have described develop with very long *lag times* before consequences materialize. One example obviously is global warming, in which the full effects of the greenhouse gases that have been released by human activities into the atmosphere will take decades to become clear, even if not another molecule is emitted. Another is cancers, such as melanoma, which are induced by anthropogenic environmental changes (thinning of the ozone layer in this case), wherein the deadly tumor may appear decades after the environmental exposure. Many lags are inherent in social trends and systems as well. Ending population growth by reducing birthrates, for instance, will take at least several more decades to accomplish, as will converting civilization to less environmentally damaging energy systems. To understand what's going on the world now and in the future will require much more attention to these rarely recognized features of human-environment interactions.[93]

There are many costs associated with humanity's rise to dominance. They include differences in well-being and influence between nations and regions, the ecological unsustainability of today's civilization and its escalating assault against its life-support systems, and humanity's growing vulnerability to dangerous new epidemics. All of these represent challenges that must be met. Now is a time of unprecedented, well-documented, and escalating environmental danger.[94] The scientific consensus holds that humanity's behavior is greatly reducing civilization's chances of becoming sustainable.[95] One group of distinguished ecologists put the necessary response this way: "Humanity's dominance of Earth means that we cannot escape responsibility for managing the planet. Our activities are causing rapid, novel, and substantial changes to Earth's ecosystems. Maintaining populations, species, and ecosystems in the face of those changes, and maintaining the flow of goods and services they provide humanity, will require active management in the foreseeable future."[96]

Humanity corporately still has an opportunity to take a series of dramatic steps to change direction and avoid its impending collision with the natural world. It is essential that we start building momentum toward shaping a world in which a sustainable number of people can all lead a decent, highly pleasurable life, able to consume at a satisfying but safe level, free from the prospect of resource wars, terrorism, and the consequences of mounting environmental deterioration. Here, the importance of leadership from the United States cannot be overstated. And no issues are more fundamental to shaping a more secure and sustainable world than those that surround the population driver of the human predicament, to which we turn next.

Chapter 3

# THE TIDE OF POPULATION

"The tide of earth's population is rising, the reservoir of
earth's living resources is falling."
FAIRFIELD OSBORNE, 1948[1]

IN 1995, we and our colleague Gretchen Daily were leading a tour
for Stanford University alumni, introducing them to some of the
environmental issues of the western Indian Ocean. Among
many other places, we visited Anjouan, an island of the Union of the
Comoros. Anjouan's hills were green, and tropical vegetation was lush
along stream courses. Palm trees waved in the breeze, half-naked children ran about laughing, and the surrounding ocean was a deep blue.
To most of our group of highly educated American tourists, it seemed
a tropical paradise.[2]

Despite appearances, Anjouan was no paradise. Along with the
other Comoros Islands, it was a society that had overshot the ability of
its environment to sustain it. Anjouan's extremely steep green hills
were cultivated to the top. There was no spare land, and the dominant
vegetation consisted of plants introduced from elsewhere. Goats, notorious agents of ecosystem destruction through overgrazing, roamed
freely. Ali, our local guide and interpreter, said that the children were
laughing because they had just caught a small fish, which they might be
able to trade for a couple of pounds of rice. "Mama will be so proud of
us, because it'll be the first rice we've had to eat in two weeks," they told
him. Like many others on Anjouan, these children lived on the edge of

starvation, subsisting for extended periods on nothing but coconuts, Ali explained. Indeed, we were begged by many of the children there, most of them showing signs of malnutrition. One child had a captive lesser Vasa parrot, tortured by being tethered with a string tied to one wing. The idea was that a tourist should buy and free it (under which stimulus, of course, another would be captured to repeat the process).

In many ways, Anjouan appeared to us much as Rwanda had in 1983—an ecocatastrophe in the making because population growth had led to severe overexploitation of the nation's limited food production resources and had overstressed the vital natural services that undergird them. The precarious situation we saw in Rwanda, to our minds, played a significant role in triggering the hideous violence that erupted a decade later.

The Comoros Islands as a group also faced an environmental crisis tracing in no small part to their exploding population, which, combined with even the limited consumption of the islanders and a government little interested in either ecology or family planning, was destroying the islands' capacity to support human life. The average family in the Union of the Comoros included almost seven children. In one of the poorest nations on Earth, Anjouan—having less than one-twentieth the affluence of Americans—the people were numerous enough to have wreaked havoc in this confined land in the struggle to gain sustenance. Between 1971 and 1986, Anjouan lost 73 percent of its natural forest, crucial to maintaining its water supplies to support agriculture (and potentially important for ecotourism). Another of the Comoros, Mohéli, lost half of its forest in the same period. In 1925 there were forty-five permanent rivers on Anjouan; in 1992 only eleven were left, and tankers had to bring water to some areas.[3]

Shortly after our visit, news reports surfaced of growing chaos on Anjouan.[4] Then, in 1997, that island and another, Mohéli, seceded from the Union of the Comoros and formed a separate Islamic republic. The rebellion was put down and Anjouan was returned to the Union, but a majority of Anjouan's population apparently would still like to secede. The Comoros have suffered nineteen coups d'état or attempted coups since they gained independence from France in 1975,[5] and local violence is still common.[6] It's hard for anyone to wield power in a desperately poor nation enmeshed in turmoil. The future looks no better. By 2050, the 600,000 residents of the Comoros are projected to increase to 1.8 million. That will give this string of tiny mountainous islands, dependent on agriculture, fishing, and tourism, twice the population density (number of people per square mile) of the Netherlands today. Think of what a paradise it still might be if its population growth had stopped at 40,000 or 60,000 people, giving it a population density less than one-thirtieth of that projected for 2050, more like that of the United States now.

The story of our Anjouan visit tells us how well-educated people from rich countries may misperceive the environmental situation in a poor country, but it tells little about the roots of the dilemma in which the children of Anjouan find themselves. After all, the natural life-support systems of Manhattan have long since been utterly destroyed, yet all but the poorest there live lives of comparative luxury—beyond the wildest dreams of those Anjouan children. Resources flow in abundance into Manhattan; they barely trickle into Anjouan. Even though agriculture dominates the economy of the Comoros, the island chain is not self-sufficient in food. Rice, the main staple, accounts for the bulk of its imports.[7]

The contrasts between Manhattan and the Comoros reflect differing historical and geographic circumstances, but even more they show that the way in which resources, economic power, and political power are distributed can create imbalances between the resources available and the needs of the population. Manhattan is the center of a vast economic empire that originally derived its power largely from an extraordinarily rich agricultural base. The United States is now able to support its huge, overconsuming population because it has built from that base the industrial and military power that allows it to co-opt resources from the farthest reaches of the planet. The Comoros have no such advantages; with a meager resource base, their population growth has brought them to their present sad state. But even abundance has its limits; the advantages of the United States might not be enough to insulate it in the long run.

## From Small Beginnings

Population growth is a nearly ubiquitous, but all too often ignored, driver of environmental and social problems. Numbers really do count, just as does the closely linked factor of per capita consumption—how much of Earth's bounty each new individual can be expected to demand. The thousandfold increase in the size of the human population in the past ten millennia is the most stunning and rapid biological change on the planet since the demise of the dinosaurs 65 million years ago. For the first few hundred thousand years of their existence, populations of *Homo sapiens* were very small and their environmental effects were localized and transitory. There was no hint that in a relatively short period (on a geologic time scale) people could rise to planetary dominance or generate the kind of ecocatastrophes that later would occur in Mesopotamia, Rwanda, or Anjouan. Rather than being on a collision course with the natural world, people were an integral part of it. As is the case with every organism, those early people and their activities altered their local environments (all living things must exchange materials and energy with their surroundings), but they had essentially no global influence. After modern *Homo sapiens* appeared, the population continued to grow and spread very slowly for many millennia, with setbacks and losses from time to time and place to place.

Some scientists believe that growth in human populations, creating higher population densities (and thus a need for better technologies to extract more food from smaller areas) was a factor in causing the "great leap forward,"[8] that little-understood revolution some 50,000 years ago which accelerated the speed at which humanity's non-genetic information (culture) changed. New technologies (such as fine blade-like stone tools and ivory needles) appeared suddenly, art bloomed on cave walls, sculptures and body ornaments were made, signs of belief in an afterlife were seen in burial practices, and perhaps there was even an advance in human linguistic ability. And it is thought that the great leap in turn sped the process of population growth by lowering human death rates. Whatever caused the leap, *Homo sapiens* was transformed into an inventive and culturally flexible animal that eventually could make its presence obvious from outer space.

Local population pressures also may have provided the impetus for the agricultural revolution about 10,000 years ago, first beginning in the Fertile Crescent, an arc from today's Israel through Lebanon, Syria, and southern Turkey to the foothills of the Zagros Mountains, northeast of Nineveh.[9] That revolution, by eventually freeing some people from the need to hunt for and gather food, enabled the appearance of new classes: scribes, professional soldiers, priests, and ruling classes able to command the labor of others. It also led to much larger populations and the kinds of institutionalized power relationships that still plague humanity. Power relationships are unavoidable in human societies, but differences in power and influence became a major factor in humanity's fate only after the agricultural revolution permitted new social strata to emerge.[10]

After the invention of agriculture, population growth accelerated. From 5 million or so people when farming first started, the world's population rose to perhaps 250 million (fewer than live in the United States today) by the time of Christ, at the height of the Roman Empire. As human populations expanded and agriculture spread across Europe and Asia (and was independently invented in several places, including in the New World),[11] people's effects on their surroundings also intensified. Increasingly, natural areas were converted for crop production and livestock grazing, at the expense of wild plants and animals.

Long before the modern age, many civilizations, like that of the Assyrians, rose and flourished for a time, then fell. Some were conquered and others simply faded as overexploitation of land and natural resources led to impoverishment and decline, often including a substantial population decline.[12] Among the civilizations that disappeared were the Mesopotamian empires, ancient Greece and Rome, the Indus Valley civilization in the Old World, and the classic Maya and Anasazi in the New World.[13] On a smaller scale, the pattern was starkly and tragically repeated by Easter Island Polynesians, who overshot their society's resources and then resorted to warfare and even cannibalism as it collapsed.[14] The island's estimated peak population of more than

7,000 plummeted to 111 by 1900. In other, less environmentally fragile and isolated regions, such as China, India, and, later, Europe, societies persisted and survived despite sporadic wars, plagues, and famines.

The world's population reached a billion shortly after the beginning of the industrial revolution. Industrialization facilitated an intensification of agriculture and better sanitation for urbanizing populations in Europe and North America, eventually improving millions of people's lives. Improved health and nutrition helped reduce death rates as the role and perceived value of children changed, and the population took off, rising to 2 billion worldwide by 1930. As life expectancies rose in industrialized societies, birthrates gradually fell, but both death and birthrates remained essentially unchanged elsewhere.

Industrialization also stimulated increased trade between continents and nations and dramatically changed power relationships among them as the early industrializers took steps to co-opt the resources of other, less technologically advanced societies. To fuel their expanding industrial systems, nations in Europe, North America, and, later, Japan increasingly sought raw materials from other regions of the world and grew richer, while non-industrial regions remained largely excluded from the benefits of modernization. At worst, in the late nineteenth and early twentieth centuries, some non-industrial societies suffered horrendous famines as a result of the first big round of globalization.[15] An exception to the exploitation of poor by rich was the introduction of improved sanitation and medical technology after World War II in Asia, Latin America, and Africa, which successfully— sometimes spectacularly—lowered death rates, although birthrates remained near their previous high levels.

That reduction in death rates set the stage for the twentieth-century population explosion: in just seventy years, between 1930 and 2000, the global population *tripled* in size, reaching 6 billion. The annual population growth rate soared above 2 percent per year in the 1960s, falling only slowly after 1970 as birthrates began to decline in some developing nations and, unexpectedly, fell further in most industrialized nations. By the end of the century, the world population was still growing by 1.2 percent annually,[16] although populations in most developed nations were no longer expanding, and some had even begun to shrink slightly. In the last quarter of the twentieth century, the combined populations of the industrialized nations increased by only about 20 percent while those of the developing world grew by some 60 percent.[17] By the year 2000, however, even in most of the poorest, least developed regions of the world, birthrates had at last begun to drop, and some of the more prosperous developing countries had attained total fertility rates (or TFR; the average number of lifetime births per woman in the population) that would soon bring an end to their population growth.

Nonetheless, because of the momentum of population growth—an unavoidable result of earlier high birthrates—continued growth in the world population to nearly 9 billion by 2050 is likely (give or take a billion or so, depending on fertility and mortality trends), with a peak size of 9 to 10 billion occurring sometime after 2050. As a result, somewhere between 1.5 and 4 billion or more people may be added to the world's population before growth ends, nearly all of them in developing countries.[18]

The prospective end of the population explosion is wonderful news, but those still-expected additions do not bode at all well for civilization's long-term sustainability and the chances of the poor being lifted out of poverty, especially if per capita consumption continues to grow among the already well-off. As things are today, even without any further increases in world population, if every person in the world were to start consuming as Americans do, humanity would require the resources of at least two additional planet Earths to support it. As Mathis Wackernagel and William Rees noted, "Unfortunately, good planets are hard to find."[19] In this context, it's important to recognize that adding 1.5 billion more people in fifty years would be infinitely better than adding 4 billion more (the difference is larger than the entire world population of 1950). Which number turns out to be closer to the one actually reached will largely depend on the population policies the United States and other nations adopt.

Sadly, most of the countries with the most rapid population growth are among the poorest, least developed, and least able to support massive additions to their populations. They are also therefore the most in need of family planning assistance. And Americans, probably the chief contributors to the population-consumption problem, broadly defined, seem mostly oblivious to the potentially massive threat posed by increasing numbers of people.

## Population on the Back Burner

Many Americans apparently have been lulled by contrary claims into believing that the population explosion is over, or that further growth doesn't matter. You would never know by reading the newspapers or watching television today that the numbers of people will greatly affect our own and our children's futures.

Oddly, the absence of population issues from public discourse has led to a failure to recognize those rather momentous *positive* changes in the population situation that have occurred in the past decade or so. Remember, only a few decades ago, the global population was expanding at 2 percent or more per year, a rate that would double it in thirty-five years or less, with no indication of any slowdown. And it did double in forty years. But now there are clear signs of a slowdown in most regions, although serious questions remain about the world's ability to keep on producing enough food and otherwise provide for an ever-increasing number of people—questions of social survival that are still very relevant.

That the good news and the not-so-good news about the population situation have become invisible in the media in the United States in recent years can be illustrated by a long segment on the Public Broadcasting Service's *NewsHour with Jim Lehrer* (among the best television coverage of such topics) on the 2002 spring drought in New Jersey and other regions of the eastern United States.[20] Many pertinent points were made, such as the inefficiency of water use and the stupidity of paving over recharge areas of aquifers, the underground deposits of water from which we pump much of our supply. Aquifers depend on rainwater filtering down through the soil to refill them, but rainwater can't filter through concrete, and concrete proliferates with population growth and increasing sprawl. Yet the program made no mention of the role of population growth on a national or regional scale in driving water consumption upward, even as subdivisions and highways coat ever more of the countryside.

Even rarer in the media is mention of the role growing human numbers worldwide play in enhancing the flow of greenhouse gases into the environment. The resultant climate change may already have begun to alter precipitation patterns enough to intensify droughts; human modification of the atmosphere is virtually certain to affect those patterns in the future.

The population connection is everywhere, and it is vastly more serious than most citizens, media pundits, and politicians recognize. Some connections are direct and obvious—for instance, to freeway congestion and smog. Others are much more subtle and complex, such as the connection of population size to global warming.

In the eastern United States, neither population growth nor water shortage is an obviously serious problem. Populations in Maine, New York, and New Jersey, for example, grew by 0.4 to 0.8 percent annually in the last decade of the twentieth century. The global consequences of those few million additional people are almost as invisible as the carbon dioxide ($CO_2$) emitted by motor vehicle tailpipes in the morning commute. Regionally, aside from prominent traffic jams, their effects are mostly subtle.

But telling nonetheless. For instance, the behavior of northeasterners is changing as they strive to avoid Lyme disease.[21] Suburbanites who moved far out of the city to enjoy nature are now staying indoors more and watching more closely where they let their children play, to prevent exposure to the ticks that carry the disease. Lyme disease is a plague made serious by population explosions of deer, white-footed mice, and deer ticks resulting from a complex of anthropogenic causes. Among those are expansion of the human population, contributing to an intrusion of automobile-centered suburban sprawl into forests; the extermination of wolves—critical deer predators—and possibly the extinction by commercial hunters a century ago of the passenger pigeon, which once competed with the mice for acorns and beech-nuts.[22]

Population surpluses are on a more obvious collision course with nature in the Mountain West, where during the 1990s human numbers were growing in New Mexico, Arizona, Colorado, and Nevada by 2.7 to 5.1 percent and in California by about 1.3 percent per year.[23] In that region, the traffic jams are growing, but the main collision is with the ability of the regional hydrological cycle to provide sufficient fresh water to support high densities of people.

Far more severe problems of water shortage are plaguing China, as we've seen. The vast expansion of China's population has been a major cause—some 700 million people, twice the current U.S. population plus that of Mexico, have been added to the Chinese population since 1950.[24] They require a lot more water, much of it diverted from the Yellow River, to meet the growing demand for irrigation, industrial uses, and domestic consumption. In addition, acid rain is a serious problem in China; ironically, a major cause is the nearly total absence of potable water as a result of high population densities and poor sanitation facilities. That requires the use of coal fires by every family to sterilize water and make it safe to drink,[25] at the cost of increased acid precipitation.

Do you suppose that if China had only 130 million people instead of 1.3 billion,[26] all of its water would be polluted? If it were, would the burning of coal to supply safe water for a population one-tenth the present size acidify rainfall to anything like today's level? Would a China with one-tenth of today's population be the number two emitter of the greenhouse gas $CO_2$—on track to catch up with number one, the United States?[27]

One factor keeping the United States in the lead in greenhouse gas emissions is the large American population, which has more than doubled since the end of World War II and is still growing more rapidly than that of any other industrialized nation. That's not the whole story in the United States or elsewhere, though; it's not just the numbers of people that count but also the way they behave, and especially the way they consume.

## The Challenge for the Rich

There are many reasons why rich nations and groups are a dominant force in undermining global environmental systems,[28] but it's fruitless to assign blame for past actions. Much of the destruction occurred long before anyone had ever heard of ecosystem services and was caused by people who were unaware of the long-term consequences of their collective actions. Those who strove to bring world resources and other people under their control so they could enjoy the assurance of more consumption usually believed it was their God-given right or manifest destiny. But today humanity must reduce its assault on Earth's ecosystems for the sake of nature and for the sake of its own future. There is ample and mounting evidence of the risks entailed, yet there still is no organized effort to make the required changes in consumption patterns, nor is there support from those who can best afford to make them.

Lacking any extra planets, civilization faces an unavoidable further expansion of human numbers on the one we have. Also inevitable will be an increasing strain on our small planet's life-support systems as poor peoples gain the chance to have decent lives. Finding ways to limit the damage from those trends is the great challenge of the new century. Part of that effort must be to bring population growth to an end as soon as humanely possible—to aim for the 1.5 billion addition rather than the 4 billion.

The affluent not only have a duty to learn the basics of how the world works; they also bear a responsibility to help their destitute cousins share in the rewards of modern life. The rich are primarily the ones who have the resources and opportunities to get the job done. To us, that implies a necessary, substantial change in the behavior of the citizens of industrialized nations, not just in how much we consume and how much assistance we give the needy but also how many children we have.

## Success Misinterpreted
## and Misapprehensions Rampant

One immediate reason for the neglect of the population topic in the United States was press coverage in the early 1970s of the achievement of "replacement reproduction" in the nation—the level at which the number of births just replaces the parent generation, an average in an industrialized country (with modern sanitation and health care) of about 2.1 children per couple—a total fertility rate (TFR) of 2.1.[29] Reaching replacement reproduction was an important accomplishment for the United States, but its most important effects were not immediate: reducing family sizes to that level precedes a halt to population growth by decades, a classic example of a time lag (the result, an end to growth, lags behind the cause, a drop in TFR, by about a life expectancy—some seventy years in a rich country).

This may seem counterintuitive, but consider for a minute. Suppose you and your spouse had two children by the time you were twenty-five years old. You would have contributed to the birthrate and replaced yourselves. But statistically it would be roughly fifty more years before you contributed to the death rate—and it is likely that by then your kids and possibly your grandchildren also would have added to the birthrate. Human beings don't drop dead as soon as they've reproduced. Reaching replacement reproduction in 1973 was wrongly interpreted as the end of the U.S. population explosion. The misimpression took over, and press coverage of population issues in the United States began to fade. Since then, we have added nearly 90 million people as a result of natural increase and immigration.

Beyond the misinterpretation of achieving replacement reproduction, there are a number of other reasons why people ignore the ubiquitous population driver. Some of them are deep-rooted, such as our being social animals who desire and love children and who tend not to notice changes that take place slowly.[30] Most reasons are cultural and involve some form of denial. Some are religious: concern among some Catholics and others that recognition of population problems will lead to increased use of contraception or abortion, both of which the Vatican and some other conservative religious groups oppose. Catholics, however, widely ignore their Church's injunctions and use both techniques; some of the lowest birthrates in the world are seen in predominantly Catholic nations (e.g., Italy, with a TFR of 1.2; Poland, 1.3; Portugal, 1.5; Spain, 1.2).[31] The global population problem is *not* by and large a Catholic problem.

Nonetheless, some reasons that population growth has been ignored are rooted in a combination of religious and political factors: fear among U.S. politicians of the animus of the Catholic hierarchy or ultraconservative protestant religious groups; fear among some Jews that their numbers will shrink if their co-religionists take the population problem seriously and further restrict their fertility; and fear among politicians of entering the minefield of immigration policy or appearing to endorse those who want to limit the size of particular groups for unpalatable reasons.

## Defusing the Population Bomb

When Paul wrote *The Population Bomb* in 1968,[32] the human population was growing at an unprecedented rate. It then was about 3.5 billion people, up from 2 billion when we were born, in the early 1930s. Since the *Bomb* was published, the population has grown by another 2.8 billion. And the world population of 6.3 billion in 2004 is projected by demographers to continue growing, as we've already indicated.

In 1968, we were deeply concerned about both the rate of population growth, at that time around 2 percent per year, and the outlook for further growth: a possible doubling and redoubling of the population within seventy years. The likely environmental impact of such a huge and rapid population expansion was alarming, with its obvious implications for Earth's ability to sustain so many billions. While some concern had emerged publicly by then about resource limitations (mainly of minerals, fossil fuels, and agricultural land),[33] connections between the size and growth of the population and environmental problems had not yet been recognized by many, nor, in any serious way, had concerns about potential limitations to food production. *The Population Bomb* highlighted these connections.

In the late 1960s, the population explosion was seen as a new problem with somewhat mysterious causes. Improvements in health care and sanitation had clearly been responsible for falling death rates—especially of infants and small children—in underdeveloped regions after World War II. But birthrates in those regions were as high as they had ever been, which led to a dramatic surge in population growth. So the assumption was made that industrial development would lift millions out of poverty and lead to a matching reduction in birthrates. This belief was based mainly on the observation that, in Europe and North America, birthrates had fallen slowly, following dropping death rates, as industrialization proceeded in the nineteenth and early twentieth centuries. By the late 1960s, the average family size in most industrialized nations was approaching the replacement level of 2.1 children. But in less developed regions, average family sizes ranged from 5 to 7 or even 8 children. The stark difference in fertility rates between industrialized and less developed nations matched the large and growing gap in wealth between the two groups of nations.[34]

It soon became evident, however, that the urban and industrial model of development was ineffective for either alleviating poverty or reducing family sizes in developing nations; a fraction of the population got richer, but most people remained poor. Although mortality rates continued to fall, birthrates in most countries stayed high. Governments in many countries where populations were doubling every twenty years or so remained complacent, not realizing that such rapid growth could soon trap them in seemingly insoluble problems of urban migration, unemployment, poverty, and social friction, to say nothing of resource depletion and environmental deterioration. The need to provide the information and means of contraception was increasingly obvious. Funding for family planning assistance was added to the foreign aid program in the United States in the 1960s, and volunteer associations such as the International Planned Parenthood Federation became increasingly active in developing countries. Within a few years, other developed nations began to fund family planning assistance as well. By the end of the 1970s,[35] family planning programs had been established in the majority of developing nations. Even so, birthrates in most of those nations stayed stubbornly high well into the 1980s. Only later were the reasons for the delay in the start of fertility reduction understood.[36]

## Politics in the Bedroom

When Ronald Reagan was elected president in 1980, his administration and its supporters opposed family planning assistance, largely because of their fierce disapproval of legal abortion. The result was a sharp cutback in funding for family planning aid, especially to multilateral agencies such as the United Nations Population Fund and Planned Parenthood. Fortunately, other industrialized countries picked up some of the lost funding, and many developing countries had taken on more of the funding responsibility for themselves. Without U.S. contributions, however, funding for family planning lagged well behind the rising demand for the services. At the 1984 United Nations International Conference on Population in Mexico City, to the dismay of delegates from other countries, the Reagan administration announced its refusal to fund any international agency that used its monies for anything related to abortion, even though funds from the United States had long been required to be kept separate from all abortion activities. This became known as the "Mexico City policy."[37] Family planning supporters referred to it as a "gag order" because it was so strict that program counselors were forbidden even to mention abortion, in any context. When President Bill Clinton took office in 1993, he reversed the policy. There is no way to know how many thousands of women may have died from quack abortions in the intervening years.

By 1990, much more was understood about the causes of persisting high birthrates. Several decades of research had demonstrated that certain kinds of development strongly influence reproductive choices, but others do not. Besides the obvious importance of making contra-

ception information and materials available for couples who desired to
limit their families, such factors as education and opportunities for
women proved crucial in lowering birthrates. Countries that provided
schooling for girls and allowed or encouraged women to participate in
economic activities outside the home, while providing basic health care
and the means of birth control, generally experienced significant declines in birthrates. In addition, societies that had also developed without great gaps in wealth between the richest and poorest groups, had the
most success in both family planning and economic development.[38]

The growing understanding of these connections became a focus
for discussion at the United Nations International Conference on
Population and Development in 1994 in Cairo and resulted in agreements to expand funding for population activities to include female
education and economic opportunities and health care centered on
family well-being. At the time, the Clinton administration pledged
substantially greater participation in assistance to developing nations,
but the Republican majority that emerged from the 1994 congressional elections undercut this pledge. When George W. Bush became
president in 2001, the Mexico City policy was fully re-established,
essentially re-igniting the Reagan administration's attack on the
world's women. The results: reduced family planning services, more
unwanted births, and more dangerous abortions.

Despite persistently insufficient funding for population programs
since 1981, though, considerable progress has been made in dampen-
ing the population explosion. Rather than doubling and redoubling in
the seventy years following publication of *The Population Bomb* in 1968,
as once seemed likely, the global population may double (from 3.5 to 7
billon) in fifty-four years, by 2012. But a redoubling is nowhere in
sight. As mentioned earlier, growth of the global population has
slowed to about 1.2 percent per year, and it appears on track to continue slowing for the next several decades, according to the United
Nations' medium demographic projection.[39]

This shift in population projections has overwhelmingly been the
result of a "birthrate solution," in which growth comes to an end chiefly
because fewer children are being born to parents in each generation—

at least so far. But we must always remember that this "good" news is occurring in the context of a planet that is already overpopulated, committed to more population growth, and almost certain to see significant increases in per capita consumption.

## The Demographic and Development Transition

After 1970, and especially in the 1990s, birthrates turned downward almost everywhere in the world. The industrialized world was no exception. By the mid-1990s, fertility had fallen below the replacement level in nearly every developed nation. By 2004, many nations in Europe, the former Soviet Union, and Japan had average family sizes (TFRs) of 1.5 or less, and some had slowly shrinking populations. Alone among fully industrialized nations after the turn of the century, the United States has a TFR of 2.0, along with a high rate of immigration, producing a population growth rate of 1.0 percent per year.[40] Canada and Australia, both of which also admit large numbers of immigrants, have much lower fertility and therefore lower population growth rates.

The developing world, where high fertility and widespread poverty prevailed in the 1960s, is no longer so uniform. Some of those societies now are more or less fully industrialized, with high incomes and commensurately low fertilities: Singapore, Hong Kong (now part of China), South Korea, Taiwan, Thailand, Israel, and the Bahamas. A larger number of middle-income countries are not far behind: Argentina, Brazil, Chile, Costa Rica, Mexico, Turkey, and most Caribbean nations, among others.

The poorest nations present a decidedly mixed picture. China succeeded in reducing its birthrate dramatically during the 1970s, reaching below-replacement fertility in the 1990s, but by employing sometimes draconian measures.[41] By 2003, its TFR had fallen to 1.7. Interestingly, China's transition out of poverty and underdevelopment began well after the birthrate began to fall. By the 1990s, though, a real "great leap forward" was well under way in China, with economic growth rates near 10 percent per year.[42] The result has been a widening disparity in China between rich and poor, the former mostly in the rapidly growing cities, especially coastal ones, the latter mostly in rural areas. Since China's 2004 population of 1.3 billion is more than a fifth of the world's people, what happens in China has significant implications for global demographic and development trends.

India, in contrast, with the world's second largest population, 1.1 billion in 2004, hasn't done so well. Some Indian states have below-replacement TFRs and others still have relatively high ones; for the nation as a whole, the TFR is 3.1. As might be expected, female literacy and economic activity are higher in the states with lower fertility,[43] but, overall, fewer than 40 percent of adult women in India are literate. As in China, incomes are rising in India, and a middle class is emerging, but wealth is not broadly distributed. The majority of the population remains very poor, with 47 percent surviving on less than a dollar a day in the mid-1990s. India has the largest number of hungry people of any nation; an estimated 57 percent of children under age five were malnourished in 1995.[44]

Outside of the two developing giants, the picture in Asia and northern Africa is mixed, but in general the trend is positive. Rapid development and falling birthrates are evident in much of Southeast Asia, even where some of the expected prerequisites are lacking.[45] In Latin America, most countries are clearly moving rapidly toward low birthrates and rising incomes. In 1990, the region's aggregate TFR was estimated at 3.5 children per family; in 2002, it was down to 2.7.[46]

The population disaster area is Africa south of the Sahara. It remains the region with the highest birthrates and lowest incomes. Fertility has only recently (since the late 1980s) begun to fall in many countries, although mostly only to a range of TFRs between 5.0 and 6.5 in 2003.[47] Unfortunately, many African countries remain embroiled in political conflict, plagued with widespread corruption, and deeply mired in poverty. Even so, the population of Africa is projected by UN demographers to more than double, rising from about 850 million in 2003 to 1.8 billion in 2050, and continuing to grow for some time afterward.[48]

A major argument over population patterns has centered on the relationship between high fertility and poverty: does poverty cause high birthrates, or does rapid population growth cause poverty? The emerging answer, for which much is owed to the pathbreaking work of economist Partha Dasgupta,[49] appears to be both. Rapid population growth clearly hinders the ability of governments and other institutions to meet the constantly growing needs of the people—to provide infrastructure, schools, hospitals, and clinics and to keep increasing food production. This is especially problematic when a very large proportion of the population—as much as 50 percent in some cases—is under the age of fifteen. Simply keeping pace with a population that is doubling in eighteen to twenty-five years is very difficult; making progress is almost impossible. And some of the poorest, least developed societies have indeed lost ground in the past few decades.

The role of poverty in generating high fertility is less clear-cut, but poverty is usually accompanied by illiteracy and lack of access to social services, including health and family planning services. A lack of paid jobs for women and cultural strictures against outside activities, along with lack of schooling, severely limit women's independence and ability to make intelligent choices about their lives. That in turn produces conditions that encourage high fertility.[50] The value of children in poor rural families as laborers, for example, to gather water and firewood, helps keep fertility high.[51] Poor families in developing countries are often marginalized and left to meet their own needs under conditions of a deteriorating environment, causing them to fall even more deeply into poverty.[52] Thus, a downward spiral can ensue, with the parents increasingly unable to produce enough food from an environment under ever-increasing pressure, and becoming more dependent on their children's labor for help, with no support from outside other than neighbors or relatives in the same fix.

The populations of many of the least developed nations are still ensnared in such impoverished conditions and are still producing very large families. As a group, the populations of the forty-nine least developed nations were growing at about 2.4 percent per year in 2002. Nevertheless, they are projected by the United Nations' demographers (in the "medium," and considered most likely, projection) to halve their aggregate growth rate by 2050.[53] Even so, the populations of some of the least developed nations, such as Chad, the Comoros, Congo, Guatemala, and Pakistan, are expected to expand 2.5 times by then and continue growing for several more decades. Populations in a handful of poor nations, such as Angola, Yemen, and Niger, may quadruple by 2050. While low-income populations will be responsible for most of the growth beyond 2050, it must be remembered that their per capita consumption and environmental impacts are negligible compared with those of high- and middle-income societies. The poorest societies have received little benefit from international programs and are likely to need the most development assistance, including family planning, in coming decades.

## Toward ZPG?

Meanwhile, in the world as a whole, the populations that are still growing are beginning to be counterbalanced by others that have begun to shrink or will do so in coming decades. Some thirty-three countries with TFRs now well below replacement level are projected to have smaller populations in 2050 than they do now. Japan's population is projected to be 14 percent smaller in 2050, while Italy and several eastern European countries, including Russia, may have as much as 20 to 50 percent fewer people.[54]

Humanity may at last be on the road to achieving a birthrate solution to the global population problem. It will not a be short road, however. Substantial growth in the human population is still ahead, if widespread high death rates from disease, hunger, or war can be avoided—and in some places they might not be.

Recently, demographers have taken rising mortality from HIV/AIDS into account in making their projections for some regions, such as southern Africa, where the disease has infected large portions of the population and has already significantly shortened life expectancies.[55] Worldwide, some 20 million people had died of AIDS by 2002. In its 2002 medium projection, the United Nations estimated that, because of AIDS mortality, the world population in 2050 will be reduced by nearly 200 million.[56] Seven countries in southern Africa, in which 20 percent or more of the people are infected today, are projected to have little or no population growth by 2050, despite continued high birthrates.[57]

The United Nations' low projection assumes a rapid drop in fertility nearly everywhere, with a peak population size of about 7.5 billion reached around 2035 and the number falling slightly to about 7.4 billion by 2050. Its medium projection has the human population approaching 8 billion in 2025 and about 8.9 billion in 2050.[58] The eventual peak population size later in the century might then be no more than 10 billion, after which a slow decline might begin.[59] Under the United Nations' high projection, the population would reach 10.6 billion in 2050 and continue growing for many years thereafter.[60] The medium projection, of course, represents a "best educated guess" extrapolated from past and foreseeable trends (including the trajectories of AIDS transmission and mortality).

Happily, then, birthrates are coming down, and, with luck, population growth should stop in this century.

So we can relax, can't we? Or can we? Obviously, our answer is no, for a series of reasons. The most important is that the greater the population increase in a world in which resources are already overstretched and ecosystems are being decimated, the greater will be the intensity of the problems that make up the human predicament. Some of the other reasons are buried in the complexities of demography (the study of population numbers and processes) that go beyond the counting of numbers and the calculation of birthrates, death rates, and growth rates. They include the composition, density, distribution, and movement of populations; the factors underlying birth, death, and growth rates (collectively, "vital rates"); and the consequences of demographic change.

## Population Momentum and Fear of the Elderly

Even though a substantial and growing portion of the human population now has below-replacement fertility, the expansion of human numbers will continue for many decades because of the momentum of population growth.[61] In rapidly growing populations, as can be seen in sub-Saharan Africa and several Middle Eastern nations, the proportion of young people under the age of fifteen can be as high as 45 to 50 percent, corresponding to TFRs of 5 to 8. These are the parents of the next generation, who most likely will produce an even larger cohort of children and live alongside them before reaching the older ages subject to natural high mortality rates. China, for example, has had below-replacement fertility for a dozen years, yet it may add another 180 million people—about equivalent to the present populations of Russia and Poland combined—before its growth is reversed, around 2025.

The proportions of people in different age classes of a population are known as its age structure. As we have seen, in a rapidly growing population a high proportion of people are young; on the other hand, the fraction of people over 65 is typically quite small—on the order of 5 percent or less. By contrast, in industrialized nations with slow or no growth, as the proportion of people under age 15 has become smaller, making up less than 20 percent of the population, the older age groups have grown to about the same proportion. Those between the ages of 15 and 65 are considered to be members of the "productive" ages—people who are capable of holding jobs and supporting children and the elderly. The UN demographers project that, as birthrates continue to fall, the worldwide proportion of people over 60 will more than triple, from about 600 million to nearly 1.9 billion in 2050, accounting for more than 20 percent of the global population and as much as 30 to 40 percent in some countries with dwindling populations.[62]

One reason that humanity may not avoid a collision with nature is that this momentous change has aroused alarm in some circles. A few demographers and many politicians and commentators have expressed grave concern about the future of social security programs to support the elderly,[63] predicting dire problems for people in the proportionally shrinking productive age groups, who will be burdened with caring for their aged parents. They want to keep populations growing, to avoid the shift toward an older age composition.

Their view neglects the trade-off represented by having proportionately far fewer children to educate and support. It also overlooks that crime and terrorism, *ceteris paribus,* would be reduced by an older age structure.[64] In developing nations that still have high birthrates, more than half the population may be under 20 years of age, and another quarter may be between 20 and 35. The youthful age composition of these populations, in the context of poverty, high unemployment, poor health care, limited education, gross inequity, repressive government, and other factors, creates fertile conditions for a desire to challenge the power of the affluent. The majority of terrorists behind the 9/11 attacks were young adult men, the demographic group responsible for most crime globally.[65] The ages of twenty suicide terrorists in the 1990s were between 16 and 28, with an average age of 21.3.[66]

High population growth rates are expected to persist in many developing nations, with a projected annual growth rate for people aged 20–34 of nearly 3 percent, as opposed to a shrinkage rate of 0.16 percent in developed countries during the years 2000–2050.[67] In the face of such growth, job opportunities in developing nations may fall even further below the numbers of applicants. And large numbers of unemployed, disaffected young men who see the West as their enemy can provide both public support and cannon fodder for terrorism.

Of course, a decrease in younger cohorts and an increase in older ones is an inevitable consequence of stopping population growth. Except to those foolish enough to believe that the population can grow forever, it is obvious that sooner or later the problems of a changing age structure must be faced. There is no compelling reason to postpone the inevitable and every reason to welcome it. After all, most people over 65 are not dependent in the sense that children are; most of them can take care of themselves and even contribute significantly to society, either in paid work or as volunteers.

In today's industrialized nations, older people are significantly healthier and stronger than were those of previous generations. Perhaps, rather than attempting to turn back the clock and revive population growth as some observers suggest, societies with aging populations should revise their retirement and social security arrangements. It seems highly unlikely that appeals such as Pope John Paul II's talk of "the crisis of the birthrate" or government bribes will lead to further population growth in Italy or most other rich countries.

Concern about aging is sometimes accompanied by panic over the prospect of a shrinking population[68]—a condition already achieved by Germany, Russia, and several other eastern European countries. People worry about too few customers for their stores, too few workers to keep wages low, too few soldiers for their armies, a loss of national prestige, and so on. Yet Germany has hardly undergone an economic or social breakdown. Eastern Europe's economic woes can be ascribed to factors other than a shrinking population, and they may be more a cause of the region's very low fertility than an effect. In western Europe, limited immigration from developing countries has been tolerated as a way to augment working-age groups. But a scarcity of labor could more wisely be viewed as an incentive to increase efficiency and productivity.

Population shrinkage in Europe and Japan is an incredibly positive trend in our view. It is, after all, the high-consuming rich who place disproportionate demands on humanity's life-support systems,[69] to say nothing of the costs of maintaining the economic power to try to keep those demands satisfied, without regard for the costs to the world's poor people and to future generations. Changing age structures and labor pools along the way will present genuine problems of equity, with consequences for patterns of consumption, migration, and the like—all tied to the ancient Socratic question of how we should live our lives. Is it fair to expect twenty-five-year-olds to pay very high taxes to support perfectly healthy sixty-five-year-olds in retirement? Is it wise to import a lot of young, cheap labor from poor nations to readjust national age structures? These and other issues are serious, as are the economic dislocations that rapidly changing age structures can cause. They demand open social discourse in all nations.

## Population Density and Distribution

In judging the well-being and prospects of a population, how it is distributed may be as important as its size. Contrarians, such as the late

Julian Simon, often cite high population densities in some prosperous societies as a reason that population growth doesn't matter. But such comparisons reveal very little about the relationships of people to the resources and the life-support systems upon which they depend. Far more important is the ratio of the number of people to the total resources and systems to which they have access in their own and other locations. Thus, the dense population of Rwanda (727 people per square mile in 2002) is dependent almost exclusively on the resources and ecosystems of that small, desperately poor country's own territory, whereas the even more dense population of the Netherlands (1,023 per square mile), wealthy for historical reasons, is able to draw resources from all over the world. That Rwanda's population is also growing by more than 2 percent per year, while that of the Netherlands is approaching zero growth, does not enhance the former's prospects. The old "Netherlands fallacy"[70]—the idea that, since New York, Tokyo, and Holland have high population densities, every place can be crowded to that level—still soldiers on in propaganda mills decades after it was fully exposed.[71]

A critical aspect of future population growth is that virtually all of it will occur in the developing countries, primarily in their cities. The urban population of the developing world is projected roughly to double in size between 2000 and 2030, although there is considerable uncertainty about how much of the increase—about 2 billion people— will go into megacities, such as São Paulo, Mexico City, Mumbai (Bombay), and Jakarta, and how much into smaller cities and towns. The world's megacities (those with more than 10 million people) are already struggling, not very successfully, with problems of air and water quality, water supply, transport, housing, unemployment, crime, health care, land use, and waste disposal. While these problems to some degree also beset the megacities in industrialized nations—Tokyo, New York, Los Angeles, and Osaka—they can become nearly unmanageable in developing nations, where urban populations have been growing by an average of 3 percent per year and infrastructures are less well established.[72]

The source of most of the urban growth in developing countries is poor migrants from rural areas, who settle in squatters' slums in the outskirts and vacant spaces of large cities. The United Nations has estimated that between 835 million and 2 billion people are living in these slums, which commonly lack even basic services such as clean water, public transportation, electricity, sanitation, and waste disposal.[73] Because the squatters' occupation of the land is illegal, urban authorities have usually ignored the needs of thousands of slum dwellers, who often settle in marginal locations (remember Hurricane Mitch), vulnerable to crime and disease. Infant mortality rates in slum settlements may run as much as three times the national average (which itself may be many times higher than those in rich nations).[74]

Officialdom's response to squatters until recently has often been antagonistic rather than helpful. City authorities have sent in bulldozers to demolish shantytowns for "urban renewal" projects, charged exorbitant prices for water delivery to slums, and impeded settlers' efforts to upgrade housing and find employment. Happily, though, a few cities, such as Lima, Peru, began extending rudimentary services such as water lines and bus service to slums as early as the 1970s. Now some experimenting has begun, with help from international nongovernmental organizations (NGOs), to organize slum dwellers in self-help programs and persuade national and city authorities to help facilitate these projects.[75] Providing access to small-scale credit, materials for housing, clean fuel for cooking, and transportation (whether buses or affordable bicycles) is an important form of assistance that costs relatively little, and much of that expense might be recouped through devices such as low-cost licensing of vendors and bicycle registration fees. These and other measures to integrate the poor migrants into the social structure of the cities could go a long way to mitigate or prevent the worst problems of rapid urbanization. If such efforts are not undertaken, the severity and extent of most of those problems could much more than double as urban populations double in the next thirty years.

The problems of megacities are classic examples of the nonlinearities that plague officials who deal with population-consumption-environment problems. When a relationship is nonlinear, as was noted in chapter 2, it means that a change in one factor is accompanied by a disproportionate change in the factor it is influencing.[76] For instance, if you double the length of the sides $(S)$ of a square, its area $(A)$ increases fourfold $(A = S^2)$. Similarly, when a city doubles in size, the problems of supplying it with water (or other amenities) may much more than double. A small city may be able to get sufficient water from a local river, but with a doubling of its population size it might require a complex set of dams, reservoirs, aqueducts, and pipes to maintain supplies. This could quadruple the costs of supplying everyone with the previous per capita water flow (and could cause far more than twice as much environmental damage in the process). Unfortunately for humanity, nonlinearities are nearly ubiquitous in environmental problems. One reason is that people are smart and normally pick the low-hanging fruit first. The same applies to supplying people with fuels, minerals, and food. Growing cities are built over some of the best soils in the world; people did not settle first on barren lands.

Some developing nations, such as China, Brazil, and Mexico, have established policies of encouraging urban migration toward smaller regional cities and away from the beleaguered capital, thereby reducing the problems that the complexity of numbers would have caused. Mexico City, with more than 18 million residents in 2002, has addressed famously horrific air pollution, along with most of the other problems of megacities, with some success. Diversion of rural migrants to smaller cities is just one of the policies the Mexican government has employed. Others have included driving restrictions for commuters and removal of the worst-polluting vehicles from the streets. Huge challenges remain, but there is little question that reducing the flow of migrants into the city has helped to prevent the problems from spiraling completely out of control.

Fortunately, such measures seem to have had an effect elsewhere too. Projections that their megacity populations would soar by 20 to 40 percent during the 1990s did not materialize for Mexico City, São Paulo, Calcutta, Shanghai, Jakarta, and several others. All increased by no more than 15 percent in the decade; Shanghai and Seoul, each in a nation with a TFR now well under 2, even lost population.

## Epidemic Impacts

Epidemics at times can significantly affect vital rates and thus population sizes; the Black Death of the late Middle Ages is a striking example. In turn, crowding, combined with other factors such as poverty, can seriously influence the risks and spread of epidemics. Even early hunter-gatherers overnighting in crude shelters or tents often crowded together for warmth and safety. The groups were small, however, and rarely stayed long in any place, so nest-fouling problems would have been minimal. Settled agricultural groups initially were relatively small and scattered but still are thought to have experienced transmissible diseases to a greater extent than hunter-gatherers.[77] Once sizable cities began to form, though, both crowding and epidemics became first possible and then likely.

Estimates are that in the third century AD Rome had a population density of 300 people per acre, comparable to densely populated modern cities such as Mumbai, Calcutta, and Mexico City.[78] Indeed, compared with the conditions suffered by most Romans two millennia ago, the squalor of some modern cities might seem a paradise. Crowding was only part of the problem—lack of running water and sanitation made much of ancient Rome a sort of high-rise shantytown, with crowded four-story tenements a common feature. Sanitation was by chamber pots, and those who lived up steep stairs in the flimsy upper stories often simply emptied them out the window—"so much the worse for the passer-by who happened to intercept the unwelcome gift!"[79] The public health conditions must have been horrendous, and it's hardly surprising that epidemics, probably smallpox or bubonic plague, swept the Roman Republic and Empire in 387 BC and in AD 65, 165, and 251, among other years. In affected areas, the worst epidemics killed as much as a third of the population.[80]

In the fifteenth to seventeenth centuries, Europe's population was not yet very urbanized, but the 100 million or so people of the continent were fairly mobile and in close enough contact to support an epidemic. Over more than a century, repeated waves of the Black Death are believed to have reduced the population by more than a fourth.

Today, many of humanity's worst scourges are diseases of large populations with urban concentrations. In 1918, at least 20 million people around the world were killed, and tens of millions more sickened, by the great flu epidemic. But medical advances of the nineteenth and twentieth centuries, such as the introduction of vaccines, insecticides, and, later, antibiotics, resulted in substantial suppression of most common infectious diseases. This, in turn, produced a sense of false security about the chances of epidemics.

Predictably, the overuse of antibiotics has led to a resurgence of old diseases as the bacteria that cause them have evolved resistance to some of the previously most powerful weapons in humanity's armamentarium.[81] And, as scientists also warned,[82] new diseases continue to emerge as ever-growing numbers of people press into closer contact with animal reservoirs of epidemic diseases. The first to emerge, HIV/AIDS, is already having a devastating effect on some populations.[83] AIDS is the fourth leading cause of death worldwide, accounting for some 3 million deaths in 2001 alone. The Joint United Nations Programme on HIV/AIDS (UNAIDS) estimates that 68 million more people will have died of the disease by 2020 unless a full-scale global effort is made to contain its spread.

## Social Effects of Population Growth

What about the social effects of population growth? Population growth must, on average, increase crowding, and crowding has long been thought to influence social behavior and, in turn, influence vital rates. In the early 1960s, some research on rats raised concerns about increased density of human beings.[84] Crowded into cages at higher densities than ever observed in nature, rats became homosexual, fought, ate their young, and so on. This was extrapolated to mean that crowded human beings would become homosexual, fight, and eat their young—something that horrified homophobes and pronatalists but suggested to others that population growth would be "automatically" controlled. Fortunately, everything we know about human behavior suggests that overcrowded rats are a poor model for overcrowded human beings.[85] People clearly can adapt to conditions of very high density, both physically (spread out; build up; soundproof rooms) and psychologically (even the worst concentration camps did not produce social pathologies such as occurred in the rat studies).[86] This adaptability may actually be disadvantageous, preventing people from recognizing the severe problems that population growth creates in other areas (such as degrading the delivery of ecosystem services) to which *Homo sapiens* has much less opportunity to adapt.

In many social arenas, it turns out to be very difficult to sort out the effects of population size itself from many other things that generally are changing as numbers increase. Most cities have bigger populations today than they had a century ago—but think of all the other things that have changed simultaneously![87] How much can the clogged freeways of most American cities be blamed on population growth as opposed to poor planning of the country's transport system and settlement patterns? Numbers of people are surely a factor, but most of the local problems could have been avoided by planning against automobile dependence and leapfrog suburbanization.

Of course, population size and growth are also factors in causing those most critical of social problems, civil violence, terrorism, and international warfare. The connection to war is not with crowding, however, but with what has become known as "environmental scarcity"—scarcity of renewable resources and a desire to secure them for a given group.[88] The classic example of a war based on environmental scarcity is the 1967 Arab-Israeli war over the desperate shortages of water in the Middle East.[89] Other renewable resources that now help generate civil conflict, and soon may generate much more, include arable land,[90] forests,[91] and ocean fish stocks (conflicts over which have occasionally led to shooting).[92] But recent headlines have focused more on conflicts connected to two *non*-renewable resources, gas and oil, in Afghanistan and Iraq.[93]

While populations with disproportionate numbers of young men are one inevitable result of rapid population growth in developing nations, many observers believe that growth itself now retards economic development, widening the rich-poor gap[94] and increasing the distress of those being left behind. Others, however, see issues related to population structure as more critical causes of stress in Arab societies.[95] These include migration, a growing number and high proportion of children seeking education, gender inequities, and stress on patriarchal family structures. One tension-causing factor making Saudi Arabia less stable, for instance, in addition to economic inequity and resentment of its government's close relationship with the United States, is its extremely high rate of population growth—a total fertility rate (TFR) of 5.7, exceeded in the Arab world only by those of Palestine, Yemen, and Afghanistan. That growth is unlikely to slow down much in the next couple of decades—Saudi Arabia's population of 24 million in 2002 is projected to grow to 41 million in 2025 and 60 million in 2050.[96]

Disparities in population growth rates among different peoples (e.g., ethnic or religious groups) may also exacerbate the conditions that breed the kinds of conflict that the West defines as terrorism. For example, one element influencing Israeli attitudes toward Palestinians is the much more rapid population growth of the latter. The TFR of Jews born in Israel is less than 3, approaching replacement level, while that of Palestinians in the Gaza Strip is more than 7, among the highest of any national-level entity today.[97]

## Migration

Migration is a worldwide phenomenon, and more than 175 million people are living in adopted countries today. Although the United States has the largest foreign-born population of any country, almost 35 million, it ranks relatively far down the list of countries with high proportions of non-native residents, with about 12 percent of the population foreign-born. More than 20 percent of the populations of traditional immigrant-receiving countries (such as the United States, Canada, Australia, and several other nations) are foreign-born; in some Middle Eastern nations, the United Arab Emirates, Kuwait, Jordan, and Israel, the proportion exceeds 30 percent. In Europe, where immigration has generally been more tightly controlled, three countries nonetheless have higher proportions of foreign-born residents than does the United States. But these proportions tell only a small part of the international migration story.

The United States, with comparatively high fertility (a TFR of 2.0) and nearly a million immigrants admitted each year (not including an unknown number of "undocumented" immigrants),[98] has the highest population growth rate of any industrialized nation, more than 1 percent per year. That amounts to almost 3 million added annually, enough to give the United States a projected population size of 422 million people in 2050.[99] With 293 million people in 2004,[100] the United States has the third largest national population (after China and India, and followed by Indonesia at 224 million, Brazil at 178 million, and Pakistan at 149 million). The United Nations' projections indicate that the United States will still have the third largest population in 2050, although India will have replaced China as having the largest.[101]

Few population-related issues arouse more ire and create deeper ethical problems than international migration.[102] In the United States, where immigration makes such a huge contribution to population growth, different interest groups have different views of immigration—legal and illegal. Generally, "open borders" are favored by liberals, and tight controls on immigration are preferred by conservatives. But some traditionally conservative groups such as industry and big agriculture favor immigration because it supplies cheap labor. In contrast, traditionally liberal groups such as labor unions are restrictionist because of the threat of competition. So are some environmental groups, concerned about the pressure that increasing numbers of Americans place on ecosystem services, not just in the United States but globally. Other environmental NGOs are concerned about environmental justice issues and remain neutral on the question of immigration. The Catholic Church in the United States favors immigration from Mexico and Central America because a large portion of the immigrants swell its ranks and add to its political power. Racists oppose Latin American immigration because the average skin color of the immigrants is darker than that of the average Ku Klux Klan member (or, at least, than his sheet). Similar economic, class, and racial prejudices pollute immigration debates in most countries—nearly all of which (including Mexico) attempt to regulate immigration to their countries far more stringently than does the United States.

Migration, whether internal or international, does not, of course, change the total number of people on the planet. But it does have many environmental consequences. Migrants understandably move toward jobs and financial rewards, and overall they appear to find them. That means that, on average, they better their condition, become more affluent, consume more, and thus add more to the overall environmental impact of human beings than if they had stayed home. International migrants may also import high-fertility habits from poor nations into rich nations, raising birthrates among the more affluent—and environmentally more destructive—people of the world. And they often bring great economic benefits to rich economies,[103] contributing to the ability of affluent local people to consume more.[104]

The migration issue is not going to go away; the flow of people from poor areas into richer ones is expected to remain vigorous for at least the first half of this century. The net population gain from migration to the developed countries is expected to be about 2 million people annually, with the United States receiving the most, an estimated 1.1 million per year, some five times that of Germany (211,000), its closest competitor. Not surprisingly, Mexico will remain the largest donor (267,000), a tribute to the U.S.-Mexico border, the longest land frontier between the rich and poor worlds. India, the Philippines, and Indonesia are expected to be the next largest donors, exporting fewer than a quarter million in each case.[105] To the degree that migration as a "safety valve" keeps poor nations from squarely facing their own demographic problems while swelling the numbers of higher-income consumers, migration will have a negative influence on the chances of reaching global sustainability.

## Household Dynamics

Population size, structure, and movement are linked to another environmentally significant demographic element that is rarely considered—household dynamics. Throughout the world, the average number of people living together in a household is shrinking, a consequence of smaller families, rising divorce rates, increasing affluence, and fewer multigenerational families living together. The decline in household sizes, of course, means there must be more homes. The trend contributes substantially to suburban sprawl, and it is further augmented by the proliferation of second homes in the United States and other rich countries. As a result, housing units are being built at a rate outpacing population growth in much of the world.

This easily overlooked change is a particularly serious threat to biodiversity.[106] Fewer people in each household leads to higher per capita resource consumption and a rapid increase in the number of households, even where population sizes are shrinking. Because fewer people are sharing goods and services in smaller households, per capita consumption of resources such as water, fuel for heating, power, and transportation, as well as demand for open space, are greatly increased.

In some affluent areas of the United States, ironically, the trend toward smaller household sizes has been accompanied by growth in dwelling size; the average size of a home built in the United States has nearly doubled in the past half-century.[107] Indian River County, on Florida's eastern coast, for instance, has seen floor space per housing unit increase by a third just since 1975. An even more marked expansion in home size has occurred in California's Silicon Valley as average-sized houses are replaced on their modest lots by "dot-com palaces." All these trends threaten biodiversity because they intensify the use of natural resources, such as construction materials, energy, and, especially, land. The effect on ecosystems of this neglected population factor is likely to escalate, since current trends in household size are expected to continue as divorce rates and affluence become more prevalent in developing nations.

## Conclusion

Since our first books on population problems were published, human numbers have nearly doubled, and the assault on Earth's life-support systems has doubtless more than doubled. That's part of the bad news. At the same time, there has been a pronounced slowing of the global population growth rate and the beginning of actual population shrinkage in many countries, especially among affluent European nations. That's very good news, as are projected drops elsewhere—as long as they result from declining fertility, as opposed to rising death rates.[108] Nevertheless, because of population momentum and still-high fertility rates in some areas, the race to curb the global population overshoot is far from over. Let's just hope that future generations will be able to have a decent life without having to find those two additional planets.

Many critical questions remain to be answered. How fast will future reductions in fertility occur, and how far will they go? Will fertility rates in the poorest regions and conservative Middle Eastern nations fall soon? Will the declining fertilities in most of today's middle-income nations fall below replacement level, as have those of industrialized nations? How rapidly might it be possible (and wise) to reduce humanely the total number of *Homo sapiens* to a level sustainable in the long term? Will fertility in industrialized nations continue to be well below replacement, or will it rebound to that level, as many demographers used to think?[109] Perhaps most important from the standpoint of the human predicament, when—and how—will the population of the United States stop growing?

On the answers to those questions hang many others that are crucial to our future: Will it be feasible economically and politically to improve the well-being of the poorest half of the world's population without risking the benefits so far achieved for the more affluent half? If the answer is yes, what will be the consequences for Earth's ecosystems and resources? Will increasing constraints and risks such as climate change and epidemiological vulnerability raise death rates and prevent the additional population growth to which humanity appears otherwise committed? If such a disruptive end to the population outbreak occurs, what kind of future will be in prospect?

In the face of these unanswered questions, perhaps the worst news is that the critical and complex demographic issues have largely dropped off the public and political radar screens—and that the equally problematic ones of overconsumption have never appeared on them. If there is to be any chance of the good news overcoming the bad, the neglect of population issues must end, so that effective strategies to address the human predicament can be formulated.

Chapter *4*

# THE CONSUMPTION FACTOR

> "It is a strange basis for a civilization, but an effective one.
> Directly and indirectly, some 90 percent of the American
> work force is in the business of producing consumer goods
> and services. Consumer products make up what we are.
> They generate most of the nation's income and employ-
> ment. And [Americans] travel, bringing both themselves
> and the desire to have more to countries that have less
> than nothing, so that one fine day those places, too, by
> getting and spending, can have and have not."
>
> ROGER ROSENBLATT, 1999[1]

EARLY IN 2002 we had the opportunity to visit some of the spectacular Mayan ruins in Yucatán. Although we had often read about them, the scale and abundance of the remains of that civilization—the magnificent pyramids, temples, and palaces, intricate glyphs, and long-abandoned ball courts of Uxmal, Chichén Itzá, and Calakmul—had an unexpected emotional impact. Here was stark evidence, like the bas-reliefs of Nineveh, of a thriving, artistic civilization that had totally disappeared. No one is sure exactly why the Classic Mayan civilization collapsed a little over a millennium ago.[2] Warfare, ecological deterioration, natural disasters, and "ideological pathology" (a sort of collective self-immolation)[3] have all been hypoth-esized, with the popularity of the hypotheses changing from the mid-1960s to the mid-1970s in apparent response to political concerns in the United States.[4] It now appears that the civilization's demise was caused by a tangled complex of which the stress of overpopulation on limited agricultural land was a key component. But it was intertwined with internecine politics, warfare, depletion of firewood supplies, climate change (drought, possibly exacerbated by local deforestation), and a relatively recently hypothesized factor of particular interest here.[5]

That last factor, best documented in an earlier Preclassic collapse, was conspicuous consumption. The consumption was engaged in not simply for reasonable use but to impress others.[6] Interest among archaeologists in conspicuous consumption was triggered by the discovery that early Mayan terraced fields, on which crops of corn, squash, gourds, and palms had been successfully grown for hundreds of years, had been buried under nearly a meter of clay sediment. The clay could not be farmed because it is rock-hard in the dry season and inundated in the wet.

The sediment came from the erosion of denuded hillsides. Why were the hillsides denuded? Archaeologist Richard Hansen has assembled data indicating that, in addition to the gathering of wood needed for household fuel and construction, the deforestation of the hills was a result of increased demand for firewood for the kilns of the Mayan lime industry.[7] He detected a fivefold thickening in lime plaster floors over a 600-year stretch—truly bizarre, since often the floors were built over pre-existing floors. "It would be like saying your sidewalk needs to be two meters thick," Hansen told us. It is estimated that, as a result of this and other conspicuous lime consumption, in the El Mirador area of North Petén, Guatemala, more than 7,000 square miles of forest annually would have been required to fuel the lime plaster industry alone.[8] That contributed substantially to the deforestation that led to erosion; erosion to clay sedimentation of farm fields; and clay sedimentation to hunger.

Profligate use of lime, with its serious consequences, was not the only example of Mayan overconsumption—consumption well beyond what is necessary to meet a basic need. Similar patterns were shown in stone construction, in which the thickness of walls was increased beyond functional purpose so as to require almost four times as much stone.[9] What compelling social need was satisfied by this otherwise unnecessary waste of resources remains a mystery—one to which we may never learn the answer.

At Tulum, on the Caribbean coast, we saw where the Mayans had enjoyed the ocean breezes some 600 years ago, protected by a steep cliff from attack by way of the sea. Some archaeologists see Tulum as an inferior site, occupied as the proud Mayan civilization declined toward extinction in the Late Postclassic phase of its history. The quality of the architecture was poorer than in earlier sites, giving Tulum's temples a slapdash appearance. But other observers believe that evidence from Tulum indicates a society less dominated by a traditional elite. The argument remains somewhat unsettled, just like that over the collapse.

On the coast both north and south of Tulum today is a sprawling, unplanned, and poorly regulated resort development. The combination of expensive hotel complexes, luxurious homes, and the skyrocketing growth of urban centers such as Playa del Carmen, where resort employees live with marginal amenities, invites comparison with that earlier proud but deteriorating civilization. It also is a microcosm of what's going on over much of the planet. And the broader picture today has similarities to Mayan history. Is the Mayan "pomp of yesterday" being mirrored by our pomp of today? After all, in today's world, politics are nasty and warfare is still common, often undertaken to gain control over resources needed to support consumption by the rich. In addition, deforestation is rampant (including once again in the Mayan lowlands),[10] agricultural land is being depleted, hunger is common, and the climate is changing. And in many places overconsumption is evident—often seemingly as senseless as extra-thick walls and floors. As a civilization, we seem to be developing our own version of thick lime plaster construction.

## Overconsumers

The problems associated with the human rise to planetary dominance are, as we've indicated, not just a consequence of how many of us there are. How we behave is also critically important in keeping humanity on that collision course. The United States, because of its population size, growth rate, and high per capita level of consumption, is the champion consumer of the world. For decades, scientists and others have pointed out the problems created by American overconsumption—both the environmental damage Americans have caused directly and the deterioration caused by others who have been inspired by our example. Only the western European bloc, with more than 400 million people and a comparable level of affluence, can rival it. Because its combination of huge population size and profligate per capita consumption puts enormous stress on Earth's life-support system, it is fair to say that the United States is the most overpopulated country on the planet.[11] This is clear when you realize that each baby born in the United States on average will cause 15–150 times more environmental damage than a baby born in a very poor country.

Further problems are traceable to America's unevenly distributed ability to consume. More than most industrialized nations, the United States has a large and growing disparity between income groups. In the late 1990s, the most affluent fifth of the U.S. population received more than 46 percent of the income while the poorest fifth received barely 5 percent. By contrast, in Sweden, the richest fifth of the population had less than 35 percent of the income and the poorest fifth had nearly 10 percent.[12] The differences between the richest and the poorest 5 percent are even more striking. America's skewed income distribution leads to power imbalances, failures of education, feelings of political impotence, and distress at being unable to keep up in the consumption rat race. The general atmosphere of frustration in much of the American population does not seem conducive to the cooperative actions needed to make the United States part of the environmental solution rather than a central part of the problem.

Yet, if the public discussion of the importance of population growth in fueling the human predicament had a short life span, public and media interest in consumption's role was essentially stillborn. While the planned parenthood and zero population growth (ZPG) movements have had a global reach and substantial success, planned consumption and zero consumption growth movements have not developed in parallel. Despite various environmental voices crying in the wilderness and individuals following "voluntary simplicity" principles, most people in both rich and poor countries still view growth in consumption as an unalloyed good, a view that has been especially hallowed in the United States in recent decades.

Americans do have some pretty good reasons for the hallowing. During the twentieth century, the industrialized world became a world of triumphant consumerism. As historian Gary Cross put it in his fascinating book *An All-Consuming Century,* the dominant belief was "that goods give meaning to individuals and their roles in society."[13] He who dies with the most toys wins. In the United States after World War II, consumption was believed to hold the key to the economic growth necessary to avoid a slide back into the Great Depression. As another historian, Lizabeth Cohen, said, there was "a complex shared commitment on the part of policymakers, business and labor leaders, and civic groups to put mass consumption at the center of their plans for a prosperous postwar America."[14] The strategy worked, and in the twentieth century consumerism, in partnership with capitalism, was largely victorious over the rival ideologies of fascism, communism, and socialism.[15] But there is little reason to believe the American style of consumerism can perpetuate its triumph through the twenty-first century without substantial modification.

## Flawed Goods

Unfettered consumerism is, in fact, environmentally a seriously flawed good. The development of the Mount Crested Butte ski area near the Rocky Mountain Biological Laboratory (RMBL) in Colorado demonstrates the point. Huge "trophy" second homes crowded together with splendid views of one another, more every year, complement the hodgepodge of hotels and condos central to the ski area. Giant second homes are not necessary to enjoy skiing—hotels, even ugly ones, are much more efficient at supplying access to that for short vacations. Moreover, the houses stand empty most of the year. Each home destroys part of the natural ecosystem directly with its "footprint," the havoc connected with construction and the building of access roads. It destroys parts of other ecosystems indirectly through its contributions to deforestation, except in the unlikely case that all the timber comes from sustainable tree plantations. Additional environmental side effects accrue from the mining of metal (for plumbing and appliances), extraction and use of oil (fuel and plastics), and manufacture of cement (foundations). And each house continues to degrade ecosystems through the environmental costs of heating and maintaining it, supplying it with water, and disposing of its wastes. Finally, there is its "eyesore" effect on the East River valley's esthetic values.[16]

The same sort of development is spreading near most American cities as "tract mansions" multiply, all with the same kinds of destructive environmental effects. But at least these mostly are not second homes; part of their ecological costs do go toward supplying necessary shelter for people. Nevertheless, the size of the average home built in the United States almost doubled in the last half of the twentieth century,[17] and the demand for heating and cooling and power for appliances increased as well. At the same time, paradoxically, average household size (the number of people per occupied dwelling unit) has been shrinking, meaning there are more homes or apartments relative to the size of the population in general. As we've seen, the shrinkage of household size has been occurring almost everywhere, even though population growth is slowing in much of the world (but not in the United States). Both larger homes and more households per 1,000 people mean more environmental impact, primarily in the forms of increased resource consumption per person and more destruction of biodiversity.[18]

By the standards of most of the world, Americans are also heavy per capita users of electric power, outdone only by the cold-climate nations of Scandinavia and Canada and by one or two oil-rich Middle Eastern nations (which presumably use it largely for air-conditioning and to run refineries).[19] Worse from an environmental standpoint, more than half of the power used in the United States is generated by

the burning of coal, the most polluting of the fossil fuels and the one
that produces the greatest amount of the greenhouse gas carbon dioxide per unit of energy gained.

Another instance of a flawed good is the mass of personal automobiles, especially sport utility vehicles (SUVs) and "road candy" (high-priced, high-performance "special" vehicles),[20] that choke American
streets and highways. In 2002, 15.7 million households owned one car,
22.6 million had two cars, 10.2 million three cars, and 4.1 million four
cars.[21] Thanks largely to such numbers, an area of the United States
larger than the state of Georgia has been paved.

Driving a grossly fuel-wasteful Hummer (ten to thirteen miles per
gallon) symbolizes what may be the single most environmentally damaging activity of *Homo sapiens* after agriculture: personal transportation
in gasoline-powered vehicles. The extent of their use is dramatic: in
2000, for example, passenger cars (including vans, SUVs, pickups, and
light trucks) in the United States used about 126 billion gallons of
gasoline, accounting for about two-fifths of the nation's petroleum
consumption for the year.[22] Most Americans take for granted the massive environmental damage caused by vehicle emissions; the building
of streets, highways, garages, and parking lots; and the resources used
to manufacture cars and trucks. Still less do we want to contemplate
the international costs of our national fixation. It's a part of life as we
have always known it.

"We constantly complain about the blank checks the Saudis write to
buy off their extremists," wrote *New York Times* columnist Thomas
Friedman about driving Hummers and the connection to terrorism.
"But who writes the blank checks to the Saudis? We do—with our gluttonous energy habits, [our] renewed addiction to big cars, and our
president who has made 'conservation' a dirty word. We never talk
straight to Saudi Arabia, because we are addicted to its oil. Addicts
never tell the truth to their pushers."[23]

Among the external costs of our auto-commuting culture is a portion of the care and feeding of a vast military machine, much of it dedicated to keeping petroleum produced in other countries flowing relatively inexpensively into American gas tanks and those of valued allies.

A conservative estimate might be that the military budget would be two-thirds of what it is today if U.S. armed forces were not deeply involved in protecting access to oil supplies in the Middle East and elsewhere. If so, the additional third amounts to a subsidy to personal vehicle drivers of about $0.38 per gallon.[24]

## Conspicuous Consumption

In his fine but depressing book *Luxury Fever,* Robert Frank makes the backyard barbecue a symbol of modern overconsumption. When his 1980s propane grill rusted out, he found that he could replace it with a stainless steel model seven feet wide, powered by either propane or natural gas, which included an infrared rotisserie, a built-in smoker system, ancillary burners, and much more. The catch? Rather than $89.95, the price of the original, the new wonder would cost $5,000![25] Simpler models were available for $3,000, $1,140, and even less, but the backyard grill had clearly become an item of conspicuous consumption, alongside Chateau Mouton Rothschild 1945, available for more than $100,000 per case.

As Frank reports, the ostentatious cooking trend has also occurred indoors.[26] Multi-thousand-dollar restaurant stoves have become the "in" thing, with burners that provide roughly double the heat of those on conventional stoves and use much more fuel. Luxury appliances, giant trophy homes, expensive cars, and even private jets don't exhaust the potential for overconsumption. Seven percent of wealthy Americans polled said that they too would willingly pay $20 million each to take a two-week flight to an orbiting space station, as American Dennis Tito and South African Mark Shuttleworth already have.[27] The sky is clearly not the limit!

Of course, human beings need to satisfy basic needs for food (and ways to cook it), water, clothing, sanitary facilities, shelter, and health care—and (in our view) also education, transportation, leisure, and recreation. Meeting those needs has inevitable environmental effects. At any one time, depending on such factors as the technologies employed and the state of the environment, those environmental effects limit the number of people who can be supported on Earth without narrowing options for future generations. Here, however, we are focusing on *overconsumption,* consumption that goes beyond satisfying basic needs and in the process greatly exacerbates the damage to human life-support systems. Overconsumption exacts large costs for small benefits.

## Conspicuous Destruction

What can only be described as conspicuous consumption is by no means confined to the rich. An example is the all-too-affordable American hobby of driving noisy, fuel-inefficient four-wheel-drive vehicles, including large trucks, off road or on steep mountain trails. A center of this activity is the twenty-two-mile-long Rubicon Trail, "a rugged dirt path from the western Sierra Nevada to Lake Tahoe . . . holy ground for millions of Americans who enjoy off-road driving."[28] Some 70,000 off-roaders cross the Rubicon annually, and that's just a portion of the approximately 3.5 million Californians, about a tenth of the state's population, who engage in motorized off-road activity. The indirect environmental results of this destructive hobby are all those involved in the construction and use of off-road vehicles (ORVs)—as well as a share of adverse environmental effects from mining, oil drilling, climate change, and so forth.

The direct effects are by no means negligible, either. Already the high country around the Rubicon is scarred where vehicles have left the trail. Erosion has reached such a level that use of the trail was temporarily blocked by a regional water agency charged with protecting runoff headed toward Lake Tahoe. And the area is fouled with a substantial portion of some forty tons of human waste deposited there annually. The ground is not suitable for latrines, and the area is too remote to permit the servicing of portable outhouses. The damage may well signal the end for the symbolic Rubicon Trail; other trails have been closed because of the damage done to terrain and related threats to endangered species. Nevertheless, companies such as the General Motors Corporation continue to advertise their SUVs with pictures of them tearing up natural areas, causing rockslides as they are driven up mountains, and the like. Even during the Iraq invasion, when American soldiers were dying for oil, DaimlerChrysler aired a Grand Cherokee ad showing the vehicle spectacularly tearing up a wetland.

While the destruction of natural areas by ORVs is often stunning, even increasing numbers of trail bikers now cause significant erosion and otherwise often degrade wilderness areas in places where some semblance of it remains. Speedboats and power skis are an aquatic parallel to ORVs—damaging riverbanks and slaughtering manatees, among other contributions to environmental degradation. Control of such activities has become almost impossible as mass use of outdoor facilities grows. In wilderness areas, even gentler forms of recreation, such as hiking or biking with some restrictions, also come with environmental costs. As the population grows and more and more people understandably seek recreation in nature, the "consumption" of wilderness makes it less and less wild. And, as affluent people increasingly seek that connection with nature, ecotourism by citizens of the rich nations, while important for consciousness-raising, is causing growing problems in ecologically fragile regions of the developing world.

## Consumption Elsewhere

The situation in other developed countries is broadly similar to that in the United States. In western Europe and Japan, however, the sizes of homes and the extent of suburban sprawl are constrained by the already high densities of populations (respectively about five and ten times that of the United States) and generally stricter zoning codes. Similarly, narrow streets and shorter inter-city distances have helped dampen (but far from extinguish) enthusiasm for large, fuel-inefficient automobiles in those areas. Also, both Europe and Japan have fast, efficient, and convenient public transport systems both within and between cities. High gasoline prices may be the most important cause of the relative shortage of gas guzzlers, however. The taxes that produce fuel prices more than twice as high as those in the United States are acceptable to Europeans and Japanese, whose cultures may not tie self-image and freedom as closely to the personal automobile as does American culture.

Nevertheless, additional berserk car cultures seem to be developing in parts of the world as diverse as Australia, Mexico, and China, and the restraints that once were found in places such as England and Japan are breaking down as more and more square miles are devoted to automobiles rather than people, agriculture, or nature. Indeed, in Japan there are now special four-wheel-drive parks where, for a fee, people can trash their SUVs by driving them over a rough course.

The case of China is special because of its enormous population. In a 1972 article, "If all Chinese had wheels," political scientist Dennis Pirages and Paul pointed out what a catastrophic increase in global consumption would be entailed if the Chinese aspired to even the 1972 U.S. per capita standard of car ownership, as they now appear to do. "The industrial nations really have two choices," they concluded. "They can continue their present course of devouring more and more of the earth's resources while destroying the environment. . . . The second choice would be for the industrial nations to deal with their own overpopulation and overconsumption . . . [and in so doing] they could provide a new kind of model for developing nations to emulate."[29] That conclusion is even more pertinent now, more than three decades later. But instead of taking steps to limit consumption by building and marketing far more efficient automobiles, while also working to reduce the need for their use in the first place, the United States, like some other rich countries and wealthy classes in poor nations, is doing exactly the opposite.

Potentially one of the greatest engines for expansion of per capita consumption will be what ecologists Norman Myers and Jennifer Kent refer to as the "new consumers." These are more than a billion people in developing and transitional countries such as China, India, South Korea, Malaysia, Brazil, Argentina, Mexico, Russia, and Turkey[30] who have a purchasing power parity (PPP)[31] of at least $2,500 per person annually. That means that in the United States they could afford to buy $2,500 or more worth of goods and services, a huge advance over the situation thirty years ago. In 2001, the new consumers around the world collectively had a PPP of $6.1 trillion, essentially three-fifths of that of the American population. The new consumers now drive some 125 million cars, almost a fourth of the world fleet, and by 2010 that could increase to more than 200 million. In one sense, that's a great part of the human triumph—more and more people are getting access to the good things of life. But the usual downside of neglected social costs will need to be dealt with. Most of the countries in which new consumers live can little afford the destruction of natural capital that, for instance, a car-dominated transport system (like that of the United States) would cause. Increasing consumption by the formerly poor will exacerbate global problems unless the rich find ways to compensate by lessening their own negative environmental effects.

## How Others Pay the Price for Us

It's easy to remain unaware of how the American lifestyle feeds into the destruction of the natural capital of distant countries. Much of the damage traces to Americans' consumption of mundane items, ranging from bananas and coffee to hamburgers, magazines, and large detached housing. The degree of destruction caused in poor countries in the service of consumption in rich countries varies, of course, from place to place. The vast banana plantations of the Sarapiquí River region of northeastern Costa Rica, where we and our colleagues have done research, now harbor only a handful of the hundreds of bird species that once occupied the forests the banana plants replaced. Those replacements, however, produce great profits for big corporations as huge quantities of bananas are shipped to the residents of industrial countries to slice over their breakfast cereal. The banana-eating habit itself was created originally by vast advertising campaigns, one of which featured a singing, dancing "Chiquita Banana."

In the Coto Brus area in the far south of Costa Rica, the landscape is dominated by small coffee plantations and degraded pastures. It is typical of the habitat that now covers a great deal of that country's previously forest-clad hill country, much of it devoted to growing coffee for rich-world consumption. A single 600-acre forest remnant and scattered smaller degraded patches are all that remain of what four decades ago was a continuous cover of magnificent mid-elevation rain forest. But this mixed landscape supports more biodiversity than the intensively cultivated lowland areas such as the Sarapiquí banana plantations; in Coto Brus roughly half of the previous community of bird species has been preserved—at least temporarily.[32]

We have personally seen the march of biologically destitute oil palm monocultures replacing species-rich tropical moist forests in peninsular Malaysia, Borneo, New Britain, the Chocó region of Ecuador, and even Costa Rica. We've watched trucks hauling huge logs out of Costa Rican forests where logging is "forbidden" but where pressures created by the advertising-fueled demand for tropical hardwoods in the homes of the rich is high (as is the desire for profits in multinational timber companies). In Sulawesi, we've seen poachers removing rattan from a national park, damaging the forest ecosystem in aid of producing furniture destined for upscale homes in Florida and elsewhere. In Queensland and on Maui, we've driven through mile after mile of sugarcane fields to find small patches of natural habitat in which to look for birds and butterflies.

A great deal of the destruction of rain forests over much of the world can be traced to activities designed to fuel consumption in the United States and other rich nations.[33] The escalating global demand for sugar, coffee, tea, rubber, beef, tropical fruits, timber, and pulpwood— much of it destined for the United States—has caused enormous but little-appreciated damage to biodiversity and human cultures. Beginning as early as the 1800s, increasing urban affluence in industrializing North America and Europe produced a middle class with a growing appetite for furniture and paneling made from tropical hardwoods such as mahogany and teak. The quantities were not so large at the time, but high-grading (removal of only certain trees) caused disproportionate damage. Many other trees were pulled down by the networks of vines that linked them to the forest giants being felled, and fragile jungle soils were destroyed when the logs were dragged to rivers down which they could be floated toward markets.

Late in that century, it was discovered that a market could be developed for bananas shipped from Jamaica to the United States and Great Britain. This signaled the beginning of the United Fruit Company and the end of many of the coastal tropical forests of the Caribbean region and Central America. By 1997, banana plantations covered some 6.5 million hectares (25,000 square miles).[34] Palm oil plantations are similar engines of destruction.[35] While some poor people may be helped by giant palm operations that need workers and supply them with cheap cooking oil, others are dispossessed.[36] So, some social benefit is derived, but it only slightly offsets the massive environmental costs incurred in the creation of the biological deserts of palm plantations, not to mention the social costs of dispossession and increased poor health among local inhabitants.

The lowland tropical forests of the Malay Peninsula, Java, Sumatra, Borneo, Sulawesi, and the Lesser Sunda Islands—collectively, the Sundaic lowland tropical forests (SLTF)—may house more plant species than any equivalent area on Earth, and they are the tallest and perhaps most beautiful of all tropical forests. In addition, they support an extraordinary array of mammals, including such charismatic species as the tiger, Asian elephant, orangutan, Malaysian tapir, clouded leopard, gaur, banteng, and proboscis monkey. The bird community of those forests is no less exciting and includes nine species of hornbill, several pheasants (including the spectacularly ornate Bulwer's pheasant of Borneo), large numbers of attractive woodpeckers, and a mass of fascinating babblers.[37] Those forests have been almost completely destroyed in recent decades, however, setting in motion, we fear, a regional extinction episode of vast and tragic proportions.[38]

K. David Bishop, a biologist with extensive field experience across the Sundaic region and adjacent areas, put it this way: "Today, August 2003, there are virtually no pristine, primary lowland forests remaining on Sumatra. Those on Borneo have less than five years before they are eradicated and those on the Malay Peninsula are in a parlous state and the attack has already begun on the foothill forests. . . . Few if any of the reserves located within the . . . region contain more than a mere fraction of the SLTF. Those reserves that do harbor SLTF are under immense and increasing pressure from illegal logging and greedy land-grabbers. As a direct result . . . hundreds if not thousands of species ranging from the tiniest invertebrate to many . . . spectacular animals . . . are threatened with extinction."[39]

The lowland forests of the trans-Fly area of southeastern Papua New Guinea, the third largest remaining lowland tropical forest in the world (the Amazon and Congo are numbers one and two), are now threatened with similar destruction. When we were in the Kiunga region of the Fly River drainage[40] in 2003, we learned that Malaysian corporations were planning a massive timber-harvesting campaign there. The campaign will begin with the clear-cutting of more than 650,000 acres under the Kiunga Forest Management Agreement. The local people will be paid roughly $0.80 per acre each year for thirty years—hardly a reasonable sum, considering that many of the dozens of trees that closely pack each acre are worth hundreds to many thousands of dollars each because of the value of the wood to rich-world consumers.[41]

The local people will have both their forests and their culture destroyed for the short-term gain of a pittance. They are already strug-gling with the problems of acculturation into the dominant global society. At one point on the Fly, we stopped to see a group processing sago palm, the traditional staple of the New Guinea diet. Both adults and children were wearing tattered Western clothes (the traditional "ass-grass" has largely disappeared since we first were in New Guinea, in 1965). And, amazingly, two of the barefoot children were playing with Game Boy computer video games. Even so, the bright, tradition-ally very political New Guineans are no match for the globalized, Chinese-backed Malaysian steamroller approaching them. They are too naïve about the ways of the outside world; national politicians in Port Moresby and local headmen are easily bribed with small amounts of money, alcohol, and access to prostitutes. The local people also will not be helped by the racist views of them held by many Malaysians.[42]

Exploitation by large corporations (often with the connivance or outright support of their governments as well as consent from the gov-ernments of the exploited countries) in aid of rich-nation consumption has repeatedly hurt people in the non-industrial world, whether indigenous peoples whose forest habitats have been destroyed, subsistence farmers squeezed off the land, or imported slave or semi-slave laborers. From Caribbean and Hawaiian lowlands to the hill country of Brazil and the forests of the Philippines, careless deforestation, erosion, and squalor have been generated by firms that bought governments and cared nothing for sustainability. It is not a pretty story, but it is a supremely important one, and one about to be repeated in New Guinea.

William Vogt was a conservationist who was deeply concerned with Central American rural development after World War II. Vogt's pioneering 1948 book, *Road to Survival,*[43] was one of the first to stimulate our interest in population-environment issues. Long ago, it stated a basic message about consumption very well: "By excessive breeding and abuse of the land mankind has backed itself into an ecological trap. . . . I do not mean the other fellow. I mean every person who reads a newspaper printed on pulp from vanishing forests . . . who eats a meal drawn from steadily shrinking lands . . . puts on a wool garment derived from overgrazed ranges that have been cut by the little hoofs and gullied by the rains, sending runoff and topsoil into rivers downstream, flooding cities hundreds of miles away."[44]

## Consumption and Agriculture

The most important activity of humanity is growing and distributing its food, and that certainly is the enterprise most critical to human health and happiness. In our heavily urbanized society, most of us are far removed from the systems that supply our food, and we tend to take them all for granted. But many of the processes involved in providing the variety of foods now demanded by consumers in developed countries carry high environmental costs. They include all the energy costs of growing, harvesting, storing, and processing food and transporting it around the world; the health costs of antibiotic resistance promoted by the intensive use of antibiotics in livestock production; and the environmental costs of overpackaging to help promote sales.

All that is on top of the ecological costs of converting the land to agriculture in the first place; still more for growth of export crops in developing countries in place of subsistence crops, plus the degradation of many countryside areas that has followed. Even the growing of staple foods can involve needless environmental damage—remember that large dead zone in the Gulf of Mexico! In addition to the ecological damage, there are still poorly understood health consequences that flow from the overuse of pesticides.[45]

The culinary demand of the well-off for exotic foods, including seafoods, as we have indicated, damages distant ecosystems and, often, poorer people. But the responsibility does not rest only with Americans, Europeans, and the entrepreneurs and corporations that both exploit the local people and overexploit the marine life. Those Hong Kong millionaires feasting on grouper lips are adding to the fishing pressures that are destroying the fauna of many coral reefs and, along with them, the livelihoods of artisanal fishermen and the nutritional security of less developed societies.

One reason for the growing concern of agricultural experts about future global food production in general is the rising demand for higher-quality foods, especially animal products, by the "new consumers" in middle-income developing nations and their growing pressure on the agricultural enterprise. China, which has more new consumers (over 300 million) than the United States has consumers (slightly less than 300 million), has virtually doubled its per capita meat consumption since 1990, making it the world's largest carnivorous nation (the power of some 1.3 billion caputs!). By 2010, with its economy expanding at 8 to 10 percent per year, there could be almost *twice* the number of new consumers in China as there are consumers in the United States, and their collective purchasing power could approach half that of the United States today.

As the Chinese increasingly use grain to feed livestock, they will put ever more pressure on their already stretched agricultural system—indeed, on a marginal world food economy. The Chinese, however, are just the leading example of rising consumption in developing countries; new consumers in many nations are pushing to emulate the consumption patterns of the world's rich. Demand for meat in developing nations, generated primarily by new consumers, is projected to nearly double by 2020. In terms of environmental damage, meat is much more costly to produce than are staple crops such as rice, wheat, and soybeans. Furthermore, the greater demand for meat will probably be accompanied by as much as an 85 percent rise in demand for feed grains to produce the meat.[46]

## Resource Wars

Demand for cheap resources on the part of the rich nations has done more than contribute to environmental rape and pillage in poor countries. In many cases, it has led to what have become known as "resource wars,"[47] conflicts either caused by attempts to appropriate the natural riches of less powerful nations or minority groups, or begun for other reasons but financed by those natural riches. It is an old story that is still being acted out and in some instances intensified. In the 1990s, resource wars killed an estimated 5 million people, created almost 6 million international refugees, and displaced between 11 and 15 million people within nations.[48]

Sometimes these struggles have been over prestige resources: one of the bloodiest recent wars was fought in Sierra Leone and Liberia over diamonds. A more important resource, copper, helped to fuel a bloody civil war on Bougainville, an island province of Papua New Guinea. Thousands died, most of them civilians, in a conflict that lasted longer than a decade. The causes included environmental damage from the world's largest open-pit copper mine and disagreement over who was going to control the revenue stream from the mine, as well as a complex of other regional issues.[49] As is so often the case, raw political power was brought to bear to make a profit, and in the process the environment was destroyed.

In the 1970s in the province of Aceh, on the northern tip of Sumatra, Indonesia, timber resources were being legally and illegally harvested by cronies of the dictator Suharto, backed by his military forces. Great environmental degradation was also being caused by the construction and operation of a huge liquefied natural gas (LNG) plant, again backed by the power of the government and a multi-national corporation. These activities led to intense local resentment because people were displaced from their homes and their agricultural and aquacultural activities were disrupted. That resentment drove the Acehnese to rebellion in 1976. The revolt was swiftly put down, but a second uprising in the late 1980s resulted in an army campaign of torture and rape and the killing of more than a thousand civilians. Fighting between rebels and the government has continued, with thousands of deaths, despite intermittent truces. As recently as May 2003, a government offensive was launched with the goal of wiping out the rebels.[50] The guerillas' major target is the LNG plant operated by the ExxonMobil Corporation. It has been alleged that Exxon-Mobil's hands have been far from clean; according to Michael Renner of the Worldwatch Institute, the company "paid the military to provide security for its operations, provided equipment to dig mass graves, and allowed its facilities to be used by the military for torture and other activities."[51]

These examples represent a tip of the iceberg of rebellions sparked by environmentally destructive exploitation of mineral resources by multinational corporations. Too often, the rebellions have been brutally put down by the host country's government at the instigation of the exploiting corporation. Among recent such upheavals have been protests over Royal Dutch/Shell's environmental destruction in the Ogoni region of Nigeria; disturbances in West Irian over damage, despoliation, and displacement of local people by the huge open-pit copper and gold mine of Freeport-McMoRan Copper & Gold; and the Occidental Petroleum Corporation's environmental impacts and resultant battles with indigenous groups in Colombia.[52] Such conflicts seem likely only to increase as demand by the affluent for resources, from diamonds, copper, and gold to oil and gas, drives suppliers to seek and extract them in places not already heavily exploited, heedless of the costs to local citizens. Governments of poor countries, needing the income from such exports, too often are unable or disinclined to exert any control over the environmental consequences.

The direct human costs of resource wars are bad enough. But the added costs in environmental degradation caused by resource exploitation by the powerful in the homelands of the poor—the deforestation, the poisoning of land with mine wastes and of rivers with long-lived industrial pollutants, and so on—adds a burden that will be passed on to many future generations. Unless the international community can find a way to regulate the environment-damaging activities of the extracting industries, the far-flung wars and destruction will doubtless continue. Fortunately, a movement is growing to push multinationals into more responsible behavior, using pressure from large stockholder blocs, unfavorable publicity, lawsuits by individual communities, and increased liability insurance costs. There are some signs that it's beginning to work.[53]

Nevertheless, imposition of environmental costs on people in developing regions seems likely to continue. Resource exploitation by giant corporations seems necessary to maintain the overconsuming way of life of the affluent and, all too often, line the pockets of the corporations' political cronies. That burden is extended to the poor in industrial countries when politicians use the pretext of terrorism to divert attention and funds away from needed environmental and social programs and into conflicts designed to maintain profits and resource hegemony.

Recent victims of wars related to fossil fuels were, in 2001–2002, the people of Afghanistan, where natural gas was the main resource in play.[54] In the case of Afghanistan, the war was incited by terrorists involved in the 9/11 attack, most of them from Saudi Arabia, who were enraged by the presence of U.S. troops in their oil-rich country. On the excuse that the instigator of the attack, Osama bin Laden, was being protected by the Taliban, George W. Bush sent American troops to attack Afghanistan. About a year later, the Bush administration got an agreement for a $3.2 billion pipeline project to carry gas from Turkmenistan's rich gas fields across Afghanistan to Pakistan.[55] Signing the deal for Afghanistan was President Hamid Karzai, a former consultant to Unocal Corporation, the U.S. company that had long pressed for the project[56] but had been thwarted by the diplomatic isolation of the Taliban.[57] Unocal will now be the lead company on the project.[58]

## Consumption and the Maintenance of Power

This brings us to one of the clearest examples of a resource war, George W. Bush's invasion of Iraq in 2003. The war was fought in no small part over the West's (and especially the United States') desire to maintain and control flows of imported petroleum. As Gretchen Daily quoted to us as Bush launched his invasion: "Do you suppose we'd be attacking Iraq if its most important export product were broccoli?"[59] (More than 55 percent of the oil consumed in the United States is imported, about a fourth of that from the Persian Gulf; Europe and Japan are even more dependent on that source.) Bush's action was not without precedent. Japan may have pioneered in destroying people's lives in weaker countries for access to precious oil when it invaded Indonesia in 1942, or we might give some credit to the British in Mesopotamia and Persia in the 1920s[60] and, later, Nazi Germany's attempts to grab the oil of the Caucasus.

In 2002, the Bush administration gave the American public the impression that Saddam Hussein was connected to the 9/11 terrorist attacks and declared the Iraq invasion to be part of a "war on terrorism." The main justification among many put forth was that Iraq had weapons of mass destruction and posed an imminent threat to Americans.[61] That Iraq has Earth's second largest petroleum reserves was never mentioned.[62] The invasion of Iraq revealed the great ease with which the powerful can manipulate the opinion of a large portion of a trusting and often poorly educated populace. The fundamental reason for the invasion was to enhance U.S. *power*—to gain solid control over an area rich in a key resource, petroleum;[63] to improve the U.S. strategic position relative to the oil- and gas-rich Caspian region;[64] and at the same time to teach the world the lesson that nothing would be allowed to prevent continued American overconsumption. A major source of petroleum for the West had been Saudi Arabia; it was the chief ally in the region besides Israel, and it was growing increasingly unfriendly and unstable (as the 9/11 attack demonstrated).[65] Stability, more than avoidance of possible oil embargoes, was clearly a major goal.[66]

Of course, many other elements may enter into wars that, like the Iraq war, are fundamentally over control of resources. They can range all the way from an altruistic desire to improve the conditions of people living under despots or to support coreligionists, to less admirable ego satisfaction and financial gain for oneself or one's friends. In the case of the Iraq resource war, interest in maintaining domestic political power was clearly involved as well. In May 2003, during the war, Bush attempted to jump-start his 2004 re-election campaign with an expensive photo op in which he was flown to an aircraft carrier in a jet. There, he bounced out of the aircraft in full flight gear and "announced" what everyone knew, that the major fighting in Iraq was over (had he announced the end of the war, he would have been forced to obey international law relative to prisoners).[67]

Wars are great generators of consumption. Part of the power that promoted the U.S. military adventure in Iraq, as Dwight Eisenhower warned so long ago, came from the corporations and individuals who make huge profits preparing for and supporting wars. During the preparations to attack Iraq, the Raytheon Company put on an additional shift to speed production of its Paveway laser-guided bombs (more than $50,000 each). As the United States moved to build a Middle East empire, Kellogg Brown & Root, a subsidiary of Halliburton (Vice President Dick Cheney's old company), minted money and consumed vast resources building military bases at home and abroad, often with questionable efficiency.[68] Halliburton has made a fortune dealing with nations that sponsor terrorism, possibly breaking U.S. federal laws by so doing.[69] Former secretary of state George Shultz chaired the advisory board of the Committee for the Liberation of Iraq, a group that lobbied hard for the war. He also is on the board of the Bechtel Group, a company that received a huge (potentially $680 million or more) contract to rebuild Iraq.[70]

All of those corporate activities are titanic engines driving the consumption of human-made and natural capital. And, by blocking local Iraqi initiatives, corporate operations don't seem to be helping much, if economist Paul Krugman is correct: "Cronyism is an important factor in our Iraqi debacle. It's not just that reconstruction is much more expensive than it should be. The really important thing is that cronyism is warping policy: by treating contracts as prizes to be handed to their friends, administration officials are delaying Iraq's recovery, with potentially catastrophic consequences."[71]

The Iraq war supplies a particularly dramatic example of how consumption interests may interact with political and economic power. But the interaction of consumption with power occurs in many other less conspicuous but no less consequential ways around the world. Both within and between nations, the consumption and power gap between rich and poor generates problems. People in impoverished areas simply are leading unnecessarily hard lives, and they may make desperate moves to escape their situation. The rich may keep increasing their consumption, but they will continue to be disturbed by problems of unwanted immigration, outbreaks of epidemic diseases, terrorist attacks, and threats of large-scale conflict, all to one degree or another generated by the widening differences in well-being between societies. The huge gap in consumption levels between the richest and the poorest seems certain to persist for some time. Where certain political conditions are present, as when a large, weak minority is (or feels) oppressed, the gap could continue to generate terrorism for many decades to come. Great deprivation not only feeds the anger that inspires terrorism; it also is commonly associated with high birthrates, which could both supply terrorist organizations with recruits and impede the development processes that might improve people's lives and prospects.

Overconsumption by the rich and underconsumption by the poor lie at the roots of many of humanity's most pressing social problems. If terrorism is an outstanding current symptom,[72] the development of vast military might is another. If the West weren't hooked on oil, there would be no need for a potent military deployment centered on the Persian Gulf.[73] And while a sane American energy policy, emphasizing increased energy efficiency and development of renewable sources, would doubtless reduce the threat of terrorism, it would also dampen America's love affair with cars and SUVs and threaten the energy interests that often govern so much of the foreign and environmental policies of the U.S. government.

In an era of declining production in the United States, roughly 65 percent of the world's proven oil reserves are in the Middle East.[74] In attempting to control that source,[75] the Bush administration was following a traditional Western policy of securing Middle Eastern sources of oil that traces back to before World War I, when warships began to be powered by oil rather than coal.[76] But the Bush administration and its right-wing "moralist" manipulators[77] have taken that policy to a new extreme as part of a program to establish a truly global American empire—as epitomized by the astonishing document titled "The National Security Strategy of the United States of America," released by the Bush White House in 2002.[78]

That document declares that the American empire will use its "unparalleled military strength" to maintain the flow of resources required to support U.S. overconsumption. As George W. Bush's father, President George H. W. Bush, said at the 1992 United Nations Conference on Environment and Development (Earth Summit), the "American way of life" is "not negotiable." He was telling an unfortunate truth—prosperous Americans show little interest in initiating substantial changes in their behavior in order to protect the life-support systems they depend upon or to help dig up terrorism at its roots. Of course, they'll have to give up that way of life sooner or later—and sooner seems more likely if current estimates of the size of Earth's supply of cheap petroleum are accurate.[79]

The new American imperialists, "drunk with sight of power,"[80] to use Kipling's phrase, have arrogated to themselves the right to attack other nations preemptively,[81] and alone if the United States cannot persuade other nations to join in the assault. Basically, these rulers are substituting aggression for deterrence, and doing it in the face of what has been an increasing international opinion that transborder attacks are unacceptable.

In other ways as well, the new imperialists have been rending the fragile and painstakingly woven fabric of international standards. They deny that the International Criminal Court has jurisdiction over them, and they have not fully supported either biological and chemical weapons conventions or nuclear non-proliferation and disarmament agreements.[82] They rejected the key Kyoto Protocol to reduce greenhouse gas emissions,[83] which is arguably the most important environmental agreement since the Montreal Protocol for controlling ozone-destroying chemicals. Simultaneously they were waging an unprecedented war on the domestic environment, fighting anything that might reduce private profits for the production of social benefits. Above all, their announced objective is a global empire in which other nations will not be allowed to compete militarily with the United States. The United States will provide them with a Pax Americana whether they want it or not.

This arrogance has not escaped the notice of commentators in friendly nations, or of friendly commentators within the United States.[84] Nelson Mandela declared: "They think they're the only power in the world. . . . One country wants to bully the world."[85] George W. Bush's renouncing of the Kyoto Protocol moved Australian commentator Richard Neville to write, "Forget the Taliban, Gaddafi or the beastly Saddam Hussein, it is the United States that is out of control, the wildest rogue nation of all."[86] *Business Week* stated of the National Security Strategy report: "Despite loose talk today about a benign new Pax Americana, many Americans and many more people overseas are uncomfortable with the image of an America acting unilaterally around the world, breaking treaties at will, giving lip service to allies and international institutions while claiming for itself the sole legitimate use of force anywhere, anytime it feels threatened."[87]

## Another Way?

Using American power to keep continually inflating the West's consumption bubble with cheap energy prices seems an exquisitely shortsighted policy—sure to build resentment elsewhere and equally sure to fail. We are convinced that the prudent course for the United States and other developed nations that wish to reduce terrorism in the short term, and avoid collision with the natural world in the medium term, is not to attempt to rule the world by brute force. A much better approach, and one more likely to succeed, is to work to ameliorate conditions for the poorest people around the world. The United States should use its power and influence to play a central role in helping to improve demographic and socioeconomic conditions in developing nations; far more than any other nation, it has the economic strength and clout to do so. Even if narrowing the rich-poor gap did not reduce the incidence of terrorism, it would be the ethical thing to do.[88] Economic growth among the already rich is not a sensible primary goal of public policy at this point in human history.

The first step toward achieving that resolution is to recognize that Earth's life-support capability is not boundless. Within constraints set by the extent of natural capital, population and consumption have a reciprocal relationship: the more people there are, the less each one, on average, can consume if the consumption is to be sustainable. If there are inequities in the distribution of wealth, the larger the population is (*ceteris paribus*), the less people at the poor end of the spectrum will be able to consume. Population and consumption together are at the heart of many human problems, many of them environmental, and some of them generating deadly conflicts. If those problems are to be solved, we must understand more about consumption patterns and about the relationships of technologies to consumption. We now turn to that issue and suggest some tentative solutions that we believe humanity must carefully test if the collision with the natural world is to be averted.

# Chapter 5

## TECHNOLOGY MATTERS

"The freedom to develop technology primarily to serve
human needs was lost with the spread of industrialization
and the growth of modern megatechnical systems in
communications, transportation, power production,
and manufacturing. These gigantic, complex, interconnected technological systems overwhelm human values
and defy human control."
GEORGE BASALLA, 1988[1]

SOMETIMES the dominant animal on Earth just gets lucky. One
of *Homo sapiens'* notable technological triumphs was the creation of Freon, a trade name for several chlorofluorocarbons
(CFCs). When first synthesized in the early 1930s, CFCs were her-
alded as one of the great inventions of the chemical industry—stable,
non-toxic compounds that were ideal replacements for the toxic cooling agents then used in refrigerators. Once Freon was installed in your
Frigidaire, you could sleep easy at night without fearing a poisonous leak. As air-conditioning and similar technologies became widely
adopted by the public, CFCs were produced in ever larger quantities.
Then a technological triumph by British chemist James Lovelock, the
invention of the electron capture gas chromatograph, permitted detection of the presence of CFCs as amazingly long-lived contaminants
in the atmosphere.[2] An atmospheric chemist, Sherwood Rowland,
became curious about their persistence and, luckily for all of us,

encouraged his post-doctoral associate Mario Molina to help him look into it.

To make a long story short, Rowland and Molina concluded that the CFCs could destroy the upper atmosphere's ozone layer, a shield extending roughly from eight to thirty miles above Earth's surface that protects all terrestrial life from damage or destruction by the sun's ultraviolet radiation.[3] Life was able to leave the oceans and colonize land only after a sufficiently protective layer of ozone (a form of oxygen) had been formed some 450 million years ago, the result of oxygen generated by the activities of photosynthetic organisms in the oceans having accumulated in the atmosphere over billions of years. Substantial depletion of the ozone layer today would be calamitous for terrestrial life, so this was one of the most unpleasant surprises of theoretical science of all time. When Rowland came home from his office after his discovery, he told his wife: "The work is going well. But it looks like the end of the world."[4]

Rowland and Molina were subjected to much abuse by corporate interests who were using CFCs in refrigeration and as propellants in aerosol cans and who claimed the scientists' conclusions were faulty. But eventually empirical science came to the rescue of theoretical science. British scientist Joe Farman and his colleagues with the British Antarctic Survey, using "old-fashioned" but well-tested instruments, documented the thinning of the ozone shield over Halley Bay and Argentine Island.[5] That thinning had previously been missed by a sophisticated satellite launched by the National Aeronautics and Space Administration (NASA) because of a series of errors in computer programming and data analysis.

There is a cautionary tale about technology here. The NASA satellite in question, Nimbus-7, carried TOMS (Total Ozone Mapping Spectrometer), an instrument that sent back several hundred thousand measurements every day, covering essentially all of the sunlit Earth. The first satellite measurements in October, the time of year the "ozone hole" forms over Antarctica, were made in 1979. For several years, they showed consistent ozone values of around 250 Dobson units; 300 is the approximate global average value at any time. But this turned out to be an artifact of the measurement system. Apparently, TOMS was programmed in its early years to reject any reading below 180 Dobson units as obviously erroneous because such low values had never been known to occur. By 1983, re-examination of the data showed that values below 175 were appearing, but a deep plunge during 1980–1982 was still not detected by analysts.[6] The way TOMS was programmed, combined with NASA's failure to make any provisions for adequately handling the flood of data that came from it, conspired to let Farman and his team first publish the news of the ozone hole. When these problems were corrected, re-examination of raw TOMS data quickly confirmed and expanded the findings of the Farman team.[7] In 1986, a brilliant young atmospheric scientist, Susan Solomon, led a team to the Antarctic and showed beyond reasonable doubt that CFCs were the culprit causing the thinning.[8]

In 1995, Sherwood Rowland and Mario Molina shared (with Paul Crutzen, another fine atmospheric scientist) a richly deserved Nobel Prize in Chemistry. They saved humanity from untold misery, and at the same time they told us a story of unintended consequences that should be engraved in the memories of all who expect technology to save us. Yes, technology can save us, as it did in detecting the fate of ozone with fancy instruments. It also found relatively ozone-safe synthetic substitutes for the ozone-destroying CFCs. But it was technology that put humanity in peril in the first place, and the possibility of unintended consequences persists. Some new substitutes for CFCs, for example, have turned out to be greenhouse gases (as are CFCs themselves) and thus may somewhat exacerbate global warming, although they are no threat to the ozone layer.[9] Above all, some technological devices stress human capacities so severely that errors—including potentially lethal ones—can easily occur at the technological-human interface, as they did in the Nimbus-7 case.

## Faulty Technologies

In confronting human-caused environmental havoc, many people are reluctant to recognize the roles of overpopulation and overconsumption; instead they find it easier to blame "faulty technologies"—ones with environmentally damaging characteristics.[10] But faulty human behavior is often more to blame. Many people who see smog or over-flowing landfills, and worry about toxic wastes, gasoline-guzzling cars, and energy-wasting appliances, believe that technological change will set things right. To a degree this is true, as it was in the case of ozone depletion. And, in some situations, straightforward solutions have been put into practice. The need for more space for landfills, for instance, can be substantially reduced technologically by re-using and recycling; in the United States, this is being done to a large extent, with cooperation from the public. Accumulations of toxic waste, some a century or more old, have poisoned tens of thousands of sites nationwide. Cleanups initiated under the Superfund legislation since 1980 have successfully remediated many of the worst ones, although many others remain to be addressed. Meanwhile, such contamination can be avoided or prevented in the future by technological improvements in handling wastes or by substitution of more benign substances for toxic ones.[11] Some of the country's worst corporate offenders in the past have more recently pioneered in developing safer new processes and substitutes.[12] Most industrial societies today realize, in the case of toxic substances, the wisdom of an ounce of prevention and have begun putting it into practice. On far more daunting challenges such as climate change and the decay of ecosystem services, with the potential eventually to cause hundreds of millions of premature deaths, however, we haven't even started.

Some environmental impacts could be moderated by essentially simple technological changes, but political factors stand in the way. We could reduce our automobile fuel consumption by driving more fuel-efficient vehicles, which would reduce emissions of pollutants and greenhouse gases that threaten both human health and ecosystem integrity. Technology, which made the problem possible in the first place, could be used to ameliorate it. But, with automobiles, the projected increase in their use and the multiplicity of damages they cause independent of fuel efficiency (e.g., the paving over of land for roads, garages, and parking lots and, besides the spewing of widely recognized pollutants, discharge of rubber into the air from tire wear) seem likely to make it very difficult for us to reduce their overall environmental effects significantly in the near future. Indeed, the total harmful effects from automobiles seem bound to increase.

Ever since ingenuity led human beings to invent agriculture, technologies have played an important part in both enabling and exacerbating environmental damage. Sometimes technology is even the primary factor (persistent pesticides and CFCs come to mind), and a more benign substitute can solve the problem without affecting well-being or economic stability. But, in most cases, technology in a broad sense is an enabler; it underpins expanding consumption and is allowing a very large human population to be supported.

## Technology as a Chooser

Technology is rightly (or conveniently) blamed for some serious problems—which nonetheless might not be so serious but for the scale of the human enterprise. The significance of technology is overlooked in other respects, however. Perhaps the ultimate reason it matters is that, as new technologies are developed and adopted, they essentially make choices for humanity—often choices with enormous, largely unforeseen consequences. Some technologically driven choices are widely recognized: farming was a technology that set people on the road to completely new lifestyles, land-use practices, and political arrangements, as well as a greatly expanded population. The manifold changes entrained by agriculture, followed later by the industrial revolution, ultimately made possible the development of nuclear weapons, space travel, and genetic engineering, among countless other things. In the past century, the invention of the automobile generated far-reaching alterations in settlement patterns, urban infrastructures, personal mores, and, of course, transportation habits. Even more recently, mainly in industrialized nations, the development of personal computers and the Internet has revolutionized business, finance, education, and global communications. In leapfrog fashion, these electronic innovations are spreading rapidly in many developing nations, bypassing many earlier technologies and transforming emerging business communities—remember the Game Boy consoles seen in the hands of children on the Fly River in "primitive" Papua New Guinea.

Humanity has had great difficulty in reversing technology-based choices. Indeed, there are only a few well-documented instances of success—one being the rejection of guns by Japan in the mid-seventeenth century after less than 100 years of use in combat.[13] Even that, of course, was temporary; by the twentieth century the Japanese were using guns to create an Asian empire (in many ways, as historian John Dower has pointed out, by means remarkably similar to those now being used by the United States to create a world empire).[14] More often, successful technologies are superceded by more successful ones—passenger trains by airliners,[15] horses and buggies by automobiles, oil lamps and gas lighting by electric lights, typewriters by personal computers. And sometimes new technologies simply enrich the mix, as with radio, movies, and television, although these can be seen as more successful technologies than, say, storytelling or stage plays.

For all the power of modern technologies to enhance people's lives and well-being, though, they have been far from universally shared. Perhaps even more than access to resources themselves, the lack of technologies to extract and use them efficiently and effectively has kept the great bulk of humanity in poverty while others have prospered. Political and economic power wielded by people in the industrialized world impedes the transfer of technologies so badly needed by the poor, even as the economies of all nations supposedly "globalize." Two classic examples have been blockades to making affordable drugs against AIDS available for use in Africa and the complications patent arrangements pose in getting needed agricultural technologies to the poor.[16]

A proverbial two-edged sword, technology can help to reduce overall environmental impacts or it can exacerbate them. Even as technologies of various sorts have enabled the human enterprise to reach its present scale, they also have contributed mightily to the weakening of Earth's life-support systems. And sometimes efforts to mitigate the adverse effects of one technology can create other problems, as when no-till cultivation replaced plowing and reduced soil erosion but increased pest problems and toxic risks from herbicides.

How well might we do now if we made a serious effort to move toward truly environmentally benign technologies? The answer is quite well, at least potentially. In this chapter, we'll explore some of the sectors that offer us significant opportunities for reducing destructive environmental impacts by adopting improved technologies, and by changing the cultural, political, and economic practices that stand in the way of their adoption.[17]

## The Technology Factor

Travel can be considered a form of consumption; in the rich world it usually involves the use of vehicles and fuel. But to travel, a person may only need to consume food to get enough energy to walk barefoot from her hut to a well several miles away and carry water back. Another, by contrast, may consume large amounts of inanimate energy and materials in manufacturing and gasoline in order to drive a Hummer to the supermarket two blocks away. Different technological means of doing things result in very different levels of impact. Going ten miles in shoes or on a bicycle results in much less environmental impact than going by train, which in turn causes less harm than driving alone in an SUV. Population size plays a role too—if one in a hundred people drives a Hummer, a society of 100 million people obviously will have much more Hummer-caused environmental damage than a society of 1 million people. And whether one drives or walks will be influenced by population-related issues such as sprawl and traffic density. The choice of transport mode, however, is also shaped by economic, social, and political factors, including the availability, utility, cost, and convenience of various options. In turn, the choices available are largely determined by decision makers and corporations with political clout, not by the consumer. In the United States, automotive options are heavily promoted and subsidized. Walking, biking, and mass transportation are not.

Most scientists agree today that the principal driving forces behind the deterioration of human life-support systems are three factors: population size and growth, overconsumption, and the use of environmentally malign technologies. These relations are conveniently summarized in the identity $I = PAT$. Thus, the environmental impact of a society $(I)$ can be estimated by multiplying the number of people $(P)$ by the affluence $(A)$ per person, as measured by their level of consumption, and then multiplied again by the technology $(T)$ factor. The latter factor incorporates much more than just the array of technologies that facilitate consumption; it also includes the social, economic, and political arrangements that determine what is consumed, how, and by whom. The three factors are by no means independent; indeed, the technology factor is so intricately intertwined with population and affluence in generating the human predicament that it is often impossible to distinguish which one is driving another in a particular context.[18]

Within that broad technology factor, the maldistribution of power is of particular importance. The *IPAT* equation shows how the most critical and widespread damage to ecosystems and natural services can be caused not by the poor majority but by the affluent minority of the world, with their enormous collective consumption (affluence) and power. People in the industrialized world have access to the entire world's resources and often remain ignorant of, or seem to care little about, any damage they inflict elsewhere. People in poor countries, of course, also cause environmental damage, but it is mostly local in effect, mainly harms those who cause it, and is often due to their lack of capacity to prevent it.

An excellent device to help us understand the scale of the human enterprise generally, to see the connections among population, consumption, and technology, and to evaluate relative impacts among nations, is a comparison of statistics on energy use.[19] Energy use, especially use of fossil fuels (primarily coal, oil, and natural gas), is involved, directly or indirectly, in most of the activities that cause substantial environmental disruption. Fossil fuels are used to produce electricity; to heat and cool homes, offices, factories, and stores; and to provide feedstocks for toxic chemicals as well as to produce our food and to transport people, resources, and products around the globe. Their harmful effects include production of air pollutants, subsidizing of intensive agriculture, and powering of deforestation and other land-use changes. Most critically, fossil fuel use also is the chief cause of the buildup of greenhouse gases in the atmosphere, leading to global warming and climate change.[20]

Energy use per capita provides a useful index (when multiplied by population size) for roughly estimating the environmental impact of a society. Per capita energy use combines the otherwise difficult to sort out $A$ and $T$ factors of the $I = PAT$ identity.[21] At the turn of the twenty-first century, with less than 5 percent of the world's population, the United States used about 23 percent of the world's commercial energy. The 900 million people in the richest nations (including the United States), less than 15 percent of the population, accounted for about 50 percent of global energy use.[22]

Energy statistics show clearly that population growth in the past half-century has been only partially responsible for humanity's escalating environmental impacts. In the half century that the human population grew from 2.5 billion to more than 6 billion (increased 2.5 times), commercial energy[23] use rose 4.6 times. Meanwhile, the global economy (in constant dollars) surged nearly *sevenfold*.[24] The difference between population and economic growth was, of course, primarily due to increased per capita consumption, although the characteristics of the energy technologies chosen to service that consumption could have either increased or lowered the outcome.

Most of the increase in energy use has been in the wealthiest and middle-income nations, while the billion or so people in the lowest-income nations have seen little or no rise in per capita energy use.[25] Poor people in rural areas of low-income nations still mostly depend on fuelwood or charcoal for cooking and have no access to electricity. During the 1990s, per capita energy use in low- and low-middle-income nations fell by 10 percent or so; many were former Soviet Union nations, in which energy use per capita plunged about 30 percent. Meanwhile, energy use per capita continued to rise in upper-middle- and high-income regions.[26] Citizens in high-income nations use an average of 9.5 times as much energy (Americans 14 times as much) as individuals in low-income countries.

The distribution of energy use is changing, nonetheless, and developing countries will soon account for well over half the world's use. The poorest nations (the Tanzanias and Nepals of the world), until now largely left out of the energy-based industrial path, need substantially increased access to efficient energy. China is already the world's second largest energy user, but only at about one-eighth the level per person of the United States,[27] and much less efficiently on the whole. China has been making substantial progress in increasing its energy efficiency, however, by phasing out inefficient factories and power plants and thereby reducing environmental costs while increasing energy services. India and many other developing nations also have been increasing their energy use, and their populations are also still growing, if not as fast as a generation ago.

Given the attendant damage to natural capital and the enormous risk of global warming, not only must the poor be supplied with energy in the most efficient and environmentally benign ways possible, but also the rich must themselves develop much more energy-sparing economies. All this can be achieved without vastly escalating the level of human assault on Earth's capacity to sustain civilization in the long term,[28] but it will take great care and great effort.

Harvard physicist John Holdren showed many years ago[29] that efficiency improvements alone in high- and upper-middle-income nations could reduce per capita energy use enough to allow a tripling of per capita use in low-income nations. At the same time, overall energy use worldwide could thereby be limited to less than a doubling of existing levels, even with a doubling in population size (then about 5 billion). If the projected increases in energy use were derived from renewable sources instead of fossil fuels, and if the population's peak size could be kept well below 10 billion, the outlook would become considerably brighter.

## Energy Use: Prime Culprit or Prime Opportunity?

The mobilization and use of energy to carry out human activities, including agriculture and industrial production, is doubtless the prime cause, in one way or another, of most environmental damage in the modern era. This is especially true for the fossil fuels, which supply almost 80 percent of the world's energy today. Energy from fossil fuels facilitates land-use modification, powers transportation, heats and cools buildings, and generates most electric power. Fossil fuel combustion also causes air pollution and acid deposition and is the leading source of human-caused greenhouse gas emissions—primarily carbon dioxide ($CO_2$) but also methane and nitrous oxide.[30] Processes of mining and extracting fossil fuels are, in addition, important contributors to land degradation and water pollution; refining is a source of air pollution.

Although population growth and increasing consumption of goods and services per capita all add to pressure to use more energy, experts in energy technologies generally agree that most industrialized countries, especially the United States, could provide healthy, satisfying lives for their citizens on a third or less of current U.S. per capita energy use.[31] The first, and unquestionably the easiest, fastest, cheapest, and most environmentally benign, approach to reducing per capita energy use without lowering the quality of life is to increase the engineering efficiency with which the energy is produced (as fuel or electricity) and used.[32]

In the context of energy use, the term *efficiency* is sometimes used interchangeably with *conservation*, but there is a difference. Conservation is action taken by individuals to cut back energy use on a temporary basis, such as adjusting a thermostat to a higher temperature in summer or a lower temperature in winter, turning off unnecessary lights, washing clothes in cold water, and the like. In the public mind, this has become associated with discomfort and sacrifice, although it needn't be so. Nevertheless, the use of such measures by millions of Californians no doubt contributed to the significant energy savings they achieved during the "energy crisis" in the summer of 2001.

Efficiency is a more permanent, built-in way to achieve energy savings: more efficient engines (meaning less fuel consumed for the same power output), more efficient combustion in power plants, improved transmission and distribution systems so that less power is lost between power plant and user, better insulation in buildings, refrigerators, and ovens, more efficient lightbulbs and appliances, and so forth.[33] Such improvements have great potential for reducing the amount of energy used for the same benefits without inconveniencing anyone and, indeed, often with improved comfort. These measures also helped Californians reduce their energy use almost overnight in 2001, by 10 percent or more, as many invested in new, more efficient appliances and insulation for their homes, steps that can easily be taken in the short term. Businesses, for their part, invested in more efficient lighting, air-conditioning, and other energy-managing technologies.

In the 1970s, when the world price of petroleum was first substantially raised by an oil embargo imposed by the Organization of the Petroleum Exporting Countries (OPEC),[34] a move that resulted in gasoline shortages, and again in 1979, when the price of petroleum doubled, saving energy became the "in" thing to do and was promoted by the administrations of both Gerald Ford and Jimmy Carter. During the latter's presidency, solar energy collectors were installed on the White House roof (to be removed after Ronald Reagan took office) to symbolize the government's commitment to reducing energy use. That commitment was more concretely expressed by Congress and the U.S. Environmental Protection Agency (EPA) in establishing improved energy efficiency standards for a variety of consumer products. Thanks to advances in automobile engines, manufacturing processes, heating, cooling, and lighting technologies, building standards, and home appliances, the nation's energy use fell by more than 10 percent in the 1980s, despite continued growth in both population and the economy in the United States.

Then petroleum prices fell to new low levels in the late 1980s and remained low through the 1990s; a favorite comparison in the mid-1990s was that gasoline was cheaper than bottled water. Although Japan and Europe continued to make further reductions in per capita energy use, saving energy was all but forgotten as a goal in the United States. Energy use resumed its upward track, and Americans continued to be the world's leading energy users (except for a few oil-producing nations with small populations that use energy to extract and refine petroleum and natural gas for the world market). About a quarter of global commercial energy production through the 1990s and since has been used by Americans.[35]

## Short-Term Potential: Efficiency

Efficiency is clearly the best new energy "source" available to our society in the short to medium term. Most energy experts believe that we in the United States could reduce per capita energy use by more than half with no adverse economic effects, simply by using more advanced and sophisticated technologies, many of which are available now.[36] Not only will any such gains in technological efficiency help with the fossil-fuel-dominated regime we start with, but many will also be helpful when applied to alternative energy sources as they are deployed. Thus, investment in energy efficiency technology is a cost-effective strategy not only for the near term but also for the long term.

Generation of electricity accounts for a significant fraction of commercial energy use everywhere; in the United States it accounts for about 12 percent. Significant improvements have been made in the efficiency of electricity generation in the United States, spurred in part by efforts to control air pollution and reduce acid precipitation, as well as to reduce energy use. But coal still supplies more than 50 percent of the fuel for U.S. power plants, and coal burning is a major cause of air pollution and results in about 50 percent more $CO_2$ emitted per unit of energy produced than does oil, and about 80 percent more than natural gas.

Technological improvements over the past few decades have allowed electricity to be generated much more efficiently, and substantial opportunities remain for further reducing energy use in the electrical sector without reducing the quality of life. One effective strategy is cogeneration—creation of both heat and power in the same facility[37]—

which is already practiced by many industries and institutions such as universities. Considerable advances have been made as well in improving the efficiency of end-use applications such as electric appliances, from refrigerators and air conditioners to computers and electric lights. All these are positive trends, even though adoption of some of these money-saving technologies (such as efficient compact fluorescent lightbulbs) has been slower than might have been expected.[38] Some forward-thinking power companies have recognized that offering subsidies for efficiency improvements, often paid as partial rebates for purchases of efficient lightbulbs or of Energy Star appliances, are less costly than building yet another power plant.

While helpful, all these are only baby steps compared with what is needed. While energy specialists have continued to design efficiency improvements and have made progress in developing alternative energy sources, especially wind and solar power,[39] much of that new technology has remained on the shelf, thus widening the gap between what is feasible and what actually happens. A lack of interest within the U.S. government—on the part of both Congress and the administration—in reducing energy use is largely responsible for the failure to provide incentives for applying existing technologies for that purpose, despite strong economic and environmental reasons to do so.[40] Indeed, the George W. Bush administration and the 107th and 108th Congresses have done their best to cut research budgets, roll back standards, and remove incentives previously in place, although some of the states (including California) have maintained strong programs.[41]

If the greatest impediment to applying the existing technologies has been a lack of motivation, both among the public and in the government, to encourage their adoption,[42] that may change when the results of recent trends sink in. Among the salient trends are rising dependence on imported oil (remember, more than half the oil used in the United States is now imported); a growing shortage of domestic reserves of natural gas and an increasing need to import it; and rising prices of both oil and natural gas in 2002–2003.[43] Oil production in the United States peaked in 1970, and production has been declining ever since while consumption has kept growing (which is why our

imports have been climbing). Now a similar peak for domestic production of natural gas appears to be imminent. More important, the
global production peak for petroleum may occur as soon as 2010,
which is likely to lead to rising oil prices on the world market.[44] If the
terrorist attacks of 2001 and instabilities in the Middle East clearly
highlighted to members of the Bush administration the overriding
importance to the U.S. economy and the petroleum industry of ensuring access to petroleum sources, others have drawn a different lesson—
that national security requires that we begin reducing our dependence
on fossil fuels as an energy source.

Looming in the background, along with other well-known environmental liabilities of petroleum, is the increasing risk of climate change,
a threat long accepted by the majority of Americans, if not by their
president. That threat is appearing more and more real as people begin
to see changes in the weather patterns to which they are accustomed.[45]
Global warming is ultimately the most compelling reason to kick the
fossil fuel habit.

Primarily because the leaders of Europe, Canada, and Japan, as well
as other industrialized nations, have grasped the importance of global
warming, they have adopted the goal of reducing dependence on fossil
fuels, officially through the mechanisms of the Kyoto Protocol. Even
before the protocol goes into effect, its provisions are being implemented with some success through mandated reductions in greenhouse gas emissions in industrialized nations, carbon trading (whereby
polluting entities can buy rights to emit $CO_2$ from others that can
reduce their emissions more economically), joint implementation
(whereby entities in developed countries can earn carbon credits by
paying for carbon-saving initiatives in developing countries), and so
on.[46] At this writing, the Kyoto Protocol awaits ratification by the
Russian Duma to be brought into effect—without the participation of
the United States. Meanwhile, many developing countries, especially
China, though not bound by the Kyoto agreements, are preparing to
comply with the next step in the process.

The United States is the world's most profligate energy user, in
both absolute and per capita terms, yet instead of leading the world in

reducing fossil fuel use, the Bush administration, with support from most of the Republicans and some of the Democrats in Congress, is still sponsoring policies to promote further *increases* in energy use by Americans.[47] Interestingly, in the face of the federal government's total lack of interest in designing policies to address global warming, several states and quite a few local governments have taken the initiative of developing programs themselves. Also, some corporations, including some energy companies, led by BP (the British Petroleum Company), have taken responsibility for reducing $CO_2$ and methane emissions of their own operations, and they have made substantial progress.[48] At the same time, many U.S.-based multinational corporations are finding themselves losing out as European and Japanese companies take advantage of the easiest and best international carbon trades and joint implementation deals available.

## Toward the Future: Renewable Energy Technologies

Improving engineering efficiency is the essential first step,[49] but it can take us only so far. Even if every possible efficiency improvement were made, the economy would still be operating mostly on fossil fuels, though potentially much less of them. So the second indispensable approach is to develop and deploy alternative energy sources, especially renewable sources—those that don't entail the depletion of finite resources such as petroleum. Again, the potential gain is very large; several alternatives are known, albeit with varying levels of attractiveness. Some problems in deploying new energy systems are simply technical, but mainly it is economic, social, political, and in some cases environmental barriers that are impeding their adoption.

Unfortunately, too little progress has been made in this direction, and almost none has been made in the United States. Changing trends in energy use will require a concerted effort by the world community, and such an effort undoubtedly will be opposed by those with vested interests to protect and by others who fear they would have to give up a privileged lifestyle.

One important alternative to fossil-fuel-based energy is nuclear power, which currently provides about 6 percent of the world's energy (17 percent of the electricity). While not renewable, it does depend on a fuel source (uranium) that is abundant and not expensive, and it emits none of the conventional air pollutants or greenhouse gases associated with coal, oil, and natural gas. The Bush administration has been actively promoting construction of new nuclear power plants as part of its energy policy. Unhappily, nuclear power carries a set of serious liabilities, and building safe power plants is a very costly business, as we'll see later in this chapter.[50]

Hydroelectric power—that generated by turbines in dams—has long been the most important of the commercialized renewable energy sources, accounting for 18 percent of world electricity generation in 2000. At first glance, hydropower might appear to be an ideal energy source. But it has its own environmental problems, and the number of potential dam sites is limited. In most developed countries, those limits have largely been reached, although opportunities remain in developing regions. And the "renewability" of power from large dams is also constrained because dams commonly silt up over decades, ultimately becoming useless for power generation. How quickly the silt accumulates depends on how much soil erosion is occurring upstream, which in turn is often determined by the degree of watershed deforestation. Dredging of reservoirs is usually uneconomic, so dams eventually become, in essence, waterfalls. Dams also profoundly change the riverine ecosystem, among other effects blocking the migration of valued fish such as salmon to their spawning grounds.

A near-renewable source, geothermal energy—heat from Earth's interior—can be an important source of energy for some purposes. As with hydropower, high-quality resources are accessible in only a few locations. In Iceland, geothermal power is the primary source of electricity and space heating, and development of this resource is rising in the Philippines and New Zealand, among other places. It also supplies a significant fraction of electric power in California. Advances in technology may accelerate the development of lower-quality and less accessible geothermal energy sources in coming decades.[51] Geothermal energy doesn't produce greenhouse gases, but development of the resource does entail significant local environmental consequences.

Non-commercialized biomass fuels—wood, crop wastes, and dung—still constitute the largest source of energy for about a third of humanity, people who cannot afford modern fuels or have no access to them. These fuels, though not counted in global energy statistics, provide more primary energy worldwide than does hydropower. Although fuelwood is putatively renewable, in practice the rate of harvesting by the poor often exceeds the replenishment rate, and overharvesting of fuelwood is an important cause of land degradation and desertification in some regions.[52] In this form, biomass energy represents the past, not the future.

Modern applications for biomass that show promise as renewable components of a beneficial energy mix include production of fuel substitutes or additives that allow gasoline to burn more cleanly and efficiently.[53] In many developed countries, trees grown in plantations for use as fuel and residues from paper and wood production are being used in some applications to produce electricity in place of fossil fuels. Some new technologies for processing biomass into fuels may contribute as cost-effective (and less polluting) energy sources in the relatively near future. Liquid and gaseous fuels from biomass are already being used extensively in Brazil, China, and India and increasingly in the United States.[54] The burning of biomass fuels, of course, releases $CO_2$, but an equivalent amount is captured from the atmosphere by photosynthesizing plants grown for the next biomass crop. Biomass fuels also emit almost none of the often toxic air pollutants that gasoline, oil, and coal produce. Even as a supplement to gasoline, biomass fuels such as ethanol significantly reduce pollution emissions.

Besides biomass, the most promising renewable energy sources, which are now beginning to be exploited seriously, include wind power, tidal power, and various forms of solar energy.[55] While no one of these by itself could begin to replace the present fossil-fuel-based system (especially for 8 billion or more people consuming at industrial levels), each could eventually make a significant contribution in appropriate settings. In aggregate, if fully deployed they could substantially diminish, perhaps eventually even eliminate, civilization's dependence on fossil fuels.

Wind installations have been increasing rapidly in northern Europe since the mid-1990s and, to some extent, in India and China. But until very recently they have been largely neglected in the United States, after enjoying a brief boom in the 1980s. One of the chief barriers to investment in both wind and solar power has been their cost relative to the costs of cheap oil and gas.[56] But wind power in many U.S. locations has now become competitive in cost with traditional power sources, and large projects are now being built in the northern plains and in some seacoast areas. A wind project can be completed in a year or two (including planning and siting), whereas a conventional power plant requires several years, and a nuclear plant ten years or more. The principal drawback of wind power generation is that winds do not blow constantly. While wind power added to an existing power grid supplied largely by other sources is a helpful boost, especially at peak demand times, its full application awaits development of improved capacity to store electricity. So far, wind generation supplies an almost negligible portion of the electric power in most parts of the world. But this is changing very fast; worldwide generating capacity from wind power rose some 27 percent in 2002, having tripled in only four years.[57]

Solar collectors for heating and cooling of buildings or for water heating have been employed since the late 1970s, mostly on roofs of homes and some larger buildings. Passive solar techniques, which take advantage of sun exposure to warm or cool buildings, have been used in many traditions for centuries. More recently, solar photovoltaics (cells and panels that produce electricity directly from sunlight) have shown great promise as a decentralized source of electricity. Like wind power, solar energy has the advantage of being available on-site, thus avoiding transmission losses and providing insurance against power outages, but it isn't available at night or when skies are heavily overcast. Progress is being made in developing improved technologies for energy storage (particularly batteries), which may help compensate for the loss of solar input at night and for the intermittency of wind power.

As is typical of a new technology, the costs of solar photovoltaics (PV) have been a barrier to wide adoption, but rapid technological development is now bringing costs closer to levels competitive with fossil fuels, a trend that may be hastened by the rising prices of oil and gas in the United States.[58] In industrialized countries, PV cells are being installed on roofs of urban houses and commercial buildings to supplement the power grid at times of high power demand for air-conditioning. State and city initiatives in the United States (especially California, in the wake of the power shortages caused by the energy industry in 2001)[59] have helped to spur development of the PV industry and to lower costs. Although in 2003 solar cells were still supplying less than 1 percent of the world's electricity, capacity has been growing at more than 30 percent per year since 1997.[60]

In many developing regions where power grids do not exist, however, the costs of solar photovoltaics are already below what would be needed to supply power by conventional means, and much recent deployment of PV cells has been in such places. It is likely that the joint implementation provisions of the Kyoto Protocol will encourage more such installations in developing countries, especially in rural areas.

Indeed, a huge challenge for development policy is to find ways of providing modern energy services for the billions in poor societies who need them, without, as one colleague puts it,[61] repeating the Victorian age of grossly polluting, highly inefficient technologies. Ideally, new energy systems in developing regions should begin with modern renewables—primarily wind and solar—and bypass the need for fossil-fuel-generated electricity, with its cumbersome power grids, pollution, and contributions to climate disruption. Solar power may prove to be one of the greatest potential substitutes for the burning of fossil fuels, either as electricity generated directly by PV cells or in use of the sun's energy to heat a fluid and drive turbines to generate electricity. If 1 percent of Earth's land area could be covered with solar collectors, and solar energy could be converted to electricity with 20 percent efficiency, for example, more than enough electricity could be produced to power a larger and much more equitable human enterprise a century from now.[62]

## Transportation

In considering energy uses that could be made more efficient, perhaps we should start with one of the most widely consumed services—transportation. About 32 percent of energy use in the United States goes into ground transportation,[63] and about half of that for travel in automobiles. How much environmental degradation might we avoid by using more fuel-efficient automotive technology? Since the amounts of air pollutants and $CO_2$ emitted by vehicles are roughly proportional to the amount of fuel consumed, significant reductions in fuel consumption per mile driven by the nation's 210 million cars, trucks, and buses[64] would be of considerable benefit both to public health and, over time, in retarding climate change.

The sad fact is that the technology is available, but, with no incentive to minimize fuel use while gasoline prices in the United States remained low, and with no new regulatory enforcement in place since the mid-1980s, average fuel efficiency in the automobile fleet has stagnated. In the 1990s, American car buyers flocked to heavily promoted, overpowered, and fuel-inefficient sport utility vehicles—SUVs—in the mistaken belief that they were safer than sedans and station wagons. But SUVs and other light trucks (vans, minivans, and pickups) have been required to meet substantially lower fuel efficiency standards (about 25 percent lower) than cars. Improved technology has been applied instead to increasing horsepower and producing luxury gadgets for suburban drivers. So the average fuel consumption per mile of American vehicles steadily rose as SUVs replaced cars on streets and roads. By 2002, more than half of the passenger cars sold in the United States were light trucks and SUVS, causing the average fuel efficiency of new vehicles to sink to its lowest level since 1980.[65]

Meanwhile, Congress and the Bush administration refused to tighten the corporate average fuel economy (CAFE) standards by more than 1.5 miles per gallon (mpg)—far less than is technologically feasible. Indeed, it would be possible to increase mileage for new cars from the present 27.5 mpg to 40 mpg or more within a few years using existing technology, and the mileage of SUVs could be improved by a similar proportion.[66] The appearance of new hybrid electric cars (combining gasoline with electric power), which get 45 mpg or more, on the U.S. market in 2001 proves its feasibility.[67] The first hybrids were Japanese made; American carmakers expect to market diesel-fueled hybrid SUVs by 2005.

As important to total fuel consumption as the number of vehicles is the number of miles each car is driven each year. In the United States, although the number of registered automobiles changed little during the 1990s, miles driven and the amount of fuel used per vehicle per year have continued to rise. Both clearly reflect the growing popularity of inefficient SUVs as well as increasing commute distances for workers. Of course, the number of automobiles and the miles driven do not account for all the climatic consequences of automobile transport; manufacture of the vehicles and production and distribution of their fuels account for about a third of their greenhouse gas emissions.[68] Substantial additional environmental impacts result from construction of highways, streets, garages, and parking areas to serve them, from the mining of materials for their construction, and from the transport and use of fuel for those operations.

The degree to which increasing numbers of private motor vehicles lead to the paving over of prime agricultural land or natural ecosystems, as well as their relationship to urban sprawl, varies considerably between nations and between areas within nations. Americans (still believing they have frontiers to settle) have been much more profligate than Europeans or Asians in allowing suburbs to spread and have been much more tolerant of long automobile commutes to workplaces. Political and economic factors govern much of the consumption that results from suburban sprawl and mass commuting by private car in the United States. Efforts to contain and reverse sprawl could help significantly to lower overall fuel consumption and pollution emissions with no change in automotive efficiency. Some attempts to do so have been made in a number of urban areas, but they usually are strongly opposed by powerful development interests.[69]

Practical as it might be to reduce the average fuel consumption of cars, will that solve the global problem? Let's consider what could happen in practice. Suppose both the average gasoline consumption of private vehicles and the amount of materials used in their construction were both miraculously reduced by half. If the number of private cars in China alone rose to the U.S. per capita level (about 0.47 car per person),[70] and automobile numbers did not increase anywhere else, the environmental gains from those halvings would be overwhelmed by a more than 150-fold increase in China, even if Chinese cars were just as fuel-efficient and sparing of materials.[71] Such an increase in the number of autos in China would more than double the car population of the entire world, which in 2002 was about 530 million.[72] Thus, while technology clearly can help mitigate environmental impacts, those benefits could easily be swamped by growth in either population or per capita consumption, or both.

Such a colossal leap in Chinese car numbers is not imminent—perhaps not likely even in the long term. But annual production of automobiles worldwide has nonetheless been rising rapidly, jumping from about 45 million motor vehicles produced in 1985 to nearly 60 million in 2000, of which about a fifth were produced in the United States and a quarter were sold there.[73] Interestingly, auto production in the United States has not increased very much since 1985, although imports have risen significantly. Most of the increase in vehicle numbers has been in other countries, especially in middle-income developing nations such as South Korea, Mexico, and Brazil.

Even so, the United States still has more cars than any other nation—about a quarter of those in the whole world. And American cars on average are considerably larger and less fuel-efficient than those sold elsewhere. This presents an opportunity for significant reductions in fossil fuel use that would benefit all of civilization, not just Americans: simply improving the fuel efficiency of American cars. Dan Neil, automobile critic for the *Los Angeles Times,* commented on this topic: "If you ever despair that the U.S. auto industry is whirling, slowly but with gathering momentum, down the tubes of history, the second-generation Toyota Prius will give you no comfort. This is a car Detroit assures us cannot be built. No way. No how. A spacious, safe and well-appointed mid-size four-door with practical performance while returning more than 60 miles per gallon? For $20,000? Are you, like, high?"[74]

Related to the American love affair with cars, and demonstrating the indirect environmental consequences of technological choices, is the consumption of land for living space and transportation. Suburbs have spread over much of the country, and associated commuter traffic has generated much of the air pollution and traffic jams that plague most U.S. cities. The choice of commuting primarily by automobile rather than by much more efficient and environmentally benign mass transportation systems, especially rail, is, of course, not entirely a matter of consumer preference. For example, decades ago in Los Angeles, the automobile, oil, and rubber companies collaborated in a deliberate and successful campaign to eliminate the inter-urban rail system.[75] Now, very belatedly (and expensively), the city is building a modest subway system to relieve at least some of the gridlock that plagues the downtown area.

Passenger rail service is by far the most energy-efficient form of public transport (with the possible exception of waterborne carriers). Yet rail has been seriously neglected in the United States since World War II; it receives almost no support from the government compared with the huge subsidies given to air transport and motor vehicles (by funding of highways and subsidizing trucking). The lack of support for rail shows in the dilapidated condition of much of the equipment and in poor service, both of which discourage its use by the public. But the thriving rail services in Europe and Japan suggest that an attractive, well-run passenger system could succeed in the United States too.

Even a modest expansion of public surface transportation systems nationwide would go a long way toward relieving traffic congestion, improving air quality, and substantially reducing American dependence on imported oil.[76] A long-term set of technological changes that would perhaps do more than anything to reduce the environmental impacts of United States residents would be the redesign of living and working spaces around people rather than automobiles, a concept we'll return to in chapter 7.

## Hydrogen: Panacea or Red Herring?

While hydropower, nuclear power, and geothermal, wind, and solar energy can supply electricity, they cannot directly replace portable fuels for transportation. One possibility is to use hydrogen as such a fuel,[77] since it is a potentially renewable source that can be obtained by splitting water molecules, using electricity from any source. The great advantage of hydrogen is that, when it is burned to power a vehicle, the only emission is water vapor. Hydrogen is already used in industrial applications in stationary sites, and for this purpose it is currently extracted from natural gas (which is basically hydrogen-rich methane). The latter source, of course, is obviously not renewable. But a solar-hydrogen system based on the splitting of water might well be a major part of an answer to the energy problem, *if* a series of environmental problems can be engineered around (we think they could be) and *if* the political and economic will could be found to develop and deploy the technology appropriately.[78]

President Bush has put forth a plan to develop fuel-cell-powered automobiles, using hydrogen as fuel, to be available for sale by 2020. What the public hasn't been told is that the plan is based on hydrogen production by using nuclear plants to generate the electric power required for that production, and it seems to be a stalking horse for increasing the "need" for dozens of new nuclear plants. Hydrogen, however, can be produced from water using any energy source, whether solar, coal, or nuclear. And natural gas (rather than water) has been promoted as the feedstock for hydrogen production, which would result in $CO_2$ emissions.

Hydrogen does offer promise as a useful, emission-free energy source with no greenhouse gas liabilities, but a number of serious problems must first be overcome. For instance, a recent report indicated that hydrogen leakage from fuel cells might contribute to further depletion of the stratospheric ozone layer as well as possibly causing other disruptions of atmospheric interactions with the biosphere.[79] Additional impediments to developing this technology include high initial costs for fuel cell engines until economies of scale can be achieved by mass production. The Bush administration seems more interested in promoting nuclear power and natural gas than a solar- and water-based technology. Moreover, given the huge investments automobile and oil companies have sunk into service stations, refineries, and plants for manufacturing conventional gasoline- and diesel-powered engines, they are not likely to be enthusiastic boosters of this technology.

If these pitfalls can be avoided, and especially if it is produced from water using solar power, hydrogen might eventually serve as an abundant portable fuel, filling a need that renewable energy sources for electricity cannot.[80] This is one of many areas in which government subsidies could be environmentally helpful—in this case, funding research and development of technologies that might, if initial financial barriers to deployment can be overcome, significantly reduce social costs.

It is nearly impossible to overstate the importance of initiating a global transition to new systems for energy production and use. The prospect may be daunting, and many people's oxen might be gored in the process, but it also offers very exciting opportunities for inventing and developing new technologies, as well as new employment possibilities. The reward quite likely will be a chance to enhance the quality of life for most people on Earth.

Clearly, there are innumerable possibilities for reducing the human footprint on our beleaguered planet, although even the most benign collection of technologies can do no more than lighten our step. What happens in developing countries over the next few decades with respect to energy and power will be especially important. We hope that, as they establish new energy systems, developing nations will move immediately to the most efficient devices. The quicker and the more efficient, the better, for here again population growth and rising per capita consumption pose the danger of overwhelming the benefits of reduced environmental impacts resulting from deployment of the most benign energy technologies available.

## Food: Energy for Ourselves

People gain energy to run their bodies from consuming food; thus, agriculture is without doubt humanity's most important technology. If several groups of human beings hadn't invented it thousands of years ago,[81] you wouldn't be reading this book. Today we use energy, mostly from fossil fuels, to produce farm inputs, to drive farm equipment, and to transport, store, and process farm products. We've come a long way from the earliest stone-edged sickles, stone grain-grinding tools, and inadvertently selected strains of grass that made up the first agricultural technology. In recent decades, rapid advances, especially in genetics, have made it possible for an ever-growing population still to be fed—although in too many cases not very well. The most fundamental advances have been made in traditional plant genetics, the technology that was behind the green revolution.

Successful though the green revolution technology was in tripling food production in just a few decades, it also has created a wide range of problems, from pollution of water bodies by farm chemicals, accelerated land degradation, and increased pressures on water supplies to a loss of genetic variability in crops and enhanced vulnerability to pests and crop diseases.[82] It also has brought a series of social and cultural problems, including a widening of the economic gap between affluent and poor farmers. The latter commonly have difficulty paying for the seeds, fertilizers, and pesticides, and sometimes irrigation apparatus, generally required by the technology. Without the ability to maintain their land's fertility with manufactured fertilizers or to take advantage of the high-yield seeds, poor farmers usually become more impoverished.

The bottom line is that, as in the case of CFCs, even the most successful technologies can create complex, often unanticipated problems. The human predicament is not susceptible to solution simply by finding technological panaceas.[83] So we can expect that further problems will arise with many of the technical solutions that could help keep agricultural production increasing, such as drip irrigation for more efficient water use in the growing number of water-short regions. Drip irrigation systems can be expensive and difficult to maintain, and they are sometimes susceptible to blockage from chemical precipitates, organic matter, and roots.[84] Yet we have little choice but to try such solutions.[85]

The current hot issue in agricultural technology, the pros and cons of the use of genetically modified organisms (GMOs), illustrates this quite well. A mix of questions regarding costs and benefits and social and political issues is being raised by the deployment of genetic engineering technology. Caution is clearly called for, but upward of 6 billion people cannot be long sustained on Earth without technological crutches. This technology is being deployed and no doubt will continue to be. Nevertheless, it is important to make sure that the benefits get to the poor as well as the rich, which is not the trend today, and to guard against any nasty droppings that this technological rabbit may produce as we pull it out of the hat.

One rather simple measure that could substantially increase available food supplies, especially in developing countries, is to improve food storage facilities. A large portion—estimates range as high as 40 percent in some areas—of food is lost after harvest because inadequate storage places fail to keep out rodents and insects or prevent spoilage. Simply saving much of what is routinely lost today could help relieve hunger problems in many regions—especially since the greatest losses usually occur where some of the hungriest people live.

A different sort of agricultural technology that needs to be provided to farmers is one that is ecologically based. Some experimentation is proceeding along these lines, but agricultural establishments allied to agribusinesses are not especially receptive to it. American farm legislation since the mid-1980s, however, has included incentives for farmers to establish "conservation set-asides," which have helped to reduce soil erosion and provide small refuges for other organisms, such as pollinating bees and predators of crop pests (assuming the predators aren't killed by the use of pesticides). When small patches and borders of crop fields on American farms have been allowed to "go native" and have been planted with trees and shrubs, for example, they have enhanced yields and reduced the need for chemical inputs while help-

ing to preserve biodiversity.[86] A related promising advance that can
help make food production sustainable is the flowering of countryside
biogeography, the new science of maintaining biodiversity and the
ecosystem services it provides in human-disturbed landscapes.[87] Many
species are dependent on relatively pristine habitats for their survival,
but many others can persist in quite highly modified areas and maintain important ecosystem services.

The adoption of no-till cultivation, which substantially reduces soil
erosion, is another step that has found success in the United States and
some other developed countries. Some version of it could be very
helpful in some tropical areas, where soils often are thin and susceptible to erosion. Unfortunately, the main drawback to no-till cultivation is that it can enhance problems of pests and crop disease.

Another encouraging trend has been the gradual spread of integrated pest management (IPM). IPM involves a mix of pest control
strategies and requires more care and education than the simple
broadcast spraying of pesticides. But it is environmentally much safer
and economically superior in the long run.[88] It also fits into traditional
cultivation practices in many developing countries rather nicely by
focusing on use of natural fertilizers and pest control methods. Inter-
cropping and mixed crop planting are among strategies long employed
in traditional systems and now being experimented with by agricultural scientists.[89]

Finally, the growth of markets in many industrialized countries for
organically grown foods (raised without synthetic fertilizers or pesticides) may encourage a trend toward more environmentally sustainable farming practices. So far, though, organic products tend to be
somewhat more expensive than conventionally produced foods, partly
because the process is more labor-intensive and partly because of their
position as a "niche market," even though farmers reduce expenses by
forgoing commercial fertilizers and pesticides. Organic farming has
not been widely introduced in developing countries, although the
potential environmental benefits could be even greater there.

In the struggle to supply fish for the human diet, there is also one
promising recent development. That is the move to create marine

reserves (sometimes called "no-take zones") to maintain the productivity of fisheries.[90] It turns out that, if carefully chosen sections of the ocean are protected from exploitation, the fishes in them can reproduce enough to restock surrounding fished areas. Creating no-take reserves and pursuing countryside biogeographic preservation are just two of innumerable short-term steps that could help to preserve and protect at least some of the biodiversity so crucial to our food supply, even as the scale of the human enterprise continues to increase.[91]

In sum, many opportunities exist both to increase food production and to make the agricultural enterprise more sustainable through technological advances and applications of various kinds, although there are problems and pitfalls in some areas. But even more critical is the need to address the "softer" side of the technology factor—the social, economic, and political arrangements that so often get in the way of deploying truly helpful solutions. They often push us toward simple technological "fixes" that, on close examination, prove to be not so simple and sometimes not really fixes.

## Technofixes: Nuclear Power?

Some prospective technofixes for changing the ways that consumption is supported are mixed bags, to say the least. Some are even counterproductive if the goal is reduced pressure on resources and enhanced environmental security for the human population. A renewed campaign by the Bush administration, for instance, to increase the use of nuclear power correctly notes that nuclear power plants don't emit greenhouse gases and therefore would not contribute to global warming.[92] But there are several major difficulties with the nuclear approach. One is that virtually all use of energy, regardless of source, creates environmental problems, and nuclear power brings its own array of hazards.[93] Another is that the construction of nuclear power plants, using massive amounts of concrete, *does* cause significant greenhouse gas emissions. Nuclear power is not economically competitive if adequate safety standards are met; if it were, venture capitalists would be bidding for the privilege of financing dozens of new plants. Finally, expanding energy use in the United States is both unnecessary and undesirable, for reasons described throughout this book. It is thus not at all clear that it would be wise to expand nuclear power generation even if it were the safest power source.

As physicist John Holdren frequently points out,[94] a number of standards must be met before it would be reasonable to expand the contribution of nuclear energy in the United States (or world) power mix.[95] First, the costs must become competitive, which they are not in areas where fossil fuels, hydropower, or renewable energy sources are cheap. That may well change, though, as the social costs (such as deleterious climate changes and involvement in resource wars) of using fossil fuels rise and as the most favorable sites for renewable sources are utilized. Second, reactor safety must be greatly improved. In the United States, many of the few hundred reactors are operating well past their original life expectancy, and dangerous cracks and leaks have been showing up in some reactor vessels.[96] Furthermore, nuclear power plants are alarmingly vulnerable to terrorist attack.[97] Third, nuclear power plants produce large amounts of highly radioactive wastes, which pose unique disposal risks because of the intensity and long life of the radioactivity. Simply finding a place for permanent storage away from human habitation has been a major challenge in the United States—a problem that would be enormously multiplied if large numbers of new nuclear plants were built and put into service.

A completely unexpected safety hazard of nuclear power plants suddenly appeared in France as a result of the drought and heat wave in the summer of 2003. About 75 percent of the electricity in France is generated in nuclear power plants, which depend on water cooling for safe operation. But the drought had sharply reduced the amount of water in the streams that supply water to nearly all the power plants, while the temperatures soaring over 100 degrees Fahrenheit had heated the river water to levels too high for effective cooling. As a result, France's power delivery was intermittently disrupted and brought very close to a major failure before the weather changed and brought cooler temperatures. A full-scale failure would have threatened the lives of tens of thousands of elderly French people already in hospitals because of the heat wave; as it was, more than 15,000 people perished.[98] The obvious implication of this event is an unanticipated vulnerability of nuclear power plants to rising temperatures, such as are projected to be a consequence of global warming. It also is a lesson about risking overdependence on a single technology to supply so essential a service as electricity.

Holdren estimates that, if a few thousand new nuclear reactors were to be built now, safety standards would need to be increased about ten-fold to produce an acceptable level of risk (risk is defined as the product of the probability of an undesirable occurrence times a measure of how severe the consequences will be). With today's designs, nuclear reactor accidents present a version of the "zero-infinity" problem. That problem is how society should deal with the risk of events whose chance of occurring is near zero (e.g., Earth being hit by a large asteroid in the next decade) but whose consequences would be nearly infinitely bad (the end of civilization). In the case of a reactor melting down as the result of an accident or terrorist attack, the chances per reactor per year are very small, but nowhere near zero. The more reactors there are, the greater are the odds of an accident occurring. The consequences could be thousands of "prompt" deaths (those occurring immediately or without appreciable delay), hundreds of thousands of induced cancers, and an area the size of Pennsylvania made permanently uninhabitable.

The problems of achieving a level of safety ten times better than that practiced today are considerable. Doing so would probably require designs that rely more heavily on passive safety systems (ones designed with a fuel configuration that cools by natural circulation and thermal radiation and with other construction features that make meltdowns highly unlikely),[99] as opposed to the present "active" systems (e.g., with high-powered pumps, pipes, and valves, all designed to pour cool water onto fuel rods as they start to melt, and often requiring correct and timely intervention by human operators).[100]

Fourth, it must be demonstrated that radioactive wastes can be satisfactorily managed in both the short and the long term—that is, for as long as 500,000 years. Plutonium, a major component of spent fuel rods, has a half-life of more than 24,000 years, meaning that it requires about half a million years for the radioactivity to decay to more or less safe levels.

Related to that concern is a need to restore public confidence in the technology, which suffered greatly from unjustifiable optimism about safety issues originally promulgated by the industry and government agencies, followed by the industry's public relations extravaganzas at Three Mile Island and Chernobyl. People are nervous, and rightly so, about living in close proximity to either nuclear reactors or nuclear waste disposal sites. In democracies, the NIMBY (not in my back yard) phenomenon is likely to persist and make siting of nuclear facilities and transport of highly radioactive wastes problematic even beyond the point at which the technologies might be considered acceptably safe by skeptics in the knowledgeable scientific community. Persistent lying by agency personnel, as was habitual at the now-defunct Atomic Energy Commission when it had no serious congressional oversight[101] and between 1973 and 1975, when it was run by the famous anti-environmentalist Dixy Lee Ray,[102] has produced an unhappily long legacy.

Fifth, the problem of proliferation—the spread of nuclear weapons to nations not previously nuclear armed and to subnational groups—is especially difficult to evaluate. The highly radioactive wastes produced in nuclear power plants are also potential sources of nuclear weapons, as the scientific community has been warning, more or less fruitlessly, for decades.[103] The risk today is, if anything, greater than it was at the height of the cold war.[104] Suffice it to say, the marginal state of security of warheads and stocks of highly enriched uranium and plutonium in the former Soviet Union is not encouraging. Stolen or homemade warheads could soon be in the hands of terrorist groups—the problems of fabricating and arming them are not trivial, but they are far from insurmountable.[105]

We might note here that, while the risks from proliferation are daunting enough, possibly the most awesome technological threat to humanity and the environment, that of large-scale nuclear war,[106] has not been eliminated. While the West and the Soviet Union are no longer enemies, the chance of a war occurring by accident cannot be ruled out. In fact, in 1995 Russia's shaky nuclear command-and-control system mistook the launch of a Norwegian sounding rocket (designed to collect data from different levels in the atmosphere) for an attack by the United States. They got some eight minutes into a perhaps ten- to fifteen-minute countdown to a retaliatory strike before the mistake was discovered and civilization was saved.[107] This nightmarish situation has not improved. In October 2000, the Federation of American Scientists reported: "In January 1997 Defense Minister Igor Rodionov wrote an alarming letter to Yeltsin. He said the command-and-control systems for Russia's nuclear forces—including the deep underground bunkers and the early-warning system—were falling apart. 'No one today can guarantee the reliability of our control systems,' Rodionov said. 'Russia might soon reach the threshold beyond which its rockets and nuclear systems cannot be controlled.'"[108]

In the context of that near disaster and a deteriorating weapons management system, progress toward prevention of a nuclear catastrophe has hardly been satisfactory.[109] It would be an excellent expenditure of U.S. tax funds to pay the nearly bankrupt Russians enough to allow them to keep part of their nuclear submarine force and its ballistic missiles at sea. Their subs are now mostly tied up at their docks, where they are far more vulnerable to preemptive attack, and therefore are kept on a supremely dangerous hair-trigger alert.

## The Risks of Technological Complexity

In January 2000, Alaska Airlines' Flight 261 dove uncontrollably into the Pacific Ocean, killing eighty-eight people. The cause of this tragedy was the failure due to lack of lubrication of a critical part that allowed pitch control (important in making the airplane either climb or descend). The faulty maintenance was caused partly by cost-saving steps agreed to by the Federal Aviation Administration and partly by difficulties in Alaska Airlines' maintenance system.[110] The accident could have been prevented despite the human mistakes if the structure had been given a fail-safe design, but that became clear only in retrospect. Perhaps most disturbing is that, after problems appeared, requests for help from the crew on the doomed jet to airline personnel on the ground were ignored, apparently on the assumption that the problem wasn't serious.[111]

One important aspect of the human predicament that is too rarely discussed is the growing complexity (and thus vulnerability) of human technological systems. With all highly complex, tightly coupled technologies, such as jet aircraft and nuclear power plants, a major factor in accidents is operator failure. (Tightly coupled systems are ones in which processes are fast, stopping them takes time, failure in one subsystem is difficult or impossible to isolate and can propagate to other systems, and diagnosis of the problem by even alert and skilled operators may be difficult or impossible in the time available. "Tight coupling" implies, among other things, that a change in one part inevitably leads to a change in another.)[112] It's something to think about when seeking technological fixes for environmental problems, including those that might be created by acts of terrorism.

Dependence on complex systems and the risks they carry is not an issue connected only to terrorism; perhaps equally threatening are "normal accidents" such as the crash of Flight 261. As sociologist Charles Perrow points out in his classic book of that title, many modern technological systems are intrinsically high risk.[113] The best we can hope to do with them is try to lower the frequency of accidents and limit the damage done when accidents do occur. That's just another way of saying we should reduce the risk.

We have designed our enormous and multifaceted society so that it relies on the use of a great many complex, tightly coupled industrial systems. A great example of a breakdown due to these factors of complexity and tight coupling was the blackout over the northeastern United States and adjacent parts of Canada, lasting two to three days, in August 2003. The failure involved interconnected electric grids belonging to several power companies in more than a half-dozen states and much of eastern Canada. The system's vulnerability to breakdown had been compounded by recent changes in regulatory oversight and failure to upgrade obsolescent equipment. Such neglect

and penny-pinching tactics can result in disasters and substantial economic losses—and they did in this case.[114]

Society's heavy reliance on airlines provides the potential for an
even greater disaster. Imagine the effect on the American and world
economies if several large commercial jets were simultaneously shot
down by terrorists armed with shoulder-fired anti-aircraft missiles![115]
Hundreds of thousands of those are available worldwide. A few billion
dollars spent on countermeasures could reduce the chances of such a
disaster—money that would do infinitely more for our security than
the hundreds of billions being wasted trying to extend the American
empire into central Asia.

Disasters also can result when advanced technologies are inappro-
priately or inadequately transferred to less technically advanced societies. In December 1984, at Union Carbide's facility at Bhopal, India,
a combination of understaffing, poor maintenance, poor training,
inaccurate instrumentation, inadequate safety devices, general incompetence, and bad luck led to a release of extremely poisonous methyl
isocyanate (MIC) gas. A cloud of MIC gas spread over the shantytown adjacent to the plant, where workers and their families lived.
There were no alarms, authorities were not notified, and the medical
officer of the plant told police (after people had begun collapsing) that
the gas was harmless. That accident caused more than 4,000 prompt
deaths and more than 200,000 injuries.[116] That number of casualties
would not have resulted if the workers hadn't settled next to the plant
or if adequate safety precautions had been taken. Of course, the siting
of hazardous facilities away from vulnerable population centers and
installation of alarms and safety equipment often drive costs up. That
means corporate bean counters ordinarily will argue against taking
those precautions, as sometimes will poor people who would rather
have jobs and take their chances. In the end, the settlement funds
Union Carbide had to shell out to compensate the families of dead and
injured workers far outweighed what an investment in precautions
would have been.

One important but usually overlooked impediment to improving
technological systems is the attitudes of technologists themselves. In

the 1970s, we were in a conference in England with some scientists interested in developing fusion power. Paul was pressing for more use of solar energy. It slowly dawned on us why our colleagues were so besotted with fusion. It presented an enormous technological challenge, one not satisfactorily met to this day. The fusion problem involved having magnets cooled to near absolute zero close to a plasma (gas so hot the electrons are stripped from its atoms) heated to the temperature of the surface of the sun: a fascinating scientific problem. Paul's suggestion, piping water through black-painted fifty-gallon drums on roofs to provide hot water, was nowhere near as sexy. When he said this to the others, they readily admitted he was right.

Despite the appeal of dazzlingly complex technologies, if we wish to design a safer, more sustainable world, the most sensible approach is to emphasize less centralized and more loosely coupled systems, which have the advantage (especially in this age of terrorism) of being less disruptable. This is a particularly sensible approach for power systems, as the 2003 blackout so dramatically demonstrated. Both wind and solar photovoltaics, for instance, offer multiple widely dispersed small energy sources. They are not fail-safe, but a breakdown is not very dangerous and would inconvenience only a few people for a short time. The contrast with nuclear power plants could hardly be more stark.

## Judging Technologies

How should we decide, in any situation, which technologies are the best to employ? This is not a trivial question. No technology is absolutely safe—after all, even a chimp can break her toe by dropping her favorite rock on it. And few technologies are totally malign; they wouldn't be used if they were. The only exceptions that come to mind are those famous weapons of mass destruction—nuclear, chemical, and biological—though someone somewhere obviously once thought they would be needed.

Among the more beneficial options, modern society has produced a dazzling array of actual and potential technologies; the trick is to choose the best ones for any given situation, in terms of both solving a particular problem and avoiding the creation of a whole new set of problems. What should govern our choices? Economists tend to answer, "Just get the prices right and the market will solve the problem." There is truth in that argument. If all externalities were internalized, all perverse subsidies were abandoned,[117] and everyone had perfect information and behaved rationally, the entire human predicament conceivably might be solved by the market. If overpopulation threatened our civilization, the costs of having children would rise until the average family size dropped to the appropriate level. If overconsumption began to use up resources needed to support our grandchildren, the prices of those resources would escalate.

Unhappily, though, it is obviously impossible to get the prices right—or even to come very close. What is the appropriate amount to add to the cost of gasoline-powered leaf-blowers to cover the negative externalities of the headache-causing racket and toxic fumes they produce? What increase in the tax on a Smith & Wesson "chief's special" pistol would allow society to compensate law enforcement agencies for the cost of larger police forces and compensate hospitals for maintaining emergency room facilities? How much should be added to the price of coal or gasoline to compensate a future generation for possible losses due to coastal flooding from global warming? How much should a Costa Rican farmer be paid for the positive externality of keeping a portion of his land in forest, rather than cutting and burning the trees to make room to grow beans and releasing the carbon the trees contain into the atmosphere? And how, in practice, could a massive system of taxes, along with research and development subsidies (and the bureaucrats to administer the system) be instituted to do the internalizing?

So it's not possible to get all the prices right when technologies are deployed, but we certainly could do much better than we do today. There are many ways besides imposing new taxes to make prices better reflect social costs, including mandating technological standards, trading emissions permits, and so on. But simply contemplating which taxes might have to be instituted to internalize costs not captured in prices makes instructive thought experiments. Just consider today's nuclear power. Imagine the taxes that might have to be added to the price of electricity generated by nuclear plants to cover the cost of compensating the people of Pennsylvania for the loss of their state if a meltdown occurred! How much more would need to be put aside in a fund for victims of nuclear bombs that resulted from proliferation facilitated by nuclear power plants? To get a clue, consider the tens of billions of dollars being paid by taxpayers now to clean up the huge, far-flung nuclear weapons–making complex, a mess accumulated over fifty years, even though the (incomplete) market costs of creating the weapons have already been paid.[118] Or think about the prospective billions that will be needed to dispose of the wastes produced over a half-century by civilian nuclear power plants—if a disposal site and safe methods are ever agreed upon.

Making such calculations honestly about any major technological system would be difficult and controversial. If presented clearly to the public, however, they would help society decide on when, where, whether, and how to invest in nuclear power as opposed to other alternatives. A starting point in that exercise might be to make the public more aware that the nuclear industry has always refused to operate unless it was given a huge subsidy—catastrophic accident insurance underwritten by taxpayers through the Price-Anderson Act.[119] The insurance industry considers the risks generated by the nuclear industry too great to merit affordable insurance! Nonetheless, at this writing, Congress is poised to provide huge subsidies, including reauthorization of the Price-Anderson Act, all to support the Bush administration's drive to promote nuclear power.[120]

We think that nuclear power plants *could* be designed and operated with adequate safety, nuclear wastes *could* be disposed of with adequate safety, and the proliferation problems they now present *could* be solved. Unhappily, we have severe doubts that all these hurdles *will* be surmounted because factors other than technology are involved, including economics, politics, and social perceptions. But this is an issue on which honest scientists can differ. For a relatively sanguine view, and a wonderful treatment of the technical issues for the layperson, we recommend the book *Megawatts + Megatons* by Richard Garwin and Georges Charpak.[121]

## What to Do?

How can industrial societies keep important benefits while reducing crucial risks from the technological creations designed to service their consumption? First, numerous measures could be taken to address safety problems connected with complex technologies. In many situations, for instance, distance or decentralization of potentially hazardous facilities can serve to make the world more secure from calamitous accidents.[122] Charles Perrow sums up the problems of complicated and vulnerable technologies very nicely: "These systems are currently too complex and tightly coupled to prevent accidents that have catastrophic potentials. We must live and die with their risks, shut them down or radically redesign them. I include in this list nuclear power, chemical plants, genetic engineering, air transport, and space programs that carry radioactive substances aloft."[123]

Radical redesign presents society with another dilemma. Although the cost of redesigning to minimize any one of these hazards might not be too big a burden, doing them all might be financially (or at least politically) impossible. Often, people like us come up with answers like "For the cost of one aircraft carrier, we could double the salaries of every high-school math teacher. . . . " The trouble is that there are only a few aircraft carriers, but there are huge numbers of underpaid and overworked teachers, and a long list of other expensive problems that require attention. Society can't keep using the same resource to solve all its problems.[124] And prioritizing the problems requires some very difficult decisions.

## Ending Perverse Subsidies

In terms of decision making about consumption patterns and the technologies employed to service them, one of the very first things required would be a careful re-examination of systems of subsidies for various activities. Many subsidies, in the terms of Norman Myers and Jennifer Kent's fine book, are "perverse."[125] Myers and Kent point out in *Perverse Subsidies* that some subsidies may cause environmental harm but meet economic needs, such as providing electricity to low-income elderly people at less than cost. Others may do economic harm but environmental good, such as using relatively scarce capital to pay to clean up toxic waste dumps or to protect endangered species that are viewed as having no economic value. Myers and Kent define "perverse subsidies" as those that do harm in both regards.[126]

Remember that the $T$ (technology) factor in the $I = PAT$ equation includes the social, economic, and political arrangements connected with the technologies that are used to supply what is consumed. A classic example of those arrangements is the subsidizing of modern ocean-vacuuming fishing fleets to service the consumption of fish, mostly by the rich. Those subsidies allow fishers to pay for the technology that allows overfishing, the destruction of ocean ecosystems, and the collapse of one fish stock after another to economic extinction (the point at which, even with subsidies, fishing is no longer profitable). Subsidizing high-tech exploration and production of oil and other fossil fuels is another perverse example. The subsidies underwrite and encourage more use of fossil fuels, which are deeply damaging to the environment. They also impede the development of more benign and efficient energy technologies (which themselves are subsidized, but inadequately). The result is to keep fossil fuels cheap and available and the newer technologies more expensive. Other examples include the implicit subsidies given to timber companies to log, and to ranchers to graze livestock, on public lands, since taxpayers foot much of the cost and the environment suffers.

Some subsidies are simply unbalanced: corporate lobbyists and the American love of automobiles mean that highways are built and maintained by taxpayers, to the tune of roughly $20 billion annually through the federal Highway Trust Fund. This subsidy, additional hefty subsidies to the trucking industry and carmakers, plus road building and maintenance funded by state and local agencies all underwrite motor vehicle transport. Similarly, the elaborate air traffic control system and airport construction and operating costs are subsidies to the air transport system for which taxpayers shelled out another $10 billion per year in the late 1990s. Then the 9/11 disaster led to the government takeover of financial responsibility for upgraded security measures, raising costs further. Meanwhile, railroads have fallen into disarray and disrepair in the United States, in large part because of a lack of adequate subsidies; in the late 1990s they received barely $1 billion per year.[127] Yet railroads can offer safe, rapid surface transport at a far smaller environmental cost per passenger-mile than cars, buses, trucks, or airplanes.

Exposing subsidies to public scrutiny is difficult because the subject is often complex and arcane. For example, agricultural subsidies in the United States are such an insane maze that even agricultural economists are unable to explain them. That many are perverse is undoubted, as they often lead to the production of crops in utterly unsuitable areas, wasting resources and causing unnecessary environmental damage.[128] Not all agricultural subsidies are necessarily perverse, of course. Nonetheless, they provide superb examples of the barrier that subsidies can create to getting the prices right, and how political power—wielded largely in the form of money—can help keep such barriers in place. Much the same can be said of the massive subsidies to the fossil fuel, automobile, and nuclear power industries. As we pointed out earlier, the costs of maintaining a military force strong enough to enable the United States to exert control over the oil spigots are not captured in the price of gasoline. Nor are the costs of building and maintaining streets and highways, or the costs of medical care for those injured by auto-generated smog or in automobile accidents, or the social costs of the loss of biological capital to paving and poisoning. Still less included are the costs that future generations are likely to incur in trying to cope with the consequences of global warming.

It is instructive that a careful conventional analysis of the social costs of gasoline (including such items as traffic congestion and global warming externalities, but not the military one) concluded that a proper gas tax in the United States would be about a dollar a gallon. By "proper," we mean a tax that would cover most of the social costs and help reduce gas consumption, especially if combined with other devices such as regulations mandating the minimum fuel efficiency of vehicles. Taxes, however, hardly seem the ideal way to take care of the military externality—creating and maintaining armed forces to ensure petroleum supplies. Subsidizing alternatives to automotive transport could be a superior alternative.[129]

Both population and consumption are still expanding while the financial resources that could be mobilized to ameliorate their environmental impacts are limited and too often diverted into the pockets of the wealthy. That's why the insights of economists, who are specialists in thinking about allocating scarce goods and resources, will be essential to helping solve these dilemmas. There also are limits to what society can accomplish in the way of that other economic specialty— getting the prices closer to right. At present, in major economic sectors, the ability of the powerful to be certain we get those prices very wrong seems unlimited. As long as environmentally damaging technologies are priced far below their social costs, there will be inadequate incentives to develop more environmentally benign technologies.

In some respects, it is almost as if society had a death wish, because in the end even the well-buffered rich will pay a huge cost for the environmental consequences of the inefficient—and inequitable— economic behaviors that even a cursory examination of technological choices reveals. A culture dominated by short-term greed is preventing us from even starting on the task of steering away from the collision course with nature the world scientists warned us about. And until both the promises and the limits of what can be accomplished through technological solutions are recognized, and serious efforts are made to provide better technological choices, the job may never really get under way.

# Chapter 6

## BILLIONS, BIRTHRATES, AND POLICIES

"Unlike plagues of the dark ages or contemporary
diseases we do not yet understand, the modern plague
of overpopulation is soluble by means we have discovered
and with resources we possess. What is lacking is not
sufficient knowledge of the solution but universal
consciousness of the gravity of the problem and
education of the billions who are its victims."
MARTIN LUTHER KING JR., 1966[1]

OVERPOPULATION, according to an Australian politician,
is a primitive notion. Immigration minister Philip Ruddock went on to say in 2002 that he "rejected absolutely
the notion of a population carrying capacity for Australia."[2] If we can
judge by such pronouncements, he was surely an expert on primitive
notions. He actually was attacking a key element of the biological definition of overpopulation.

Carrying capacity can be defined simply as the number of individuals that can be maintained without degrading the future life-support
capability of the habitat. When the number of individuals in a population exceeds the carrying capacity of its habitat, that's overpopulation.
Mr. Ruddock's confusion seems to trace from an idea that carrying
capacity is a fixed number, but for any animal it actually varies with the
quality of the habitat and the behavior of the animal. The carrying

capacity of an area in the Sierra Nevada of California for a population of Edith's checkerspot butterfly that feeds on a plant of the genus *Collinsia* may be quite limited if that plant is scarce. If the butterflies were to evolve the capacity to feed on a common weed of the genus *Plantago*, the carrying capacity for the checkerspots would be greatly increased.

So it is for people. Earth can support a much smaller number of human beings who obtain their food by hunting and gathering than of people who live in primarily agricultural societies. In turn, Earth's carrying capacity for simple agrarian societies is smaller than for industrial societies. Carrying capacities are difficult to calculate for any organism, but, contrary to Mr. Ruddock's belief, it is often quite easy to tell when a carrying capacity has been exceeded—that is, when support of a population is degrading the capacity of the environment to support future generations. Anjouan's situation, described in chapter 3, illustrates the point very well as that island's soil, forests, and rivers disappear. Changes in habitat quality or human behavior at any time might increase or reduce carrying capacity, so it is often a useful exercise to estimate where one is at present compared with future carrying capacity.[3]

There is no question that, for Earth as a whole (including those parts of it we call Australia and the United States), human beings are far above carrying capacity today. Humanity in the early twenty-first century, as we have seen, is living not on the interest from its natural capital but on the capital itself. Earth's deep, rich agricultural soils are being eroded away in many areas much faster than they can be regenerated, fossil groundwater is being depleted, and biodiversity is being exterminated at a rate unmatched in the past 65 million years. Every year, politicians pride themselves on writing a bigger check against their nation's natural bank accounts—their repositories of natural capital ("the economy under my stewardship grew 2.3 percent")—but they never check the balance in the account, which might be declining precipitously.

The depreciation of natural capital is one fundamental reason why the view of some economists a generation ago that population growth could continue without limit is wrong. On the contrary, economic analysis shows that standards of living can be maintained *only* if the population stops growing.[4] Indeed, ordinary common sense tells us that infinite growth on a finite planet (or in a finite universe) is impossible.

Clearly, then, civilization must come to grips with the two principal drivers of the ever-expanding scale of the human enterprise: growth in population and growth in consumption. We can set aside reserves for biodiversity until we're blue in the face, burn fossil fuels ever more efficiently, and recycle assiduously, and civilization will still go down the environmental drain unless population and consumption are addressed. Even though improved technologies can help, they can't help enough by themselves. As populations burgeon, desperate people will, as they already do in many areas, invade nature reserves to kill what's edible, harvest what's marketable, and settle on any land that's farmable. As more and more people place pressure on the land, changes to preserve natural capital will be increasingly difficult to institute or maintain.[5] As ecologist Peter Vitousek and his colleagues wrote, "we live on a human-dominated planet—and the momentum of human population growth, together with the imperative for further economic development in most of the world, ensures that our dominance will increase."[6]

## Optimal Population Size

Fortunately, it appears that the end of the human population outbreak is now in sight, although growth is still far from over. Yet consumption is still escalating as people in wealthy countries find themselves "needing" more and more goods and services relentlessly promoted by increasingly competitive companies. Meanwhile, more and more people in developing regions are adopting the overconsuming habits of those in affluent societies. It is still an open question whether it will be possible to avoid a population crash (a dramatic reduction in population size due to a greatly increased death rate) caused by a gross overshoot of carrying capacity as both numbers of people and per capita consumption expand. Obviously, addressing the population factor must be a crucial part of any successful global strategy for achieving a sustainable civilization.

How many people should we aim for to achieve a sustainable civilization for the long term? What would be an "optimal" population for Earth? It should be apparent that there is no simple or scientific answer to that question. Any answer will depend upon assumptions made about future technological capabilities as well as about people's desires and aspirations in the future. Will they be content to live like factory ("battery") chickens,[7] with a maximum number of individuals crammed into a minimum space along with enough food to keep them alive and reproducing, and with minimal lifestyle choices? Or will they prefer to emulate wild eagles, constrained somewhat by their environments but able to soar high with a wealth of choices about where to go and what to do? In other words, will people accept a society that maximizes the numbers and densities of human beings in a world where resources are stretched thin, or should we work now to create and maintain a society in which individual freedom and access to the natural world are maximized and resources are abundant in relation to the numbers of people?

With our colleague Gretchen Daily, we took a first cut at this question a decade ago.[8] We assumed that an optimal population size would be one for which the minimum physical necessities of a decent life could be guaranteed for everyone. We also assumed that the optimum had to be few enough people that basic human social and political rights could be ensured for all. We thought the population should be large and dispersed enough to encourage maintenance and development of humanity's cultural diversity and to provide a critical mass in numerous areas of high density so that intellectual, artistic, and technological creativity would be stimulated. But the population should be small enough to permit the preservation of natural ecosystems and biodiversity at a level that could sustain natural services. Hermits and outdoor enthusiasts could find plenty of wilderness to hide in or enjoy; lovers of opera, theater, and fine food could have large, vibrant cities.

We tried to find a population size that would maximize options overall and hedge against disasters. On the basis of energy statistics and assuming more or less contemporary (largely Western-style) aspirations and technological capabilities, highly efficient energy systems and resource use, and a closing of the rich-poor gap, we came up with an optimal population of around 2 billion people—less than a third of today's.[9] This is hardly an outlandish or insane number—it's the number of people who were around in 1930, a time when both extensive wilderness areas and large cities existed. Utopian? Maybe. Maybe technological advances and changes in cultural attitudes about such things as freedom and wilderness will make it look just plain silly in a few decades. But for the moment it seems to us an excellent—and achievable—target to aim for over the next century.

How can we go about approaching that target? The obvious and humane way is by limiting births (as opposed to allowing death rates to rise).

## Family Planning

At the simplest level, there clearly is a need to extend birth control services in societies that still have rapid population growth. So one solution might seem to be simply ensuring that contraceptive materials and services are available to all sexually active human beings. That was how family planning assistance began back in the 1960s: with the establishment of programs to provide the information and means for birth control in developing nations. Before long, though, it became apparent that simply providing contraceptives did not always have much effect on high birthrates. Some societies quickly took advantage of the services; their birthrates dropped, and in most cases they experienced success in their economic development efforts. In some other societies, by contrast, family planning programs seemed to make little difference in birthrates, and progress in development was uneven at best.

Social scientists made great progress in the past thirty years in elucidating the factors that influence childbearing,[10] and eventually the mystery of different family planning outcomes was solved; it became clear that educating women and giving them job opportunities were associated with sharply declining birthrates. Female literacy in particular is negatively correlated with family size.[11] Women's education and smaller families are both connected with successful modernization and development. Indeed, it is difficult to think of any nation that has successfully developed without educating its women and providing them with some measure of independence.

Of course, the general importance of education for modernization has long been recognized, but it was widely assumed in many societies that educating girls was of secondary importance compared with educating boys. The difference is that, while men apply their educations to finding better jobs and earning more income, women apply their knowledge first to providing better health care and nutrition for their families. And women with schooling not only can contribute to enhancing family well-being and modernizing their societies; they also become receptive to the idea of family limitation.

The classic experience that indicated the importance of women's education was that of the state of Kerala in southern India, where for generations girls have been educated and women have enjoyed a relatively high degree of independence. Fertility fell rapidly during the 1960s and 1970s (well ahead of the slow national decline), dropping below replacement level before 1990.[12]

Other factors also are associated with declining total fertility rates (TFRs): improving basic health care and reducing infant and child mortalities seem to be essential prerequisites because, with improved assurance that their children will survive to adulthood, people feel less need to have many of them. A related factor is the role that offspring perform in providing old-age security for their parents in traditional societies. In order to be sure of having a surviving son to support them in old age, parents must have at least four children (daughters usually are responsible for their husbands' parents). Governments, by providing some form of old-age social security for their population, can thereby remove one important incentive for having a large family. Requiring education of all children is another factor; children who must go to school incur expenses (books, writing equipment, sometimes uniforms and tuition) rather than contributing to the family's income.

In the drive to improve the status of women, however, those involved in family planning programs have sometimes forgotten that "it takes two to tango." The attitudes of men cannot be neglected. For example, Costa Rica's family planning program had substantial success at first in lowering birthrates by providing information and services to women. Education of girls through grade school was required, and efforts were made to inform the public about family planning. But progress then slowed. A study of the Costa Rican fertility "plateau" by ecologist Karen Holl and her colleagues concluded, "There is some tendency to neglect the critical roles of men not only in familial reproductive decisions but also in creating the all-important social milieu in which both men and women make those decisions."[13]

A very successful family planning program in Tamil Nadu, another state in southern India, does not neglect men. Indeed, hairdressing salons (which are patronized by men, not women) have been turned into centers of contraceptive delivery.[14] Hairdressers are trained as family planning missionaries, and big jars of free condoms are placed at doors so that men can scoop up a handful on their way out. As a result of this simple measure, along with emphasis on educating children of both genders and giving them nutritious school lunches, and providing a comprehensive maternal and child health program, Tamil Nadu's TFR fell by roughly half from the 1950s to the 1990s, and it is now probably lower than that of the United States.[15]

Although laying the social groundwork is essential for creating receptivity to family limitation, the ability of couples to practice birth control also depends on the necessary knowledge and materials being available and convenient. Lack of success has sometimes resulted when family planning programs were poorly run; some have failed to provide follow-up care for clients, or facilities were available only in large cities and provided no outreach to rural families. Programs in some countries have offered only a very limited choice of contraceptive methods, and many women found those options unsuitable. There are advantages and disadvantages to various contraceptive methods; the best choices depend on each woman's age, lifestyle, physiology, and personal preference.[16] In many circumstances, condoms are a desirable method of birth control; besides greatly reducing the chances of conception, they can help retard the spread of AIDS and other sexually transmitted diseases. Exchanges of information about successes and failures, fostered by the United Nations Population Fund and the UN population conferences held every ten years, along with social science research that uncovered some of the failings, have helped to remedy many of these problems.[17]

In rural areas of many poor countries, especially the least developed countries, fertility rates have hardly budged and people have not been much touched by the modern world. They have little or no education and no access to modern fuels or electricity, sanitation, or clean water. In these situations, both children and women play important economic roles at a very basic level. In parts of sub-Saharan Africa and southern Asia, for instance, they often must spend many hours daily trekking to distant sources to gather fuelwood or to retrieve water for the household.[18] This sharply limits their ability to partake of other activities, such as schooling for children or other economic activities for the women. And it keeps the family highly dependent on the children's labor for survival.

In many African nations, women are often left to run the family farm while their husbands seek jobs in cities or even in other countries. Female farmers by tradition have no property rights, so they are given no support in the form of extension services, farm credit, or access to irrigation water. In this situation, they depend on their children to help with the farm work. Large families are therefore a short-term necessity, but later the children's inheritance (the farm) must be divided among several, resulting in farms being repeatedly subdivided until too little land is left to support a family. The lack of external support also is a recipe for gradual environmental impoverishment since, without services and credit, the female farmers usually lack the capacity to maintain the land's productivity.

Thus, more subtle yet important pathways to population limitation can be seen in seemingly unrelated strategies such as supplying cheap kerosene fuel and digging wells for poor villagers in the least developed countries. In addition, changing property rights (who can inherit what), opening up lines of communication and exchange through electronic media, building farm-to-market roads, providing schools and access to newspapers and magazines, and generally finding ways to increase the economic security of the poor are all measures that can help bring down fertility levels. Indeed, most of these measures, as well as maternal and child health services and education, usually need to be in place before people will have very much interest in family planning.[19]

## Abortion

Abortion is a particularly contentious matter in the United States, where religious conservatives have maintained strong opposition to the procedure ever since the movement to legalize it began in the 1960s.[20] The original reason for outlawing abortion in the United States in the late nineteenth century was that it was highly dangerous under the medical practice of the time. By the mid-twentieth century, safe procedures had been developed, but abortion, except to save the mother's life, remained illegal. In the 1960s, the invention in China of the vacuum device used everywhere today made abortion even easier and safer. That may have been a factor in the push to make it legal in the United States. Before the *Roe v. Wade* decision of the Supreme Court legalizing abortion in 1973, the number of clandestine abortions performed was very roughly estimated as about 700,000 per year.[21] After the decision, the number of the procedures was about 750,000, rising to 1.43 million in 1990 before falling again by 17 percent in the late 1990s to 1.19 million per year, when there was a considerably larger number of women of reproductive age in the population.[22]

By the mid-twentieth century, abortions were being performed legally in some other parts of the world. In the Soviet Union and eastern Europe, contraceptives were often unreliable and usually unavailable, so abortion was the primary means of birth control. It was also widely used in several northern European countries and in Japan, where it facilitated that country's rapid reduction in birthrate after World War II, when modern contraceptives were not yet available. Today abortion is still illegal in much of the world, including many developing nations. The result is a high rate of illegal abortion under abysmal conditions, with all the danger to women's health that entails. The World Health Organization has estimated that as many as 20 million unsafe (that is, illegal) abortions are performed each year and that 50,000 to 100,000 women die unnecessarily as a result.[23]

Abortion is a difficult issue for most people, and most people probably would prefer to see safe and effective contraception widely available to, and used by, all sexually active individuals. If this were to happen, the abortion controversy, perhaps *the* biggest source of ethical dispute in our society today, could go away. That is certainly our view. It was expressed once by Bill Clinton as "I want abortion to be safe, legal, and rare."

The issue of when human life starts is often considered important to the abortion debate, and here biologists' insights can contribute neutrally, regardless of one's ethical views. Human life started (depending on one's definition of *human*) sometime between a few hundred thousand and a few million years ago. Since then it has been continuous, from parents to child. Sperm and eggs are every bit as much human life as is Rush Limbaugh.[24] The time that society wishes to define as the start of personhood is an ethical and legal question, not a scientific one. A society must determine what rights it is appropriate to impute to fetuses at certain stages, as well as newborns, and that opinion may well evolve with time and technological advances. Legal decisions in recent decades have generally indicated that a fetus' rights increase relative to the mother's as the time of birth approaches. The law also discriminates before birth between a child who is wanted by the parents and one who is not.

One technological advance, the invention of ultrasound technology to monitor the progress of a pregnancy, has had some unexpected and significant consequences. A parent who has seen a three-month-old fetus on an ultrasound screen may bond to the fetus more closely than he or she would have before such visualization was possible and thus may decide against a contemplated abortion. Anti-abortion groups have made extensive use of photos of developing embryos and fetuses to convince people that abortion is "murder of an unborn child." Such emotional appeals are undeniably effective, but whether they lead to wise decisions is another question. On the other hand, in China, India, and some other developing countries where tradition puts a higher value on sons than on daughters, ultrasound examinations have been used to determine a fetus' sex so that females could be aborted. Even though this use of ultrasound is technically illegal in both countries, it is widely practiced.

The provision of safe and legal abortions would save many women's lives, but it might not do much to solve the problems of population growth, since where abortion is not legally available, quack abortion and infanticide (to an uncertain extent) are used as substitutes. Obviously, effective contraception is far preferable to abortion as a way to limit family size. But mistakes happen, and a backup method is sometimes necessary.

## Influencing Reproductive Decisions

The numbers of people in a society or inhabiting the entire globe are clearly a matter of social concern. Society therefore automatically has an interest in individual reproductive decisions, just as it has an interest in decisions about how fast people drive or whether they can smoke in hospitals. But in most societies, people do not want governments or experts to tell them how many children they should have. So policies to influence family limitation, if they are to play a positive role in dealing with the population driver of environmental problems, should lead people to *want* to take appropriate actions.

In many countries, it might be useful to employ market mechanisms, such as taxes and financial incentives, to influence people's reproductive decisions. Yet it is worth noting that policies intended to encourage larger families, such as family allowances, long a traditional measure in Canada and France, have been notoriously ineffective. Financial incentives for smaller families might work in some societies, but much would depend on the type of incentive and the level of development that has been achieved. Some policies that were tried in the past, such as payments for vasectomies, were abused and ultimately backfired. In most low-income countries, practically speaking, policies involving taxes would affect only the small wealthy elite groups (who usually do have small families). Most programs in developing nations try instead to get the desired results by persuasion and public promotion, as well as indirectly by provision of basic health care for families (which ideally has family planning as an integral part) and education and opportunities for women.

China has followed a different path. Faced with a population passing the 1 billion mark and a clearly deteriorating resource base in 1979, China tightened an already rather draconian "birth planning" policy, mandating a one-child family for much of its population.[25] The program had substantial success but caused significant suffering for some parents (or, in the language of economics, incurred some social costs). The policy was national but was planned and implemented locally, and it was at the local level that abuses appeared. The one-child policy, however, had been preceded and supported by programs to provide universal education and basic health care, including family planning services, and during the 1970s China's TFR dropped by half. Incentives were given for compliance with the policy, such as better housing and educational opportunities for the children, but penalties for failure to comply were also meted out. Usually, privileges and good jobs were withdrawn, but in some cases (in some localities) forced abortions and sterilizations were imposed. The latter were not approved by the central government, according to its stated policies, and this was confirmed by Chinese feminists we interviewed.[26]

One result of the one-child family policy was a severe skewing of the sex ratio, with boys of a given age outnumbering girls by as much as 120:100 or more. This was not a new phenomenon; Chinese culture has favored sons for uncounted generations, and during the great famine of 1957, when millions of families were faced with starvation, many sacrificed infant daughters in favor of sons. Thus, the age group born around that time had a skewed sex ratio as high as 140:100, and young men twenty to thirty years later were unable to find wives. When the one-child policy was imposed, the practice was revived. A resurgence in abortions, and even some infanticides, of females in the mid-1980s caused the Chinese government to relax the policy somewhat and allow many families to have a second child if the first was a girl. Even so, by 2003 China's TFR had fallen to 1.7, and the population was expected to peak around 2030 at about 1.5 billion.[27] Had the one-child policy not been implemented, China's population would now be larger by several hundred million people, and a humane end to its growth might not be a likely prospect. Even more important, the serious environmental and food supply problems the country faces today, along with associated social ones, would surely be far worse.

Obviously, China's policies to lower the birthrate, which began when its TFR was about 6, would not work in a country such as the United States, where collective decision making about family size (fortunately, in our view) would be unacceptable. Of course, the United States, like other industrialized nations, has a relatively low fertility rate, so it has less reason to impose a stringent birth control policy. The United States' TFR is currently about 2.0, slightly below replacement level—though not as low as those in most of Europe or Japan. The high U.S. growth rate of 1 percent per year, as mentioned in chapter 3, is due to the combination of a moderate TFR plus a high rate of immigration—roughly 1.4 million people per year (more than a quarter of them illegal immigrants).[28]

## Population Policies

Intelligent public discussion of the population issue has been notoriously lacking in the United States for the past two decades. Indeed, Americans have repeatedly been treated to heated discussions for or against immigration conducted with little understanding of existing policies or social and economic consequences of immigration. But there has been no parallel discourse, informed or not, on population policy overall. Asking legislators (or bureaucrats) to determine immigration policies without considering the desired size of the national population is like asking an aircraft designer to build a jet transport that can load twenty people per minute without specifying its passenger capacity. No American policy explicitly addresses population size or growth. But some policies, seemingly unrelated to population, are implicitly pronatalist (e.g., income tax deductions for each child).

Educating—or re-educating—the public on the population issue is clearly the first step to be taken. Few Americans could tell you approximately what the present U.S. population is (more than 294 million in 2004), let alone what the best estimates are for 2025 or 2050—about 350 million and 420 million, respectively. Thus, the U.S. population is projected to increase by the equivalent of France's population in some twenty years, or another of Japan in forty-five. And few Americans ever seem to think about the larger social and environmental consequences of reproductive decisions. Discussions of population issues should ideally be made part of the regular public school curriculum and be the subject of frequent programs in the media. Any serious discussion of population should include the role of population growth in generating or exacerbating problems about which many in the public *are* concerned—sprawl, traffic congestion, disappearing open space, lack of affordable housing, and the like. And the public could be informed about other adverse consequences, such as the fact that degradation and losses of natural capital, including prime farmland, forests, and wetlands, impoverishes us all and might well lead to high prices and constrained supplies of food, increased water shortages, and more pollution, among many other problems.

We think that one sensible and humane approach to increasing awareness of the costs of population growth in a nation such as the United States would be to use the tax system more judiciously to influence childbearing decisions. After all, parents impose costs on society through their childbearing; additional children increase the need for public schools, water and sewage systems, recreational facilities, police forces, and so on. These social costs are not captured in the "price" parents pay for having children—they create a "population externality."[29] It therefore makes sense to remove the standard child deduction from income taxes for third and subsequent children. When we first suggested restricting child exemptions on income taxes and imposing luxury taxes on goods for babies to help internalize those costs,[30] people complained that such taxes would be burdensome for poor families and would hurt children. Thinking that criticism correct, we stopped suggesting them. But later an economist colleague persuaded us to change our minds. "If you want to help poor children, do that directly. Don't send the message that having large families without paying their social costs is okay."[31]

Other measures could include strengthening the government-supported family planning facilities available to low-income families and increasing their outreach capabilities to immigrant communities. Improving public education about reproduction, relations between the sexes, and family limitation would also help, at the least to reduce the high incidence of unplanned pregnancies and the numbers of abortions. The teenage pregnancy rate in the United States has been significantly reduced since 1990, but it is still among the highest in the developed world. Counterintuitively, subsidizing day care for young children can help lower birthrates, as studies have shown, by making it easier for mothers to work outside the home. Also (as in developing countries), encouraging young women, especially in low-income groups, to complete their education can have two results—delaying marriage and childbearing, and equipping them for better jobs and the eventual ability to improve their families' well-being.

Parents who can afford it should pay the full social costs of their children's upbringing as long as overreproduction is a problem, especially in families with more than two children. There is too much subsidizing of the rich in the United States while many other citizens struggle, and some fail, to make ends meet. For instance, rich homeowners with large families have the cost of their giant houses subsidized by the mortgage tax deduction; minimum-wage workers struggling to pay for rental housing in cheap apartments or motel rooms, and struggling to feed and clothe their kids, usually get no such handout. The well-off often get expense accounts that cover costs of meals;

the working poor are lucky to get enough time to buy themselves some cheap junk food.[32] We have, as someone pointed out long ago, a system of socialism for the rich and capitalism for the poor.

If the U.S. population growth rate is to be reduced toward zero in the reasonably near future and eventually become negative, *both* factors—fertility and immigration—clearly must be reduced significantly. How much each factor should decline is a matter of social choice, for, ideally, each immigrant admitted should be balanced by at least one birth forgone. There is no "scientific" way to make decisions between restricting reproduction and restricting ingress, and no obvious direct way for enforcing any decisions made—though from a global ecological perspective fewer births probably would be preferable to fewer immigrants.

All of these points highlight the ethical issues related to regulating population size. How does one deal with the classic problem of conflicting moral "imperatives"? On one hand, many people think it's morally imperative to limit government interference in the private lives of citizens; people should be free to reproduce as they wish. Others emphasize the imperative to behave responsibly toward other members of society and toward future generations. It's an old story: individual freedom versus social responsibility. In this case, the ethical choice is a no-brainer, since population growth forever is impossible, and, as populations grow, freedoms are inevitably curtailed. Unless we seek the "freedom" enjoyed by factory chickens, we'd better go the socially responsible route.

If we know what needs to be done to halt population growth humanely and start a slow decline to a sustainable human society, why isn't it happening everywhere and more rapidly? One answer, of course, is that not only are people uninformed about the key roles that human numbers play in our present dilemmas and future prospects, but also in many cases they are misled about them by powerful organized forces, ranging from religious organizations to business interests. Some conservative religious groups not only abhor abortion; their goal ultimately is to ban contraception. They see population growth as desirable, whether to increase their memberships or simply to fulfill the biblical injunction to multiply and "fill the Earth." Business interests are often focused on local situations, where they see population increases, especially through immigration, as a source of new customers or potential cheap labor. Large resource-extracting industries also want more customers and prefer to deny that resources might be limited. Neither group is especially cognizant of environmental deterioration; they help keep our culture disconnected from the reality of the population driver of the human predicament.

In both the affluent developed societies and the poor, struggling ones, resolving the population problem will require further changes in awareness, attitude, and behavior. For the United States, this includes changing ideas about giving aid to poor nations. At least in democracies that have achieved a level of development that includes an educated electorate, an important first step is generating a public discussion of the issue. In the least developed nations, which generally have the highest birthrates (and also the highest infant and child mortality rates), much more effort needs to be made toward basic modernization before people are likely to become receptive to the idea of family planning.

In sub-Saharan Africa, people desperately need an end to the wars and corruption that have plagued them for several decades, as well as assistance in combating HIV/AIDS and other rampant diseases that often attend AIDS. Family planning understandably is not a top priority for their governments, although well-designed programs could certainly aid in treating and, especially, preventing sexually transmitted diseases. All these changes nevertheless need to be achieved despite organized resistance from a variety of groups who think their short-term interests are being threatened. In sub-Saharan Africa, the greatest impediments to preventing diseases, especially HIV/AIDS, and establishing effective family planning programs are strong pronatalist traditions, lack of education, widespread profound poverty, and weak health-care infrastructures in most countries. Ending the wars and corruption poses a huge challenge to the global community, which is only beginning to come to grips with these related problems. Leaders of corrupt governments are understandably not interested in changing their ways or giving up their power; the conflicts are often the result of the damage they do to their people and resources, frequently with encouragement and even help from international corporations seeking access to those resources. If these sad conditions can be changed, family planning (along with such things as education for women) could make invaluable contributions toward creating sustainable African societies.

## Population Politics: An Example

It may be instructive to look at the current status of population issues in another industrialized country, where, unlike the situation in the United States, population size has been the subject of prolonged and often heated debate.[33] It can give us a preview of what some of the issues and differences will be if and when the United States as a nation ever faces up to its severe population problems—indeed, when *any* other rich nation does. Superficially, the issue in Australia seems straightforward. Among those who are familiar with the country, only someone who thinks that population density is a reasonable index of under- or overpopulation would fail to recognize that Australia, with some 20 million people, is already overpopulated. Yes, Australia has only seven people per square mile—but then the western Sahara has only three, and the moon has zero people per square mile, and few think they're underpopulated. Most of Australia is a miserable desert (only about 6 percent of its land is arable),[34] its few rivers are already dwindling and polluted from overuse, much of its limited agricultural land is salinized, and its biological capital—its native flora and fauna—has been in continuous decline for at least a century.

Indeed, the impacts of the human population on ecosystem services are probably more obvious in Australia than in any other developed country. Many world-class Australian environmental scientists have repeatedly warned about this deterioration of their nation's fragile life-support systems. In 1999, Professor Harry Recher of Edith Cowan University, for example, a world expert on the ecology of birds and a leader among Australian environmental scientists, predicted that

"Australia will lose half of its terrestrial bird species in the next century."[35] Dr. Frank Talbot, director emeritus of the Smithsonian Institution's National Museum of Natural History, past director of the Australian Museum, and a leading marine ecologist, recently expressed foreboding to us at the thought of further Australian population growth: "I can't imagine the [Great Barrier] Reefs persisting in anything like their present form if there were 25 million of us—even if Aussies were the only ones exploiting them."[36] Coastal development—the vast majority of Australia's population is concentrated in five coastal urban areas, centered on Brisbane, Sydney, Melbourne, Adelaide, and Perth—overfishing, and poorly managed tourism are all causing damage and degradation of the fragile reef ecosystem. Talbot wrote in 2000, "Without fresh thinking and fundamental attitudinal and management changes, the Great Barrier Reef . . . will be slowly and continuously degraded both biologically and aesthetically."[37]

In 2002, a report from the Commonwealth Scientific and Industrial Research Organization (CSIRO), Australia's national science organization,[38] pointed out some of the problems that would need to be faced if the nation's population were to keep growing until 2050: deteriorating water quality, the disappearance of "iconic" resources such as plentiful seafood and Australia's unique flora and fauna, and the possibility of ninety new cities the size of Canberra.[39] This was greeted by much ignorant commentary in *The Australian,* a newspaper owned by one of the world's richest (and most powerful) men, Rupert Murdoch.[40] Murdoch's newspaper worked hard to kill the report, saying it was "discredited," "dogmatic," "fuzzy," "religious," and so on.[41] In an unsigned editorial, the paper claimed that the report exposed CSIRO's "ideological predilections" and was pervaded by "the anti-growth green agenda that links economic expansion and more people with environmental degradation."[42] Imagine that!

Some Australian academics also have ignored the conclusions of their ecological colleagues. For example, sociologist Jerzy Zubrzycki, in an address before the Australian Population Association in November 2000, played to chronic Australian fears of invasion by populous Asian neighbors and concerns about labor shortages and called on

Australians to have more babies to keep the population young and growing. Zubrzycki, as *The Australian*'s editorial page noted, thus joined "a growing chorus of academics, commentators and politicians concerned about the number of women having fewer children."[43] Perhaps he believes the population can grow forever.

*The Australian*'s lack of concern about overpopulation is largely rooted in its owner's interest in economic expansion. After all, more people may mean more customers at your restaurant or hardware store, more buyers of your automobiles or tract homes, more students paying high tuitions to hear you lecture, more travelers for your package tours, more watchers of your television show or subscribers to *The Australian*. The pro-growth approach to population owes a lot to narrowly trained economists in the past who developed a series of models of economic growth that viewed indefinite growth in population to be beneficial. Contemporary growth models include an assumption that the creation of ideas (technological progress) is positively linked to demand created by population growth.

These economic growth models also assume a world where the natural resource base constitutes a fixed, indestructible factor of production—in other words, a world where humanity's natural capital never depreciates. Economist Partha Dasgupta put it succinctly: "The problem with the latter assumption is that it is wrong."[44] Dasgupta is one of a growing group of economists who understand the vulnerability of humanity's stores of natural capital. A fundamental hidden assumption in those growth models is that the past couple of centuries represent a suitable base from which to extrapolate into the future—even though for most of some fifty centuries before that, economic growth was hardly perceptible.[45]

The fallacy of economic growth over millennia was demonstrated long ago. An old-time growth economist, Wilfred Beckerman, stated that economic growth had "gone on since the time of Pericles" and that it could continue "for another 2500 years."[46] A British social scientist, Jack Parsons, did a simple calculation. He showed what would be implied if growth had gone on since Pericles at 1.0 percent per year, if there had been English families and coins at the time of Pericles, and if the value of British currency had remain unchanged (no inflation or deflation). Under those circumstances, the calculated average family income in Pericles' day would have had the annual buying power of less than a millionth of a penny.[47]

Dasgupta looked at the same issue in a different way. As he put it, the notion of indefinite growth of economic output in the future is a vision that places "an enormous burden on an economic regime not much more than 250 years old. . . . Extrapolation into the past is a sobering exercise: over the long haul of history (say 2000 years), economic growth was for most of the time not much more than zero until about AD 1700, even in regions that are currently very rich."[48] Dasgupta assumed that, at the time of Christ, per capita income was roughly a dollar a day (which is the minimum people can survive on today). So, over those 2,000 years, income has risen about fourteenfold, from about $350 per year to today's average of about $5,000 per year. That means an annual growth rate of 0.14 percent per year. That figure is not very far above zero, and considering that substantial growth since AD 1700 is included, it tells us that there was hardly any growth before 1700.

So we can see that an important reason for lack of concern about population growth (or even for its promotion by *The Australian*) is misinformation[49] about the critical importance of natural capital and the potential for continuous economic growth. And, especially in the United States, the lack of concern can also be traced to the idea that the population problem has been "solved." Unfortunately, it hasn't been, either globally or nationally.

The editorial in *The Australian* also wrapped expansion of the Australian population in a cloak of humanitarianism. In discussing a decision by the government of Prime Minister John Howard to increase immigration, the editorial stated, "We cannot turn a blind eye to the problem of overcrowding beyond our shores." Skipping the point that overcrowding is rarely a "problem" in itself, the editorial writer (who had accused CSIRO of doing "fuzzy maths") might have tried some simple arithmetic herself. If Australia were to try to alleviate misery overseas by admitting just one year's population increase in East Asia and Southeast Asia, Australia's population would instantly be boosted by 18 million, nearly doubling it, and the Asian societies would hardly notice the difference. Genuine concern for the state of poverty-stricken people is a valuable thing in rich nations, but encouraging the poor to immigrate, while helping a relatively few individuals, tends to make global problems worse in the long run.

That editorial was followed by another one emphasizing that scientists ignore how adaptable human beings are and how "people will change their behavior in response to new situations."[50] It assumes incorrectly that Australians can maintain a reasonable life regardless of the number of people on the continent. Neither editorial in *The Australian* mentioned the possible "ideological predilections" of Murdoch and his friends to keep Australia's population booming as long as possible in order to line the pockets of the powerful people who benefit in the short term from growth—such as real estate developers and peddlers of mediocre newspapers. As the *Sydney Morning Herald* reported, "Many corporate leaders are lobbying for a substantial increase in the immigration intake, arguing that at under 20 million Australia lacks the domestic markets necessary to sustain it economically."[51]

This might be a legitimate argument, but it rings a little hollow in a globalizing world economy. To take it seriously, one would first have to see a careful economic analysis with clearly stated assumptions, showing how and why more people would provide greater economic benefits. It would also need to project how those benefits would be distributed. Most important, the analysis would need to calculate the general social benefits and costs (including environmental costs) of that population growth and show whether further population growth would be a net cost or benefit. And a parallel analysis would be required for the benefits and costs of population shrinkage.

As we have indicated, some of Australia's most knowledgeable ecologists have calculated that the environmental costs of substantial further population growth would be staggering. Charles Birch, professor emeritus of zoology at the University of Sydney and one of the world's most distinguished ecologists, told us: "Considering what is known of the ecological situation in Australia, I believe that a maximum sustainable population for Australia, with anything like today's patterns of behavior, would be about ten million people. Over 50 percent of the land is seriously deteriorated from salinity or wind erosion. We cannot manage sustainably with close on 20 million. How can we cope with even more people?"[52]

Professor Andrew Beattie, head of Macquarie University's Commonwealth Key Centre for Biodiversity and Bioresources and a leading expert on Australian biodiversity, put it bluntly: "We're already squandering our natural capital. . . . Australian population growth is undermining the very ecosystem services required to support today's mob."[53] Harry Recher expressed his continuing distress at the negligible attention many Australian politicians pay to the information made available by the scientific community: "They and the government bureaucracy are more interested in elections and power groups than the future of Australia's children. Disgracefully, they often even try to censor the reports of the scientists they pay to discover and tell the truth."[54]

Such censorship is more severe in Australia than in the United States; in Australia, government ecologists normally must give their scientific papers to their bosses for political approval before they are permitted to publish them. Government agencies becoming for all practical purposes wholly owned subsidiaries of those they are supposed to regulate is a pervasive problem of governance, and the United States is not immune. Indeed, the problem appears to have become epidemic in the George W. Bush administration.

On a more optimistic note, there is a movement toward sustainable agricultural practices in Australia, one in which some farmers and graziers are leading the way in efforts to restore some of Australia's lost carrying capacity and make it possible to sustain the population already in place. We saw this personally in the work of the Tammin Land Conservation District Advisory Committee in Western Australia in 1991.[55] The committee was working in collaboration with CSIRO to restore native vegetation around salinized wheat fields. In the past century, when almost all native shrubs and trees were removed to make way for wheat fields, the natural pumping action of their roots drawing water from deep underground ended, and this allowed the water table to rise. With the rising water came salts that had been spread over Western Australia for millions of years by winds off the Southern Ocean. When the salts beneath a field rose to the level of the wheat roots, the land went out of production. Salinization, which has so far affected about 3 percent of the cleared wheat lands, costs Western Australian farmers some $150 million annually.[56] But when the native vegetation was replanted around the margins of a salinized field, the water table could be lowered again, the salt flushed from the soil by rain, and the field restored to production. In addition, habitat for many native organisms could be restored. Recently, a distinguished collection of Australian environmental scientists known as the Wentworth Group has taken up the crusade to make revolutionary changes in the way the Australian landscape is treated in some of the other states, and to make it a more suitable habitat for *Homo sapiens*.[57]

Another reason for optimism is that not all Australian politicians are automatically stuck in the antique "growth at any price" rut. Bob Carr, the premier of New South Wales, stated that the idea of the population growing to 50 million people, a goal proposed by some politicians, was "nonsense."[58] Carr is convinced that the vast majority of Australians agree with him about the need for their country to limit its population, despite the efforts of some pressure groups.[59] We think he is correct. They are voting in their bedrooms, it seems; Australia's TFR in 2002 was 1.7. And they don't seem inclined to support a great increase in their moderate immigration rate.

So, when we look at Australia, the best case we know of for vigorous discourse on issues related to the size and growth of the human enterprise, we can see room for both dismay and hope. Dismay that, even with a broad public discussion, the obvious conclusions are not turned into policy; hope that a broad discussion clearly can occur. The Australian example really brings home how far behind the United States is in getting a debate under way. This is especially worrisome because of the magnitude of American overpopulation today and the projected increase to more than 420 million by 2050. This makes clear the urgency of the United States' once again having a national dialogue on population and related issues.

Americans had a dialogue three decades ago about population, both domestic and global, and now seem to think the matter is settled. It is past time for a fresh round of public education on the subject and a discussion about the nation's goals for its own future population size and growth. It also is time to resume the leadership role the United States once held in designing and supporting humane policies and programs as part of the international community. If our small planet is to remain hospitable to human life, we should strive to hold the remaining increment of population growth to fewer than 2 billion people, if at all possible, and commence a gradual decline to a more sustainable population size—an optimal size yet to be determined. Challenging as that might be, what choice do we have but to strive toward sustainability?

All the same, the overshoot in global population size is not the only factor in the human predicament we have to contend with; it may not even be the hardest. Common sense about appropriate population size and resource conservation is clashing with the growth-manic ideology of the West and the powerful forces behind it. The basic problems are cultural attitudes and practices that have not changed rapidly enough for us to come to grips with the deteriorating situation created by rapid cultural evolution on the technological side combined with a destructive consumption-oriented economic ethic.[60] Governance, ethics, and the distribution of power are more and more where the action is, and, unfortunately, that's where the human enterprise is falling further behind.

# Chapter 7

## CONSUMING LESS

"We all need a growing economy."
TRENT LOTT[1]

FOR MUCH OF the economic history of the industrial nations since World War II, there has been general agreement among academic economists, government decision makers, corporate leaders, and the public at large that economic growth is highly desirable.[2] The war-generated recovery of the American economy from the Great Depression of the 1930s was explained in a Keynesian framework that focused on the deferred consumer spending of the war years and emphasized the importance of increasing aggregate demand for goods and services. As historian Robert Collins put it, "Most Americans simply assumed that the consumer culture *was* America and vice versa."[3]

The motives behind growthmanship and consumerism, at least in the United States, were diverse. Corporate interests in expanding markets and increasing profits were obvious ones. Also, right after the war, many liberals saw economic growth as a generator of wealth that could supply the wherewithal to solve the many problems of economic inequity in society—to use economic growth to ameliorate class conflict. But consumerism and the politics of the era were tightly intertwined, often in ways that perpetuated inequities.[4] After the unprecedented prosperity of the extended post–World War II boom, the

United States entered a period of slower growth in output, increasing unemployment, and pessimism in the 1970s, following the turmoil of the anti–Vietnam War movement and fueling a growing environmental movement. Then, after recessions in the early 1980s and again in the early 1990s, the boom times returned in the mid-1990s, only to end in a turn-of-the-century bust. Through it all, the view has consistently been that a "healthy" economy is one showing overall growth in output.

Economic theory holds that people will be rational in their view of the future course of events. Individuals may make mistakes, yet they will not expect, for example, that market prices will always rise; they will recognize that prices fluctuate. In this view, people are assumed to have sufficient information (and appropriate psychological characteristics) so that they will not behave irrationally. There has been much discussion of whether the assumption of rationality is sufficiently robust to keep the economic theory that rests on it a good basis for understanding short-term economic behavior.[5] But when one considers the long term, the non-rationality of consumers, many economists, and most politicians is manifest. They have the most irrational of expectations; they think that there has always been growth in the physical economy and that it can and must go on forever. Evidently, they lack crucial information.

Nonetheless, politicians (such as U.S. senator Trent Lott, quoted in the epigraph to this chapter) and pundits are eternally saying that, by consuming more, people can help boost the economy. And they're right in the short term, where the majority of politicians dwell. But one of the most vexing questions related to economic growth is, how long can it be sustained? Sustainability is an extremely complex topic, in no small part because economic growth is also complex. Growth in exactly what, where, and for whom are major questions that are central to considerations of humanity's long-term survival.[6]

We can be sure, however, that growth in the United States economy cannot long continue at the sort of rates expected by George W. Bush's secretary of the treasury, John Snow: 3.5 to 4.0 percent annually.[7] At such rates, in 100 years' time—that is, within the lifetimes of some babies born this year—and if the population remained around 300 million, the average yearly income of an American family of four would be about $5 million in 2004 dollars.[8] In 200 years, it would jump to some $150 million. Assuming no less equitable distribution than today's, one wonders what the highest-income families would spend it on. Would they be satisfied if making money were their only objective? Remember, there's no price inflation for goods in those hypothetical numbers, so a family with a $5 million income could easily buy a dozen homes a year around 2104 and a couple hundred around 2204. But we suspect that maids, gardeners, roofers, dishwashers, and garbage collectors would be hard to recruit in this imaginary wonderland.

Nobel laureate economist Robert Fogel noted recently that "we have become so rich that we are approaching saturation in the consumption not only of necessities, but of goods recently thought to be luxuries, or which were only dreams or science fiction during the first third of the twentieth century."[9] Indeed, if Snow's dreams of economic growth were to come true and those rates persisted worldwide, not just in the United States, the average human being in 2204 would have an annual income (in 2004 dollars) of more than $7 million. A favorite expression of those focused on overall growth of the economy, such as Snow (and many politicians), is that "a rising tide lifts all boats." Snow used that as justification for Bush's plan to substantially reduce taxes for the rich, claiming it would cause a surge of investment and spending that would increase economic growth. But a critical question for social policy is whether further lifting of Bill Gates' or Rupert Murdoch's boat would be a good thing. To Gates' credit, along with Warren Buffett (whose boat has also been lifted very high), he expressed strong disapproval of the Bush tax-cut policy.

Significant long-term economic growth is mostly a phenomenon of the past two centuries; as we saw in chapter 6, continuous growth at, say, even a quarter of 1 percent annually cannot have been a feature of the global human economy for thousands of years. Even the enormously successful Egyptian civilization could not have enjoyed such a growth rate over its 3,500-year history. But if the economy can't grow at a significant rate for very long, doesn't that put us in a terrible bind? Could society possibly survive without economic growth?[10]

Actually, yes, it could, as the vast majority of economists would admit (although many think more growth even in rich countries is desirable). Once we reached the point at which the average person's production was sufficiently high—so that people's real incomes were sufficient to give them what they need (and a little more)—we wouldn't need further growth of per capita output (or income) to assure satisfactory living standards. We wouldn't need further growth of *absolute* output either if the population size were constant or diminishing. What is crucial is that real income (or output per person) be adequate, and that could remain sufficiently high without growth of output if there were no increase in the number of people.

In the foreseeable future, of course, the world's physical economy will need to grow simply to keep an expanding population from becoming progressively more impoverished, because a constant-sized "pie" would have to be sliced into ever smaller per capita pieces. But once the population stops growing and begins to contract toward a sustainable size, per capita income could increase even if there were a non-growing economy because there will be fewer people to share its output. And even if physical throughput—the rate at which natural resources are processed, used, and converted to rubbish—were held constant or reduced, the economy almost certainly could continue to grow for a long time in other dimensions through technological innovation.

Even if the economy didn't continue to grow for some reason, that wouldn't necessarily be disastrous. Some economic effort could be diverted into maintaining essential infrastructure, and the workweek could stabilize at a level at which enough labor would be done to maintain the needed flow of goods and services. People could concentrate not on always having more gadgets, or on reaping scandalously high economic rewards, but on growth in intellectual and spiritual areas.

Not only is a non-growing economy possible in theory; it is also possible in practice. For long periods in the Middle Ages, people didn't expect their economies to grow, and, as pointed out in the last chapter, economies rarely did. That's one reason why they were willing to participate in building massive cathedrals that wouldn't be completed within their life spans. They didn't expect growth in wealth and technologies to expand capabilities so much that their efforts would soon be superceded. Of course, we're not recommending a return to a medieval lifestyle; we're just suggesting that a non-growing economy for a non-growing (or even slowly diminishing) population needn't be viewed as unthinkable or frightening.

Some economists, at least as far back as Kenneth Boulding, a brilliant scholar of two generations ago,[11] have recognized that growth in the physical economy cannot go on forever.[12] Those interested in an exposition for non-economists of how a steady-state economy might work should consult the writings of a pioneer in that area, economist Herman Daly, and his colleagues.[13] While not many other economists have tackled the question, it might be a good time to take up the challenge. Designing a transition in collective expectations away from seeking *more* to seeking *enough* shouldn't be all that hard, if it could be approached as a cooperative enterprise and an ethical issue, if economists applied their professional expertise, and if ample time were allowed for the idea to come to full fruition. Everyone will eventually need to understand, as someone once remarked, that perpetual growth is the creed of the cancer cell.

## A New Economic View of Consumption

The unalloyed good of consumption has classically been associated with increases in a nation's gross national product (GNP) or its close relative, gross domestic product (GDP). GNP is an index of the level of economic activity at any given time, the sum of consumption of goods and services, investment in capital (such as the purchase of new machinery for an automobile plant or the printing of a new stock of books by a publisher), and net exports.[14] But GNP (which perhaps should more usefully be named the gross national cost, its exact equivalent) is a lousy predictor of the present or future well-being of a people.[15] As economist Partha Dasgupta put it, "It would be wrong to regard a country as rich simply because its GNP per head is high: it could be blowing its capital assets on a consumption binge."[16] GNP, in other words, doesn't tell us the state of a nation's capital, the social worth of its current expenditures, or what, if anything, the nation is investing in its future.[17]

In place of GNP as a measure of well-being, some have proposed net national product (NNP). NNP is simply GNP adjusted for capital depreciation. That seems an obviously needed correction. If GNP is growing at 5 percent per year in a poor nation dependent on exporting its forest products, and the forests are being cleared at 10 percent per year, there's a threat to the country's well-being that NNP, properly calculated, would reflect, but GNP would not. So NNP is an improvement over GNP as an index of well-being, but it is not flawless. It turns out, for technical reasons,[18] that NNP can increase for a while even as a nation suffers a decline in wealth and quality of life.[19]

Leaders in economics now consider that the best measure of a society's sustainable well-being is not GNP or even NNP but whether genuine wealth, the social worth of its capital assets, is increasing or declining.[20] Capital assets include the society's manufactured capital (homes, factories, computers, etc.), natural capital (freshwater springs, forests, pollinators, oil deposits, etc.), human capital (the skills, technical knowledge, and satisfaction of individuals in the labor pool), and social capital (skills, general knowledge, and satisfaction embedded in social networks and institutions).[21]

Remember, the terms *social cost* and *social benefit* refer to costs and benefits that include not only those captured directly by the participants in market transactions but also the external costs and benefits suffered or enjoyed by society at large. For example, the social cost of a coal-fired power plant is generally greater than its market price because of external costs (e.g., damage from air pollution resulting from the generation of electricity by the plant). Of course, many aspects of natural capital are especially difficult to measure—as are many aspects of human capital (e.g., the positive social worth of leisure time, which can be socially negative if it's the leisure time of hoodlums). Also hard to measure are externalities (costs not captured in

market prices) related to the *distribution* of wealth. They obviously can
be a crucial aspect of evaluating social capital—just ask Louis XVI or
Nicholas II, who died because of the social costs of maldistribution, or
ask poor people about the myriad difficulties they encounter in dealing with the health-care system in the United States. But economists
too often ignore those costs.

The most recent analysis based on genuine wealth suggests that
many, if not most, nations *are* growing poorer today. A study of Bangladesh, India, Nepal, Pakistan, sub-Saharan Africa, China, the United
States, and the United Kingdom found that all the developing nations
considered except China had lost a substantial portion of their productive base—that is, their natural capital, physical capital, and human
capital—in the past few decades, reducing their per capita wealth. In
other words, they are overconsuming relative to the resources they can
command—although, of course, not in terms of what we think they
*ought* to be able to command; their absolute levels of consumption are
often pitifully low![22]

The study's findings contrast starkly with those of conventional
measures of well-being such as per capita GNP and the United Nations
Development Programme's more recent Human Development Index
(HDI), both of which show rises everywhere except in sub-Saharan
Africa. In Pakistan, the HDI suggests that the average Pakistani was
twice as well-off in 1996 as in 1965, when in fact he or she was almost
twice as *poor* because of the decline in Pakistan's aggregate wealth (a
trend that sooner or later will depress its HDI). An average citizen of
Bangladesh became more than twice as poor in the same period that
substantial portions of the nation's stock of natural capital were consumed. Tragically, in sub-Saharan Africa, the average person has
become twice as poor every twenty-five years.

According to the study of aggregate wealth (including natural capital), per capita wealth is projected to rise in China and India, however.
The study also indicates that the United States and the United Kingdom may be investing enough to assure increased future wealth per
person. Some of this future benefit, though, is most likely due to the
ability of those countries to import goods and services at prices below

their social value. This appears to be especially the case for natural resources or resource-intensive goods. Thus, some of the projected future increases in U.S. and UK wealth are almost certainly made possible because substantial portions of their consumption will be supported by a decline in the resource bases of poorer countries from which the resources are extracted.[23] So the rich appear to be overconsuming relative to the resources they can command, which means relative to the resources of the planet. In essence, the rich are being subsidized by the poor—hardly a new phenomenon. In the 1980s, Willy Brandt, former chancellor of West Germany, called the flow of funds from poor to rich nations, as the former struggled to service their debts, "a blood transfusion from the sick to the healthy."[24] The flow of resources is just another form of the transfusion.

The modern form of this subsidy traces back at least to the Victorian age, when the behavior of the emerging industrial nations and the first economic globalization helped to create the "Third World."[25] Countries such as Bangladesh are becoming poorer because they suffer from highly inefficient production of both capital goods and consumption goods. Their inability to command enough resources forces them to underinvest; that is, they cannot invest enough even to maintain today's standard of living into the future. In very poor nations, increasing the consumption of nutrients can amount to investment in critical human capital. Overconsumption—in the sense of consumption far beyond necessity and reasonable comfort—is a phenomenon of rich nations and growing affluent classes in some poor ones. Ironically, the world is thus faced with a complex dual problem. If civilization is ever to achieve sustainability, it must find ways both to increase necessary consumption in poor nations and to simultaneously reduce wasteful and harmful consumption in both rich and poor countries.

Studies of the genuine wealth of a country also sometimes fail to assess accurately what is happening to its natural capital. In the sample of poor nations in the wealth study discussed earlier,[26] only commercial forests, petroleum and other minerals, and the atmospheric sink for carbon dioxide ($CO_2$) were considered as elements of natural capital. Not measured were surface water and groundwater supplies, fishery

stocks, and biodiversity, which provides such services as carbon seques-
tering, nutrient cycling, pollination, pest control, flood management,
and erosion prevention on farmlands and shorelines. If those critical
components of natural capital had been included, the decline in wealth
of the poor nations in the sample (and quite likely some of the rich
ones) would have been even more dramatic. Indeed, consumption by
an ever-expanding human population would be seen as making
humanity *globally* ever poorer—despite superficial impressions to the
contrary. Focusing exclusively on growing GNP as the measure of success has allowed much of society to miss the deeper issues that convince scientists that humanity is indeed on a collision course with the
natural world. Will our impoverished descendants consider those
superficial impressions humanity's "pomp of yesterday"?

But even if global wealth were shown to be increasing under a "most
likely" future trajectory of growth in population and consumption,
and economists continued to neglect issues of equity (distribution of
wealth), there are good reasons not to be complacent. Much uncertainty surrounds potential responses of natural systems to changes,
which, as you'll recall, are often nonlinear. A small change in one factor
influencing the system might produce a large change in it. For instance,
a seemingly small increase in gasoline consumption, causing emission
of more $CO_2$ into the atmosphere, might be just enough to trigger a
dramatic, and relatively rapid, change in global climate.

To take account of all potential outcomes, conservative estimates of
the consequences of consumption for the sustainability of civilization
will have to incorporate a wide range of scenarios for the responses of
those natural systems. For instance, we can't assume that climate
change as severe as the Younger Dryas rapid cooling event will not
occur. The climate system appears to have alternative stable states, as
noted earlier, and we must consider the possibility that it may be
pushed into a very different one.[27] Rather than assume a relatively
smooth pattern of change in response to increasing global consumption and consequent strains on Earth's life-support systems, we should
be prepared for more dramatic shifts as well. In other words, we should
hope for the best and plan for the worst. From what is known at the

moment, civilization's ability to maintain even its current overall level of consumption (however measured) over the long term is certainly in doubt.[28]

## Consumption and Satisfaction

With rising consumption calling into question the sustainability of the human enterprise, it seems appropriate to inquire into the deeper reasons for its continued expansion. Increased consumption, at least at the individual level, is generally considered an unqualified blessing. But what is the evidence for this? Certainly, if a poor African farmer is consuming a diet of mostly maize meal that supplies 1,900 kilocalories per day, she would benefit greatly by an increase to 2,400 calories provided by a 500-calorie supplement of nuts, milk, and meat. But an American stockbroker who adds 500 calories in the form of a small fast-food hamburger to the 3,500 fat-rich calories he already takes in may find the pleasure of increased consumption rather seriously diminished by the resultant heart attack.

In the aggregate, there is abundant evidence that, once basic biological needs for food, shelter, clothing, and health care are met and a standard of living providing some leisure time and recreation is adopted, further consumption doesn't provide much increased satisfaction.[29] The data for this are relatively unambiguous.[30] In the United States, per capita real income (a surrogate for consumption) doubled between 1957 and 1992, but public opinion polls showed no increase in reported happiness. There also was no increase in happiness in Japan between 1958 and 1987 despite more than a quadrupling of GNP.[31] A near tripling of personal income in European countries between 1960 and 1990 similarly produced no increase in reported satisfaction.[32]

A dramatic example of the disconnect between consumption and satisfaction is the phenomenon of the "suffering rich" in industrialized nations. A recent survey revealed that 62 percent of Australians believed they couldn't afford all the things they needed. This included 46 percent of the richest households in the country—those with annual incomes above A$70,000.[33] At the same time, people in a fifth of the poorest households in Australia (with incomes less than $20,000) thought they could afford everything they needed, which is consistent with reports that some older pensioners claim they are doing well. So the holders of the most wealth apparently aren't the most satisfied group in our utterly wealth-oriented societies.

Maybe it's time for a careful reconsideration of society's true goals. It might be useful for newspapers to report regularly on statistical indicators of such items as the state of the environment, the functioning of the health-care system, and the knowledge of graduating high-school students, with equal prominence as is given to stock market averages, which are largely an index of the psychology of gamblers.

If increasing consumption beyond the meeting of basic needs doesn't really enhance satisfaction, why do so many well-to-do human beings strive to consume ever more? One possible explanation might be called the "rat race" theory of consumption. It says that, once basic needs are met, people get satisfaction not from absolute measures of income or consumption but from their position and prestige relative to the peer group with which they identify.[34] As biologist Donald Kennedy once put it, "welfare detectors are disparity detectors."[35] We feel satisfied if we are able to consume as much as—or, better, more than—other members of our peer group; we are dissatisfied (suffer relative deprivation)[36] if we can't consume as much as our friends do. A person's self-worth is tied up in his net worth; money allows us to display our success in achieving status. It gives people what economist Thorstein Veblen a century ago called "pecuniary decency."[37] This leads to the rat race of competitive acquisition,[38] attempts to keep up with and get ahead of the Joneses. Interestingly, though, our health is better and our life expectancy is longer if we live in a nation with a relatively equitable income distribution, where the opportunities to outdo others are fewer, as are the chances of being outdone.[39]

What makes it a rat race is that, while aggregate consumption increases, the average individual does not gain in satisfaction. In addition, as Robert Frank analyzes in great detail in *Luxury Fever*, substantial social costs can be inherent in the wasteful consumptive competition.[40] Resources are limited, and those diverted into competitive

consumption by individuals could instead be allocated to public benefits such as repair of crumbling roads and rickety highway bridges,
cleanup of water supplies, and refurbishing of disastrously bad educational systems. Many individuals doubtless would prefer to have safer
transportation, better health care, and superior education for their
kids over more consumption for themselves, but they don't see that
they have those choices.

Young professional families may be able to buy larger houses and
fancier cars than we did when we were starting out in the 1950s, but is
the price they pay in reduced leisure time, job insecurity, worries about
affordable health care, and the need for both members of the couple to
work, worth it? Most families today obviously don't really believe they
can choose more leisure time instead of the moneymaking grind—cultural and institutional arrangements militate against it. People are
increasingly competing in markets in which the chances of real success
are limited.[41] At the same time, they are constantly inundated with
visual images of "success" linked to conspicuous consumption—consumption that sends a signal of success. A luxury car, the glossy ads tell
us, is a symbol of success and freedom. An attorney who might prefer
to keep driving her battered old Dodge knows she would be sending a
subliminal signal to potential clients that she's not likely to win their
cases.

We are "sight animals." Thanks to a sojourn our ancestors millions
of years ago spent in shrubs and trees, snatching bugs and lizards with
nimble fingers, vision is our dominant sense.[42] But rather than using
our eyes to spot a tasty grasshopper, we now employ them to absorb
the glories of a new Mercedes or Lincoln Navigator, or even, for a mere
$308,000, the extravagant new twenty-foot-long DaimlerChrysler
Maybach (not including a $50,000 stereo and other accessories).[43]

Such images of the lifestyles of the rich and famous, brought to us
first via photos and films and now, especially, by television, not only
show us what others have but virtually bring those others into our families. Movie and television stars, rock stars, royalty, and other prominent people become "pseudokin,"[44] members of a reference group
with whose consumptive behavior we compare our own. The real kin

relationships that once were central to each individual's life are increasingly being replaced by those of pseudokin, and our connections to them are often promoted by purely commercial interests. Just consider the great popularity of television soap operas and how easily we "relate" to some of the characters. And when we see images of our pseudokin driving Lamborghinis, living in 45,000-square-foot homes, and sitting on yacht bar stools upholstered with sperm whale foreskins, we know we're not keeping up.

If a transition from seeking *more* to seeking *enough* is to become possible for our civilization today, we will need familiarity with what lies behind the grow-and-consume craze—behind the desirability of whale foreskins (for us, not for the whales). Are physical needs and a desire to "keep up with the Joneses" all that we are attempting to satisfy by acquiring road candy and trophy homes? The trend toward ever more consumption evidently is driven by other factors besides perceptions of comparative status. In many cases, increased consumption may simply carry absolute benefits considered well worth the personal costs. The convenience and dependability of two new cars for a two- or three-driver family may be judged a vast improvement over having a single older one. In a seemingly ever more frantic world, more gadgets may seem some compensation for less free time. And some gadgets may become "ritually marked," as one anthropologist claims refrigerators often are when they become centers of symbolic display, as in our house, where that appliance is coated with magnets supporting drawings and messages from grandchildren.[45]

Then there is, of course, the steady drumbeat of advertisements urging people to consume, and politicians saying they should do so for the good of the economy. The pressure to consume comes from all sides in modern societies, and many people have come to see increasing consumption as a central goal in their lives, be it a more lavishly furnished home in the country, the latest clothing fashions, or vacations on distant continents.

But that's not the entire story. How does one analyze the influences behind purchasing a Hummer, running an air conditioner, or buying a five-foot-wide television set? To what degree are corporations essentially manufacturing the public's desires for their products by preying on consumers' emotions? To what extent are they responding to real desires while benefiting themselves in the bargain? Are they manipulating other people to behave in ways that most of them, even if fully informed, might choose on their own anyway?

The last question is probably the most difficult of all. We personally are certainly not uninformed about environmental problems, and we're well aware of efforts to manipulate our behavior. Yet we find that many of our own patterns of consumption, for example, do not conform to what we intellectually believe is ideal. Yes, we've given up swordfish and we had only one child, but we certainly travel more (and generally consume more) than the average person should in today's world. Some of the consuming we do is enforced by the logistics of suburbia and is thus outside our control, and some is connected to our work. This is surely true for many, perhaps most, Americans, the majority of whom have even less of the flexibility that a relatively high income provides than we have. We are lucky enough to live near our workplace, unlike most people. But we have no public transport near our home, nor are shopping facilities within easy walking distance, so using a car for many everyday activities is necessary. Still, if we don't change our own patterns of behavior as much as we think is appropriate, how can we expect others to change theirs?

## Superconsumption

The urge to compete through ultimately unsatisfying consumption seems much more puzzling than the question of why human beings have recently tended to overreproduce. Continuous growth in the number of people seems easily explicable—people like to reproduce (sex is fun, and so are kids), and with lower death rates, numbers grow. That much is biology. Over billions of years of genetic evolutionary history, maximizing an individual's reproduction was the name of the game. Differential reproduction is the basis of natural selection; individuals that fit into their environments better than others in the same population out-reproduce them, and more of their genes are represented in subsequent generations. All of us are descendants of champion reproducers.[46]

In contrast, maximizing consumption of anything beyond physical and ritual needs of individuals, and sometimes of close kin, is a recent development. It started some 10,000 years or so ago with the advent of the agricultural revolution—an eye-blink compared with an evolutionary history at least 250 times as long. It was not physically possible for nomadic hunter-gatherers to engage in much conspicuous consumption, beyond that of successful hunters distributing meat, perhaps in return for sexual access; there are limits to how many possessions can be carried. Besides meat, well-made tools, weapons, and clothing have doubtless been prized for tens of thousands—perhaps millions—of years. In fact, there are reports of chimpanzees carrying specially selected rock tools around with them.[47]

Once the agricultural revolution started generating some abundance and a sedentary lifestyle that allowed for permanent buildings and storage space, acquisitiveness could have come to have a payoff in that most useful human currency—prestige. That, in turn, could have had a payoff in reproductive success. For instance, a study of the isolated Trinidadian village of Grande Anse found that men with bigger patches of land had more mating success. And, of course, the famed emperor of Morocco in the eighteenth century, Mulay Ismail the Bloodthirsty, managed to co-opt enough power and resources to father nearly 900 children.[48] Possibly, then, besides the apparent cultural rewards to individuals who acquire more than others in their society, there could be genetic evolutionary advantages as well.

The potential for superconsuming—which we define as getting *way* ahead of the Joneses and almost everyone else—appeared when human beings became more efficient farmers. With the eventual capacity of farmers to supply food for more than one family, the door was open to cities, class stratification, and Bill Gates' 45,000-square-foot home.[49] And the opportunities that appeared may have functioned as superoptimal stimuli—if prestige or mates could be attracted with a few pounds of meat, what might one get for a 5-million-ton pyramid? Or for 3,400 pounds of Porsche 911 Turbo, or a few ounces of Patek Philippe Calibre 89 wristwatch (one of which sold for $2.9 million)?[50]

Superconsumption itself goes about as far back as does recorded human history, which began roughly halfway between the agricultural revolution and today. After about 3000 BC, the Egyptians gave up simple sand-pit burials and began to leave the first thoroughly documented record of wealthy classes consuming far beyond the capacity of most members of a society. The richest Egyptians, primarily the pharaohs, began building elaborate tombs, a practice that culminated in the construction of gigantic pyramids.[51] This reached a climax with the construction between 2589 and 2566 BC of the Great Pyramid of Khufu (Cheops to the Greeks), among the outstanding examples of conspicuous consumption of all time. The structure contained some 2.5 million two- to three-ton blocks and was constructed by Khufu's workers with phenomenal precision on a level base covering more than thirteen acres.[52]

Most of the stone for the Great Pyramid was quarried from the Giza plateau itself, but the fine, white, homogeneous limestone for the structure's cladding was quarried east of the Nile and brought across in boats (all Egyptian tombs were on the west side—the side of the setting sun, which was associated with death). The wood required for levers, sledges, and fuel had to be largely imported; the biggest timbers doubtless were cedars from Lebanon.

An idea of the income gap between the pharaoh and the average Egyptian can be seen in conservative calculations showing that the Great Pyramid was built in about twenty years by a paid labor force of 20,000 to 25,000 men. Few individuals in any society have had the power and money to mobilize in their service that sort of effort over such a long period. However it was built, Khufu's monument has already endured almost 5,000 years, and its traces may be detectable 10,000 to 100,000 or more years in the future.[53]

The effort commanded by Khufu's conspicuous consumption of resources was by no means unique in Egyptian civilization. The Egyptians believed not in reincarnation (rebirth in new bodies) but in resurrection—raising of the dead. That's why they simulated the natural mummification of early Egyptian sand-pit burials with ritual mummification, to ensure there would be a body to resurrect. Mummies were then buried, accompanied by everything an individual could afford to take along to supply the comforts enjoyed in this life over a much longer afterlife. That practice, along with successful translation of the huge hieroglyphic legacy of Egyptian civilization,[54] explains how we know so much about ancient Egyptians in general, and the tendency of their god-kings and other wealthy people to superconsume in particular.

Khufu, Rameses, Tutankhamen, and other Egyptian pharaohs had a huge advantage over John F. Kennedy, George H. W. Bush, George W. Bush, other wealthy modern political leaders, and the super-rich in general. They had no cause to hide their wealth and power from a public suspicious of the very rich. Consumption by the Egyptian pharaohs was truly and proudly conspicuous. So was the superconsumption of the proud rulers of Nineveh. The great and ruthless King Sennacherib (704–681 BC), in whose reign Nineveh became the capital of Assyria, "erected 'The palace without a rival,' a royal dwelling that outshone all others in splendor. It was so richly embellished with gold that 'the whole city shone like the sun.'"[55]

More than two millennia later, the 1990s were also an era of superconsumption, but with a much larger number of wealthy consumers. Various factors have been suggested as driving the rush to be superconsumers in the 1990s. One factor is that the individuals with the highest incomes in the United States are largely those who have enjoyed disproportionate growth in their incomes. The sources of the income have varied: wildly exorbitant salaries of corporate executives; huge salaries and bonuses paid to Wall Street operators (in 1997–1998, about a thousand got bonuses of more than $1 million); cash-outs of new dot-com multimillionaires and Enron-style crooks; gigantic salaries for sports and rock stars; rewards reaped by the already well-off from the 1990s stock market bubble; and so on. Other founts of ready cash, though at a smaller individual scale, were those of middle-class baby boomers who finally got their kids through college and found money suddenly available. All of this produced a lot of surplus buying power looking for something to buy—and the behavior of the rich and near rich sets the consumption pace.

Unfortunately, it seems unlikely that income disparities between the superconsumers and the rest of us mere overconsumers will do anything but increase. A persuasive case has been made by social scientists Robert Frank and Philip Cook that the industrialized countries, especially the United States and Britain, and to a lesser extent some developing countries such as Brazil, China, and Indonesia, are becoming "winner-take-all societies."[56] Winner-take-all markets are those in which the pay for marginally superior performers is vastly greater than it is for the also-rans. Ballet is a classic example: superb performers who are not quite as good as the prima ballerina are relegated to minor roles or to the chorus and paid a pittance. As movies and satellite television transmissions allow actors to perform for larger and larger (now virtually global) audiences, the number of people who can make a living by acting declines. Furthermore, the cadre of superstars itself shrinks, such that recently Julia Roberts could command at least three times the salary of any other female star. Similarly, Frank and Cook point out, a century ago there were many thousands of opera houses in the United States alone, employing thousands of tenors; now everyone can listen to Luciano Pavarotti in his prime on a CD, and it's difficult for a tenor 95 percent as good as Pavarotti to make a living in a vastly diminished number of opera houses.

Frank and Cook claim that the kinds of winner-take-all markets that once were largely confined to sports, the arts, and entertainment have increasingly spread to other professions, such as investment banking, corporate management, fashion design, surgery, law, and so on. The rise to dominance of Wal-Mart among discount chain stores is an excellent example, as are best sellers in book publishing, which account for a huge proportion of sales. All this engenders more super-rich, superconsuming individuals, the winners who are lauded and serve as role models for a mass society of wannabes.

## The Price of Overconsumption
## and Superconsumption

Ancient Egypt had a single growing season, timed to the annual flooding of the Nile. That meant that during off-season months the large agricultural labor force could be employed in building pyramids. Furthermore, Egyptian agriculture was so productive that many people were freed of the need to produce food and instead could become artisans to produce the stunning goods and art objects consumed by the rich. Whether superconsumption by rich Egyptians had the same kinds of negative social effects that superconsumption in the United States has today can only be guessed. But it is hard to imagine that the simple housing, water supplies, and bread-and-beer diets of most of the population would not have been improved if the rich had capped the size of pyramids at 10,000 tons, limited the amount of funerary goods that could accompany an individual to the next world, and distributed the freed surplus directly or by creating infrastructure and provision of services for the majority of Egyptians.

As Robert Frank put it, in the context of modern America, "paying for luxury consumption has also meant having to curtail spending in the public sphere."[57] Tax cuts for the rich may encourage more purchases of superexpensive cars, but they limit the availability of funds to repair the potholes in the roads those cars must drive on. There is, after all, no such thing as a free lunch.

Critics such as Frank are primarily concerned about the social inequities and crumbling infrastructure that have accompanied superconsumption. Others have begun to register concern about supply constraints as shortages of natural gas become manifest in North America and the global peak of petroleum production appears imminent.[58] These realities make even more problematic the aspirations of developing nations to provide energy and power to their citizens, who now have little or none at their disposal.

The story of gasoline consumption, discussed earlier, is a case in point. If the average fuel consumption of private vehicles and the materials used in their construction were both reduced by half, those changes alone would substantially reduce the assault on our life-support systems. Of course, there are limits to what technological advances can do: if the number of cars were to keep increasing world-wide, the aggregate assault on the environment would soon surpass today's level.

The same goes for the average size and number of homes per capita, a factor related to household size. Factors important here include the "footprint" of the home; a three-story, 5,000-square-foot home will occupy less land and, other things being equal, have a smaller environmental impact than a single-story home of the same square footage. More, larger, and less compact homes also require more energy for heating and cooling.

## Can We Stop Consuming So Much?

Dealing with the problems of overconsumption and superconsumption in the United States is extremely difficult, given that many powerful people—and not just people who are impervious to environmental concerns—believe the economy owes its health to the actions of consumers. At the annual meeting of the Society of Environmental Journalists in Baltimore in 2002, Maryland's governor, Parris N. Glendening, addressed the group. He had a good environmental record, but he said, and obviously believed, that it was essential to keep the economy growing.[59]

If humanity is to have a decent future, we all will have to reconsider such attitudes and the behavior accompanying them—to make major changes in the victorious ideology of the past century or so. That will be no small task, considering that it means we must, in part, redefine ourselves. Consumerism has delivered great benefits to a substantial portion of humanity, benefits that clearly have enormous appeal to most of the rest, who are increasingly aware of the lifestyles others have attained. Not only are we in the world's rich nations going to have to retreat from many aspects of our consumerism, but also the poor will necessarily need to modify their dreams of emulating us. Tough goals, to say the least.

But there are some factors that weigh in favor of success. As we have seen, ever-increasing consumption has not led to ever-increasing happiness. There have been minor rebellions against rampant consumerism, as in the voluntary simplicity movement and phenomena such as green labeling (certification of an environmentally benign origin of products). And, perhaps most important, the negative environmental and social consequences related to unfettered American consumerism—suburban sprawl; deteriorating roads, bridges, and schools; degradation of national parks and forests; the growing gap between rich and poor—are increasingly being noticed.[60]

Leading people to recognize those negative effects and presenting viable alternative visions for the future, we believe, holds the most promise of effecting the necessary change of attitude, especially in the United States. (We focus here on the United States because it is Americans who are indulging in the greatest consumption binge and because Americans' behavior serves so much as a model for the rest of the world.)

The crowning achievement of U.S. consumerism in the twentieth century was to provide virtually every American with a motor vehicle, many of them now sport utility vehicles. Not only is the car-centered society emblematic of overconsumption; the automobile may also be the single most environmentally destructive device on the planet. Mass transportation suffered greatly as the United States was converted to the service of the car. Between 1923 and 1940, streetcar rides dropped from 15.7 billion annually to 8.3 billion.[61] By the 1950s, the entire nature of the country was being transformed from urban and rural to urban-suburban, with vast numbers of suburban dwellers commuting by automobile to their urban places of employment.

It took about sixty years for the automobile takeover to be fully accomplished; the next sixty (better yet, thirty or forty) years could be spent on the re-conquest. It could be started with a steady increase in gasoline taxes, with the revenue being earmarked for the development of modern, safe, efficient mass transit systems connecting suburbs and city centers. Safe bicycle routes and sidewalks could be part of the plan. The railroad system could be rebuilt and expanded to serve cities short distances apart—routes that have been served increasingly poorly, if at all, by the airlines, primarily because serving those routes is economically (and energetically) a losing proposition for them.

Overhauling the American transportation system to reduce the population's environmental footprint effectively would involve complex planning and coordination among the various transport modes. Revision of land-use planning activities would also be needed. The mix could include systems of subsidies and taxes that would promote small-footprint high-rise dwellings near both workplaces and transit lines; security systems that would make mass transit nearly crime-free; restructuring of political units to avoid sprawl-inducing tax considerations,[62] and a campaign to wean Americans from the idea that a big, fancy car reflects a high-quality owner.

Such profound changes would not be easy to make, since an estimated one-sixth of the U.S. workforce is in some way dependent on making, selling, and provisioning automobiles or on building the infrastructure that gives them paved access to most of the country. Past attempts to change the transportation system in an environmentally and humanly benign direction have largely failed. Big corporations that sell automobiles, fuel, tires, or auto parts, or that build and repair roads, will doubtless continue to resist the re-conquest fiercely, supported by many of their employees.

To have a successful re-conquest will almost certainly require significant changes in attitudes and governance, some of which we'll discuss later. But some aspects will automatically favor the changes. One is that they would allow urban planners to give free rein to imaginations long confined to finding band-aid solutions for the car-strangled cancers our cities have become. And people would be healthier and less stressed. Many commuters could be reading newspapers on their way to work (or on their way to shop in refurbished city centers) in quiet trains and enjoying a glass of chardonnay on the way home. Many others could be walking or biking to work, adding years to their life and sleeping more soundly. Still others would be working from home in housing clusters designed for telecommuters. All this would surely be much nicer than crawling along bumper-to-bumper on a smog-choked freeway!

Fortunately, the schlock construction of many of today's strip malls and slums-of-tomorrow housing developments will make them more than ready for demolition in the next few decades. Restoration ecology could flourish as some of those maldeveloped areas are reconverted into something resembling natural ecosystems that could help cleanse the air, reduce flooding, purify water, shade and cool neighborhoods, and make living generally more pleasant. In the future, automobiles should be superefficient and retained for jobs they do exceptionally well—for instance, for family vacations in locations not well served by bullet trains or as secluded places where teenagers can make love (using condoms, of course).

Such a re-conquest would be an undertaking worth trying as people become more aware of the costs that the nation's (and world's) environment pays for an auto-commuting society, to say nothing of the social and economic costs, including the huge cost incurred in attempts to exercise control over foreign sources of petroleum. The time spent in the transition necessarily would be long enough that the economic burdens could be eased. The process might be helped along if prices of gasoline and natural gas continue to rise as they have in the first few years of this century. The technical challenges of managing the transition would be many, but some tactics are rather obvious. Some automobile manufacturing, maintenance, and support capacity could be switched to the manufacture, maintenance, and support of buses, trains, and bicycles. Many of the jobs phased out would not need to be replaced once the United States was moving toward a smaller population size and a less hectic lifestyle, with more time for leisure and community activities.

If the United States were to take such a route to "redesigning the country," no doubt other nations would follow suit. Most important, this might encourage developing countries *not* to turn their societies over to self-propelled, energy-guzzling metal boxes but instead to use energy-efficient automobiles as convenient tools for transportation only where they have real advantages over feet, bikes, urban mass transit, trains, planes, and boats.

## The Role of the Rich Nations

The key to putting on a "consumption condom" thus clearly lies in the overdeveloped nations and especially the United States. They are the main locus of the overconsumption problem,[63] and solutions they find will very likely be emulated and adopted, when appropriate, by developing nations. At the moment, far from actively helping those nations take a new path, the conspicuously rich are encouraging overconsumption, often provided by outdated, inefficient (and thus more environmentally destructive) technologies.

Traditions already in place that could help in tackling this problem are both customs and sumptuary laws (laws limiting private expenditures on extravagance) designed to reduce excessive consumption or at least restrict it to those able and willing to pay a very high price for it. In the United States, the excesses of conspicuous consumption displayed by the super-rich in the late nineteenth and early twentieth centuries led, by the middle of the twentieth century, to a middle-class consumption ethos among the wealthy. Huge mansions staffed by numerous servants were eschewed, and the rich were becoming, in the words of Kevin Phillips, "'inconspicuous consumers' either suffering from a guilt complex or afraid of giving visible offense."[64]

In the West, leading economic thinkers, from Adam Smith and Alfred Marshall to Milton Friedman and Kenneth Arrow, have pushed for consumption taxes, and virtually all front-rank economists now agree that taxing consumption rather than income is the smart way to go.[65] Indeed, most European nations now tax consumption via a value-added tax (VAT), basically a national sales tax on manufactured products, usually a little less than 20 percent. In 1995, a consumption tax bill was actually introduced in the United States Senate to replace the present income tax. That proposed USA (Unlimited Savings Allowance) tax would be a progressive income tax (one in which the rich pay a higher percentage of income tax than do the poor) that exempts all savings from the tax, thus focusing on income used for consumption.[66]

Robert Frank makes a persuasive case for the use of a graduated tax on consumption as a way of lowering incentives for people to engage in rat-race consumptive behavior; of increasing the savings rate, thereby strengthening the economy; and of diverting resources toward needed improvements in infrastructure. The details of his plan needn't concern us here—basically, people would be taxed on the difference between their annual earnings and their annual savings, and the tax would be progressive.[67]

Frank's proposal for a tax on consumption really focuses on an externality related to consumption. Those who consume more create more envy and make others feel worse off, so this consumption tax improves efficiency. One great advantage of such a system, however, could also be its Achilles heel. A simple consumption tax doesn't require the government to determine which goods are socially desirable and which ones aren't. Such a tax doesn't attempt to influence the *composition* of consumption as does a luxury tax. But from the standpoint of maintaining humanity's critical natural capital, influencing the composition of consumption is exactly the goal. Ten million dollars spent on a Van Gogh painting is conspicuous consumption with negligible environmental impact; the same amount spent on buying and flying a private jet aircraft would contribute significant environmental damage.

Certain consumption taxes, specifically designed to internalize externalities (include social costs in market prices) are called Pigovian taxes by economists, after welfare economist Arthur Cecil Pigou, who first proposed them.[68] A Pigovian tax might be a gasoline tax designed to encourage people to shift from cars to alternative forms of transport. A tax on electric appliances that was higher on inefficient models would also be Pigovian. Both would help to capture social costs of energy generation or use not now included in the price of gas or electricity. By internalizing externalities, such taxes improve market efficiency. VATs are not Pigovian, since they are blanket taxes, not explicitly targeted to influence externalities. VATs can be very regressive, hitting the poor harder than the rich, as can Pigovian taxes unless carefully designed.

In contrast, ordinary taxes, such as personal income taxes, corporate taxes, and sales taxes, do not generally address externalities. As a result, ordinary taxes tend to distort markets and make them less efficient.[69] But efficiency here has a limited sense; an efficient market maximizes the gains (satisfaction) of the winners minus the losses of the losers. There is no consideration of distributional effects. A market could be efficient even if it led to an Enron executive "winner" being able to afford a gold toilet and an Enron former employee "loser" struggling to buy junk food. In the view of most thoughtful economists (and other human beings), it is important to consider both efficiency and distribution in regulating markets.

An indiscriminate consumption tax is therefore a blunt instrument. A preliminary way to sharpen the instrument might be to combine a progressive consumption tax with some form of progressive (Pigovian) energy-use tax. Economists generally tend to favor a carbon tax—a tax on fuels to increase their price on the basis of the amount of $CO_2$ they emit. Carbon taxes are designed to discourage wasteful use of fossil fuels, especially high $CO_2$ emitters such as coal, and to encourage technological improvements that increase the yield of services per unit of fuel burned. Since energy use, especially use of energy derived from fossil fuels, is central to virtually all of humanity's assaults on its own life-support systems, more general taxes on it would be appropriate.

In economic terms, the goal is to bring market prices in line with social costs. The details of the taxes needn't concern us here; the complexities of minimizing the disruption and inequities often caused by badly designed taxes can be, and are being, worked out by economists such as our colleague Larry Goulder.[70] The basic strategy is to combine Pigovian taxes and revenue recycling to produce the desired social result.[71] For instance, a high gasoline tax (say, a few dollars per gallon, phased in over several years), constructed to encourage a redesign of the transportation system and land-use patterns in the United States, would be an insurmountable burden to people who now must commute perhaps two hours each way by car to low-paying jobs. But if the huge revenues from that Pigovian tax were recycled by eliminating much or all of the extremely regressive FICA[72] (Social Security and Medicare) taxes, those commuters could be kept in the workforce, and the redesign might even allow them to find work nearer home.

The use of taxes as tools to control the adverse effects of consumption has two great advantages. One is that individual consumers, not government bureaucrats, make the ultimate consumption decisions. The role of the taxes that we have in mind (besides raising revenue for the government) would be to limit environmental damage by incorporating its costs into the prices of the items or services consumed. The higher prices then presumably would discourage the purchase of those items or services. Moreover, to garner political support, the revenue could be used to repair damage or compensate affected individuals. The Van Gogh painting carries close to zero external cost, so there seems little reason, on environmental grounds, to tax Van Gogh paintings. The jet plane, on the other hand, has a wide variety of external environmental impacts associated with its construction and operation, ranging from pollution stemming from aluminum mining and smelting and fuel consumption to its share in the costs of constructing airport facilities and operating the air traffic control system. But a person who could afford to do so would remain free to "consume" the pleasure of owning the Van Gogh or the convenience of the jet.

The other great advantage of using taxes to influence consumption is that they are familiar instruments, with social structures already in place to collect them. They can be instituted with the stroke of a pen, and, if they fail to produce the desired social results, they can be altered or removed in the same way. In this respect, they contrast with speculative technological schemes such as dumping iron filings in the ocean to "cure" global warming. The iron putatively would work through a fertilizing effect, encouraging the growth of algae and photosynthesizing bacteria, which would remove $CO_2$ from the atmosphere and sequester it in ocean depths. Several such vast geochemical experiments have been proposed to counter the effects of greenhouse gases.[73] They tend to be expensive, highly uncertain in their effects (which might be disastrous), and often utterly irreversible (think of trying to remove the filings from the sea). Taxes are a far more attractive and less risky instrument of policy change. It is a pity that the right wing has so demonized taxes that a sea change in public opinion will be required to make them much more effective tools for efficiently protecting our life-support systems.

Finally, we can imagine carefully designed taxes helping to reduce the contribution that the accumulation of surplus wealth makes to the weakening of liberal democracy. Wealth far beyond that required to live a fulfilling and secure life is often used not only to superconsume but also to wield disproportionate political power—for good or for ill (often depending on one's viewpoint!). In a media-saturated nation, wealth-based power has contorted a one-person, one-vote system into a one-person, one-*million*-votes (or one-million-dollars, one-million-votes) system. The disproportionate influence of wealthy donors from major industries on legislative and administrative decisions is notorious.

The time may be ripe for more public discourse on the ethical implications of surplus wealth in the United States because of the CEO scandals. Is it ethical, for example, for the twenty chief executive officers with the highest salaries to average $50 million annually when that includes, as Jim Hightower wrote, "several who drove their companies straight into bankruptcy, sank their shareholders' stock value to worthless levels, and presently are under criminal investigation"?[74] Probably of greater concern, as a cynical friend of ours commented, are those who are *not* under investigation. Charitably assuming an eighty-hour workweek for fifty weeks a year, $50 million per year works out to $12,500 per hour in CEO wages, in a country where many Americans are struggling to get by on $6 or $7 per hour.[75] These top dogs get about 2,000 times as much as the working poor, but overall, CEOs in the United States average only about 200 times the compensation of their employees. That may explain why the George W. Bush administration thought the CEOs and other overpaid executives needed a tax break. Such concentrations of money, and thus of the power not just to super-consume but to continue concentrating wealth and power, might be countered with the institution of a surplus wealth tax.[76]

## Action on the International Scene

Lester Pearson, former prime minister of Canada and president of the United Nations General Assembly, said in 1969: "A planet cannot, any more than a country, survive half slave, half free, half engulfed in misery, half careening along toward the supposed joys of almost unlimited consumption. Neither our ecology nor our morality could survive such contrasts."[77] As we have seen, those differences, now far greater than they were three decades ago, have grim environmental consequences; they also are causing people increasingly to question the morality of the current world system. And the relatively powerless who do the questioning sometimes turn to terrorism.

In the long run, understanding the connection between overconsumption and terrorism would help America economically, environmentally, militarily, and ethically. It is one more very good reason why the United States and other rich nations should move as rapidly as possible toward energy-efficient economies that minimize, and perhaps eventually eliminate, dependence on imported oil and gas. At the same time, much more effort should be put into limiting wasteful consumption of all resources and narrowing the rich-poor gap.[78] By finding ways to restrain their own aggregate overconsumption, wealthy nations could help themselves and the rest of the world. By setting an example and raising global public perceptions of fairness, they could enhance what Joseph Nye Jr., of Harvard University's John F. Kennedy School of Government, calls their "soft power." Soft power is getting what you want by behaving in ways that make others want to emulate you; it derives from the quality of your culture, particularly its values and institutions.[79] It played a substantial role in the successes of France in the eighteenth century, Britain in the nineteenth, and the United States in the twentieth. But in the initial years of the twenty-first century, the United States government may have squandered much of the good will the nation had previously earned.

We might win back much of that good will by adopting a consistent policy of promoting, rather than suppressing, the modernization of developing societies. Today, the United States and other industrialized nations give development aid and support humanitarian activities through international agencies while at the same time encouraging exploitation of poor nations' resources by multinational corporations and conducting trade policies that undermine those generous efforts. Just by insisting that U.S.-based multinationals apply in developing countries the same environmental protection and labor relations practices (not necessarily wages) that are required domestically, the United States could earn important points in the world prestige game. Rich nations could also gain by being less protective of corporate interests and more willing to share technologies and work for fair trade practices. As one example, the industrialized nations could help both ends of the economic spectrum by creating new markets for their energy- and resource-efficient technological advances. Indeed, this is being practiced by some European and Japanese companies and by some American companies, but so far with little or no support or encouragement from the U.S. government.

What is really needed is a powerful rededication to the goal of helping developing countries, especially the poorest ones, to modernize and become economically viable. While setting an example as a global citizen, the United States should also bolster its pathetic level of international aid, carefully targeting much of that aid on efforts to improve social and demographic conditions (e.g., increasing employment and helping to lower fertility rates) in developing countries. Aid for education, particularly of women, and for development of labor-intensive enterprises, with care to minimize the creation of sweatshop conditions, are two examples. Such efforts might well speed the transition of population sizes everywhere toward more satisfactory and sustainable levels.[80] They would especially help the least developed nations, which need it most, especially in sub-Saharan Africa; however, major progress toward modernization would require a serious international effort through government foreign aid, United Nations agencies, or the World Bank.

Success will require innovation, vigilance, international cooperation, and unwavering diplomacy, and it will not be achieved overnight. But that is all the more reason for changing American attitudes, announcing our good intentions, and showing the changes to be genuine by getting started right now.

The current situation on the consumption front was eloquently summarized a decade ago by David Korten, a distinguished specialist in organizational structures: "No sane person seeks a world divided between billions of excluded people living in absolute deprivation and a tiny elite guarding their wealth and luxury behind fortress walls. No one rejoices at the prospect of life in a world of collapsing social and ecological systems. Yet we continue to place human civilization and even the survival of our species at risk mainly to allow a million or so people to accumulate money beyond any conceivable need. We continue to go boldly where no one wants to go."[81]

# Chapter *8*

## A CULTURE OUT OF STEP

> "A long-run vision, as it were, of the deep crisis which
> faces mankind may predispose people to taking more
> interest in the immediate problems and to devote more
> effort for their solution. This may sound like a rather
> modest optimism, but perhaps a modest optimism is
> better than no optimism at all."
> KENNETH E. BOULDING, 1966[1]

LET US ENVISION a world in which diverse societies will be able to
last for centuries without disruption by serious internal strife, war,
or environmental disaster. How could a transition to such a
peaceful and sustainable world be accomplished? A first step would
seem to be to develop awareness of the discrepancy between the way
society is now organized and the basic goals most people share. We
must be cautious in characterizing those goals, to avoid as far as possible
mistaking our own goals, those acquired from our culture,[2] for more or
less human universals. A starting point for considering basic goals for
a sustainable civilization might be the statement of the "four freedoms" expressed by Franklin D. Roosevelt more than six decades ago:

In the future days which we seek to make secure, we look forward to a
world founded upon four essential human freedoms. The first is freedom
of speech and expression—everywhere in the world. The second is freedom of every person to worship God in his own way—everywhere in the
world. The third is freedom from want, which, translated into world

terms, means economic understandings which will secure to every nation a healthy peacetime life for its inhabitants—everywhere in the world. The fourth is freedom from fear, which, translated into world terms, means a world-wide reduction of armaments to such a point and in such a thorough fashion that no nation will be in a position to commit an act of physical aggression against any neighbor—anywhere in the world.[3]

The need for freedom from want and fear (thrill-seeking aside) is biologically based and can safely be considered a universal value. If freedom of religion is translated as freedom to believe whatever one wishes, that might also be a universal human desire, but others would argue, along with Adolf Hitler, that many, if not most, people crave strong leadership, someone to tell them what to believe.[4] The desire for freedom of speech is similarly suspect as a human universal. It has been valued in Western tradition at least since the golden age of Athens (when freedom of speech was awarded only to adult male Athenian citizens), but it may not be so highly valued by individuals raised in, say, Chinese culture.

So here we'll assume that most people would consider that a central role of their society is to provide them (and their descendants) dependably with access to food, clothing, and shelter and to protect them from enemies, domestic and foreign. And it can be argued that at least half of all human beings receive those things from their societies. Advances in some countries, such as China, however, are uneven; freedom from want may be increasing, for example, but freedom from fear may still be a distant goal.

But, regardless of their views of various freedoms, all societies function within cultural parameters, and, as we hope we've convinced you, never before in history have most human cultures been so maladapted to the biophysical realities of our planet.[5] Furthermore, like the technological systems we rely upon, the world itself is becoming a more complex, tightly coupled, and arguably dangerous place. Unfortunately, the scientific community has proven remarkably ineffectual at communicating what it understands about the dangers to society at large, in part perhaps because most people don't want to hear the message. Thus, politicians who don't know a kilobyte from a kilobase from a kilowatt from a kiloton are making decisions that affect all of our futures, and many leaders of society remain oblivious to the collision course with nature that scientists warn we are on.

This cultural disconnect between what people think is going on and the scientific evaluation of their situations has developed very recently. *Homo sapiens* has come a long way from the time, now some ten millennia in the past, when every normal adult human being was the repository of nearly the entire culture of his or her society. Even three centuries ago, the vast majority of people were still much closer to that state. Disaster may have been just around the corner, but everyone knew as much (or as little) about it as everyone else.

In the past few centuries, though, cultures have changed with unprecedented speed, in unprecedented ways, to produce an unprecedented situation. Today in technological societies, culture—the information not stored in our genes but embodied in our brains, books, films, CDs, paintings, structures, stories, customs, art objects, computer databases, satellite images, electron micrographs, and so on[6]— has become vast almost beyond belief. A 747 jetliner embodies much more information (that is, knowledge or meaningful structure) than all of the DNA packed into its pilots' cells. No human being in a modern technological society is the possessor of even one-millionth of his or her culture's information. The transition to this state of ubiquitous cultural ignorance has occurred in an evolutionary blink of the eye, and humanity is having great difficulty dealing with it.[7] It's now commonplace for "well-educated" individuals to be utterly unaware of critical aspects of their changing environment.

## New Dimensions of Power

The evidence the scientific community has amassed on humanity's peril is overwhelming,[8] and its interpretation is clear to those who care to consider it. Only a few seem interested at present. Yet the issue is not one that can be put off; our children's and grandchildren's quality of life will surely depend on the actions we take now.

Why, then, has there been no determined action by leaders of the

United States, the world's leader in science, to encourage smaller families and restrict dangerous consumption? It can be summed up in that
one important word we have used a great deal already—*power.* Power is
what permitted Khufu to get his pyramid built and General Dwight
Eisenhower to defeat the world's best-trained army in Normandy.
And power is what keeps population limitation and consumption control off the political agenda of the United States and access to petroleum near the top of the nation's priority list.

Great power is something relatively new in the organization of
human societies—a feature of the last two-tenths of 1 percent of the 5
million years of human history.[9] Hunter-gatherer societies were relatively egalitarian, the principal differentiations often being those
based on physical traits connected with age and gender.[10] The agricultural revolution, starting some 10,000 years ago, gave rise to stratified
societies that today have massive inequalities in access to power.[11]
Stratification in modern, nominally democratic industrial societies,
with many levels of education and skills, a division of labor exemplified
by a plethora of specialists, and a heavy burden of well-placed but relatively useless managers and manipulators in the private sector,[12] leads
to extremely complex and difficult-to-evaluate power relationships.
The rich, of course, have much more political power than the poor, but
that's not where it ends. Judges have power over chief executive officers; university professors, over rich students. But sports stars, media
moguls, business executives, stock market analysts, corporate lawyers,
religious leaders, and many others (including some prominent professors) can have power not easily measured by their specialist positions,
though it is usually related to the institutions in which they function.

Industrial societies, in turn, create international power differences
in part through economic leverage and in part through their possession of advanced technologies, especially weapons technology. A U.S.
Army special forces unit equipped with Predator unmanned surveil-
lance aircraft is vastly more powerful than a force of Afghan fighters,
even if the latter are armed with Kalashnikov rifles imported from
another high-tech society. But the power relationship holds only if the
Afghans are willing to fight by the same rules as the Americans (which

they are not). The rapid cultural evolution of technology has produced new dimensions of power that create disparities so great that they are virtually different in kind from those of just a century or so ago. The United States, with its extensive military forces and thousands of nuclear weapons, is now by far the most powerful nation in the world. And a powerful segment of American society, imagining they have a superior moral culture, want to use that unprecedented power to create a rejuvenated post–cold war American empire, most recently under the leadership of George W. Bush.[13]

Like all the power relations of history, this one will not be eternal; indeed, compared with the duration of those in which ancient Egypt was enmeshed, the life span of the relatively new American empire may be just a passing moment. The United States may already be rapidly replaying a pattern that helped lead to the downfall of the Roman Empire almost two millennia earlier. The military of the American empire now leans heavily on technological "mercenaries" (smart bombs, carrier battle groups, nuclear missiles) and soldiers drawn heavily from relatively disenfranchised elements of society—blacks, Latinos, poor whites, and in some cases legions from coerced allies.[14] The Romans increasingly depended on barbarian mercenaries to man their legions as the empire declined. The personal involvement of the Roman elite in actual combat likewise declined—Caesar led his troops in battle; Nero did not. Claudius had a faux campaign in Britain,[15] complete with an elephant. He paraded up and down the beach collecting seashells and the like, which he took back home as booty. It was the first-century equivalent of prancing on the deck of an aircraft carrier in a military costume you haven't earned.

## Getting to Know a World of Wounds

The Anjouan experience we described in chapter 3 was an extreme instance of nearly ubiquitous environmental deterioration, the consequences of the mismatch between the dominant culture's view of the world and the world as revealed by scientific analysis.[16] To ecologists, environmental devastation is one of the most depressing facts of life, and their experience with it generally is long-standing. Many, if not most, ecologists began immersing themselves in nature as children. One can understand the human predicament intellectually by simply examining the literature, but ecologists usually have also gained a vivid emotional understanding through their fieldwork.

Many of the things that attract tourists from developed nations to the less developed world are disappearing, and ecotourists are less and less likely to see anything that resembles unaltered habitat. The truth is, of course, that there is no truly natural habitat left. All of Earth's surface has been influenced by *Homo sapiens*. As described earlier, much of the world has been grossly altered by deforestation, human-caused wildfires, erosion, cities and infrastructure, wetland drainage, dams, river canalization, and so on. More subtle but nearly ubiquitous changes have also been wrought by people transporting organisms to places where they did not naturally occur. Through habitat destruction and overharvesting, humanity has dramatically changed the communities of organisms found in virtually every region. The best "birding" we found in late 1996 in lowland West Java, for example, was in the Pamulka Passarum caged bird market in Jakarta, with perhaps 60,000 individuals of some 160 species, captured both legally and illegally.[17] The countryside around that Indonesian capital was, in contrast, remarkably devoid of land birds. Even places that look totally pristine have felt the influence of our species through climate change and the deposition of synthetic chemical compounds and novel radioactive isotopes generated by nuclear weapons testing and use.

It's not just ecotourists who find that what they go to see is disappearing. Increasingly, tourists visiting developing countries find only the crowded open-air markets selling mass-produced junk, squalid temples, run-down palaces, and other signs of poverty that make up the obligatory "city tours." There is little chance to make contact with the marvelous cultural diversity that was once one of humanity's great resources; that too is rapidly disappearing. So many people visited the Lascaux Cave in southern France, with its fabulous prehistoric paintings, that it was forced to close. The moisture from the breathing of thousands of tourists was causing the paintings to deteriorate. Now visitors must make do with Lascaux II, a magnificent re-creation, but a re-creation nonetheless.

The world is losing key components of its precious biological and cultural diversity, globally and very rapidly. McDonald's and CNN are everywhere. In Jerry Mander's words, we're moving rapidly toward a "global monoculture."[18] Over the next decades, terrorism permitting, international travel may become even easier for those who can afford it, at least to those areas where political stability makes it advisable. But there will be less and less incentive for doing it, so those with the most influence may become even more insulated from increasing numbers of poor people and the deteriorating state of the world's ecosystems. The disconnect between culture and the facts of life will then be even greater. Museum collections can travel; natural wonders can be preserved on videotape or disk and enjoyed in one's living room without the risk of falciparum malaria or other resurgent diseases that are now ravaging much of the globe.[19] Virtual reality seems to be arriving at just the right time, as real reality is being phased out.

The present situation underlines Aldo Leopold's famous statement of decades ago: "One of the penalties of an ecological education is that one lives alone in a world of wounds.... An ecologist must either harden his shell and make believe that the consequences of science are none of his business, or he must be the doctor who sees the marks of death in a community that believes itself well and does not want to be told otherwise."[20] The marks are evident the world over: we are unraveling the very fabric of life. Our culture is out of step with the biophysical realities of what is required to perpetuate it. As the world scientists warned, humanity is indeed on a collision course with the natural world.[21]

Recognition of that course is utterly critical to humanity's future well-being, yet most people are unaware of it. That is one important form of environmental ignorance. But there is another as well: lack of knowledge about, and intelligent public discussion of, policies and practices that might provide effective ways to repair the fabric, and even make those of us alive today—not just future generations—better off.

## Promoting Environmental Ignorance

That lack of awareness is no accident. It is rooted in two kinds of power. The first is the power that government and pressure groups exercise directly through the control of information. The second kind of power is that wielded to keep most elementary, high school, and college education partial and often second-rate. A classic example of direct control came in 1980, late in the Jimmy Carter administration, when *The Global 2000 Report to the President*,[22] prepared by the Council on Environmental Quality and the U.S. Department of State, was published. It contained a version of the same message that was later embodied in the two 1993 scientists' warnings. Its letter of transmittal to President Carter stated:

> Our conclusions . . . are disturbing. They indicate the potential for global problems of alarming proportions by the year 2000. Environmental, resource, and population stresses are intensifying and will increasingly determine the quality of human life on our planet. . . . At the same time, the earth's carrying capacity—the ability of biological systems to provide resources for human needs—is eroding. The trends suggest strongly a progressive degradation and impoverishment of the earth's natural resource base.[23]

The incoming Ronald Reagan administration promptly destroyed all the copies of the report it could and ignored its recommendations, actions that helped retard needed progress and left the current generation with an unnecessarily larger task of remediation. Such denial and direct control of information have been dramatically illustrated recently by the attempts of the George W. Bush administration to restrict or distort public knowledge of scientific findings, especially on population, environment, and health issues.[24] For example, the administration has altered government Web sites to slant information about reproductive health issues in a direction favored by the religious right. A Web page of the Centers for Disease Control once said, accurately, that there was no evidence that educating people about the use of condoms caused sexual activity to increase or to commence at a younger age. The Bush administration removed that statement, presumably to please "abstinence only" advocates—even though increased condom use is essential to reducing the incidence of sexually transmitted diseases, especially AIDS. Similarly, the news of a large Danish study, which found that "induced abortions have no overall effect on the risk of breast cancer," was deleted.[25]

The administration has also tampered with the makeup of scientific committees dealing with topics sensitive to its big-money backers or to Christian fundamentalists (especially in the area of abortion).[26] After the intervention of two organizations of major pesticide polluters, CropLife America (the cutely renamed American Crop Protection Association) and RISE (Responsible Industry for a Sound Environment), the latter a trade association of pesticide suppliers and producers, three of America's top experts on the health effects of pesticides on children were blocked from speaking at a conference for health-care professionals funded by the U.S. Environmental Protection Agency (EPA). The conference was postponed and the experts were not re-invited, even though many thousands of children are affected every year by pesticide poisoning.[27]

Such actions, of course, are nothing new. The pesticide industry and its supporters have a long history of trying to deceive the public about the toxicity (and efficacy) of its products, as has the chemical industry as a whole.[28] They have managed to toxify the entire planet,[29] have loaded our blood with a cocktail of synthetic organic chemicals whose interactions are unknown,[30] and have produced an absurd situation in which the burden of proof of damage to health or the environment rests not on those coating Earth with toxins but on individuals who suspect they have been directly affected. No precautionary principle— that is, no commitment of resources in advance to guard against future negative effects of a decision—here!

In general, polluting companies and their lobbyists have been supremely successful at exposing all of us to risks that we ourselves are required to discover. We then must prove any damages in court while being opposed by the lawyers hired by multi-billion-dollar industrial firms. Worse yet, individuals who use their free-speech rights and raise

issues of hazards to their own or environmental health are often subjected to SLAPP suits (strategic lawsuits against public participation)
by the polluters, charging them with slander, harassment, libel, or
interference with contracts, in an attempt to squelch any opposition.
Even though the company may not win, the costs of defense are so high
that critics are often silenced.

Some of the most important direct attacks on the environment
have been made by Gale Norton's U.S. Department of the Interior and
by the EPA under Christine Todd Whitman's direction. A 2003 report
by the Democratic Staff of the House Committee on Resources, not
written by friends of the administration but accurate, according to all
our other sources,[31] summed it up thus: "Over the past two years, the
Administration has ignored, manipulated, challenged, suppressed and
dictated scientific analysis in order to implement an agenda harmful to
the environment and to roll back Clinton-era protections."[32]

When Whitman resigned as head of the EPA in May 2003, Eric V.
Schaeffer, former director of the EPA's Office of Regulatory Enforcement, wrote: "In the last two years, important EPA decisions seemed
increasingly driven by forces outside the agency, degrading its reputa-
tion for integrity and independence. As a result, it currently markets
environmental policies that its own staff opposes, stonewalls inquiries
from skeptics in Congress and in the media and, at times, functions
like an extension of the White House's public relations machine."[33]

Jeremy Symons, former climate policy advisor for the EPA's Office
of Air and Radiation, chimed in: "When President Reagan pursued a
more overt agenda of undermining the EPA's ability to regulate industry, aggressive congressional oversight led to the resignation of EPA
head, Anne Gorsuch Burford.[34] Despite the similarly far-reaching
impact of the current administration's proposed rollbacks in clean
water and air protections, Congress has been largely held at bay, and
the public kept in the dark, by the White House's adroit control of
information."[35]

Although Whitman did eventually support some positive environmental initiatives, such as the Clinton administration's restrictions on
diesel exhaust and arsenic in drinking water, she gave up attempts to

limit the flow of carbon dioxide ($CO_2$) into the atmosphere, allowed
confined animal feeding operations (CAFOs) to pollute more, and
disabled laws requiring the installation of upgraded pollution controls
when old coal-fired power plants are expanded.[36] The administration
also tried to remove or curtail requirements for environmental review
and public comment on proposed logging, mining, drilling, and other
development projects in national forests, monuments, and reserves.[37]
The administration (and its largely captive Congress) talked a lot
about its concern for the environment while quietly allowing the fuel
economy of private cars in the United States to reach a twenty-two-
year low, pressing for oil drilling in the Arctic National Wildlife
Refuge, and pushing for a bill to allow business owners to deduct as
much as $86,000 of the cost of a new giant sport utility vehicle (more
than 6,000 pounds).[38] That's a federal income tax saving of more than
$33,000 for those in the top bracket. The government thus is subsi-
dizing waste and inefficiency (especially by the rich) while doing nothing to promote energy efficiency or to create transport systems that
would help wage earners who must commute to work. More socialism
for the rich and capitalism for the poor, all handled in ways that only
those who pay active attention to environmental policy would be likely
to notice.

The Bush administration has also used national military security as
a smoke screen to weaken national environmental security. It has tried
to exempt the military from many environmental rules, weakened corporate accountability by restricting access to firms' pollution records,
and instructed the U.S. Army Corps of Engineers not to disclose pollution (including oil spills) at its dam sites. The administration is also
withholding funds where they are desperately needed. As Craig Miller
of Defenders of Wildlife succinctly put it, the administration is "stran-
gling the Fish and Wildlife Service to stop endangered species programs."[39] And it has attempted to minimize awareness of all this activity by releasing news at times when press coverage would be minimal
(e.g., on weekends or around major holidays) and by developing
double-talk labeling in which logging of national forests became "thinning," logging of old growth was called the "Healthy Forests Initiative,"

and a rollback of regulations to reduce air pollution was announced as the "Clear Skies Initiative."[40] It's an easy time to be a curmudgeon.

The proof that the assessment by the staff of the House Committee on Resources was on target came in June 2003 when the Bush administration tried to manipulate an EPA report to distort the content on global warming. The administration wanted the report to neglect the consensus of the scientific community and give the false impression that uncertainty about climate change was so great that no action could be contemplated.[41] Its behavior was so egregious that eventually the EPA report came out with *no* statement on that key problem. Had the report appeared as originally drafted, it would have pointed out that U.S. $CO_2$ emissions had risen 17 percent in the previous ten years.

Russell Train, who headed the EPA in the Richard Nixon and Gerald Ford administrations, stated categorically that during that time he was never subjected to such interference by the White House. He said, "I can appreciate the president's interest in not having discordant voices within his administration. But the interest of the American people lies in having full disclosure of the facts, particularly when the issue is one with such potentially enormous damage to the long-term health and economic well-being of all of us."[42]

## Science and Public Education

Much more effective in the long run in keeping public awareness of environmental issues at a minimum, though, is the tactic of not struggling to rescue the deteriorating American educational system (while loudly claiming to do so). For politicians who want a free hand to enrich themselves and their buddies, to get re-elected despite failed policies, or to pursue dangerous or ignorant policies for any reason, the worst enemy is a well-educated, alert electorate. Education systems have been fraught with problems and have raised difficult issues since at least the time that Pericles decided (wrongly) that Athens' system was so superior to Sparta's that it would guarantee military victory.[43] Today, it is generally agreed by even the most ideological of politicians and their backers that education to provide literacy and mathematics and computer skills is a necessary underpinning of industrial society. But education systems that raise questions of life goals other than wealth and consumption, promote open discussion of sexual behavior and ethics, impart understanding of humanity's evolutionary history, examine flaws in our own political system, discuss the ways in which money and power constrain the free flow of information, carefully and evenhandedly examine the motives of our enemies, and avoid promoting organized religion are anathema to the Bush administration, as they have been to many others.

To be sure, really first-rate, open educational systems are also anathema to many citizens, school board members, teachers, educational administrators, and even some professors. Most Americans, like people everywhere, are rarely interested in examining the assumptions of their culture, concepts learned at their mother's knee and now from television. Indeed, many are threatened by the very idea. A most basic problem, we suspect, is the low value placed on learning (as opposed to the earning of degrees) in most American homes. But education that examines the cultural disconnect and what is happening to the natural world is precisely what is most needed today.

Responsibility for the disconnect between the common cultural view of where society is going and where it is actually headed rests in part with the lack of communication between scientists and society. It is a major barrier to a successful transition to a sustainable society. The deplorable ignorance of most Americans about science, and especially about its skeptical nature, is in no small part due to the difficulties of getting more competent teaching of the natural and social sciences firmly and broadly established in American schools and universities. We're not resolving the disconnect in formal educational systems, and we're certainly not resolving it in education of the general public through the media.

When scientists try to inform the public about today's environmental situation, the media are often the key to success. Members of the press are usually more sympathetic to environmental concerns than are most people, and better educated about their subtleties. But scientists frequently are ineffectual in communicating with the press and the public; they have never been trained to do so. That is especially sad, since most people are supportive of science; they realize that it's responsible for many of the good things in their lives and are curious about its findings. One of the bright lights on the horizon is that some members of the scientific community are now taking steps to improve the flow of information to the public by training scientists to communicate more effectively with the media and give clear, concise, understandable testimony before legislators. An outstanding example is the Aldo Leopold Leadership Program, established by leading ecologist (and past president of the American Association for the Advancement of Science) Jane Lubchenco. It has already graduated dozens of top environmental scientists.[44]

Still, the communication gap between scientists and citizens who support and value their work remains large. Besides a lack of sufficient knowledge about scientific findings, the public view of how science works is often based on misapprehensions. How often, for example, have we heard about an "absence of scientific proof" or an "absence of scientific certainty" on an issue as an excuse for inaction? Scientific proof (or certainty) is something that cannot exist, since science never "proves" anything. It does the best it can in trying to understand how the world works. But scientific conclusions are never certain or final—they can always be altered by new data, new experiments, new theory, or just new ideas. Scientists must constantly re-examine their assumptions. When some politician or public relations person says no action should be taken because there's no scientific proof, despite substantial evidence behind a scientific consensus, it's a safe bet the message really is "never take action."

One cause of the frequent misrepresentation of science is the press' pursuit of "balance," resulting in the treatment of scientific disputes as the same class of phenomena as differences of opinion between politicians. Journalists usually take the implicit position that there must be something in both viewpoints, that "the truth must lie somewhere in the middle." But science usually doesn't work that way; it doesn't discover compromise solutions to differences of opinion. Science suffers from an "elitism": better explanations displace worse ones. But it is an elitism based on experiment and systematic observation, theory, intense internal debate and competition, and the test of conclusions in the real world. In debates in the natural sciences, the truth almost never lies in the middle. Earth goes around the sun; both bodies don't go around each other. There is no phlogiston or even a compromise "phlog." As turn-of-the-twentieth-century physicists Albert Michelson and Edward Morley showed, there is no "ether" filling space whereby Earth could cause an "ether wind" as it travels (and no compromise "ether breeze" either!). And "intelligent design" is not a satisfactory middle ground between evolutionary theory and the oxymoronic "scientific creationism."[45]

For some complex issues, ongoing debate may make it perfectly reasonable for the press to present opposing views. But not always. Whether dangerous climate change could be caused by human activities is no longer debatable. The evidence that greenhouse gases are building up in the atmosphere and that climate change is a likely result is overwhelming, as is the consensus of the scientific community on the need for a measured response to the potential threat. The likely speed and magnitude of change and its precise global and regional consequences are uncertain enough, however, that the steps that should be taken to slow change *are* debatable, and presentation of opposing or varying views is imperative. The issue now is largely one of social science and practical policy: how can we best cope with the causes of climate change to reduce the odds of disastrous changes?[46]

The scientific enterprise generally works because scientists can enhance their reputations by revealing other scientists' mistakes, or can gain even more kudos by demolishing entire paradigms (as did Newton, Darwin, and Einstein). Frontline scientists are expected to be wrong sometimes, and there is no disgrace attached to it, since much progress is often made in the enterprise by correcting errors. But to gain respect and recognition, the heterodox scientist, one who disagrees with the dominant view in her field, must use careful reasoning, show deep knowledge of the orthodoxy with which she disagrees, thoroughly test her ideas, have her results critiqued by colleagues, and publish her conclusions in respected, peer-reviewed journals. You can be sure that any scientist who neglects that process and only appeals directly to the public to support his or her scientific claims is a charlatan.

Environmental scientists, environmental journalists, and environmentalists have learned many lessons from encounters with powerful people in industry and government who believe that environmental concerns are either trivial or threatening to their interests. Many, whose profitable activities create environmental problems, attempt to allay public concern by suppressing information about those problems. They use the mushroom-culture approach to informing the public on crucial issues: "keep 'em in the dark and feed 'em shit." One law of mushroom culture is that spokespeople can always be found to push their anti-environmental agenda as if it were science—to generate what is known as the "brownlash," a backlash against "green" policies.[47] Such distortions emanate from the misinformed staffs of public relations organizations such as the Competitive Enterprise Institute, the Heritage Foundation, the American Enterprise Institute, the George C. Marshall Institute, and the Cato Institute—organizations largely funded by far-right foundations.[48] And the Luntz Research Companies[49] produced a notorious detailed memo for Republican politicians on how to mislead the public about the environment and environmental policies—how to *sound* like an environmentalist while wrecking the environment. For example, ignoring the consensus of the Intergovernmental Panel on Climate Change (IPCC), Luntz advised Republican politicians: "Voters believe there is *no consensus* about global warming within the scientific community. Should the public come to believe that the scientific issues are settled, their views about global warming will change accordingly. Therefore, *you need to continue to make the lack of scientific* CERTAINTY *a primary issue in the debate*" (italics in original; caps added).[50] We highly recommend that everyone with an interest in environmental policy browse through the Luntz document—particularly noting the "Words That Work" boxes.

Of course, some individuals, who have made few, if any, intellectual contributions to an understanding of environmental problems on their own, have made names for themselves by attacking prominent environmental scientists and disagreeing with the consensus of the scientific community. In so doing, they have become heroes of those right-wing public relations organizations and are beloved of the editorial page staff of the *Wall Street Journal,* editors of the *Economist,* conservative politicians fighting to prevent environmental regulation from cutting into the short-term profits of their corporate supporters, and, to a lesser degree, some left-wing ideologues who fear that attention to environmental problems will divert public attention from their social agendas.

The recent Lomborg affair shows clearly how powerful interests, especially those that run media outlets, can promote these individuals in an effort to manipulate the way people see the world. Bjorn Lomborg, a Danish statistician, wrote a wide-ranging attack on environmental science and scientists, including us. It was an error-riddled book, full of selective and misleading examples that purported to demonstrate scientifically that concerns for the future of human life-support systems were misplaced. Among myriad examples, he ignored the central environmental issue of ecosystem services, claimed that Paul and Edward O. Wilson of Harvard University were supporters of a non-existent plan to move all Americans to make way for wilderness, and reported statistics on the extinction of forest birds in the eastern United States that were totally at variance with the published facts.[51] Lomborg's tract was greeted with joy by right-wing commentators, and it hoodwinked much of the journalistic community.[52] The book gained momentum by being published by Cambridge University Press (CUP), which gave it the aura of a peer-reviewed work even though it clearly lacked competent scientific vetting.[53] Chris Lehmann, deputy editor of the *Washington Post Book World,* for example, said later that his newspaper staff had been fooled by the volume because it was published by CUP and they assumed it had been "subject to a level of critical scrutiny that other titles are not always."[54]

The *Economist* magazine promoted Lomborg's book heavily, inviting Lomborg to write a 2,500-word essay based on it.[55] The magazine then gave the book a glowing review, stating: "This is one of the most valuable books on public policy—not merely on environmental policy—to have been written for the intelligent general reader in the past ten years. Its target is environmental pessimism, the defining mood of the age. By the end, fair-minded readers will find that most of the concerns they had about the future of the planet have given way to fury at the army of dissembling environmentalists who have dedicated themselves to stirring up panic by concealing the truth."[56] The *Economist* followed this up with a drumbeat of attacks on environmental scientists, ignoring the condemnation of the book by the scientific community. The Committee on Scientific Dishonesty of the Danish Research Agency—Denmark's equivalent of the U.S. National Academy of Sciences—carried out an investigation of Lomborg's work. Its conclusion, announced in January 2003, was that Lomborg's book violated Danish standards of scientific practice and met the criteria for "scientific dishonesty."

This didn't stop the *Economist*, which then attacked the Danish committee.[57] Of course, the *Economist*'s incompetence is not restricted to environmental science. As Sir Partha Dasgupta, Frank Ramsey Professor of Economics at the University of Cambridge and one of the world's most distinguished economists, wrote in connection with the treatment of Lomborg, the magazine's economic analysis "is rarely above the sophomoric. . . . As far as we can tell, the magazine's writers have no understanding of the price system, their constant show piece. . . . So we would urge you not to infer the state of modern economics from the *Economist*."[58]

The purpose of the magazine is not always to record an approximation of the truth; sometimes it aims to push its owners' political agendas—often ones that widen the culture-reality disconnect. Shortly after the largely failed World Summit for Sustainable Development in Johannesburg in 2002, for example, the *Economist* editorialized that "if the world needed saving, it would have been wrong to expect an event such as the UN summit to rise to that challenge in the first place. Happily, though the world does not need saving. . . . [I]t is ludicrous to suggest that the earth is in grave peril."[59] Small wonder the magazine leans on Lomborg and ignores the scientific community.

In addition to charges of being wrong, environmental scientists are often accused of having a "political agenda." Political scientist Roger Pielke, for example, wrote an editorial claiming that the scientific community's disagreements with Lomborg were political.[60] This is misleading at best.[61]

The far left, of course, has its specialists in denial just as the far right does—not as well funded or powerful, but at times generating an equally counterproductive stream of nonsense.[62] Those on the far left are often just as disconnected from the biophysical facts of life as are the fellows of the Competitive Enterprise Institute (CEI) or the Heritage Foundation. They tend to believe that all population and environmental problems can be blamed on maldistribution and capitalist greed, and they often assume that, in an equitable world, population and consumption could grow forever.

Environmental scientists (and environmentalists) can have political agendas as well, of course, and on occasion may selectively cite data and take other steps in an effort to strengthen their cases. There is a difference, though. Environmental scientists must subject their work to peer review if they are to maintain their reputations in the community, and their reputations are vital to getting the rewards that community has to offer. The scientific community is large and diverse, and the penalties for scientists who do bad science are severe. Scientists don't have to be right, but they do have to be honest—the system keeps them that way if they want to retain any respect from their colleagues.

Like scientists in other fields, environmental scientists hold a broad range of political views and often fulfill their obligations as citizens by pointing out a danger or recommending what they believe is the best course of action to take. When medical scientists say that the evidence shows that smoking is harmful to health or that there are risks to smallpox vaccinations, they are not said to be "politicizing science."[63] Medical scientists are not accused of advocacy when they recommend use of condoms to avoid contracting HIV, press for quarantines in the face of an epidemic of severe acute respiratory syndrome (SARS), or point out that severe obesity is frequently lethal. They are viewed as meeting their responsibilities to the public. When environmental scientists try to alert people to the hazards of population growth or the risks of rapid climate change, or try to counter those who deny those risks exist, they are likewise not politicizing the issues at hand; they are meeting a public responsibility.

## Religion and Its Disconnects

Of course, all of the disconnect between today's dominant culture and the biophysical facts of life cannot be traced simply to the self-interested manipulations of the powerful. The more general cultural factors that maintain the disconnect include an overlapping complex of popular denial, fear of change, distrust of science and scientists, dislike of activism, faith in authority, and, in some cases, religious beliefs. We'll let cultural evolution of the last stand in for all of these, to get some idea of the problems and promise of developing greater awareness of the collision course with nature and of generating grassroots support for steering toward a sustainable society.

Some roots of the disconnect run very deep. The great leap forward (or "cultural revolution") 50,000 or so years ago[64] and the agricultural revolution 10,000 years ago set *Homo sapiens* on the road to civilization, high technology, and the population explosion. Both of those early revolutions, ironically, may have occurred partially in response to expanding populations.[65] With the occupation by humanity of essentially the entire globe, geographic variation in environmental settings produced variations in the kind and pace of cultural evolution,[66] an astonishing diversity of religions, and an increasingly dramatic divergence in the technological capabilities of societies. Western civilization went down the path to population and consumption explosions and to the creation of complex "high" technologies, all of which together now threaten the persistence of a humane civilization, possibly the ultimate survival of *Homo sapiens* itself. And while the fruits of Western technological development have transformed the population and consumption explosions into global phenomena, cultural evolution has been just plodding along on the social side. There has been no parallel development of a worldwide social, ethical, or religious system suited for a twenty-first-century civilization that is occupying an ever more crowded and resource-depleted planet.

For a very long time, human religious beliefs made little difference to the state of humanity as a whole. Religious wars and persecutions were sometimes incredibly vicious, but not global. That is no longer the case. The religious fanaticism of Islamists such as Mohammed Atta killed thousands of New Yorkers in a couple of hours and triggered a response that led to the deaths of thousands of people in Afghanistan. It subsequently also provided the Bush administration with an excuse to invade Iraq, killing many thousands more, in an attempt to assure the West's stable access to oil, and it led to the administration's establishment of an international precedent that could eventually kill many millions—reinforcement of the idea that so-called preventive international aggression is permissible.[67] The 9/11 atrocity has also provided political cover for Bush to escalate his war on the environment nationally and internationally. The whole mess is ultimately traceable jointly to the religious conflicts that have long plagued the Middle East and, of course, the oil-fueled lifestyles of rich nations.

On the issue of population, the religious dogmatism of Pope John Paul II and George W. Bush (the latter aided by many conservative Protestant legislators) has also harmed millions. It has hampered efforts to make contraceptives (especially condoms) and safe abortion available everywhere in the world, thus contributing to the deaths of many thousands of women in botched illegal abortions every year, and to the misery of millions more poor women in the world who want to control their reproduction or simply need medical help from groups defunded by the U.S. administration. Columnist Nicholas Kristof called that Bush policy "killing them softly."[68] It is both instructive and frightening to realize that the leader of the world's only superpower views the complex and dangerous modern world through the lens of religious fundamentalism.[69]

Fortunately, large portions of populations are not controlled by the pronouncements of such powerful leaders. Tens of millions of Americans don't share the religious views, real or putative, of their elected leaders. As noted earlier, Catholics widely ignore the pope's injunctions and use both contraception and abortion, and some of the lowest birthrates in the world are seen in predominantly Catholic nations.[70] Former priest Daniel C. Maguire, professor of moral theology at Marquette University, wrote of Karol Wojtyla's "failed and disappointing papacy":

> Two areas especially signaled his inadequacy as a world moral leader: his demeaning view of half of the human race—women—and his obsessive concern with what can be called pelvic orthodoxy. . . . The Vatican has also forced its opposition to condom use—even to prevent the spread of AIDS—onto the U.N. stage and elsewhere. This kind of ignorance is not just unfortunate; it is murderous. And this energetic pope has personally taken this message around the world.[71]

Despite widespread Catholic resistance to the pope's views on birth control, powerful people in the Church have been able to make religious dogma a national problem in one large and geopolitically important nation, the Philippines. There, the well-named Cardinal Jaime Sin (recently retired) promoted population growth, responding, "The more the merrier" to an inquiry about that nation's population explosion. Because of the Church's power and influence, the Philippine government fights the use of modern birth control.[72] A fifty-seven-year-old schoolteacher in the tiny village of San Roque, Manuel Musingi, has nine children, and one of his neighbors has thirteen. Contraceptives are not available in the village, and they are widely mistrusted because of popular misinformation not countered by the government. "If you have many children, you are a man," said Musingi. As a result of such attitudes, in 2003 the total fertility rate (TFR) in the Philippines was 3.5, one of the highest in the world outside Africa. Ironically, before Cardinal Sin gained so much influence, the Philippines had one of the first family planning programs and a head start in reducing fertility. But in 2003 the population was growing at 2.2 percent annually, food production was increasing by 1.9 percent, and that island nation, with only half again the area of New Zealand, is, at those rates, projected to have more than *twenty-five* times New Zealand's population in 2050.

Many other religious notions besides pronatalism may help retard any progress toward sustainability. One attitude often seen is that, whatever happens, we should not concern ourselves because the future is in God's hands and things are proceeding according to His plan. Similarly, we shouldn't worry about the poor, for they will be rewarded in heaven. Or, a woman's place is in the home, and women should be subservient to men and kept "barefoot and pregnant." The list of religious and related notions that make it difficult for people to perceive the human predicament is nearly endless, but some people are raising ethical concerns rooted in religion that are helping to bridge the gap. An example is the growing advocacy of some religious groups, including some fundamentalist Protestant groups, for protecting God's Creation. An outstanding example was the recent announcement by the Orthodox Patriarch of Constantinople that exterminating another species is a sin. People of most religions believe in tolerating others' views and in practicing the basic human compassion and cooperation that could be crucially helpful in avoiding a collapse of civilization. The ethical concerns of religious as well as non-religious people need to be aired much more publicly in an attempt to reconcile differences and, in particular, to develop a common ethic for dealing with both the environment and other human beings.

What can be done to encourage these positive trends and to discount the religious beliefs that contribute to the disconnect? How can grassroots support be generated to re-examine other widely and dearly held beliefs (for example, belief in the omnipotence of markets or the superiority of white men) for which in this discussion we have used religion as a stand-in? We have no master blueprint for guiding human ethical systems in general and attitudes toward population and consumption in particular. But we do have some ideas about how society could be encouraged to change direction in ways that would be more helpful in dealing with the human predicament. Those ideas are encapsulated in the notion of conscious cultural evolution ("conscious evolution" for short), an approach that might substantially alter society's understanding and attitudes toward both the natural world and fellow human beings in a relatively short time.[73] This would entail extensive use of public discourse and changes in education as essential starting points, because people cannot be expected to seek a rational path to sustainability until they understand their situation.

In the process of healing the disconnect there also needs to be much discussion of how power relationships work in our civilization and what might be done to restrain their more dangerous aspects. Developing broad-based public discourse on such topics could be the path to weakening the powerful and empowering the weak. But if it is not done in a context of education about how both fellow human beings and our life-support systems should be treated, the results might not be what we wish. Out of ignorance, the newly empowered might keep us on the collision course. We need to understand much better how cultural evolution could produce either human or biological holocausts or triumphs of love and preservation. And then we must direct its course toward the latter.

## Sustaining the "Third Chimpanzee"

So here we are, small-group, highly social apes, suddenly thrust into a position of planetary dominance. Our nearest relatives are chimpanzees and pygmy chimpanzees (bonobos), which led evolutionist Jared Diamond to put us in an appropriate genetic and cultural context as the "third chimpanzee."[74] *Homo sapiens* is a transformed chimp, struggling to update its ancient primate social system to deal with the governance and ethical problems of living in a global, half highly technological, half traditional society of more than 6 billion individuals. Our genetically evolved background has permitted us to acquire language and develop ethics, and it may have given people the tendency not only to recognize but also to favor kin and, indeed, to invent pseudokin.[75] That same background presumably made us a small-group animal by limiting the accounting or record-keeping capabilities of our brains and forcing us to culturally evolve legal systems in order to live in large groups.[76]

Evolution provided human beings with a nervous system with perceptual constraints that make it hard to deal with slowly developing environmental problems. We don't easily notice changes that take place over decades, whereas it's a cinch to grasp those occurring over seconds.[77] In other respects, the evolution of human social and ethical systems does not seem seriously constrained by genetic proclivities.[78] Whatever "building blocks"[79] our nervous systems provided for developing ethics, however, would clearly have been the result of natural selection driven by relationships with other members of social groups, and not geared for ethical treatment of our environment, including non-human animals. Thus, those who wish to change humanity's course should concentrate on finding ways to direct cultural evolution consciously. There is no reason why cultural evolution can't be steered so that humanity does much more to husband its natural capital and the flow of essential services generated by that capital.

Can we be successful? Can we find ways to channel cultural evolution more strongly toward an environmentally sustainable global society, assuming that is the goal most people desire?[80] One starting point for society to develop the "long-run vision" Kenneth Boulding sought (in the epigraph to this chapter) is for all of us to look at what we, in own professions or positions, can contribute to the channeling of cultural evolution in the desired direction. We believe that humanity's chances of avoiding a global Mesopotamia could be enhanced if many more social and natural scientists got behind an effort to make people aware of all the dimensions of the human predicament, and to work personally to bridge the disconnect. Scientists should try to improve understanding of cultural evolution and use that knowledge to change its course. Even more important will be undertaking various tasks, from generating the necessary understanding and concern among decision makers and the public about the human predicament to the hard social, political, and biological work necessary to preserve humanity's natural capital.[81]

For scientists to make substantial contributions to the battle for sustainability, there will need to be accelerating changes in the professional norms and ethics and in the ridiculously outdated structure of academic disciplines.[82] Answers to the human predicament cannot be found within the boundaries of conventional disciplines,[83] nor by multidisciplinary teams. Multidisciplinary teams are composed of individ-

uals each working separately on his or her "piece" of an overall problem. Needed instead are *interdisciplinary* teams—groups of people who
focus not on "their" component of a problem but collaboratively on
the entire problem through the lens of their particular expertise.[84] So,
one place where a breakthrough could occur is in the universities,
especially American universities, which are among the best in the
world. But they are in danger of losing their leadership role in society
by concentrating on producing not thinkers but primarily technologists and managers for a consumption machine. Perquisites (perks)
and money still flow down disciplinary lines to old-fashioned departments, but sooner or later academicians will recognize the increasing
drag of university structures on teaching about and finding solutions
to human problems. Although it is difficult to overestimate the con-
servatism of many university faculty members and administrators, we
hope that one day soon the leaders of some university will recognize
the challenge and dramatically reorganize their institution into the
first true twenty-first-century university.[85] If such change does not
come from within the community, and especially from the faculty, it
will be imposed from without—and both academia and society at large
will suffer.

It may be possible for the scientific community to help direct cultural evolution by systematically marketing a set of environmental
ethics: doing the necessary market research, selecting appropriate
goals, and carefully monitoring performance of the "product." The scientific community conducted a small-scale experiment in the mid-
1980s with its "nuclear winter" campaign.[86] That was a program to
investigate and then publicize the potential environmental and climatic consequences of a large-scale nuclear war. The entire exercise
was funded by only about $1 million, but the results were presented to
the public and the press using professionals in public relations. The
effect on attitudes in both the military and the general public in the
United States and the Soviet Union was substantial; it was a pioneering exercise in conscious evolution by scientists in several disciplines.

Maintaining the flow of ecosystem services upon which society
depends is just as important as avoiding a large-scale nuclear war, and

launching a publicity campaign to steer cultural evolution toward that goal would seem well worth the effort. The resources could be made available—a single donor recently gave more than 100 times the amount used in the nuclear winter campaign to an environmental organization.

But one needn't be a scientist or other professional in order to contribute significantly to solutions. In developed nations, everyone with some spare time can get involved in politics and join organizations whose goals one believes are to make the world a better place. The latter have already been quite effective worldwide,[87] and we hope they will become even more so in the future. One compelling factor is on our side: the very life of our civilization is now threatened, so everyone has a stake in ensuring that the misuse of power is curbed, for that misuse is now the principal obstacle to building a sustainable society.

# Chapter 9

## HUMAN BEHAVIOR
## AT THE MILLENNIUM

"Gradually . . . man has been accustoming himself to the notion of the spherical earth and a closed sphere of human activity . . . it was not until the Second World War and the development of the air age that the global nature of the planet really entered the popular imagination. Even now we are very far from having made the moral, political, and psychological adjustments which are implied in this transition from the illimitable plane to the closed sphere."
KENNETH BOULDING, 1966[1]

ECONOMIST Kenneth Boulding was right when he wrote that, nearly forty years ago and three years before astronauts viewed the spherical Earth from the moon. And the process of accustoming ourselves to it has been gradual indeed. Human behavior today is still, by and large, "empty world" behavior;[2] it evolved in a time when people were a minor ecological force, when ecology and environmentalism were non-concepts and wars might be bloody, but neither wars nor human-induced ecocatastrophes had the potential to devastate continents, let alone the entire planet. Something clearly needs to be done to face the human predicament and start to solve it, but how rapidly must we move? How close are we to the collision with the natural world that Earth's leading scientists are so alarmed about?

264

## Estimating the Limits

No scientist who doesn't need to take off his shoes to count up to twenty doubts that, sooner or later, if the product of human population size and per capita consumption of material goods continues to grow, it will become evident to everyone that humanity has disastrously overstressed its life-support systems. But how can we convince the world of the risks we are all running? Is there any way we can get a clue as to how close humanity is to a catastrophic situation? In the mid-1980s, Peter Vitousek, Pamela Matson, and the two of us estimated what proportion of the food available to all land animals was actually being commandeered by *Homo sapiens.* We used a measure called net primary production (NPP), the total product of photosynthesis less the energy needed by photosynthesizing organisms for themselves.[3] When we added up all the NPP that is consumed directly (as food, fodder, and forest products), that is produced in human-controlled systems but not consumed (crop residues, pasture grasses, forest wastage, etc.), and potential production that is lost because many human systems (including areas paved or built over) are less productive than were the natural systems they displaced, we found that human appropriations amounted to more than 40 percent of all the planet's potential production on land. That portion has undoubtedly risen further since the mid-1980s as expansion of agricultural production and further decimation of tropical forests—among the most productive ecosystems on Earth—have continued essentially unabated.[4]

Thus, human beings have already appropriated for themselves nearly half of the productivity of the land-based natural systems on which non-human life, as well as civilization, utterly depend, and we have degraded a significant portion of it in the process. Moreover, the human population is likely to increase by 2 to 3 billion or so in the next several decades. So a further human takeover of the planet is virtually inevitable, although a great deal could be done to moderate its effects.

Given the built-in lag times in the responses of many natural systems and processes to change (e.g., the reaction of the climate system to increased greenhouse gas emissions), and similar lags in social responses to slowly developing problems (such as the refusal of the George W. Bush administration to encourage a reduction in fossil fuel use), a very conservative guess as to how long it will take to double today's human impact on the global system would be thirty to fifty years. Implementing corrective action also takes time; population growth can be humanely and sensibly slowed only if it's done gradually. Innovative ideas rarely take hold rapidly, and converting the world's industrial system to a sustainable basis will take many decades even if we start tomorrow. With both population and per capita consumption growing simultaneously, neither one would have to double for their joint (multiplicative) effects to double. The critical question is whether we can avoid doubling the total impact altogether.

## The Spaceman Paradigm

Most people are still focused on the classic social, political, and economic problems that have afflicted *Homo sapiens* for at least several thousand years, since the rise of states. These problems—racism, religious conflict, war, dictatorships, poverty, and the like—are still important and are critical components of the human predicament because they have become global concerns. But humanity's prospective collision with the natural world has made it essential for us to look beyond those traditional, mainly social and economic, problems. Given the rate at which the human environmental impact is increasing, it seems clear that the start of a conversion to Boulding's "full world behavior," behavior more appropriate to a crowded planet without frontiers, where everything is interlinked, is needed now. And, given the lag times and thresholds that will inevitably delay corrective actions, it is needed fast. All of that demands a major shift in ways of thinking about human behavior and nature.

Boulding's idea of the world being filled up, of spatial constraints on human activities, is related to an important theory about the rise of nations that was developed by social philosopher Herbert Spencer in the late nineteenth century and refined by anthropologist Robert Carneiro in 1970.[5] That theory is of circumscription, in which states evolved when barriers (which could be physical barriers or opposing social groups) prevented future subjects from fleeing from those who would rule them and extract taxes from them.[6] Island societies were thought to be classic examples. So, possibly, was the emergence of the monarchical Israelite state under David;[7] the Philistines of Palestine's southern coastal lowlands formed a social barrier that kept the Israelites from fleeing domination by a king. Circumscription probably led to the earliest development of states, the essence of which is a set of relations in which power is ceded to a ruler or ruling class in return for protection of property rights.[8]

We think it is now time to develop a theory of *super*circumscription. In the twenty-first century, all of humanity has been forced into a single global society, hemmed in not just by the physical barrier of outer space but also by less clearly defined yet no less severe environmental restraints. No one now can escape the influence of the global society. As a global society, we must shift our focus from the old paradigm to one that comes to grips with the social, political, and economic problems of supercircumscription. Those problems are likely to be much more difficult because of the size and complexity of the new global entity and the absence of similar entities to give it legitimacy (as the existence of other states did for early states)[9] or a new bonanza of resources to avert collapse (as was provided to Europe by the conquest and exploitation of the rest of the world).[10] The new paradigm therefore must focus on how we can adjust power relations, institutions, and behaviors to make the human future as pleasant, equitable, and sustainable as possible. We must keep in mind the collapses of previous civilizations; when they disappeared, there were other places and other peoples to create new civilizations. What is at risk now is a *global* civilization.

To capture one dimension of what in his view such a change might entail, Boulding described the need to shift from a "cowboy economy" to a "spaceman economy."[11] Cowboys, he wrote, were "symbolic of the illimitable plains and also associated with reckless, exploitative, romantic, and violent behavior, which is characteristic of open societies." The spaceman economy would lack "unlimited reservoirs of anything, either for extraction or pollution. . . . The difference between the two types of economy becomes most apparent in the attitude toward consumption. In the cowboy economy, consumption is regarded as a good thing and production likewise." By contrast, in a spaceman economy, Boulding suggested, the basic measure of success "is not production and consumption at all, but the nature, extent, quality, and complexity of the total capital stock, including in this the state of the human bodies and minds included in the system."

Boulding's insightful analysis never made a dent in the world of his mainstream colleagues in economics, who, as he said, had become "obsessed with . . . income-flow concepts to the exclusion, almost, of capital stock concepts." But it made a deep impression on us and our colleagues when he published it, and, as you have seen in the discussion of genuine wealth in chapter 7, decades later it has become part of the background thought of some of the world's leading economists. Today his message is more urgent than ever; numerous important issues await discussion by the national and international communities while too many national leaders continue to behave according to the norms of the nineteenth century.

Among issues that need to be placed high on the national and international agendas, perhaps the most important is simply this question: is it the proper economic role of most human beings to be primarily instruments for funneling more wealth to the already wealthy? That seems to be the role played by most people today. Immanuel Kant surely would have said no to that question, as would have John Stuart Mill, with his utilitarian viewpoint.[12] We suspect most people today would agree with Kant and Mill if the question were put before them; happily, cultural evolution seems to be moving human ethics in that direction.[13]

A second question for national and international agendas is whether limits should be placed on the accumulation of wealth. Wealth gives power, both the power of increased personal consumption and the power to direct others' consumption through control of corporate operations and political behavior. This second issue is also becoming increasingly prominent in public discourse as more and more people realize that the world is being run by the superwealthy, not just through the politicians they are able to buy directly but also, and perhaps even more, through their manipulation of the levers of giant corporations. In the United States, those corporations often exert influence over politicians even more effectively than rich individuals do. Corporate power is a major force behind the human predicament, typically promoting consumption among the already rich, encouraging the use of environmentally malign technologies, expanding economic inequities that threaten global political stability, and, in some cases, skewing the direction of society's discourse.

The limits-to-wealth question really has two parts. One, discussed earlier, is how personal consumption might be constrained to reduce the ecological footprint of the wealthy. The second part is whether it is ethical to allow individuals to accumulate personal wealth simply to accrue power, how to judge when this is happening, and how, if such behavior is determined to be inimical to the goals of society at large, it might be limited. Not easy questions, but ones that must be raised.

A third important issue (especially in the United States) is a reconsideration of the rights and responsibilities of property owners. The conferring of property rights[14] is central to the functioning of markets, but all too many people today erroneously believe that such rights are absolute. They never are, except perhaps for tyrants. It is perfectly clear that there should be ecological limits to private property rights, since most private property is connected with other private (and public) property globally through the atmosphere and regionally via water flows and the movements of animals, plants, and microorganisms. To one degree or another, what happens on private property is everyone's business. Some environmental constraints on those rights are already commonplace; one cannot raise hogs on most suburban properties— the right of neighbors to be spared the smell of pig feces overrides the financial benefits to the potential hog farmer who owns the property. Now that virtually any development impinges on other people's interests and threatens Earth's shrinking pool of biodiversity, more of the ethical and legal burden of saving our life-support systems will need to be shifted to private landowners. They should be required to show that the social benefits of building one more subdivision or clearing new land to farm exceed the social costs. Restraint of development, not promotion of development, should become society's default position.

## Ethics and Cultural Evolution

So far we have mostly discussed ways in which today's economics-dominated system could be redirected in a campaign to achieve sustainability. But, in parallel, society could try to reduce that economic dominance by developing alongside it a much greater emphasis on human spiritual fulfillment, stressing the importance of maintaining excellent relations not only among individuals and groups but also between people and nature. The need for improving human relations has been one motivation for religious activities since the dawn of history, and that is made infinitely more pressing by the evolution of weapons of mass destruction and the spread of small arms, both of which have been converting *Homo sapiens* into a species of deadly predators.

Nothing less is needed than a rapid ethical evolution toward re-adjusting our relationship with nature so that the preservation of bio-diversity becomes akin to a religious duty.[15] That view was recently expressed by Australian ecologist Harry Recher, who is dismayed by the need to promote conservation largely on economic grounds:

> By demonstrating the dependence of human economic and social systems on global ecosystems and the services they provide . . . proponents of nature conservation seek to exploit the dominant paradigm of human society. Humanity venerates unending economic expansion, with prestige and accolades, as well as wealth and power, to whomever can control the world's resources and people. By using economic arguments, conservation becomes part of the human economic system and the need for a revolution—that is changing the paradigm and the values on which the system is based—is avoided. We can almost feel the desperation as conservation scientists set aside ethics, their sense of identity with nature, and submerge their awe of life and compassion for other species as they search

for some way to change human attitudes towards other species . . . as year by year humanity mindlessly eats its way across the planet and consumes the future.[16]

Eloquently put, but what social scientists have not yet figured out is why some of us feel that way as individuals and many others do not. Why people make the choices they do is often difficult to determine, and how their individual choices become aggregated into social choices is even more mysterious.[17] Fortunately, the cultural evolution of groups is more readily interpreted than that of individuals—just as climate is more predictable than weather, which in turn is more predictable than the effects of a butterfly's wing-beat on the surrounding air. Besides the averaging effects of large sample sizes, group behavior is better documented historically, depends less on interview data, and can be observed over longer periods than can the development of individuals' unique natures. Group behavior is a typical example of biocomplexity—the emergence of large-scale organization from interactions at a smaller scale.[18] The literature on social revolutions is instructive; it shows that many common features can be discerned in the conditions that lead to revolutions regardless of the interacting behavior of particular individuals.[19]

An understanding of how different human natures evolve culturally could help humanity deal with myriad issues connected to the human predicament, from abortion to zealotry, because the basic task will be to help direct future evolution away from the collision course. There is abundant evidence that different behaviors toward the environment are not in any significant way programmed into the human genome.[20] The environmental factors that shape the diversity of attitudes and behaviors are unknown in detail, as are the interactions of more than a trillion changing neurons as they react to constantly varying sensory inputs from the environment and to new thoughts. But understanding those interactions between brain, environment, and culture becomes progressively more crucial as the human predicament deepens.[21]

## Leaders and the Process of Change

Enlightened political leadership obviously will be essential to help us to deal with overpopulation, overconsumption, and environmental abuse. Perhaps the best current example of such political leadership on the environmental front is provided by the tiny nation of Bhutan in the Himalayas, sandwiched between India and China. Its king, His Majesty Jigme Singye Wangchuck, in June 1998 voluntarily transferred much of his power to the National Assembly (which now can remove him by a vote of no confidence)[22] and is leading the country in developing a program of gross national happiness (GNH). The program is based on four principles: economic development, environmental preservation, cultural promotion, and good governance.[23]

On a visit in early 2000, we and colleagues were impressed by many aspects of this program, especially by the ubiquity of cultural symbols and children going to school, and the goal of retaining some two-thirds of Bhutan's forest cover intact. Forest-clad mountain ranges stretching as far as the eye could see were the most common vista in Bhutan, a stunning contrast to neighboring Nepal, which has lacked environmentally oriented leadership. Whether Bhutan can be a success story in the long run will depend in no small part on how its government handles the problems of globalization, especially the anticipated intrusion of large corporations and the enormous pressures put on the nation by its gigantic neighbors. For example, when we visited, television had just been allowed to penetrate the nation. Its long-term effects are unknown; when we asked the minister of education about it, he said: "So far its main influence seems have been to regularize the dinner hour." That it will not gain much more influence may be a vain hope.

Ignorant and corrupt political leadership, of course, can have an effect on the environment opposite to that of Bhutan's government, as is clear from the environmental messes created in many parts of the world. An example is Florida, where crooked politicians, rampant development, payoffs by the sugar industry, and rapid population growth largely due to in-migration from other states have created, especially in the south and around the everglades and Florida Bay, an environmental disaster area.[24] Florida's problems are among the more blatant, but they are by no means unique in the United States. Political failure relative to the environment is also endemic in other developed countries, as shown, for instance, by the horrible mismanagement that has undermined the efficacy of laws designed to protect the Great Barrier Reef in Australia.[25]

Leadership, good or bad, operates through what is probably the most potent and widely discussed process of cultural evolution: contagion[26]—that is, the process wherein ideas, innovations, and attitudes are copied through networks, gradually "infecting" most or all of a population, and sometimes spreading with unexpected rapidity.[27] Contagion (and conformity) have been invoked to explain everything from patterns of resistance to change to the rapid decline of total fertility rates.[28]

Contagion or imitation, and social learning in general,[29] can explain how ideas and attitudes spread, but these mechanisms do not explain either their origins or their frequent failure to propagate. For instance, contagion does not allow us to understand the long gaps between Captain James Lancaster's experiment demonstrating the efficacy of lemon juice in warding off scurvy in 1601, its confirmation by Dr. James Lind in 1747, and the adoption of citrus fruits to wipe out the vitamin C deficiency disease in the British Navy (1795) and merchant marine (1865).[30] One factor may have been that Dr. Lind was not an influential figure in the navy, and Captain James Cook, who was, did not report that citrus fruits were an effective anti-scorbutic.

Kings and presidents can obviously use their influence to have their ideas propagated through networks much more effectively than most of us can. The same is true of other political leaders; consider the effective spread of the American right wing's agenda when it was promulgated by Newt Gingrich while he was speaker of the House of Representatives. The campaign to ban land mines and remove them from old battlefields took off only when Diana, Princess of Wales, took up the cause.

Failure of ideas to propagate may often be traced in part to class barriers and relationships. An interesting case put forth by sociologist Katherine Betts is the failure of growing anti-immigration sentiment in Australia to have a strong influence on government policy there in the past few decades. Her basic argument is that a new, prosperous cosmopolitan liberal class has arisen in Australia that is anti-racist, unlike many more parochial Australians. According to Betts, this internationally oriented class has been able to "buy immunity from the costs of growth and even make a profit as growth boosts property values."[31] Members of this group, who can afford to live in pleasant surroundings and don't fear competition from new immigrants, see high levels of immigration as anti-racist (politically correct). Their attitude is promoted by a consortium of pro-growth interest groups centered in the housing and construction industries. That much of anti-immigration sentiment in Australia *was* racist in origin added to the pro-immigration bias of the cosmopolitan liberals, most of whom were not in a position to perceive the non-racist, especially the environmental, reasons to question a relatively liberal immigration policy. As prosperous constituents, they no doubt have significant influence on political decisions.

The failure of some ideas to propagate may also be traceable to a phenomenon known to economists as "stickiness," the influence of traditional ways of thinking and acting that do not change in response to even the most compelling arguments for change (as in the religious pronatalism discussed in the previous chapter).[32] Stickiness, however, does not explain the differential longevity of ideas, attitudes, and trends—for example, why Christianity survived in ancient Rome while many other oriental mystery religions faded from the ancient Roman scene.[33]

One general sociological explanation for cultural persistence centers on the way groups construct notions of deviance to define themselves.[34] One can certainly attribute the longevity of organizations, from religions to environmental non-governmental organizations (NGOs), to a combination of feelings of group solidarity and the common interests of the members.[35] The great sociologist Max Weber partially agreed with Karl Marx that the fate of ideas was closely coupled with those of associated interests: "Not ideas, but material and ideal interests, directly govern men's conduct," Weber said.[36] In this context, many environmental and anti-environmental groups may well have the same social roots and need for solidarity—and their persistence may not bode well for the needed conversion of most people into a new breed of "environmentalists," since groups cling so tenaciously to old ideologies. One can see this in the near-automatic resistance of some environmentalists to the "heresy" of proposed market-based solutions to environmental problems, no matter how promising. Contagion, of course, can be the enemy of environmental quality in other ways; emulation of the development patterns of today's rich nations by societies that are struggling to "develop" is a clear example.[37]

## Where Do We Go from Here?

One of the elements most lacking in our society is any broad-based discourse on key ethical issues—that question of what spaceship ethics ought to be like. Even when the United States was gearing up to invade Iraq, there was pathetically little discussion of the many deep ethical issues raised by that action. And, with the outstanding exceptions of issues raised by the civil rights and women's liberation movements (with abortion a subtopic of the latter), there has been too little formal discussion in the post–World War II period of the ethical obligations of human beings in general, and citizens of rich nations such as the United States in particular, toward their fellow human beings and the natural systems that support their lives.

A couple of caveats seem appropriate here: in the following discussion of ethics, politics, and power, we are to a large degree expressing personal beliefs; and our use of the term *society* is shorthand for *contemporary society in the United States,* although some statements may apply more broadly. Our own ethical approach is relativistic[38] with a substantial dose of utilitarianism.[39] We should note that we don't think we've led exceptionally ethical lives according to our own standards; we're probably not even as holy as thou. Being holy is difficult for a social animal, which is probably why so many holy men have been hermits. But we do believe that unless we all start getting holier—or, at least, less self-indulgent—fast, our descendants (and some of *us*) are likely to pay a very high practical price.

On average, people's commitment to thinking about ethical issues, promoting discussions of them, and acting on their conclusions is too small.[40] Virtually all of us spend far too little time trying to come to grips with the critical issues that confront civilization and helping to shape cultural evolution to make our society more ethical.[41] In recent decades, technological products of an expanding human enterprise, from the printing press to the Internet, have transformed formerly more or less local ethical debates into global issues of freedom, justice, and governance. At the same time, the communications revolution has enabled us to mobilize much more rapidly against actions widely viewed as ethically flawed. Self-righteous megalomaniacs who think the entire world can be controlled through power politics need only look to the history of the Third Reich, imperial Japan, European colonial empires, and the Soviet Union to find reasons to rethink their assumptions.

The age of mass communications has been increasingly inhospitable to autocrats precisely because it is now so much more difficult to stop the spread of ideas than it was just a half-century ago. Hitler, a brilliant orator, was able to use radio effectively to spread his poisonous notions, but there were not hundreds of other communications channels in Germany, nothing akin to Radio Free Europe, to spread countervailing ideas. Indeed, the growth and spread of modern communications—particularly fax technology, satellite television transmission, and telephone links—doubtless hastened the breakup of the Soviet empire. People today, especially those with ready access to the Internet, in one part of the world often know instantly what is going on in other parts. Despite the persistence of a few dictatorial or theocratic states, democracy in one form or another seems to be traveling hand in hand with the openness that is promoted by the communications revolution and the growing role of science (a truly international cooperative enterprise) in nearly everyone's lives.

Widespread approval of the downfall of dictators, from Chile and Romania to Iraq, has been a cheering sign of the spread of the ethical goal of enabling people everywhere to enjoy "human rights" and, in retrospect, at least a taste of FDR's four freedoms. This goal is still somewhat incompletely defined but is widely understood and virtually universally acclaimed (even if, like the United Nations' Universal Declaration of Human Rights,[42] it is too often honored in the breach). Indeed, the invention of new "rights" has become a cottage industry for the moral entrepreneurs (reformers)[43] within our increasingly complex societies.[44] But with exactly which rights and how much freedom each citizen should be endowed remains controversial.

All too often in the West, *spreading freedom* has been code for *civilize the natives,* and talk of human rights has been a cloak for gaining control. Thus, the American passion for democracy at times has not extended to peoples (such as Chileans and Nicaraguans in the recent past) who have made the "wrong" choices. Some political commentators still prattle on about "democratizing" Arab nations, fully confident that they know what is right for others.[45] But do they?

Nevertheless, the debate has shifted in recent decades, and ethics have evolved; most of the world community now agrees that running a vicious dictatorship is unethical. Even those who, like us, were opposed to the invasion of Iraq from the start, are happy that Saddam Hussein was deposed. Three hundred years ago, the morality of distant rulers was rarely, if ever, an issue. Now the discussion is about ethical ways of ending totalitarian regimes when the process is likely to harm large numbers of innocent people, especially children. How does one balance innocent lives lost in a "preventive war" against innocent lives that might be saved in the future by that war? Is a relatively stable, democratic, and sustainable world more likely to be created by the use of lethal force by a lone superpower, its leaders convinced of their own righteousness, or by employment of soft power?[46]

If humanity fails to create a more equitable and sustainable world, it faces the prospect of nuclear weapons exploded in anger, human-made plagues, chemical terrorism, and economic collapses. One need only consider South Asia, where a weapons-exporting Pakistani society, armed with nuclear bombs and packed with dedicated Islamists, confronts a nuclear-armed Indian society increasingly dominated by Muslim-hating Hindu hard-liners.[47] A nuclear war between those two nations, sparked perhaps by another attack on Indian politicians by Muslim terrorists, could put an overstressed global society into a downward spiral from which it might not recover for decades. Dozens of nuclear explosions would kill many millions, subject vast areas to radioactive fallout, create foci of disease, and most likely disrupt the global economic system and further destabilize an already shaky international peacekeeping system.

Such confrontations have long been foreseen, as has the possibility of nuclear terrorism that might trigger large-scale nuclear conflicts.[48] The world has largely wasted the post–cold war opportunity to make the use of nuclear bombs less likely, and the United States has been one of the leading culprits in, among other things, failing to meet its obligations under the nuclear non-proliferation treaty. Squandering that opportunity has led to a frighteningly real prospect of nuclear weapons being used by terrorists in American cities,[49] while the United States continues to spend money on technically and politically questionable missile defenses. Long-range missiles are likely to be the last way in which rogue nations would choose to attack us; we would know immediately where the bomb came from, whereas determining the origin of a smuggled weapon would be much more difficult.[50] In addition, there continues to be a very real, continuing threat, generally unrecognized by the public, of an accidental nuclear war between the United States and Russia.[51] Remember the Norwegian rocket incident.

Ethical questions thus have grown much more complex for Americans. How does the nation that possesses the largest effective nuclear arsenal on the planet now deal ethically with accelerating proliferation? How could the greatest contributor by far to global warming defect from the international endeavor to solve the problem? How does one of the world's richest overconsuming nations explain the ethics of being the stingiest with foreign aid? And why has there been no national debate on these and other ethical failures, the last of which may have helped generate recent terrorist attacks, attacks that may be followed by much worse?[52]

Fortunately, at least for the moment, new forms of electronic communication show the potential for becoming a new forum for discussion of such issues. The Internet, e-mail, and fax technology have proven to be powerful forces indeed in a giant global society that is increasingly interdependent and attempting to live beyond the carrying capacity of Earth. Among other things, they have reinforced the view that, in the world of ideas, personal freedom (autonomy) and its close relative political freedom have broad appeal, even in societies such as China's, which traditionally placed much greater emphasis on the social responsibilities of individuals than have Western societies. The Internet's potential power is suggested by the efforts of China's repressive government to censor Web sites it finds offensive,[53] and also by the speed with which the Web became flooded with information and commentary on the Bush administration's foreign and environmental policies.

But the communications revolution has been a two-edged sword. The Internet is not only a source of information; it is also, like much of the media, a cesspool of disinformation.[54] This raises the same issue as for other media: how can people best be encouraged to compare, analyze, question, and ultimately build a picture of what's going on in which they have confidence? As with many other technological decisions, both people and governments are apparently going to have to learn to live with the Internet. We're not in the position of the long-ago Japanese government that simply turned its back on a technological revolution and gave up guns after they became a potent weapon in local wars among the Japanese.[55]

Furthermore, the spread of Western values has tended to undercut the sense of community that once was a prominent feature of human societies, and the process of democratization itself seems to increase the chances of international conflict, since domestic political conflict frequently follows the breakup of autocracies.[56] And the spread of Western economic values has helped to produce a dog-eat-dog world in which immediate financial gains too often govern people's relationships with their environment and with one another (including political relationships), upon both of which their lives and happiness ultimately depend.

The communications revolution nourishes that commercial ethos: the idea that unrestrained markets and ever-growing consumption can solve human problems gushes from every radio, television set, and pop-up Internet ad. Low levels of voting and confusion of celebrity and wealth with competence to govern suggest a political malaise (at least in the United States) that bodes ill for generating interest in improving governance and coping with the human predicament. Indeed, a dearth of forums exists in which those problems can be addressed and debated in front of a substantial portion of society. Whether that reflects a lack of interest by the public as a whole or a lack of interest by corporate sponsors is not clear. We suspect more the former because, if demand were there, someone would come forward to fill it. At a time when ethical issues related to overpopulation, overconsumption, globalization, international equity, weapons of mass destruction, and the like require increasing attention, they actually seem to be receiving less from most citizens.

## Spaceman Ethics

Peter Singer has been an important voice arguing, in effect, that the species that invented ethics is now obliged to extend them beyond the limits of *Homo sapiens*.[57] That idea is now almost universally accepted in the West, at least with regard to the treatment of domestic animals and those used in research. But the current concern about the rights of domestic animals should be enlarged to deal with the issue of the rights of the planet's biota as a whole.[58] That means answering some tough questions. Should all plants, animals, and microorganisms, or even entire ecosystems, have "standing"?[59] Is it ethical to consider that nature has only instrumental value (the value of what it can do for us), or should we assign it intrinsic value? If our civilization is to have a long-term future, ethics must evolve to encompass deep concern about the preservation of humanity's living capital and maintenance of the planet's human carrying capacity. This raises the question of whether we should also value natural capital for its own sake, apart from its importance to our life-support systems. Our own view is similar to that of Harry Recher, quoted earlier—that developing a broad spiritual concern for our only known living companions in the universe is the best way of maintaining their instrumental value.

Ethical practice in a gigantic, globalizing society surely must also extend to consideration of the human behaviors that are degrading the ecosystems supporting society, thereby creating additional threats to the health, happiness, and security of the human population. Globalized ethics must embrace questions such as those Singer has raised:[60] How far do each of our ethical duties extend in space and time? Should people do more for the welfare of their fellow citizens than they do for that of citizens of other countries? How much of humanity's heritage of natural capital should we save for people ten generations in the future, given great uncertainties about future technological change, population sizes, and the preferences of our descendants? Perhaps the most vexing question on the issue of equity and power is, what is the optimal level of inequality?[61] Put another way, how does society create an incentive structure that is both efficient and humane?

All responsible American citizens today face some crucial ethical issues. Is it ethical to insist, for example, as George Bush père stated, that "the American way of life is not negotiable"? Is it ethical for the rest of us to pursue that way of life, regardless of the rest of the world's needs or opinion? And does the nation have the right to wage a so-called preemptive war to preserve our overconsuming lifestyle?

Of course, our own ethical conclusions, as implied by some of this section, will be disputed by many people. Some may believe it's highly ethical for a government to apply sanctions against couples who have more than one or two children, in an attempt to maintain a national population within the government's perception of its nation's carrying capacity. Others may consider such sanctions a grossly unethical intrusion into individual rights and believe that the threats perceived in global change by scientists will be automatically neutralized by free markets. We all continually must learn to live with different ethical views and protect people's rights to their differing opinions. The key thing is to get the discussion going, ventilate the issues, and educate ourselves and others. There has never been a better time to stand up and be heard. And there has never been a better time for the United States government and American citizens alike to rejoin the growing global discussion.

## A Millennium Assessment of Human Behavior

In that discussion, how can we promote public consciousness of the value of a Boulding-style worldview? Perhaps the paradigm shift needed for us to recognize and repair humanity's predicament could be started by a dramatic step. The nations of the world, through the United Nations, might be persuaded to inaugurate a Millennium Assessment of Human Behavior (MAHB)—so named to emphasize that it is human *behavior,* toward one another and toward the planet that sustains all of us, that requires rapid modification. The idea is that an MAHB might become a basic mechanism to expose society to the full range of population-environment-resource-ethics-power issues and thus be a major tool for conscious evolution.

The Intergovernmental Panel on Climate Change (IPCC) could serve as a partial model for the MAHB. The IPCC involves hundreds of scientists from nearly every nation representing diverse disciplines, from atmospheric physics, chemistry, and ecology to economics and other social sciences. They are conducting an ongoing evaluation of the current and projected effects on the world's climates of increasing greenhouse gas concentrations in the atmosphere, and attempting to reach consensus on the technical, economic, and policy issues related to that contentious topic. A major role of the IPCC is to sort out the scientific validity of claims and counterclaims of competing interests. It also puts a strong emphasis on finding *equitable* solutions, which may be one reason members of the Bush administration are not fans of the IPCC's efforts. The sessions are open and transparent, and representatives of various governments, interested industries, and environmental organizations also participate as observers.

An endeavor that might serve as another model for an MAHB is the Millennium Ecosystem Assessment, which has been developed by environmental and social scientists to assess the condition of Earth's life-support systems.[62] Hundreds of ecologists and earth scientists all over the world are gathering information to feed into a major report that will be released in 2005. The report is intended to be useful at the global, regional, and local levels. It includes not only an assessment of the current state of the world's ecosystems but also projections of alternative future trends and consideration of related policy choices.

Like both the IPCC and the Millennium Ecosystem Assessment, the MAHB would work best if it included broad participation from a variety of non-scientists, ranging from ethicists to business interests to representatives of public interest groups. It would especially need to recruit social scientists from diverse fields such as sociology, psychology, economics, and political science, as well as experts in resource and environmental law, into its global effort to assess and seek ways to escape the human predicament.

The MAHB could be kicked off with a world megaconference like the United Nations Conference on Environment and Development (UNCED), held in Rio de Janeiro in 1992.[63] The purpose of this conference would be to initiate a continuing process; the MAHB should be created as a semi-permanent institution. It should be designed as a broad forum for integration of information and insight from many disciplines in the natural and social sciences (and philosophy), debate among diverse interest groups, and public education. It would be a way of washing *Homo sapiens'* dirty linen in public and trying to reach agreements on how to live within increasingly tight environmental constraints. The forum would explicitly review and support modern research on the behavior of complex systems subject to irreversible change[64] and, in the light of historical precedents, would develop scenarios to examine the possibility of a collapse of the emerging global civilization.[65] It would then recommend actions that a consensus of participants believed would reduce the likelihood of such a denouement. If successful, the MAHB might supplant and extend the United Nations' environment and development conferences, which have been

convened every ten years since 1972, and might also become a foundation for reorganization of international environmental efforts.[66]

The MAHB would strive to generate strategies for dealing with
supercircumscription by designing and helping to create an environmentally sustainable, socially and economically equitable global society. A broad base of support already exists worldwide for individual
elements of such a strategy, including support for maintaining environmental quality (usually too narrowly defined); ending gross economic, racial, and gender inequities; providing family planning services to those who want them; and stopping economic globalization
from making poor people even poorer.

The last, especially, is a hot-button issue today. The first attempts at
globalizing markets in the latter part of the nineteenth century started
a process that continues to this day.[67] As the population continues to
grow, trade between regions and nations becomes increasingly necessary for reallocating resources that are abundant in one area to other
areas where they are scarce. So liberalizing trade should be good thing
to do. And it would be, in a much more equitable world. But in the
world as it is now, deeply inequitable both economically and politically,
it too often becomes another route for exploitation.[68] Despite the
interests that block progress in making trade more fair and equitable,
the MAHB could well play a constructive role in resolving these
dilemmas.

A vital task the MAHB could take on would be to initiate and maintain a dialogue on human aspirations, issues of equity, and the use and
abuse of power.[69] With regard to the latter, the MAHB could generate discussions of ways to overcome institutional and political obstacles
to effective public policy. A priority would be to consider not only government power and the power vested in corporations but also the relationship of the two in areas as diverse as military procurement and the
arms trade, control of the airwaves, and management of pollution and
various kinds of hazardous substances.[70]

Finally, participants in the MAHB would need to recognize that the
exercise of power is subject to severe environmental constraints.[71] The
long-term problems of irrigation proved beyond the ability of the

rulers of empires in ancient Mesopotamia to control, and that inability eventually sapped their power. So far, our society has shown a similar inability to recognize and deal with gradually rising threats.[72] Central to developing enough interest to permit widespread discussion of such issues, obviously, is the universal need for better education about the environment. People are unlikely to be convinced of the importance of placing strictures on wealth if they actually believe that growth in aggregate wealth has no biophysical limits.

A step in this direction by the MAHB might be to explain the real limitations that civilization faces and to disseminate that information through the Internet and the mass media—if the latter could be convinced to cover them adequately. Persuading people to change their reproductive and consumptive behavior is difficult enough when they are aware of the stakes; it seems well nigh impossible when they think environmental problems are no more serious than most other problems facing society. Think what a different world it would be if the majority of wealthy and influential people, including national political leaders, understood that environmental security is fully as important as military security, if not more so!

A global consensus on the most crucial behavioral issues is unlikely to emerge promptly from the MAHB—or any other international forum. And open discussion of the role of maldistributed power in the human predicament will not be easy to generate or maintain. But, since the MAHB is envisioned as an ongoing effort, not all the goals would need to be reached immediately. And if the scientific diagnosis of humanity's approaching collision with the natural world is accurate, what alternative is there to trying?

## Toward a Better International Regime

Many related issues ripe for attention are already on the international agenda, from dealing with greenhouse gases and sustainable fisheries management to control of weapons of mass destruction and the legitimacy of preemptive strikes against terrorism. The IPCC is already exploring pathways to an international consensus on global warming with considerable success, and the Millennium Ecosystem Assessment is making parallel progress in evaluating the condition of the biosphere. Also, the United Nations' environment and development conferences of past decades have laid much of the groundwork for managing human interactions with Earth's natural systems, notably the Rio Declaration on Environment and Development and Agenda 21, both adopted at UNCED in 1992.[73] Some progress has been made in meeting the goals of those very ambitious agreements, which have been formally accepted by many, perhaps most, nations, although more often they have been neglected or only partially met.

The United Nations system at large addresses many important problems, from emergency food supplies to peacekeeping in many areas around the world, sometimes successfully, sometimes not. But, through influence on their government delegations, vested interests too often swing decisions to favor themselves or to impede action. The United Nations itself suffers from an outdated structure (especially that of the Security Council) and a far-flung set of agencies with too little coordination among them. In short, the UN system needs revision, as well as much more consistent and concrete support from member nations. Fortunately, discussion of these needs is already under way.

We can offer no easy answers on how to increase empathy or control the misuse of power (or, indeed, in many cases, to decide when misuse has occurred). And the difficulty and cultural risks of bringing Masai and Bhutanese herdsmen, Mexican, Nigerian, and Chinese villagers, New Guinean and Amazonian forest dwellers, Caribbean and Malagasy fisherfolk, and many others into a global discussion are truly daunting. Those discussions might be dominated, at least at first, by American and European values and technologies and by organizations such as the World Bank and the International Monetary Fund. Contributors from rich countries, as in other international negotiations, will have great advantages in staff and resources, and special efforts will be required to keep the playing field level—indeed, to decide what "level" is.

But humanity has no choice but to face such challenges and struggle to improve human systems of governance, and to do it fast. The stakes of political error have become much larger for everyone. If the United Nations were to fail to intervene in a dispute between India and Pakistan, or between the United States and China or Russia, hundreds of millions of people could die, and civilization might be headed toward a breakdown. If responsible nations do not cooperate to reduce the flux of greenhouse gases into the atmosphere, the negative consequences might be almost as devastating (although probably not so sudden). Thus, *is* is departing ever further from *ought,* and the past is becoming an ever less reliable guide to the future.

In sum, an unknown process long ago changed *Homo sapiens* from an evolutionary to a revolutionary animal.[74] That process put all humanity on a course toward the fate of the ancient Mesopotamian civilizations symbolized by Nineveh. The cultural, agricultural, writing, scientific, industrial, and (perhaps) computer and information revolutions have placed humanity in a totally unprecedented position. Our species is overshooting the capacity of its planetary home to support it in the long run; our margin of error has shrunk to almost nothing. The penalties for continued ignorance, malfeasance, and folly among opinion makers, the leaders of society, indeed, all of us, have escalated enormously—and often those penalties may be paid globally rather than merely locally or regionally. We have utterly changed our world; now we'll have to see if we can change our ways.

# Chapter 10

## SUSTAINABLE GOVERNANCE IN AMERICA

"Times of trouble prompt us to recall the ideals by which we live. But in America today, this is not an easy thing to do. At a time when democratic ideals seem ascendant abroad, there is some reason to wonder whether we have lost possession of them at home. Our public life is rife with discontent. Americans do not believe they have much to say in how they are governed and do not trust the government to do the right thing."

MICHAEL J. SANDEL, 1996[1]

IT WAS IN the spring of 2003 that the U.S. Environmental Protection Agency (EPA) submitted its draft report to the George W. Bush White House indicating that, among other things, emissions from smokestacks and vehicle exhausts were adding to the greenhouse effect—heating our planet.[2] When the White House sent the report back, it had substituted its own wording based on a report commissioned by the American Petroleum Institute. Outgoing EPA administrator Christine Todd Whitman decided to leave out the discussion of climate change, characterizing the text with the White House's editing as "pablum." According to an internal EPA document leaked to the *New York Times*, the White House had so modified the report that it "no longer accurately represents scientific consensus on climate change."[3]

In parallel with the administration's actions, the U.S. Senate's Republican Policy Committee wrote a polemic on global warming,[4] replete with quotes from a few scientific contrarians funded by the Organization of the Petroleum Exporting Countries (OPEC) and the fossil fuel industry as if they were a credible scientific majority on climate change. They ignored the consensus of the hundreds of mainstream scientists who wrote the assessments for the Intergovernmental Panel on Climate Change (IPCC) or the National Research Council.

Senator John McCain, a conservative Republican, courageously stood up to this engine of disinformation, co-sponsoring with Democratic senator Joseph Lieberman the McCain-Lieberman bill, which actually would require the United States to cut its greenhouse gas emissions, rather than acquiescing to the Bush administration's position that volunteerism—under which U.S. emissions have been growing steadily—somehow would be an adequate response to climate risks.[5] McCain's and Lieberman's collaboration shows again, as did the joint efforts of the late Republican senator Jack Heinz and Democratic senator Tim Wirth in the 1980s, that critical environmental issues can be addressed on a non-partisan basis.[6] Unfortunately, such bipartisan cooperation is increasingly rare, and the tendency for U.S. political leaders to view serious problems as political footballs is a major obstacle to solving them.

## Reforming the American Government

The United States is now the dominant nation on a planet dominated by human beings. Sadly, our nation is also at present the biggest engine of ecological destruction on Earth, the chief (but by no means only) force keeping humanity on a collision course with the natural world. To our minds, reform must begin right here at home, first because we are Americans and second because, hated as the United States has become in many quarters, it is also still much admired and emulated. If this nation can change its ways, there is hope that others will follow its example.

What would it take for the United States government to move

toward a more environmentally responsible position? How might the non-partisan spirit exemplified by McCain, Lieberman, Heinz, and Wirth be brought into ascendance? What reforms in governance might lead the way to U.S. cooperation and even leadership in steering the world away from its collision course and toward sustainability? In our view, the EPA–climate change incident offers some clues to crucial areas needing reform. First, the use of overweening executive power to interfere with regulatory agencies and to distort or ignore consensus findings of science, at levels uncharacteristic of previous administrations, must somehow be restrained. And second, it is more urgent than ever to curb undue corporate influence in the processes and outcomes of American government and, perhaps most important, on public discourse and elections. While we're under no illusion that our suggestions in this chapter will be readily adopted under present conditions of unchecked hubris, these two changes could make a significant difference. In any event, we are certain about the impracticality of the United States and other nations continuing on their current courses.

The first step in changing deep-rooted social behavior in any country is putting ideas on the table, and it's important to get that process under way immediately because novel policies can't be designed and deployed overnight. The fundamental changes that are needed may even take a few generations. Nonetheless, numerous shorter-term measures could be instrumental in starting us on the path to a more sustainable future.[7] Some measures are already being taken in different parts of the world, and many more could be taken to avoid, delay, or at least cushion the impending collision between the expanding human enterprise and its natural life-support systems.

Even so, larger questions need to be resolved: How can we end the cultural disconnect between what people think is going on and the actual environmental situation and then move toward sustainability? How can the present economic structure be modified to lessen the pressures on the environment while increasing equity, on ethical grounds as well as to bolster social stability? How can we become more social and less lethal and avoid the fate of the Mesopotamian civilizations? Society as presently constituted obviously is not on that course, largely because of maldistribution and misapplications of power. If the latter are to be corrected, we all must confront some difficult issues of governance.[8]

Some people think that the solution to governance in the United States is to restrict government's domain to a few functions, such as providing policing and military security. Other possible functions, such as education, health care, environmental protection, and old-age insurance, they believe, should be left to the private sector, and especially to the magic of markets. It is true that markets are critical to the smooth functioning of modern societies—at least, no one has come up with a good substitute for them. Many people, however, have drawn the wrong conclusion from the collapse of the centrally planned economies and decided that the best system of all is one based on unfettered markets. They are wrong because, as we have seen, market failures are ubiquitous.

Market failures occur when Adam Smith's "invisible hand" doesn't function properly—when self-seeking by individuals and corporations does not maximize the welfare of society.[9] Most common is a failure to get prices right, especially by failing to internalize environmental externalities. But also problematic are failures caused by unequal access to information,[10] as in the Enron fiasco and other corporate disasters caused by criminal executives who knew the true state of corporate finances but denied the information to employees and investors, thus ensuring that social welfare was not maximized.

The prevalence of market failures makes it clear that close government oversight of markets[11] and corporate practices is necessary, a view that Adam Smith would strongly support. Since U.S. government agencies so often climb into bed with those they are putatively regulating, it seems essential that market reform, corporate reform, and government reform should proceed in lockstep, accompanied by a careful examination of how chasing profits can distort human priorities and worsen the human predicament. Markets can easily provide incentives to make short-term profits, but only with difficulty can they promote trends that solve long-term environmental or economic problems.

Reforming markets so that prices more accurately reflect environmental costs and benefits will be no small task, but it is an absolutely essential one.

## Reforming American Democracy

If history teaches us any lesson, it is that we're unlikely to reach any kind of near-perfect governance system in the foreseeable future. The steady acceleration of history,[12] especially since the industrial revolution, has greatly raised the stakes in the governance game, as we've seen. When Assyria and Babylon went to war more than two and a half millennia ago, they couldn't destroy the world. Weapons were not capable of mass destruction, civilizations were too scattered and disconnected for plagues to become global, and the environment was vast and resilient in comparison with the scale of the human enterprise. Those conditions no longer obtain.

Lacking the carefully trained philosopher rulers who Plato thought should run society for the benefit of all, we should heed Winston Churchill's comment that democracy is the "worst form of government except all those other forms that have been tried from time to time."[13] There is now considerable debate about the connection between liberty and democracy,[14] and, while we agree with Churchill, there is no guarantee that society will automatically evolve culturally in the direction of either freedom or democracy.[15] History and psychology[16] suggest that freedom and democracy are fragile creatures, ever vulnerable to totalitarian attack.[17]

The founding fathers of the United States were very concerned about the possibility of concentration of power within the government, and they developed a system of checks and balances to try to counter any tendency toward dominance by the executive branch.[18] James Madison was very explicit that the separation of powers was "essential to the preservation of liberty."[19] What was not a great "check and balance" issue in Madison's day now is—the balance of power between governments and giant corporations whose wealth and power may exceed those of even quite large nations.

Sadly, from that viewpoint, the United States seems well on its way to losing many valued aspects of its democratic tradition and becoming a corporate kleptocracy as well as a theocratic plutocracy. (Aren't those terms wonderful? In case they're unfamiliar, a kleptocracy is a government by stealing; a theocracy is a government by those claiming divine sanction; and a plutocracy is a government by the wealthy.) Of course, the corruption that money and power bring to politics is still worse in nations without America's pretensions of democracy or a free press. Even in strong dictatorships, central governments are often powerless to deal with corrupt officials.[20] Nevertheless, corrosion of the political process of the United States, the lone superpower and a nation to which many have looked for inspiration, does not bode well for extricating us from the human predicament.

The task of reforming American democracy to make it more accountable, transparent, and responsive to the needs and environmental security of all citizens in the twenty-first century will be difficult, but far from impossible. The principal needs are interrelated and already well recognized. They include the following:

1. Reduction of the power of special interests, in particular large multinational corporations.
2. Election reform so that elected officials are not so beholden to special interests.
3. Diversification of information channels so they are less subject to control by special interests (or at least so that many such interests can be represented).
4. Reform of regulatory bodies to insulate them more thoroughly from the power of those they regulate.
5. Creation of some new institutions and reorganization of some agencies to deal with novel environmental and social problems.

In what follows we'll briefly explore each of these. Ideally, attempts to address these needs should be coordinated with an ongoing examination of overriding worldwide issues under the auspices of an institution, such as the Millennium Assessment of Human Behavior (MAHB) that we proposed in the preceding chapter. It should never be assumed that structures of governance that worked yesterday will necessarily work today or tomorrow. Governance in the United States when it was still a developing nation largely focused on domestic issues; governance today, when we have global (and, in the view of some, imperial) responsibilities and a greater concentration of power in the executive branch, is a very different issue.

## Governance of Fictional Animals

The problem of special interests in the United States is largely centered in the activities of corporations. A corporation is a legal fiction;[21] as Chief Justice John Marshall said in 1819, it is "an artificial being, invisible, intangible, and existing only in contemplation of law."[22] However, the law treats corporations in some ways as natural persons: they can own property, go into debt, make contracts, sue and get sued. Corporations are important economic instruments, and there is general agreement that they are essential elements in modern capitalist economies—even though there is disagreement over such questions as how "democratic" giant corporations are and how significant is the emergence of a class of professional managers.[23] Corporations are central not only to the way the American environment is treated and consumptive behavior is encouraged but also to controversies over trade and globalization. We need to know much more about the use of the power concentrated in giant corporations, which in many circumstances allows them to dictate policy not just to American politicians but also to other nation-states.[24] The primary goal of a corporation is to make a profit, and everything else is secondary to that goal. The only real constraints are legal requirements and the company's public image (which, if not positive, can make it difficult for the corporation to sell its product or service).

There are powerful reasons for reforming the status of corporations and for imposing high ethical standards on them from without. The need, in our view, has a biological basis in the evolution of the human brain. One major step in that evolution was the development in our ancestors of a "theory of mind"—the realization by each of us that other individuals have thoughts, knowledge, and aspirations just as we do.[25] Signs of these and other human mental attributes can be seen in our closest relatives, chimpanzees,[26] but neither they nor any other living animal has yet developed a human level of empathy. And the evolution of empathy is what allowed the evolution of ethics. It led to the development of ideas of right and wrong in the ways others are treated and eventually to the Golden Rule: "In everything, do unto others as you would have them do unto you."[27]

Corporations can invent ethical codes for themselves or have them defined for them.[28] But they can't have empathy, and therein lies the rub. No mechanism has evolved that could give corporations automatic insight into the needs of natural persons—either immediate needs or future needs represented by the necessity to maintain environmental quality. As English jurist Sir Edward Coke commented long ago, corporations "cannot commit treason nor be outlawed, or excommunicated, for they have no souls."[29]

That's why people from Thomas Jefferson onward have battled to prevent corporations from imputing to themselves rights that most of us would probably assign only to real human beings—such as free speech, and its corollary, the "right to lie."[30] But that battle was lost in the nineteenth century under pressure from the immensely wealthy railroads and their lawyers, curiously as a sequel to the passage of the Fourteenth Amendment, which gave full legal rights to freed slaves. In 1886, the corporations succeeded in gaining the same rights as individuals, to the enormous cost of American democracy.[31]

The issue is still very much alive. For example, Nike, Inc. recently received much media attention over allegations that its overseas employees were subjected to poor working conditions. The company mounted a heavily funded public relations campaign to portray its distant operations in developing countries in a more favorable light, but it was then sued for misrepresenting those working conditions. As part of its defense, Nike claimed the right of free speech to protect it from liability for making allegedly false and misleading public statements; but the California Supreme Court held that the claims were "commercial speech," for which Nike could be held civilly liable.[32] The *New York Times* opined in 2002: "By refusing to grant the company the same broad First Amendment protection enjoyed by its critics, the ruling poses an immediate threat to robust debate and reporting about globalization, and other important issues."[33] The U.S. Supreme Court let the ruling stand,[34] much to the distress of corporate interests that would still like to broaden their legal right to mislead consumers.[35]

Entrepreneur Paul Hawken summed up the issue thus: "By invoking the First Amendment privilege to protect their 'speech,' corporations achieve precisely what the Bill of Rights was intended to prevent: domination of public thought and discourse."[36] The very notion that a gigantic multinational corporation such as Nike could have the same one-voice, one-vote sort of standing in the political system or public discourse as you or we do beggars the imagination. Most of us don't have hundreds of millions of dollars to buy television time and politicians, thousands of employees dependent on us, and armies of lawyers to write the laws our hirelings will pass or to defend us in court. And now these financial Gargantuas are claiming the same right to "free speech" (including the right to lie in their own self-interest) with which flesh-and-blood people are endowed. This is not to say there are no complex issues involved here, such as what rights to lie might or might not be permitted environmental non-governmental organizations (NGOs, most of which are non-profit corporations) or right-wing public relations organizations such as the Heritage Foundation[37] (also a non-profit), but to us the answer for profit-making corporations is clear—it should not be permissible to lie to the public to sell products, to improve your image, or to promote politicians or political positions.

It is ironic that in the United States there are legal constraints on what corporations can claim with regard to their products, services, and operations,[38] but no legal limits on what they can whisper in politicians' ears about policies that will either threaten or enhance their bottom lines. Many corporations constantly strive to have environmental and safety regulations rolled back (although some have taken a more socially responsible course).[39] Perhaps most egregious has been the support by some corporations of a campaign of misinformation to persuade the U.S. government and the public that global warming is unimportant and doesn't warrant any policies to curb energy use.[40]

In what follows, we can be interpreted as tough on corporations and on the rich. Since by world standards we are rich and have owned stock for perhaps forty years, we are in a sense being tough on ourselves. "Do as we say" is always easier than "do as we did." But we want to emphasize that we think corporations need to be carefully reformed, not eliminated. We are well aware that very rich people can be extremely socially responsible and that many of them are willing to go to considerable lengths for important causes—be it Warren Buffett criticizing the Bush tax cuts that would make him even richer,[41] Ted Turner buying up large tracts of land in order to save the biodiversity there and dedicating vast resources to help the United Nations and reduce the danger of nuclear war, or Bill Gates trying to cure the sick of the developing world single-handedly. Examples of the generosity of the rich in trying to pay back what society gave them are myriad—just consider the good done by great foundations such as the diverse Carnegie-endowed organizations, The Ford Foundation, The Rockefeller Foundation, The William and Flora Hewlett Foundation, The David and Lucile Packard Foundation, and The John D. and Catherine T. MacArthur Foundation, among many others. We tend to agree with our colleague Gretchen Daily that if the current human predicament is to be solved, much of the action will come from the well-off, often mediated through corporations that they control.

When we criticize ourselves and other relatively well-off people, it's because we think that we (and many corporations) have both the means and a special responsibility to see the world through to a place where virtually everyone can have secure and satisfactory lives. We all can do better, especially the rich, who generally give a smaller proportion of their income to charitable causes than do those making much less.[42]

In a recent provocative book, *The Divine Right of Capital*,[43] Marjorie Kelly effectively challenges the basic idea that corporations should function purely for the benefit of stockholders. As she says, "Because corporate revenues represent the bulk of GDP, and the wealthiest own the bulk of corporate equity, running corporations to serve stockholders means running the economy to benefit the wealthy." That notion that only owners should benefit indicates the direction in which most people who are directors or shareholders in corporations look to find "ethical" principles. It was enshrined decades ago by Nobel laureate economist Milton Friedman in an article titled "The Social Responsibility of Business Is to Increase Its Profits"[44] (profits that, of course, usually go to the stockholders directly or through reinvestment, but may be appropriated by managers). He argued that as long as corporations didn't break the law, that was the extent of their commitment to the broader society in which they were embedded, ignoring the large hand corporations themselves had in writing those laws.[45]

Kelly has a deeper insight about the place of corporations in society. She argues that, rather than being viewed as a piece of property co-owned by investors, a corporation should be seen as a human community with obligations to the stockholders, the employees, and the external community as well. Under the present system, though, a corporation functions largely to make the wealthy wealthier. In aid of this, the financial returns to those who make the productive contributions, the employees (with the exception of upper management),[46] are minimized. If the flow of income to stockholders can be increased by firing or pauperizing employees, the employees get the sack or the lowest wages and stingiest benefits possible. High rewards (the prospect of high stock prices) are supposed to provide capital holders with the incentive to invest or lend. But such investment is not the only contributor to corporate success, even if success is defined only by the bottom line. More important is the need to supply reasonable financial incentives to employees to perform and innovate; as Kelly noted, "efficiency is best served when gains go to those who create the wealth."[47]

Perhaps most critical from our perspective, some corporations also attempt to shift as many costs (such as those of toxic waste disposal or the military costs of maintaining access to foreign resources) as legally—or even illegally—possible onto the communities with which they interact. Those negative externalities, often damaging to the environment or human health, no doubt boost the stockholders' stream of income, but they lessen the chances for their children to have a happy future.

## Reforming Corporations

Because of these problems, society is challenged to examine and redefine how corporate success ought to be viewed, especially with respect to the communities within which the corporations function. Action on this front is essential since, in the words of physicist turned activist Vandana Shiva, "for many corporate interests, sustainability means the sustainability of return on investment, and very often all other concerns and definitions are lost. Such businesses ignore nature's economy and the people's economy. The only economy they consider is that of the company, and it must continually be growing."[48] *In principle,* a series of positive changes that could be made in the United States (and in many cases globally) to help curb the power of the expanding plutocracy, serve the common good, and help prevent humanity's collision with the natural world might include the following:

- Amend the United States Constitution to include a presumption favoring the individual over the corporation, stating that corporations are not "persons" and are not entitled to the protections of the Bill of Rights. As attorney C. J. Mayer noted, "Only then will the Constitution become the exclusive reserve of those whom the Framers sought to protect: 'real' people."[49]
- Forbid corporations to make any contributions to political campaigns or parties or to do any sorts of "favors" for politicians (free vacations, transport in executive jets), with meaningful penalties for both corporations and politicians if the law is breached. Restricting the possibilities for corporate lobbying would greatly reduce the undue influence of corporations in policy making. Lobbyists, after all, according to John Ralston Saul, "are in the business of corrupting the people's representatives and servants away from the public good." In England, where the extent of lobbying is less extreme than in the United States, one lobbyist

nonetheless said of members of Parliament, "You can rent them, you can do what you want, you can rent them exactly like taxi drivers. They will do anything for you."[50]

- More frequently enforce the laws enacted in all fifty states that allow, when cause is shown, the dissolution of corporations, sale of their assets, and redistribution of the proceeds (minus any fines as determined by courts) to investors. The usual grounds for these actions are that the corporation obtained its articles of incorporation through fraud or that the corporation has continued to exceed or abuse the authority conferred upon it by law.[51] Exxon, for example, should have had its charter reviewed after the disastrous *Exxon Valdez* oil spill, as soon as it became clear that there was massive malfeasance behind the "accident," which in the opinion of some was no accident at all.[52]

- Pass new anti-trust laws that forbid any corporation to own directly (or control through subsidiaries) more than one major newspaper, national news magazine, or radio or television station in a given market. If networks were co-owned by participating stations, and individuals were prohibited from having large investments in more than one media corporation, it would go a long way toward breaking the grip of a few individuals on what the media tell us.[53] Laws could also be passed that forbid advertisers from attempting to censor print or programming content adjacent to their ads, with heavy penalties for doing so. Media groups should not be permitted to refuse advertising simply because it is critical of business practices or consumerism—a common malpractice today.[54]

- Make other legal changes to the financial system to favor smaller and more local enterprises, to discourage speculation,[55] and to limit the size and power of corporations. Limiting size is essential, even occasionally at the cost of loss of economies of scale. As David Korten put it, "the bigger our corporations, the greater their power to externalize costs and the greater the need for big government to protect the public interest and to clean up the consequent social and environmental messes."[56] Big corporations also foster big government; a small government wouldn't have a prayer against the armies of attorneys and public relations people that a corporation like Exxon, Bechtel, or Microsoft can deploy—indeed, even big government has problems doing so.

- Take actions that change the view that corporations are responsible only to their stockholders. Boards could be legally required to have fiduciary duties to employees and to the community at large, to better integrate corporations into society. There are some difficult details to work out in establishing such requirements (such as how to delineate community responsibilities and enforce the corporation's duties in regard to them), but such actions are critical. Many suggestions can be found in Kelly's *Divine Rights of Capital.*[57]

Some moves along these lines are already under way. Many corporations are beginning to change their own views of corporate responsibility, some voluntarily, some under stockholder pressure.[58] In recent decades, there has also been phenomenal growth in mutual funds that screen corporations for social and environmental responsibility, of which the Sierra Club Mutual Funds are only the latest.[59] Large pension funds and investors of church funds have been leaders in pushing corporations to meet community responsibilities, but there is still a very long way to go.

## Governance: Whose Representation?

The need to establish a broader and more widely recognized set of ethical standards that citizens can share, and can expect their elected representatives to observe, is critical in today's large technological societies. Those standards need to address not only how individuals and groups treat each other but also how they treat Earth's life-support systems and how they take into account the long-term interest of society in the perpetuation of those systems.

A major problem of governance in the United States has been not just the potential power of fictitious persons (corporations) to overwhelm the influence of real voters but also the collapse of our republican (small *r*) form of government into a more ostensibly democratic (small *d*) one. The founding fathers wanted a republican government, as opposed to a direct democracy, which is basically unworkable with large populations. Unlike the situation in ancient Athens, where all citizens met together to make decisions, a republic is a *representative* form of government. The original idea (and theoretical ideal) was basically that voters[60] would select representatives[61] who were the wisest and most trustworthy among them. Those representatives would be delegated the power to make laws and develop budgets and decide upon war and peace, judicial appointments, and the like. Above all, the authors of the Constitution thought that a republican form of government would help guard against the pressures of special interests ("factions") that otherwise could organize to foist their narrow views on the entire polity.[62] This could lead, for example, to a tyranny of the majority, in which the rights of minorities would be trampled.[63]

But the original plan of the founding fathers has not worked out. Gradually, the legislative process has been exposed to public view, as one might argue it should be. And technology has made it possible for the media to report that messy process continually (even in real time). Add in rule changes such as ballot initiatives that regress directly toward a direct "democracy" (people voting to enact specific laws) and continual electronic polling, and the gigantic United States has been changed into a grotesque analog to the Athenian citizens' assembly. It's grotesque because what the Athenian voters knew or thought they knew was not being largely manipulated by media conglomerates and many millions of advertising dollars.

That manipulation, which might be described as "mediacracy,"[64] has exacerbated a problem we mentioned in chapter 2—mobilization bias. Minority groups, including corporations and citizens' groups (such as the National Rifle Association, which also functions as a lobby for corporations that manufacture firearms) whose members care deeply about an issue, can politically outcompete majority groups (such as the gun control lobby) whose individual members are not as active in their commitment to the issue.[65] In the environmentally critical area of agriculture, for example, agribusiness is fully mobilized. It gets the American taxpayer to subsidize the production of crops such as corn, soybeans, and sugar. In 2002, after the farm states had favored the Republicans in the 2000 election, agribusinesses' political contributions were $53 million (up from $37 million in 1992), and the Republicans' cut increased from 60 percent to 72 percent. It was a small price to pay for a $40 *billion* subsidy *increase.*[66]

Even without heavy corporate influence, mobilization bias may cause difficulties in governance. Two hundred fishermen who seek a government subsidy worth $10,000 each will mobilize much more political effort in favor of it than 200 million taxpayers, each on average contributing one cent to the subsidy, will mobilize against it. This can be a problem in a direct democracy, and it doubtless was in Athens. But it appears worse in a modern republic. The constantly wide-open lines of communication between constituents, corporate interests, and legislators has greatly enhanced the ability, and thus the incentives, to mobilize. Since World War II, the number of lobbyists and lobbying organizations has exploded. In the 1950s, there were some 5,000 registered lobbyists in Washington. Today there are more than 20,000—averaging about 38 for each member of Congress—and more than 100 are retired congressmen themselves.[67] In 1999, lobbying organizations spent $1.45 billion in Washington.[68] Philip Morris alone had an amazing 245 lobbyists working state and federal legislatures.[69]

## Leashing the Media

The need for delegation of authority to well-informed and well-intentioned representatives has become ever greater as the human population has grown and government responsibilities have become greater and more global in scope. A serious error by the Athenian assembly could at most cost the loss of a regional war or the death of a great philosopher; an error by the U.S. Congress could have disastrous global consequences.

Major General Victor Renuart, director of operations for the United States Central Command, said at a press briefing during the 2003 Bush invasion of Iraq that "the media is reality in free societies like ours."[70] All too often, all too true. But government by media can make it very difficult for lawmakers to have much success, even as their responsibilities have expanded far beyond what their equivalents in the eighteenth and nineteenth centuries could imagine.

The turn toward direct democracy in a world awash in mediacracy has had serious consequences. With the emergence of the electronic mass media, heavily funded by corporate interests, it has become easier to manipulate public opinion (although newspapers used to do a pretty good job of it—as when the American press, especially William Randolph Hearst's newspapers, helped foment the Spanish-American War).[71] High-speed communications now inform members of Congress of the concerns of their constituents in real time, and few are courageous enough to vote their own conscience (as was originally intended) rather than go along with their highly manipulable constituents.

Congress also is vulnerable to lies promulgated by the executive branch—lies that often are boosted by the media. A classic case was that of the events leading to the Gulf of Tonkin Resolution, which launched the Vietnam War. The resolution was based on a total fabrication by the Lyndon B. Johnson administration about attacks on U.S. ships that was swallowed whole by Congress and reported uncritically by the media.[72] A more recent example was the George W. Bush administration's brazen invention of a series of excuses to attack Iraq, when its true reasons appeared to include securing a better strategic position in the Middle East, especially to gain more control over the world's oil and natural gas supplies, winning the 2002 midterm election, and making money for some of the administration's corporate supporters—all with nary a peep from the mainstream media about some of those obvious motives.[73]

In attempting to reduce the problems caused by mediacracy, one advance that might work in society's favor would be the development of new channels of communication that are more difficult for the powerful to control. Today, Rupert Murdoch can encourage *The Australian* to publish nonsensical editorials on population and, through his control of American media outlets, can support the dissembling of the

Bush administration. George W. Bush and his associates could happily and repeatedly make misleading statements on national television about his administration's motives for invading Iraq, who would benefit from his tax cuts, and what the administration was doing environmentally—and be assured that the Fox News Network would expose none of it.[74] And yes, most of the media "informing" the American public about issues relative to the predicament are predominantly conservative, often (especially in the case of radio talk shows) radically so.[75] Individuals who would simply have been run-of-the-mill fools haranguing a few dozen people on street corners in 1904 can command the attention of tens of millions of radio or television fans in 2004.

The success of the right's takeover of sources of information and entertainment (which are increasingly blended) has been facilitated by the public's preference for news about murder and rape trials, celebrity scandals, horrific accidents, sports spectacles, and wildfires and its lack of interest in events and trends that actually will affect the lives and futures of so many, many people. All the commercial communications outlets pander to this preference at some level and give scant attention to issues of real import.

Perhaps, if the airwaves could be recaptured so that more time were devoted to public discussion, the United States could have a sort of electronic version of the Federalist–Anti-Federalist debates. Yes, people now want entertainment, and we admit to enjoying commercial programs such as *Law and Order* as well as *The Sopranos* and *West Wing* ourselves. And people like junk food. But these are acquired tastes, and there is no *a priori* reason to believe that most people could not also acquire a taste for intense political debate and thoughtful analysis, if well presented. After all, serious programs such as *60 Minutes* are highly popular, and millions of people watch public television and listen to National Public Radio. In Abraham Lincoln's day, political debates could be exciting and informative spectacles—a far cry from most of the sanitized television and radio discussions of today, moderated by avuncular figures, or the scripted "battles" of the *Crossfire* or, worse yet, *Hannity and Colmes* ilk, the political equivalent of junk food. They could be exciting again. There is no reason that public affairs programs on television need be restricted to the same few hours on Sunday morning and largely depend on the small array of inside-the-Beltway political pundits who masquerade as intellectuals today.[76]

Some means of democratizing information channels and returning to more reasoned, civil commentary is needed, either by the appearance of alternative information channels or by some other mechanism. But consolidation on the Web is already even greater than in the traditional media.[77] If anything, the need to maintain media diversity has been made even more critical by the recent Republican attempt through the Federal Communications Commission (FCC), which is charged with protecting the public interest, to allow ownership of major news outlets to be consolidated further in a few giant corporations. That would reinforce the growing plutocracy in the United States. It was a classic example of the behavior of a regulatory agency captured by those it is supposed to regulate.[78] All this was in the wake of an earlier sell-off of the nation's airwaves to those same media corporations that have failed to inform the public about the scientific consensus on population-consumption issues.[79] Few things are more important to making democracy work than accountability, transparency, and easy access to information from diverse sources—qualities disgracefully lacking in today's public discourse.

## Fixing Governance in the United States: Delegated Delegation

Government by human beings is never perfect, but there is clearly a need to modernize that of the United States to make it more effective in dealing with the nation's critical issues in the twenty-first century. That there is no easy or complete cure for the messiness of politics doesn't mean that reforms are impossible. They might even be quite popular. In an article that should have been more influential than it was, Princeton University economist Alan Blinder suggested that Americans are estranged from their politicians because they believe that "the process of governing has become too political."[80] Political analyst Fareed Zakaria basically concurred with this observation in his recent book, *The Future of Freedom.*[81] As politicians in the United States have increasingly pandered to public opinion, citizens' trust in politicians has plummeted. Zakaria observed, "The American people have watched their leaders bow and scrape before them for the last three decades—and they are repulsed by it. Perhaps they sense that this is not what democracy is all about."[82]

What to do? An obvious step is to search for ways to make the government of the United States *less* of a corporate-controlled democracy—and to do that by placing more of it in the hands of carefully selected and monitored specialists, distasteful as that may sometimes be. Many issues require technical knowledge, long-term attention, and freedom from day-to-day political interference if the best interests of the public are to be served—indeed, if civilization is to be assured of persistence.

This is not a novel idea. As Blinder points out, several areas of our government (besides the Supreme Court) have already been to one degree or another insulated from the vagaries of politics. Blinder's main example is the Federal Reserve System, in which "the pace is deliberate, sometimes plodding. Policy discussions are serious, even somber, and disagreements are almost always over a policy's economic, social, or legal merits, not its political marketability." The Fed is not completely beyond political control—its seven-member board of governors is appointed by the president of the United States and confirmed by the Senate, and in an extreme case its decisions can be overturned by Congress. Perhaps its biggest failing is a considerable lack of transparency in documenting the reasoning behind its decisions. But it is an excellent instance of what we call "delegated delegation"—the people choose representatives, who then, in the name of the common good, delegate some of their delegated authority.

The Fed is far from the only government agency that was designed to be at least somewhat insulated from day-to-day politics. Others include the U.S. Food and Drug Administration, the Federal Trade Commission, the U.S. Securities and Exchange Commission, and, most recently, the Base Realignment and Closure Commission. In the last case, the commission recommended a number of military bases to close, and Congress had to vote yes or no on the list as a whole. As Blinder noted, Congress in some cases may be very happy to delegate power, when it is the power to allocate pain rather than pork. Indeed, Congress started this sort of "flee from the battle (and responsibility) strategy" when, in the midst of tariff wars of the Progressive era a hundred years ago, it ceded its constitutional duty and told the president to set the tariffs. Congress would then rubber-stamp the tariffs—a superior modus operandi to tearing itself apart in disagreement over what were often very minor issues.

Nowhere could delegated delegation be more important, and spare politicians more pain, than in areas of fundamental constraints. One can think of the messiness of politics as a sort of market in which ideas, interests, and jurisdictions compete with one another. Just as financial markets need government constraints, so does the chaotic political market need strict institutional limits set on the impacts of the human enterprise. Our society needs laws that will establish such limits, and institutions similar to the Federal Reserve System could be created to set and monitor them. Elected representatives should be delighted to be distanced from many of the tough decisions necessitated by humanity's collision course with the natural world. Exactly what the constraining mechanisms should be is beyond the scope of this book, but some of the directions in which to look are not hard to discover.

In the late 1960s and 1970s, the United States passed a series of landmark laws for environmental protection, beginning with the National Environmental Policy Act of 1969 (NEPA), which led to establishment of the Environmental Protection Agency (EPA) and required environmental impact statements for major government-funded development projects. NEPA was followed by the Clean Air Act, the Clean Water Act, and the Endangered Species Act of 1973 and, later, the Superfund legislation. By 1980, a remarkably strong body of laws was in place to protect America's environment and public health—laws that were admired and emulated by many other countries around the world. But much of the regulatory structure has been weakened or lost in political battles and simple neglect. At the same time, the gravity and scope of environmental problems have enormously escalated, including the unanticipated early arrival of the threat of global warming.[83]

Establishing new institutions specifically designed to develop policies with respect to consumption, population, and humanity's effects on the natural world would constitute a dramatic step toward resolving the human predicament. Also needed is reconstitution of the quasi-independent regulatory structures that have been recklessly emasculated or dismantled by the administrations of George W. Bush and other recent presidents.

Because of the diversity of environmental and social issues intertwined in humanity's predicament, it seems crucial that the nation institute a comprehensive and coordinated strategy to alter its direction. At the federal level, departments and agencies with prime environmental elements in their portfolios include the EPA and the Departments of Agriculture, the Interior, and Energy, although the Departments of Health and Human Services, Housing and Urban Development, and Defense, the Office of Homeland Security, and the National Oceanic and Atmospheric Administration also have environmental responsibilities. Conceivably, many of their major environmental policy-making (not administrative) responsibilities could be centralized in a relatively insulated independent agency, a Federal Environment Authority (FEA). The FEA, like its predecessor, the now largely inactivated Council on Environmental Quality, would be an independent entity, ultimately, like all agencies, under congressional budgetary control. It would need a staff large enough to analyze and coordinate information from the other departments and formulate policy recommendations, and its leader would be appointed by the president with confirmation by the Senate.

The FEA could be delegated a number of tasks that require more political courage than most legislators can muster—the environmental equivalent of cutting off pork distributed in the form of surplus military bases. One such task would be promoting a shift of the burden of proof when proposals are made for development of new land. The FEA should strongly advise all jurisdictions to move the basic burden

from where it is now—on those who wish to preserve what is left
of relatively undisturbed ecosystems—to the developers. Until now,
mobilization bias has put most of the political cards in the hands of the
developers; a change in the national ethos will be required to reverse
that, and the FEA should champion that change. The FEA might start
by recommending a very tough federal land-use policy (just as the Fed
sometimes sets a very tough discount-rate policy).

It could insist, for example, that not a square inch of still-pristine
federal land would be developed without demonstration of compelling national need and compensatory restoration of twice the area
of already developed land—close to the present law, which, sadly, is
poorly administered. The Bill Clinton administration tried to have the
remaining sizable roadless areas in federal lands that weren't already in
wilderness areas (mostly in national forests) protected from logging,
road building, and mining. The George W. Bush administration has
been fighting to reverse that and other of Clinton's conservation
efforts, even in the face of strong public opposition.

State and local governments would be encouraged to establish anal-
ogous policies on development of state and private lands; since the
exact circumstances and needs in each area are likely to be different,
zoning or planning regulations should be tailored to them. The FEA
could promote the idea that all development of never-developed land
should be banned. Such restriction of development seems hard to
imagine now, but with creation of some federal incentives, and gradual
education of the public (perhaps by the Millennium Ecosystem Assessment), it might eventually become possible.

If strong restrictions on land use and development were established, the free market could still operate within them. Developers
could compete for contracts to redevelop blighted or underdeveloped
areas; state legislatures could fund the tearing down of strip malls and
subdivisions to make room for more freeways (or vice versa); munici-
palities could still attempt to zone and rearrange property rights in
ways that maximize tax revenues; rich people could lobby local officials
to make the beaches in front of their mansions private beaches, and
civil rights lawyers could sue to open those beaches to the public; all of
us could strive to get public subsidies, and so on. In short, it would be

messy political business as usual in a more limited sphere, but our elected legislative delegates could escape much of the political heat on the most basic issues relevant to societal survival. They would just need to monitor carefully and adjust the constraints as required—but their votes would be up or down on packages of constraints.

Another charge that could be given the FEA would be designing constraints on the extraction ("severance") of resources (timber, minerals, etc.) from federal lands, taking into consideration the immediate environmental impact of such extraction and its probable effects on the life-support systems of future generations. It might recommend, for example, some version of economist Herman Daly's "depletion quota" scheme,[84] designed to constrain material consumption by limiting the quantity of resources that could enter the economy and eventually leave it as wastes and pollution. The entire flow of resources to material goods to wastes and pollution is known as "throughput."

The FEA could also advocate other policies that, without its imprimatur, might be difficult politically for Congress to enact. A simple (though often impractical) one to improve water quality would be to mandate that any firm or any government entity that withdraws water from a stream or river and returns water to it would be required to have the discharge pipes upstream of the intake pipes. It could collaborate with economic entities in the administration to develop new measures of economic status to replace gross national product (GNP) and gross domestic product (GDP)—measures that, among other things, would take into consideration the depreciation of natural capital.[85] With establishment of the FEA, one might see some genuine long-term planning for sustainability injected into government activities. For example, today the environmentally crucial questions of how many people can live sustainably in the United States and at what average level of environmental impact are not even discussed. More than a third of a century ago, we suggested establishment of a Department of Population and Environment (DPE).[86] That was when the United States had a population of about 200 million people instead of the almost 300 million of today and when immigration was at roughly half its present rate and was not a significant political issue. An FEA today could be charged with considering demographic trends in the United

States (and elsewhere when those trends strongly impinge on U.S. affairs) and recommending policies that could lead to sustainability.

Such actions as discouraging rampant "development" obviously would be very unpopular unless the FEA's leadership carefully explained their necessity. But members of Congress would be somewhat insulated by their partial delegation of responsibility for policy making to the FEA, as they would not be if they did the right thing on their own by imposing such measures as carbon taxes. Since there is no question that the physical throughput of the economy will need to be limited sooner or later (we think it should have been done twenty years ago, but that's beside the point), it would be wise to establish the appropriate institutions as soon as possible. Radical though they might seem, these suggestions are not far from the sorts of reforms already being discussed in academic literature and settings, and now is the time to get ideas on the public table.

A first small positive step in moving beyond the idea stage in reorganizing our government would be for Congress to revive the Office of Technology Assessment (OTA), which between 1972 and 1995 supplied it with excellent independent evaluations of technical issues. OTA was killed in a frenzy of downsizing, as summarized by a first-rate scientist, M. Granger Morgan: "Through a comedy of errors, oversight and political machismo, Congress had 'chosen' ignorance, and ended the 23-year history of its best and smallest agency."[87] Its reestablishment could be one sign not only that public opinion was starting to move in the right direction but also that members of Congress had awakened to the realization that they need the availability of sound, independent analysis of critical issues.

Another crucial area that could benefit from more delegation, for which Blinder made a good case, is taxation, a topic hardly popular with either citizens or the Congress. A Federal Tax Authority (FTA) could be created, whether as an advisory body to the administration or to Congress, perhaps beginning as an adjunct to the congressional Joint Committee on Taxation. Congress could perhaps relieve some of the political stress of shifting toward carbon and other consumption taxes less painful for itself by establishing the FTA. The authority could be given a mandate, say, to plan the transfer over five years of a substantial portion of the tax load from income to consumption and perhaps (horror of horrors) to design a surplus wealth tax. Congress could then promulgate taxes that are needed, as is its constitutional duty to do, perhaps in self-mandated up or down votes on the entire package, as in the base closure case.

One can imagine many areas in which carefully delegated delegation could improve the functioning of society: strengthening the FCC and charging it to reverse the growing monopoly control of the media, improving allocation of health care, and maintaining separation of church and state come to mind immediately. But both Congress (especially to inform its use of budgetary power) and the public will need to monitor carefully the operations of their delegated entities; there clearly are dangers in turning over too much power to specialists. Even so, in a world swamped with technological problems, it is clear that society can ill afford *not* to take more advantage of available technical knowledge.

Properly concentrated on key leverage issues, though, delegated delegation might reduce the negative effects of too much direct democracy, perhaps giving politicians some relief from the plethora of special-interest pressures. That might give them the will and the time to make needed decisions for the good of the nation and the world. Of course, we know that more delegation would not be a panacea. The present system is so abused, however, that experimental changes will carry little risk of making it worse. But eternal vigilance will remain the price of sustainability. Nor do we think that much new delegation is likely to be instituted until there is some change in the culture of politicians, a shift to more frequent examination of how well the government is actually fulfilling the nation's needs. Public activism could play a major role by insisting on public accountability and attention to central issues of the time.

## Addressing Inequality

Conservatives are fond of saying that our system does not guarantee equality of outcomes, but a situation in which some people are living in upward of 10,000-square-foot houses and a million or more others are homeless is a degree of inequality of outcomes that many, including ourselves, find unacceptable. The American system of socialism for the rich and capitalism for the poor today is actually *guaranteeing an inequality of outcomes*—an inequality that makes cooperation toward avoiding the collision with the natural world less likely. Why should the poor, often unable to get by, be moved to support actions requiring sacrifices for the good of a nation that coddles the rich and increasingly dismantles programs designed to improve the security and well-being of the poor and middle-class? Why should people care about aggregate throughput or the selection of energy technologies when they are hungry and may not even be able to afford a secondhand refrigerator?

For instance, state after state has allowed environmental deterioration to continue, infrastructure to crumble, school systems to decay, and the elderly to be forced to choose between buying needed medication or food. At the same time, these states have poured many millions into subsidizing gigantic corporations—huge welfare programs to no one's advantage except stockholders and perhaps state politicians.[88] Tax breaks in Louisiana saved Borden Chemical, Inc. some $15 million over a decade in which it was responsible for a number of serious pollution episodes. New Jersey, Connecticut, and New York pass out about $2.5 *billion* annually in corporate welfare, bidding against one another to get corporations to create jobs in their states. Ohio forgave corporations $2.1 billion in corporate property tax relief, yet property taxes are needed to fund schools, libraries, and police and fire departments. Shareholders make money while education systems and public services decline. The list goes on and on.

Making the distribution of wealth outcomes in the United States more equitable not only would make it a more pleasant country for many of us to live in; it would probably also make us healthier.[89] And it would give us a better chance of uniting to solve the tough problems of our predicament by allowing us to spend less time and effort on dealing with class antagonisms and more on pursuing sustainability.

## Knowledge and Power

Reducing income and wealth inequalities would also reduce power inequalities. Therein lies a rub. Some will argue that the rich and a largely bought-and-paid-for Congress will never permit that to happen to any significant degree. They may be right, but we hope not. The best way to counter the corruption of the democratic system, of course, is to have an informed and engaged public. It goes without saying that the educational system needs to be strengthened to spread knowledge more broadly. All citizens need to become familiar with the problems we face and the remedies we can institute, especially with both the benefits and costs of expanding technologies.

One way to improve public education and to put a damper on the present system of corporations buying politicians and elections would be to remove all election-related commercials from television and radio and substitute broader debates among candidates and more in-depth interviews, discussion, and political analysis controlled by, as one possibility, a Federal Elections Authority[90] (delegation again) and similar authorities at the state level. Perhaps one way to get campaign reform would be to give Congress the authority to regulate elections, as has long been proposed by Senator Ernest "Fritz" Hollings.[91] An elections authority would make the tools available to reduce the opportunities to "buy" elections. Only government funding of elections might be allowed, so that a system of one person, one vote would start to replace the current system of one dollar, one vote. The notion that money is a form of speech (enshrined in the preposterous 1976 Supreme Court decision *Buckley v. Valeo*)[92] needs to be expunged from any society that doesn't want to perpetuate plutocracy.

## Rules of the Game

To summarize our view, a major role of government should be to create "bounded fields" on which the messy decision-making processes of a liberal capitalist republic would be played out, and to generate rules for how those political games must be conducted. Having boundaries on a football or soccer field, rules for whether the teams are amateur or professional, for how each game must be played, how many players may be on the field at one time, what drugs players may or may not use, and so on, makes the game more disciplined and enjoyable. And within leagues there are often rules on trading players that keep one or two teams from winning too much. Similarly, bounding our political, economic, and ethical playing fields and establishing rules of the games, including rules to limit disparities in outcomes, will greatly increase society's chances of becoming sustainable (and thus much more enjoyable).

These are not new ideas, as anti-trust laws, campaign contribution laws, and many others attest. Also not novel is recognition of the need for the setting of fundamental rules to be as abstracted from the everyday political fray as possible. The founding fathers saw this clearly when they wrote the Constitution. For example, they forbade the establishment of a national religion, wishing to avoid a tyranny of the majority (and realizing it would be impossible anyway, considering the great religious pluralism in each original state)—something that seems to have escaped the notice of some who believe the government should allow prayers to be part of the routine in public schools.[93] Our own view is close to libertarian on this: the government should stay out of areas of personal morality, belief, and behavior as long as the behaviors, no matter how outrageous, do not directly harm others, incite others to harmful acts, or promote religion. Passing laws that would constrain those behaviors would be out of bounds, as would be laws mandating the preaching of creationism (or other religious dogma), or racial, religious, ethnic, or gender intolerance, in public schools.

On the other hand, for governments (state or federal) to set limits on population size and development, establish rights to real and intellectual property, exert control over the structure and behavior of corporations, determine sanctions for anti-social behavior, attempt to make economic opportunities and outcomes more equitable, and provide security are clearly not only within bounds but also, as long as done within constitutional limits, absolutely necessary. What *is* new is that Americans need to learn that their playing fields are laid out on a spaceship, not in a vast wilderness. Restrictions on consumption activities must be much tighter today than was needed even fifty years ago, and, if current trends continue, they will need to be tightened as much again in a mere decade or so if our society is ever to become sustainable.

The suggestions we have made here are just that—contributions to ongoing discussions of governance, discussions that need to be greatly expanded. Working out the details of necessary changes in national governance is the major political challenge of the twenty-first century, a challenge that all too few people (and all too few politicians) are aware of, let alone are trying to meet. But almost all adults can vote, and votes can be used to support politicians who pledge to work to reduce the maldistribution of power and brighten the future for the children of the poor (and the rich as well). And, since that seems unlikely to produce quick results, individuals can find other ways to make themselves heard, from talking to fellow citizens and pressuring representatives to participating in consumer boycotts and mass demonstrations and protests. The Bush administration has waged a determined and successful war on the environment, women, international governance, and civil liberties, while failing to address intelligently the extraordinary threat of terrorism. We now need to build a new movement, incorporating the very best of the existing environmental, justice, and peace movements, that will design and strive for a much more secure and sustainable world.

Unless America's interest in ethics and politics can be regenerated, global sustainability will be a steadily receding dream. But if Earth's most powerful nation reasserts its leadership in positive directions, empowered by a new comprehensive campaign of united activists for sustainability, it might even be possible to resolve the dilemmas of international governance.

# Chapter 11

## HEALING A WORLD
## OF WOUNDS

"Modern globalization is no accident of evolution. It
was created by human beings on purpose, and with a
specific goal: to give primacy to economic—I should
say corporate—values, above all other values, and to
install aggressively and codify globally those values."
JERRY MANDER, 2003[1]

"The stresses on the planet have achieved a new level
because of the intensity and scale of human activities. . . .
Contradicting projections of collapse is the possibility
that human foresight and innovation can reverse those
trends and develop paths that sustain natural diversity
and create opportunity."
HOLLING et al., 2002[2]

THE REFRAIN of Rudyard Kipling's poem "Recessional," the
source of this book's title, is "Lest we forget." A combination of
hubris and ignorance of history has caused people around the
world to ignore the environmental degradation that helped usher previous civilizations off the world stage; Kipling in 1897 appeared to have
been mindful that the British Empire might follow them into oblivion.
Now we have a global civilization that threatens to become "one with
Nineveh," yet that fact is rarely even part of international discourse.
Few people realize that we're living in what agricultural economist

Lester Brown has called an "environmental bubble economy," an economy in which "output is artificially inflated by over-consumption
of the earth's natural assets."[3] Clearly, many actions must be taken to
deflate that bubble gradually before it bursts, and, equally clearly, that
will involve reorganizing the way nations deal with global problems
and one another. In a world where the rich-poor gap seems likely to
widen, this represents a special challenge to the industrialized nations
that play such prominent roles in the overconsumption—lest we
forget.

The problem of reforming governance in the United States to make
it compatible with achieving long-term stability is tough enough. But
at least there is an American government to reform. At the global level,
there is no real government—just a wounded United Nations and a
complex of agreements and power relationships that are in almost
constant flux, with an American empire a central factor.[4] In a sense,
this is a paradigmatic case of cultural evolution in technology outpacing cultural evolution in the ethics of human relations. Transportation
and communication technologies have made the entire planet a more
interconnected, integrated unit than the United States or even Great
Britain was a century ago. Long before then, Americans and Britons
had organized governments that could help them adapt to changes.
But earthlings have not yet managed to take that step, and global society is the unit that now must be made sustainable. The world's population must be an appropriate size, balanced by an appropriate average
level of consumption, and with mechanisms in place to maintain that
balance. That means, among other things, that the world must become
more equitable, if for no other reason than that the vast majority of
humanity will then be more likely to support a cooperative effort to
achieve sustainability.

## The Free Market and the Human Predicament

Achieving a more equitable world will be a big challenge, considering
the growth of inequity—and resentments—generated on the international front by unbridled greed concentrated in multinational corpo-

rations combined with the immense power of the nations and financial institutions that support them. They fuel a struggle for endless and increasingly rapid economic growth ("hypergrowth"),[5] and their quest for increasing privatization tends to push aside the public good. The stories are grim—of poor people in Rio de Janeiro going without power when their country's formerly government-owned electrical system was "privatized" into a monopoly (sold to two multinationals, which axed services and raised prices); of poor people in Bolivia forced to pay great increases in water prices as a result of similar privatization (to the benefit of a Bechtel subsidiary); of unemployment ravaging Argentina's economy because the International Monetary Fund (IMF) dictated severe restrictions on government spending while the economy was on the edge of a deep recession. The last, and other recent privations on top of already deep poverty, can be traced to possibly well-meaning but draconian policies, originally called "structural assistance plans" and now euphemistically and misleadingly renamed "poverty reduction strategies." These have been pressed on poor nations by the combined power of the World Bank and the IMF, both international institutions established to help developing countries financially. Those policies are also supported by the Inter-American Development Bank and the World Trade Organization (WTO), among other international agencies.[6]

Ironically, the policies recommended to developing nations today tend to be the exact opposite of those that created today's rich nations. Britain and the United States developed behind high tariff barriers; Switzerland and the Netherlands pulled it off in no small part through stealing other nations' intellectual property (by not recognizing patent rights in the late nineteenth and early twentieth centuries).[7] Furthermore, the developed world still subsidizes its agriculture to the tune of some $300 billion annually, which makes a joke of the "free market" and devastates farmers in poor nations.[8] The average European Union cow is paid $2.50 a day in government subsidies, while almost half of Earth's population lives on less than $2.00 per day and 1.2 billion people survive on less than $1.00 per day.[9] Nor is this simply a holdover from the past; thanks to $53 million in campaign contributions from agribusiness, the 2002 U.S. farm bill *increased* subsidies by $40 billion. In other words, today it's free trade in agriculture for the developing nations but financial barriers to protect the rich. Small wonder that, in September 2003, representatives of developing nations walked out of the WTO's trade talks in Cancún.[10] One possibly positive result was the reaction of South American nations, which pushed to form a trade alliance for themselves in an attempt to balance the power of the United States as it tries to organize hemispheric trade in its own favor.[11]

One of the main problems with globalization as presently practiced is that it is globalization of business and profits but not of social services or environmental concern. Within the United States, as within many other countries, there is a national economy and some sense of responsibility on the part of national and local government for the basic welfare of its citizens. Governments, usually with the general approval of the public, allocate resources extracted from richer citizens and areas to aid poorer citizens and areas. After California's legislature, "inebriated by long draughts of utility political donations,"[12] partially "deregulated" the electricity market, the state suffered blackouts and steep rises in energy prices resulting from corporate manipulation of energy sources. One of the biggest accused of such manipulations was Reliant, a co-owner of the multinational that gouged the unfortunate citizens of Rio over water.[13] California's plight attracted national concern, in part because several other states, including New York, also had been deregulating energy, making themselves vulnerable to similar problems. Limited corrective action came late, forcing the governor to borrow billions of dollars to give the state a reprieve. So the taxpayers were saddled with a substantial debt and corporate gougers made gigantic profits, but at least there was a state response and, eventually, a weak national response.[14]

The key point here is that a political framework existed that assumed some responsibility for the problems of California consumers. In no circumstances would substantial portions of the population have been obliged to live in the dark for long periods. And California's citizens were not victimized bystanders; they took an active part in reducing energy use until the crisis was over. In contrast, the globalized citizens of Rio were not perceived to have a problem by any government, global or local, and the Brazilian national government was itself largely being controlled by outside corporate and organizational entities.[15] Nor did individual citizens have any power to remedy the situation. The globalized poor of Bolivia were in a similar situation; when they protested, what Nobel laureate economist Joseph Stiglitz called an "IMF riot" ensued. The price was 6 people killed and 175 hurt (including two children blinded) when the military attacked the demonstrators.[16]

The depth of resentment about World Bank and IMF policies among the poor in Latin America is difficult to overestimate. As one unemployed Bolivian miner put it, in protesting a plan to export natural gas to the United States, "globalization is just another name for submission and domination. . . . We've had to live with that here for 500 years, and now we want to be our own masters."[17] That view is understandable; the history of exploitation is very real and very long. As a writer for the *New York Times* commented, aside from the curbing of runaway inflation (an important accomplishment), "the average Bolivian has had little to show for the government's embrace of policies urged on it by the United States, the World Bank and the International Monetary Fund, now the focus of so much resentment."[18] The effect of these privatization policies all too often is to generate a flow of wealth from poor to rich, and an increase in the wealth of the rich often at a huge environmental cost (such as the decimation of tropical forests), paid mostly by poor local peoples and future generations.[19]

The value of free trade is explained by the standard economic notion of "comparative advantage," which traces to Adam Smith. The basic idea is compelling: through specialization every nation should gravitate to a position of comparative advantage that would make it richer by making its resource use most productive. According to the theory, a country does best by specializing in products that, for it, are relatively less costly to produce. Suppose China's comparative advantage recently had been in the growing of edible beans, and Costa Rica's advantage had been in growing coffee. The two countries would then be better off if China grew beans and imported Costa Rica's coffee and Costa Rica grew coffee and imported China's beans (this is an over-simplification of what has happened). This should be true even if, in the absence of trade, Costa Rica could produce both beans and coffee at a lower cost than China could. Costa Rica would have an absolute advantage in producing both commodities, but its relative (compara-tive) advantage in coffee should nonetheless lead it to specialize in exporting coffee and to import beans. China then could make money by exporting beans to Costa Rica, despite its absolute disadvantage relative to Costa Rica in their production. Comparative advantage should thus drive international trade to create a win-win situation for everyone.

While there is much merit to the idea of comparative advantage, unhappily what works well in theory often doesn't work so well in practice. A basic problem, as indicated earlier, is that those with power often manipulate the system or impose economically antique ideas to further enrich the rich.[20] Another is that the specialization encour-aged by comparative advantage may create serious difficulties for econ-omies, especially those of smaller developing nations, when global eco-nomic conditions change. A glut of coffee on the world market that caused prices to plunge has been catastrophic for many Costa Ricans, who now have trouble finding the cash to buy food they could have been growing for themselves. Comparative advantage, by itself, takes no account of factors such as national food self-sufficiency, which may, in some circumstances, prove critical.

There are other problems on the trade front. Since World War II, both modernization and globalization have largely meant American-ization (or Westernization). Little attention has been paid to whether people in different cultures might wish to set different rules for polit-ical and economic games. Certainly, Americans usually want the play-ing field as large as possible and the rules as few as possible; the Chinese, we suspect, would prefer a smaller field and more social constraints. Even in the West, there are clear cultural differences over how the play-ing field should be designed—what kinds of environmental boundaries should be placed on business, industry, and development, for instance. The French put more constraints on their real estate markets, trying to protect their countryside in general and their agriculture in particular from the assaults of urban sprawl. Americans often promote sprawl, often for simple private profit, sometimes even in the name of property and sales tax revenues.[21] These cultural factors often add to the complexity and misunderstandings found in trade negotiations.

Furthermore, advocates of free trade generally view national environmental regulations and standards as barriers to trade and a drag on hypergrowth; thus, they often resist the very social and environmental protections that will in the long run be essential to achieving sustainability. Finally, the whole notion of comparative advantage was developed by Adam Smith and David Ricardo in an era when they could not imagine today's instant international mobility of capital (as, for example, when the Chinese buy up Costa Rican coffee plantations; does Costa Rica then still have a comparative advantage in coffee production?).[22] This is not to say that trade is bad or that nations, whatever economic diversity they decide to encourage, shouldn't generally try to produce to their comparative advantage—obviously they should, but with an eye to economic resilience and security. And high tariffs are generally a bad idea, since they greatly reduce the efficiency of markets. We simply emphasize that comparative advantage is just one of many factors to consider when establishing trade policies.

## Localization

In humanity's present situation, it is clear that total globalization is neither possible nor desirable. Most people do not speak a language of globalization, are not familiar with computer technologies, let alone other cultures, take comfort in their own traditions and ways of life, and are not world travelers. Thus, one clear need in the contexts both of modernizing political units and of making trade arrangements is more emphasis on maintaining people's sense of place. Biophysically and culturally, Earth is a complex planet; while there certainly are advantages to globalization, there are also clear advantages to localization. Perhaps most important is that localization can strengthen that sense of place, that attachment to an immediate environment, which is still a major part of the identity of most human beings.[23]

An understanding of local surroundings permits many people to gain awareness of the ecosystem services upon which their lives depend. Localization allows development of "laws of the land" that are appropriate to local cultures and biophysical circumstances. But there is much more to law than the protection of private property, which is the legal structure the rich press hardest for the poor to adopt. For example, in traditional societies many local non-governmental social devices besides privatization have evolved to regulate common-property resources—fishing grounds, community pastures and forests, and so on. Too little attention is sometimes paid to them, though, and well-meaning outside aid can destabilize them.[24] Localization also helps maintain humanity's rich cultural and linguistic diversity and established community rights, all of which are also essential for governments to safeguard.

There are many ways of relating to other peoples and the human environment besides those promoted by Western corporate globalizers, and place-based knowledge of those ways may be badly needed in the future for everything from finding new natural medicines to discovering new ways of settling disputes. Increased localization would permit billions of people to orient to a world they know, not to be uprooted and marginalized in a global society they neither understand nor desire, as hundreds of millions already have been. As analysts Richard Barnet and John Cavanagh noted a decade ago, "unlike peripatetic lawyers, executives, rock stars, and other jet-age nomads who see the world as a giant menu of personal and professional choices, most of these people have no better prospects than marginal employment in a capital city or a life of insecurity in a faraway land."[25] In addition, localization helps maintain food security and other forms of self-sufficiency in a world with a trade system that is increasingly vulnerable to disruption by terrorism, regional warfare, and epidemic disease.

Work, like a sense of place, is also an important aspect of most people's identities, identities that give them a base from which to consider larger issues, such as the viability of the environment for their children and their children's children. In today's complex, globalizing, and increasingly inequitable society, how can people find fulfilling work? One thing is crystal clear: that unfulfilling toil is hardly restricted to poor people in poor countries—as Charles Birch and David Paul show for the case of Australia in their fine new book *Life and Work*.[26] The working poor in the ultra-rich, ultra-consuming United States often lead lives of quiet desperation—as dramatically illustrated in Barbara Ehrenreich's *Nickel and Dimed*.[27] Read that book and you'll get an emotional feel for what it's like to work in Wal-Mart's simulation of the brave new world or to toil as a rent-a-maid—even if doing so were to pay a living wage, which it doesn't. It will make you leave large tips for hotel chambermaids. And it will make you even more thoughtful about a society organized so that several million people are able to earn thirty or more times the wages of the working poor.[28]

Maybe, though, most work has never been fulfilling. Did !Kung women find digging roots fulfilling? Did an Inuit man crouched freezing and immobile for hours over a seal's blowhole in the ice, hoping to spear the animal when it came up for air, find that fulfilling? Actually, we suspect so. At least there was a direct connection between the work and the reward—a full stomach and approval of peers followed success in either case. After the agricultural revolution, work fulfillment certainly declined, especially when people began to labor for the benefit of others. One imagines that building a Conestoga wagon from scratch in 1840 was more rewarding than installing the same transmission in car after car on Henry Ford's assembly line a century later. Even a mother in the Conestoga days heating water in a copper boiler, using it to wash clothes for her six children, and carrying the wet wash fifty feet to a clothesline to dry probably got more fulfillment from having the children in clean clothes than do many people today from serving customers in fast-food joints for a pittance. The issue is complex, since, for example, poorly paid workers at Wal-Mart make it possible for other poor people to get some goods more cheaply than they could elsewhere. But there are some signs that disaffection of the workforce is one more serious and increasing problem in the organization of a growing and globalizing society, one that could cause strife that would make a cooperative change of course toward sustainability ever more difficult.

## Curing Corporate Globalization

Jerry Mander's opinion of globalization as designed to give primacy to corporate values, quoted in this chapter's epigraph, is an increasingly widespread view.[29] And many specialists in international economics generally agree with Joseph Stiglitz' critique: "Globalization today is not working for many of the world's poor. It is not working for much of the environment. It is not working for the stability of the global economy." In most cases, the transition from centrally planned economies to market economies has been butchered (China has been the primary exception), and "poverty has soared as incomes have plummeted."[30] Not much of an endorsement.

Stiglitz' proposed cure is not to abandon corporate globalization. That seems infeasible and might neglect potential benefits of certain aspects of globalization, which, for example, has brought millions of people in East Asia out of poverty. Rather, Stiglitz wants globalization's management reformed. He doesn't believe that the WTO's passion for free trade should be an excuse for allowing the use of shrimp nets that also catch sea turtles; he is concerned about the ethics of the IMF having billions to bail out banks and next to nothing to provide food subsidies for those impoverished by IMF policies. In short, he argues that the economic playing fields should be constrained by social and environmental considerations. Stiglitz thinks the basic motives of most managers of the World Bank, the IMF, and the WTO, as well as those of the associated government ministers, are good and that they genuinely believe their failed policies, if pursued long enough, will eventually work to the benefit of all parties. He's probably right—few individuals appear to believe their role in life is to make millions of people miserable in order to line the pockets of others.

But many people do support policies that have that effect. The

WTO's actions, from the viewpoint of the health of human beings and the environment, or of human rights in general, have frequently been atrocious, and its deliberations are anything but transparent.[31] It seems doubtful to us that, in the long run, its benefits (largely in keeping tariffs low) outweigh the very high costs its decisions incur. This is especially true since powerful countries are much more successful at applying protectionist policies against producers in poor nations than vice versa. In 2003, relations between Vietnam and the United States were seriously damaged by moves led by Senator Trent Lott and others designed to bar the importation of Vietnamese farm-raised catfish into American markets. The Vietnamese were simply too competitive for Mississippi Delta catfish farmers. Once again, socialism for the rich, capitalism for the poor.[32]

A basic solution to the inequities in the international system suggested by Stiglitz is similar to an element of the one we've outlined for the United States.[33] The relatively new international public institutions, such as the IMF and the WTO, are in desperate need of reform. And, in this case, they may be suffering from too much delegation of power. Accomplishing the needed reforms would require the maturing of a new global ethos of increased fairness and equality. That ethos could lead to efforts to greatly diminish the dominance of the rich countries, which is abetted by wealthy bankers and trade ministers from poor countries. More representation of people of average means from developing countries could then be possible (almost all have more than enough Westernized plutocrats who work against their own people's interests, given the chance). And people from environmental and social non-governmental organizations, along with interdisciplinary ecologists, economists, anthropologists, and the like, could inject human values other than economic growth into the discourse. Perhaps then most decision makers wouldn't view "the market" narrowly as a single, freestanding cure-all, and market efficiency as the sole social goal—something world-class economists have understood since the days of Adam Smith. Rather, they would see it as a complex, culture-dependent and development-stage-dependent class of economic institution that, when guided by appropriate government functions, could serve diverse societies and strata within those societies in different ways, and usually very well.[34] Of course, given that complexity and the lack of agreement even among thoughtful economists on appropriate restraints to put on markets, the entire system would need to be constantly monitored and managed in order to ensure desired results.

One prerequisite of efficiently functioning markets is a free flow of information.[35] But the world's poor people (who generally have much less information than rich people and often lack the time or means to seek it), as well as representatives of developing countries to international organizations (who usually lack the large, sophisticated staffs that assist representatives of rich countries), are easy victims of "friction" in market operations. In his recommendations, Stiglitz rightly emphasizes increasing the transparency of deliberations in order to make it more likely that environmental concerns will be acted upon.[36]

One more general, and drastic, solution that Stiglitz does not discuss is altering the status of corporations and the rules governing them, along the lines of our discussion in the previous chapter concerning corporations as individuals. He also does not recommend substantially modifying or shutting down entirely the World Bank, the IMF, or the WTO, which, under their present policies, may produce much greater long-term costs than can be justified by the limited benefits. For instance, there is considerable doubt as to whether creation of the superproducing, superconsuming "Asian tigers" (e.g., Malaysia, Singapore, Korea, Taiwan, and coastal China) will prove to have been a positive step toward global sustainability. And the WTO's insistence on giving property rights priority over all other human rights makes clear the sort of antique attitudes embedded in those organizations. Recently, for instance, the WTO decreed the abolition of Indian patent laws designed to make foods and medicines more widely available because they were deemed unfair to corporations' desires for profits.[37]

The WTO is also vulnerable to special-interest pressures from the United States and other rich nations. In a notorious example, the United States leaned on the WTO in favor of the huge fruit multinational Chiquita, at great cost to banana producers in small Caribbean countries who wanted to sell bananas to European nations. Carl Lindner, who owned 37 percent of Chiquita,[38] gave $1.4 million to Democrats and $4.2 million to Republicans to get the job done.[39] It is not clear whether the WTO and related international institutions can be adequately reformed (as Stiglitz hopes) or will need to be closed (World Bank) or replaced (the IMF and the WTO) by new bodies fully accountable to the United Nations, the direction in which David Korten leans.[40] What is clear is that the human predicament demands that the pace of discussion and action in dealing with international trade-related organizations be accelerated before they do even more damage to the world's environmental and social fabrics.

## International Governance

A final crucial globalization issue is one of international governance. For a long time we, and many others, placed our hopes in the United Nations. Despite its structural and other defects, it's been the only game in town. But recent events may have greatly reduced what effectiveness the United Nations had in increasing global security (as opposed to its various successful relief, educational, and monitoring functions). But there might be a bright lining to that cloud. World disgust at the actions of the only superpower might lead to a restoration of the United Nations' influence and challenge the hegemony of a renegade United States.[41] The institution's structure could be redesigned to be more realistic, especially the ridiculous Security Council arrangement that gives veto power to the victors of a war now six decades in the past. And some way should be found to allow better representation of people everywhere, not just of governments (many of which are not democratic),[42] perhaps in part by better organizing and integrating non-governmental organizations (NGOs) into the structure.[43]

Much of the needed discussion about UN reform could be centered in the context of the Millennium Assessment of Human Behavior (MAHB) discussed in chapter 9. A parallel discussion in the United States would fulfill one of the findings of the Clinton administration's

President's Council on Sustainable Development: that the administration should support "a forum for thoughtful consideration of sustainable development issues by high-level leaders in all sectors."[44] Both discussions might call for a redistribution of power, which very likely would be opposed by many people now at the top. These individuals are convinced that their lofty positions are proof of their own righteousness, proof that they've gotten their deserved rewards, that the system favors the best, and that any discussion of reforms would be a waste of time.

Yet, if humanity is to deal successfully with issues of population, consumption, and power, the governance of the world clearly needs to be reorganized.[45] Impractical? Not at all; nothing could be more practical to do. Unrealistic or even politically impossible? Maybe. Once again, nothing is bound to prove ultimately more impractical than ignoring the global maldistribution of power, since it is one of the main driving forces of the human predicament. Corporate behavior, as we have seen, is directly responsible for much of the deterioration of the human environment, has played a major role in the generation of resource wars, and is indirectly responsible for many of the world's consumption patterns. Corporations have begun to slip out of civilization's control. These fictional individuals, functioning as the tools of very real individuals and the governments they often control, are becoming a law unto themselves in their effects on Earth's environmental systems. Those who worry about the world being taken over by computer robots actually should have a more immediate concern.

## What Should We Do?

What, in summary, does humanity need to do to achieve a sustainable, thriving, and humane planetary society? How can a civilization that is now both global and vulnerable avoid causing the environmental deterioration that made the ancient Mesopotamian region no longer a suitable home for proud and thriving empires? One critical action, previously mentioned, would be reintroducing population, consumption, and the distribution of power (equity) into public and political discourse as urgent issues.[46] But talking about these problems is far from enough—humanity needs to assemble the collective will to *do* something about them. We believe the required socioeconomic and political changes can be achieved only if our species can take advantage of everyone's brains and good will. Societies must find ways to reduce the time, energy, and talent wasted because of ancient hatreds based on racial, religious, gender, and affectional differences. That will require a speeding of the gradual transformation toward more tolerance in private attitudes that has been under way since before the abolition of slavery in Britain and then in the United States.

Private attitudes among well-off Americans about helping the less fortunate need to be translated into national actions that, for instance, greatly enlarge the international humanitarian aid the nation supplies. Today, contrary to much of its rhetoric[47] and the personal generosity of most of its citizens, the United States is the stingiest of the rich nations in terms of providing development assistance to poor countries. It ranks fifteenth in the world by donating 0.1 percent of its gross national product (GNP), while Denmark, the Netherlands, Sweden, and Norway all give more than eight times that proportion, and all but Italy in the list give more than twice as much.[48]

But this is not because Americans individually are cheap or uncaring. The majority erroneously believe that the United States spends about 15 to 18 percent of the federal budget (roughly 3 to 4 percent of GNP) on foreign aid, but they would be willing to give 5 to 8 percent, *more than ten times the amount actually expended.*[49] So the public will is there to allow the United States to start on a path to true leadership, if the public could be informed of both the enormous need and what is not being done by our nation to meet it. And leadership from the world's most powerful nation is desperately needed if the global society is to reorganize itself to resolve the human predicament successfully. While there are huge problems in appropriately allocating and delivering aid, there is also no question that the rich must try harder to help the poor.

Unfortunately, we're long past the era when incremental changes can save the day; our natural and technological environments are changing too rapidly.[50] We face the addition of at least 2 billion more people to the planet in the next half-century, even under optimistic assumptions, and we're already overconsuming natural capital and disrupting planetary systems at a rate Earth cannot long support. The ancient Mesopotamians had plenty of time to avoid their fate, but they couldn't foresee the future. Today's society *can* see what its fate will be if business as usual prevails. Every single state and empire of the past sooner or later collapsed—as attested by, for instance, the desolate remains of Nineveh found by Austen Henry Layard, numerous similar traces of other previously proud cities, and the dissolution of the British Empire and, more recently, the Soviet Union. And, in virtually every collapse, environmental and resource (consumption) factors broadly considered played some role—not just political or military factors. Now we have a global state-corporate empire centered on the United States.[51] There is still a limited time to circumvent a long-term environmental collapse that would destroy this new state-corporate empire and be the first *global* collapse. But the empire must change its ways.

There is no instant cure or magic bullet, of course: the scale of the problems, the rapidity with which they are worsening, and the recalcitrance of the power structures in place are simply too great. But with new tools in hand, it may just be possible for us to change direction and start building momentum toward a better world. In that world, a sustainable number of people could all have decent, pleasurable lives. They would be able to consume at a satisfying but safe level, free from the prospect of resource wars and of continuing, eventually catastrophic, environmental deterioration. People could enjoy a society largely purged of the antique attitudes that so hinder efforts to find cooperative solutions to the problems of consumption, population growth, power, and equity.

Helping to build momentum in that direction is what we must all endeavor to do. *Homo sapiens* is the most culturally adaptable species that has inhabited Earth, and over millennia that has benefited us greatly. We all have different talents, skills, and interests, and we can all find some tactics, individually and in concert with others, to press for the needed changes in human and institutional behavior. We're now facing the greatest adaptive challenge of our history. It is highly unlikely that human beings will ever create a utopia, but collectively we can create a sustainable world.

Human societies can change dramatically when the time is ripe. That is demonstrated by events such as the rapid shift in American race and gender relations and the swift reorganization of international arrangements following World War II; the sudden decline in the birthrate and the institution of modern environmental regulations in the United States in the early 1970s; and the unexpected collapse of the Soviet Union in 1991. The causes of those episodes of rapid cultural evolution[52] are little understood, but it seems obvious that groundwork by farsighted, often courageous individuals and extensive social discussion preceded these major shifts. We believe that engaging in similar groundwork and public discussion is a central task for citizens everywhere today. We may not be able to predict when the time will be ripe for a sea change in attitudes toward the sustainability of our civilization, but we must all work to ripen the time.

In the midst of writing this book, deeply concerned about the state of the world, we were quite depressed. We realized that goals such as we've described would be considered much too idealistic by many people. And yet we believe that "idealistic" solutions have become the only realistic ones. Then something cheered us a little. The occasion was a television rebroadcast of Martin Luther King Jr.'s famous 1963 "I Have a Dream" speech.[53] Listening to King speak words that traced back to Thoreau via Gandhi with a bit of Rousseau and Marx mixed in, we were reminded that all is not dark; that many human beings have had, and many still have, a vision of a world of peace and equality—and that substantial progress in that direction has been made. Even though he was assassinated five years later, Martin Luther King Jr. changed the world. In the face of pervasive injustice and massive environmental need, idealism can be realism.

# Afterword to the Paperback Edition

We began this book with a description of two 1993 warnings by the world's scientists of an impending environmental catastrophe if humanity continued on the course it was on. Now there is a new report out by a different group, this one the result of a gargantuan effort involving 1,300 leading scientists from ninety-five countries who evaluated the state of Earth's systems that support human life. In its final form, the Millennium Ecosystem Assessment (MEA) was released in March 2005.[1] Walt Reid, coordinator of the effort, described its main results: "The bottom line of this assessment is that we are spending Earth's natural capital, putting such a strain on the natural functions of Earth that the ability of the planet's ecosystems to sustain future generations can no longer be taken for granted."[2]

Will this warning be as completely ignored as the two 1993 warnings from the scientific community?[3] Or is it possible that many more human beings will finally figure out that, unless action is taken soon, the future viability of civilization will be in doubt? Relatively little has happened to give us hope for substantial movement in that direction in the time since we wrote *One with Nineveh*—no concerted worldwide effort has yet been made to reduce human dependence on fossil fuels, to help develop sub-Saharan Africa, to limit population growth as much as is humanely possible, or to limit wasteful consumption among the rich. Moreover, India and China seem largely bent on repeating many of the mistakes of the Victorian industrial revolution, becoming more and more nations of motorists and superconsumers.

Unhappily, much of the power structure of human society, especially in the United States, seems opposed to making any of the necessary changes. While many nations and some elements of industry are, for example, increasingly interested in doing something to avert catastrophic climate change, the government of the only superpower remains adamantly against it. Consider the 2004 American national elections. The roles of power and marketing in politics were never more obvious. The Republican Party's national campaign was a brilliant extension of a program designed to promote a plutocracy and to weaken the government's role in environmental protection, civil rights, and social services. It was a program that was largely initiated during the Reagan administration. George W. Bush's entire campaign for a second term was framed as one of preserving national security and promoting a putatively biblical set of "family values."[4] Yet, during Bush's first term, the domination of the government by corporations operating in their own short-term interests was obvious, and the failure of the mainstream media to expose what was happening was glaring, to say the least.[5]

Before the election, the predictable (and predicted) disaster in Iraq grew steadily worse, and American military and environmental security declined. Iraq, previously essentially uninvolved in promoting terrorism elsewhere, became after the invasion a recruiting ground and rallying point for Islamic militants,[6] and nations such as North Korea and Iran increasingly came to see nuclear weapons as a way of deterring American attack. The Bush administration's Iraq invasion, a military attempt to secure sources of fossil fuels in central Asia (and to increase the potential profits of American oil companies), exacted a high price. It diverted attention and funds from the needed transition *away* from dependence on those fuels. Within the United States the administration's anti-environmental policies, from promoting the opening of the Arctic National Wildlife Reserve to speculative drilling for oil, to instituting what some have called a "no tree left behind" plan for national forests,[7] to relaxing pollution controls, threatened the future well-being of Americans. A substantial portion of the public clearly either got insufficient information (or too much misinformation) about what was happening, was scared by the terror-mongering of the administration and its allies, or simply didn't care. Millions voted against their own economic interests in favor of false security or those "family values."[8]

So why should we care deeply now? Yes, more people will be hungry, more Hummers will roll on streets and highways, more pollution will be generated, and civil liberties will be further restricted under this administration. But isn't American politics cyclical? Surely the Democrats soon will regain some power. All people need to do is wait.

Unhappily, we can't take such a relaxed view; we are afraid these "current" events represent a sea change in public attitude—a rapid move away from the Enlightenment's "question-and-test" approach to the world, and back toward "believe and obey." One reason is that many of the problems outlined in the preceding pages can hardly be laid only at the door of right-wing Republicans. If the Clinton administration was vastly superior to its successor in many respects, it was still unable (and largely unwilling) to take the steps toward curbing the growth of the American population, reducing overconsumption, and moving toward more benign technologies that would be required for the long-term protection of the ecosystem services we rely upon. A return of Democratic business as usual would be a major improvement, but at present there is no sign that the Democrats as a party would have either the will or the skill to do more than slow the rate of environmental deterioration that scientific studies reveal. The Democrats seem unlikely to campaign vigorously for a renewal of American enlightenment and progressive global cooperation or to pay closer attention to the underlying issues of equity and military and environmental security.

The public most recently has been distracted from the seriousness of the human predicament by the rise of fundamentalist religion and its intrusion into political affairs. Fundamentalism played two important roles in the 2004 election. On one hand, fear of fundamentalist Islamist terrorists, who labeled the United States the "Great Satan" and mounted attacks against American troops in Iraq and Afghanistan, allowed the Bush administration to pursue its interests under the cloak of a "war on terrorism." On the other hand, prominent Christian fundamentalists at home further poisoned the atmosphere by claiming, among other insults, that "Islam was founded by Muhammad, a demon-possessed pedophile,"[9] igniting the fears of the uninformed and encouraging a believe-and-obey approach to foreign policy, based on rhetoric about (but not the reality of) the Crusades of the Middle Ages.[10]

A moment's thought shows that "terrorism" is not an enemy but a tactic, and having a war on terrorism is like having a war on amphibious assaults. With this clever (if transparent) ruse, the administration developed a way of frightening many Americans into submission and readiness to surrender hard-won civil liberties. Administration allies among neoconservatives who were interested in central Asian fossil fuel reserves did a brilliant job of mobilizing the large Christian fundamentalist portion of the American public to support Bush's new "Crusade."

Within Christianity, however, there remains substantial diversity, even among fundamentalists. For example, the Evangelical Environmental Network has been promoting preservation of Earth's biodiversity—God's creation.[11] And many mainstream Christians are appalled at the activities of the Bush–right-wing fundamentalist combine.[12] At the other extreme are members of the "end time" sects, who believe that the end of the world is nigh, that signs such as gay marriage foreshadow it, and that any effort under present circumstances to preserve Creation is a waste of time.[13] That element ties in both support of Israel and the invasion of Iraq with prophecies in the book of Revelation.[14] This last view and similar ones are now shared or encouraged by a significant portion of congresspeople and Bush administration officials.[15] The gap between the believe-and-obey crowd and those in the question-and-test school seems never to have been wider, and the former are presently in the political saddle in the United States. Donald Kennedy, editor in chief of *Science* magazine, put it this way:

> U.S. society is now experiencing a convergence between religious conviction and partisan loyalty, readily detectable in the statistics of the 2004 election. Some of us who worry about the separation of church and state will accept tablets that display the Ten Commandments on state premises, because they fail to cross a threshold of urgency. But when the religious / political convergence leads to managing the nation's research agenda, its foreign assistance programs, or the high-school curriculum, that marks a really important change in our national life. Twilight for the Enlightenment? Not yet. But as its beneficiaries, we should also be its stewards.[16]

The religion-politics convergence goes hand in hand with organized Bush administration disinformation campaigns. Shortly after the 2004 presidential election, it was officially disclosed that excuses given by the Bush administration for the Iraq invasion had been outright lies. There were no weapons of mass destruction in Saddam Hussein's regime, and Saddam posed no threat to the United States.[17] There is no sign at present that the United States, notwithstanding the administration's new rhetoric about nation building and the spreading of democracy, will deviate from the current position, designed in part to gain more control over the fossil fuel resources of central Asia. This position was succinctly expressed by the Hudson Institute's Irwin Stelzer, who stated that "the key to a sound energy policy is a strong military" and "our aircraft carriers are the principal instruments of our energy policy."[18]

The Bush administration has further promoted the dissemination of misinformation to the public and decision makers by continuing to ignore the seriousness of rapid climate change[19] and by pressuring scientists to distort or conceal results that don't fit with its ideological biases.[20]

As Brooke Allen put it, although it is doubtful that George Bush ever read George Orwell, he seems to have grasped the Orwellian axiom "If you repeat a lie often enough, people will believe it."[21] But the posture of the Bush administration may eventually prove to have consequences far beyond those imagined by the fabricators themselves, who seem clueless about the threats embodied in a deteriorating global physical and epidemiological environment.[22] The nasty consequences of these policies are likely to be felt most, however, where people are generally poor.

Late in 2004 we took trips to developing countries that gave us new glimpses into the environmental situation around the world. The first trip was to the islands of Polynesia, which in some ways are a microcosm of the planet. First, they are already heavily modified by human activities. Land has been extensively degraded, bird species have gone extinct, many coral reefs have suffered deterioration, and local fisheries have declined. In addition, these island societies have become heavily dependent on supplies of petroleum, not just for powering activities on the islands but also for importing critical supplies and bringing in ecotourists. In general, their economies, already marginal, are dependent on subsidies from developed nations, especially France and New Zealand. Finally, the islands are very vulnerable to the sea-level rise that will accompany global warming. Even in the short time since this book was first published, evidence has accumulated that changes in climate are likely to occur more rapidly and more dramatically than earlier predictions suggested.[23] The threat is most obvious for atolls where the highest point today is only a few meters above sea level, such as Funafuti in Tuvalu (Ellice Islands).[24] But even on high islands like Bora Bora, most economic activity is concentrated in vulnerable coastal lowlands. Of course, the unfortunate accompaniments of sea-level rise will not be restricted to Polynesia. Indeed, there are now warnings about rising sea level forcing the abandonment of major continental cities as coastal aquifers are salinized.[25]

Another dimension of humanity's effects on natural processes and their consequences was brought into sharp focus by the Indian Ocean tsunami tragedy at the end of 2004. Although the impending sea-level rise can be traced mainly to human use of fossil fuels, human activities played no role in causing the huge earthquake that led to the devastating tsunami. Many of its consequences, however, were not "acts of God" but a result of acts of people, because our species had greatly reduced the protective coastal mangrove forests.[26] Extensive mangroves make excellent buffers against tsunamis, as can coral reefs, another type of natural ecosystem being degraded by human activities.[27] Indeed, according to the MEA, about 27 percent of Earth's coral reefs and 35 percent of its mangroves have been destroyed in the past few decades.[28]

How many lives would have been saved in the Indian Ocean basin if coral reefs had been better protected and vast areas of mangroves had not been cleared to make way for resorts and various types of aquaculture? How many people died in the tsunami because of shrimp farms producing shrimp they could not afford to eat or because of the construction of resorts they could not enjoy? If the human population had been stabilized at, say, a sustainable 2 billion instead of rocketing past

6 billion, would unsustainable fisheries exploitation and ecologically damaging aquaculture have been needed at all? And what does one say about the ethics of the stance taken by U.S. Secretary of State Condoleezza Rice, who described the tsunami as "a wonderful opportunity," since it wiped coastal areas clean of traditional communities that blocked development of more resorts and shrimp farms to benefit the already rich?[29]

How many thousands of lives might have been saved in the past, and might be saved in the future, with policies in place to discourage the trend of mass population movements toward seashores? In addition to making populations more vulnerable to storms and tsunamis, extensive coastal development often harms oceanic fisheries by degrading or destroying coastal wetland "nurseries" and, in some areas, generating a runoff of silt that destroys coral reefs. If the Indian Ocean tsunami had occurred after a few more inches of sea-level rise, how much worse might it have been? Sea-level rise is one of the certainties with current global warming, and contrary to intuition, a very small rise can greatly influence tsunami and storm-surge effects on coastal communities.

Similar questions could be asked about recent floods in the Philippines, Haiti, Nicaragua, and eastern Europe. In the Philippines and Europe, governments have recognized that deforestation, by corroding the free ecosystem service of flood control, was largely responsible for the disasters. In Nicaragua, the death toll from Hurricane Mitch in 1999 was greatly swollen by a combination of deforestation leading to floods and mudslides and an inequitable income distribution that had forced many poor people to live in environmentally vulnerable areas. How much of that deforestation was done to meet demand from overpopulated and overconsuming rich nations, such as the United States, for forest products? How many people die annually in the poor South of the world or have their very cultures destroyed so that we can have tropical hardwood furniture and floors in our second homes? And what will be the costs if not an "act of God" but anthropogenic climate warming increases the power of the most extreme tropical storms, including hurricanes?

Another trip, to Venezuela, produced some cheery moments but also a close-up look at a nation of potentially great importance to the world's resource wars—and one that should be fully developed instead of "developing."[30] Among the pleasures was meeting with old friends and colleagues at the Instituto Venezolano de Investigaciones Científicas, and spending more than a week in the field with a brilliant young agronomy student. But in a country so rich in natural resources (Venezuela has the world's sixth largest oil reserves—the largest outside the Middle East, at 78 billion barrels), the divisions between rich and poor, and especially the slums housing the poor, remain shocking. That oil may be in the gun sights of the Bush administration, which does not like the democratically elected President Hugo Chávez, who is determined to have Venezuela's oil under Venezuela's control. We wondered whether he will follow Ecuador's Jaime Roldós Aguilera, Panama's Omar Torrijos Herrera, and Chile's Salvador Allende, all democratically elected, in meeting an untimely demise for resisting control by American corporate and government interests.[31] Or will the U.S. oil wars in central Asia give Chávez a stay of execution? It's a great benefit for a nation to have rich natural resources, but they can attract lethal attention to national leaders who can't be easily subverted or bullied.[32]

From Venezuela we traveled directly to the adjacent Caribbean island of Trinidad to do fieldwork, and there we revisited a site where we had done research more than three decades ago. That early research had been on a population of butterflies in a dense tropical rain forest—a species-rich habitat that has since been disappearing globally at a frightening rate. On Christmas Day, at the top of the Arima Valley in the Northern Range, we explored our old haunts at Andrew's Trace—a trail along the top ridge of the mountain range. Much of the rain forest we had worked in had been cleared by squatters, and most of the giant trees were gone, replaced by low second-growth forest with tangled undergrowth. Miraculously, we found a metal sign marking position 7 in our transect still bright and legible on a tree trunk. It looked as if it had been nailed in place three months before, rather than in 1969!

We also found that the species of long-wing butterfly we had studied so long ago,[33] and the passionflower vines their caterpillars feed on, were still present. But our pleasure was muted by another development. We had always assumed that most of Trinidad's Northern Range rain forests would be protected by steep slopes and high rainfall. We had thought logging there would be too tough and dangerous to be practical, and agriculture impossible on most slopes. But we were wrong. Large areas had been cleared and were now covered with netting that supported vines of a squash called christophene, a delicately flavored local staple we had often enjoyed when doing fieldwork on the island. The green of the extremely diverse forest had been replaced with the green of squash leaves. It will now become the job of conservation biologists to evaluate the threat of christophene cultivation to the biodiversity of the Northern Range forests and the ecosystem services (flood control, carbon sequestration, pollination) they supplied —and to try to find ways to make areas of christophene cultivation more hospitable to tropical forest organisms.

We returned home from our travels at the end of 2004, impressed with the precariousness of the environmental situation virtually everywhere we had been. Back among the rich, the signs of the human predicament, obvious to us, are virtually absent as topics of public discourse, especially in the electronic media.[34] Coverage of the death of a religious leader, the political maneuverings surrounding the fate of a brain-dead woman, reactions to the desire of some homosexuals to marry, and the trial of an accused celebrity child molester filled the tube.

The threats of rapid climate change and sea-level rise, the potentially lethal consequences of biodiversity destruction, the real reasons behind the Iraq invasion, the long-term results of cutting the taxes of the super-rich, and similar topics were not brought home to television audiences. The amount of coverage with an undertone of religious issues, combined with so little analysis of the behavior of the Bush administration, is, we think, a sign of the sea change. After decades of careful planning and infiltration of the political system from below,[35] far-right Christian fundamentalists and arch-conservative Republicans have finally gotten into place an administration and a congressional majority all too willing to support their agenda and cooperate in turning the country toward a Christian theocracy. The mainstream media have even gone so far as to support the "rapture" (end time, when believers are swept up to heaven) enthusiasm of many fundamentalist Christians. Undoubtedly inspired by the financial success of Mel Gibson's ultraviolent video-game rendition of his imagined version of the crucifixion and by the enormously successful *Left Behind* novels, NBC actually ran a series called *Revelations.* It was lured not by the supernatural but by an opportunity to shake more dollars from the pockets of advertisers anxious to cater to fundamentalists.[36]

The sea change in the political atmosphere is leaving most Americans unable or unwilling to dig for the truth and facing a flood of intellectual pablum from corporate-controlled electronic and print media in which the bottom line seems to be the only line. They are hardly likely to dwell on the plutocratic interests of many of the administration's backers or on the Bush administration's attempts, by a combination of tax cuts, escalating military spending, and ballooning government deficits, to destroy the government's power to help the poor or educate the population. Renaming the estate tax (once strongly supported by Republican president Theodore Roosevelt) the "death tax" helped shift, as tax journalist David Kay Johnston put it, "the burden of taxes off of rich dead people and onto living wage earners."[37]

In the face of this sea change, people of the question-and-test school are too quick to assume that politics *is* cyclical, and that all this too shall pass. Perhaps so, but unhappily Earth's ecosystems don't know that, and evidence is accumulating that very dangerous trends are under way and gathering momentum. Environmental systems, you will recall, are classically nonlinear and involve thresholds.[38] More and more evidence has come to light that we are approaching such thresholds, especially in the area of climate change, since this book was first published.[39] We must move quickly to increase the chances that our children and grandchildren might avoid the massive suffering that will accompany continued global environmental deterioration and its social and economic consequences.

Wide recognition of how our patterns of life contribute to the extent of such deterioration is long overdue; indeed, it might have occurred automatically if a Millennium Assessment of Human Behavior (MAHB) had been in place. Remember, an MAHB would be a rough analog to the Millennium Ecosystem Assessment (MEA) mentioned at the start of this afterword, but centered on the social-behavioral issues raised by such assessments of the human predicament. It would focus on how and why we *act* the ways we do, and especially on the disconnect between what natural scientists know is required to maximize the chances of achieving a sustainable society, and actions that the public and politicians are willing to take. An MAHB would keep the connections between human behavior and the state of the environment under continuing discussion in transparent forums. For instance, economists, ecologists, journalists, and policy makers could be encouraged to start gathering and disseminating data on the costs of "natural" disasters, such as the Indian Ocean tsunami, Florida's rash of severe hurricanes in 2004, or Hurricane Mitch. What portion of those costs is attributable to the increasing size of the human population, its distribution, the consumption habits of the rich, the environmental vulnerability of the poor, and the use of damaging technologies and unsustainable sociopolitical arrangements? It could be a regular activity of the MAHB to examine a whole series of cost-benefit questions about such disasters, questions that all too often are ignored in public discourse.

A second crucial way in which the MAHB would differ from the Intergovernmental Panel on Climate Change (IPCC) or the MEA would be in having the dissemination-communications functions built right into its structure. Including such exercises as deliberative polling would be critical.[40] In deliberative polling, random samples of the public are queried on their attitudes toward an issue. The group queried then participates in an opportunity to deliberate about the issue, being exposed to a balanced assortment of publicly available expert briefing materials and having small-group access to expert panels. They are then re-polled to see how being informed might have changed their views. The MAHB itself would provide much of the background; the deliberations and views should be transparent to the media, made available on a Web site, and, wherever possible, broadcast over television (as has already been done in some cases). The very existence of a widely recognized MAHB could, among other things, help keep the mass media more honest in their reporting.

One goal of the MAHB would be to communicate the basic framework of such key issues as climate change to the general public—both its scientific background and its policy implications. It would add value to the work of groups such as the IPCC by framing the limits of responsible discussion. That might make it more difficult for commentators like Rush Limbaugh and those who write for the editorial pages of the *Wall Street Journal* to find "experts" to back their antienvironmental screeds, and fewer listeners or readers, now better informed, who might take them seriously.

There will still be those who, even while acknowledging the existence of ominous environmental trends, unfailingly put their faith in technological solutions that they believe ultimately will bail us out. The irony is that numerous technological means already exist, for example, to reduce profligate American use of fossil fuels. But the political activities of those who refuse to acknowledge the findings of the world's scientists, or whose interests lie elsewhere, stand in the way of their adoption, despite the potential for economic and environmental advantage many of these technologies offer. Rather than address the problem as an opportunity for progress, well-compensated antienvironmental forces work to maintain the status quo for those who profit from it. Thus, when Jared Diamond expressed great concern in his book over the possible collapse of our global civilization,[41] journalist Gregg Easterbrook advised readers not to worry: "If the phase of fossil-driven technology leads to discoveries that allow Homo sapiens to move into the galaxy, then resources, population pressure and other issues that worry Diamond will be forgotten."[42] Against that level of analysis there is little defense.

Even so, while the United States government is charging toward plutocracy and theocracy, that is not happening in Europe or Japan or China, whose governments show greater concern for and awareness of the human environmental peril. Nor is it happening at all levels in the United States. The state of California is enacting a series of carbon emission—reducing actions, including tighter fuel-conserving requirements for automobiles, that are being emulated by nearly a dozen other states and Canada. Meanwhile, more than 130 mayors around the country have recently pledged to promote Kyoto goals of emissions reductions in their cities. The release of the MEA is a bright spot, as is the large portion of the U.S. population—now exceeding 50 percent—that does not support the Bush administration.

Furthermore, there has been a rather positive response to the idea of initiating an MAHB, especially at our home institution. Stanford University, under the auspices of the new Stanford Institute for the Environment, is starting a model MAHB, first focusing on the wide range of behavioral and ethical issues surrounding California's positive actions to mitigate global warming. A broad range of Stanford faculty is involved, drawn from the natural sciences, social sciences, the humanities, law, engineering, and other disciplines. It could be one tiny start on a new way of tackling the enormous educational challenges we face globally.

Is it possible for a small-group animal, with such a large built-in tendency toward irrationality and faith, ever to evolve a sustainable worldwide society with many billions of individuals? Perhaps through persistent effort, another sea change could overtake us, one that would bring more of the question-and-test group of human beings to power, not just in the United States but also in the Middle East and elsewhere. Perhaps the time has finally come for what Sam Harris called an "End of Faith,"[43] and for human beings to come together in a more rational search for a sustainable society. We see little choice but to try.

# Notes

INTRODUCTION: HOSTAGES TO HUBRIS

1. "Recessional" (Kipling 1942, p. 893). Although the poem may appear to present second thoughts about imperialism, what is known about Kipling's views when he published it shows that it "was never intended as in any sense anti-imperialist" (Ricketts 1999, p. 237). "Recessional" led to considerable controversy at the time over the degree of imperial caution being urged (e.g., see also Gilmour 2002; Mallett 2003).

For brevity, the last two stanzas of the poem were omitted in the epigraph to this book. They read as follows:

> If, drunk with sight of power, we loose
> Wild tongues that have not Thee in awe—
> Such boasting as the Gentiles use
> Or lesser breeds without the Law—
> Lord God of Hosts, be with us yet,
> Lest we forget, lest we forget!
>
> For heathen heart that puts her trust
> In reeking tube and iron shard—
> All valiant dust that builds on dust,
> And guarding calls not Thee to guard—
> For frantic boast and foolish word,
> Thy Mercy on Thy People, Lord!

2. Cotterell 1980.
3. Leick 2001, p. 242.
4. Leick 2001, pp. 222ff.
5. Dalley 1997.
6. Layard 2001 (1882), p. 5.
7. Leick 2001.
8. E.g., Roaf 1990, pp. 18ff.
9. E.g., Jacobsen and Adams 1958.
10. Cotterell 1980.
11. E.g., Redman 1999, pp. 136–139.
12. Roux 1980, pp. 391ff.
13. Sadly, the remnants of the Assyrian people were subjected to intense persecution by Turks, Kurds, Persians, and others from World War I to after World War II, with tens of thousands of deaths (Yacoub 1986).
14. The decline was actually quite an uneven affair of complex social-ecological interactions (Adams 1978; Tainter 1988; Tainter 2000; Yoffee

and Cowgill 1988). The Mesopotamian collapse is now being studied in the context of complex adaptive systems (Gunderson and Holling 2001; Levin 1999) and resilience theory (Redman and Kinzig 2003).

15. For details, see Leick 2001.
16. Diamond 2003a.
17. Central Intelligence Agency (CIA), Iraq, in *The World Factbook* 2003 (CIA, Washington, DC, 2003), http://www.cia.gov/cia/publications/factbook/geos/iz.html#Geo.
18. Green 1979, p. 272.
19. For a while, they even collected tribute from the once great maritime city of Tyre (Cotterell 1980, p. 131), sited in what is now southern Lebanon. Tyre was captured by the crusaders and then recaptured by Muslims and destroyed in AD 1291, to be remembered along with Nineveh in Kipling's poem.
20. Healy 1991.
21. Nagle and Burstein 2002, p. 40.
22. Quoted in Starr 1991, p. 133. This is the source for much of the material in this paragraph.
23. Union of Concerned Scientists 1993. The entire statement is reprinted in Ehrlich and Ehrlich 1996, pp. 242–250.
24. National Academy of Sciences USA 1993. The report is reprinted in Ehrlich and Ehrlich 1996, pp. 233–242.
25. E.g., Ehrlich 1989; Sapolsky 1997; Bazzaz et al. 1998.
26. E.g., Pirie 1966; Blanko et al. 1967; Oak Ridge National Laboratory 1968; Dyson 1975. For analysis, see Cloud 1968; Ehrlich and Holdren 1969; Ehrlich 1975; and Ehrlich and Mooney 1983.
27. Pirie 1966, 1969.
28. Oak Ridge National Laboratory 1968.
29. Newman and Kenworthy 1989, pp. 106, 148, 164; Kay 1997, p. 15; Freund and Martin 1993, p. 7.
30. For an introduction to the drawbacks of modern agricultural technology, see Ehrlich et al. 1993, 1995; Smale 1997; Shiva 1999; and Smil 2000.
31. It can also be defined as one that has resilience, that is, the ability to absorb shocks and stresses without losing fundamental valued properties. What exactly is meant by a sustainable society (or ecosystem) is a more difficult technical issue than it may appear. See, e.g., discussions in Gunderson and Holling 2001.
32. Ornstein and Ehrlich 1989.
33. For a recent pertinent analysis, see Rosa et al. 2003.
34. Union of Concerned Scientists 1993.

CHAPTER 1: THE HUMAN PREDICAMENT
1. "Recessional" (Kipling 1942, p. 893).
2. World Resources Institute 2000.

3. Study of Critical Environmental Problems 1970. The first mention we have found of humanity being a geological force is in Osborne 1948, chap. 3. For a more recent assessment, see Vitousek et al. 1997.
4. Ehrlich 1993.
5. Schneider 1997b; Intergovernmental Panel on Climate Change (IPCC) 2001.
6. This has been summarized in a simple identity: $I = PAT$. All the equation says is that the environmental impact of a society $(I)$ can be estimated by multiplying the number of people $(P)$ in the society by the affluence $(A)$ per person, measured by the level of consumption. ($A$ is used for affluence instead of $C$ for consumption simply because $IPAT$ is euphonious and $IPCT$ isn't.) That product is then multiplied by the technology factor $(T)$, which includes the social, economic, and political arrangements connected with supplying what is consumed (Ehrlich and Ehrlich 1990; Ehrlich and Holdren 1971; Holdren and Ehrlich 1974; Ehrlich 1995).
7. Vitousek et al. 1986, 1997; Pimm 2001.
8. E.g., Diamond 1997; Sachs and Warner 2001.
9. E.g., Ehrlich 2000.
10. This is the subject of a large and somewhat contentious literature. See, e.g., Landes 1999; Davis 2001; Easterly 2002; Acemoglu et al. 2002, 2003.
11. Population Reference Bureau 2003.
12. Pritchett 1997.
13. Recent advances in India and China may have brought about a small reversal of this trend (World Bank and International Monetary Fund 1999).
14. World Bank and International Monetary Fund 1999, p. 2; World Bank 2001.
15. There is evidence that some hunter-gatherer groups, besides being culturally integrated and not jealous of the condition of others, were able to supply their material needs in a relatively few hours per day.
16. GDP is the total flow of goods and services produced in a nation over a year. Gross national product (GNP) is GDP with the income earned by people living in the country from investments outside the country added in, and the income accruing to foreigners living abroad subtracted. Average per capita GDP in North America and Europe rose from about $7,500 in 1950 to more than $25,000 in 1999 (in constant U.S. dollars) (Worldwatch Institute 2000). Per capita GDP for sub-Saharan Africa was $500 in 1999, and it was even lower in many countries, such as Burundi, Chad, and Ethiopia.
17. Here we have used figures on per capita GDP (gross domestic product— the sum of all goods and services produced in a society divided by its population size) as a measure of wealth. More recently, economists have

devised another measure, PPP (purchasing power parity). PPP is essentially the per capita GDP corrected for price differences between nations in the dollar value of goods and services one could buy in the United States with a given amount of money. We use this measure for some later comparisons. Purchasing power in very poor countries often differs considerably from that in the United States. Thus, in terms of purchasing power, sub-Saharan nations, excluding South Africa, have an average per capita income of about $1,000 (World Bank 2001).

18. World Bank 2000. Some Asian countries, especially in East Asia, have per capita GDPs resembling Europe's, whereas some others are among the world's poorest. The two largest nations, China and India, are still ranked as lower-middle and lower-income, respectively, by the World Bank, although China's GDP has been increasing rapidly in recent years. Latin America has made some progress, if unevenly, and per capita GDPs there have roughly doubled since 1950, to $6,500 in 1999; see Worldwatch Institute 2002.

19. E.g., Feshbach and Friendly 1992. Average per capita GDPs of the former Soviet bloc are barely one-fifth those of the market-based industrialized nations.

20. The United States, Canada, Japan, Australia, New Zealand, and countries in Europe, except for the former Soviet Union and its eastern European satellites.

21. World Bank 2000.

22. Pritchett 1997.

23. While *purchasing power* gives a more accurate view of the buying power of individuals, given differences in costs of essential goods and services, most people in sub-Saharan Africa are surviving on two dollars a day or less. Purchasing power figures here are from Population Reference Bureau 2003.

24. Directly or indirectly—much of the grain is fed to animals that in turn are eaten by people. The leading cereals are wheat, rice, maize, and a variety of coarse grains such as oats, rye, millet, and sorghum.

25. Worldwatch Institute 2002.

26. Ehrlich et al. 1993. International food agencies were also created in the 1970s to stockpile food surpluses and distribute emergency supplies in areas threatened by famine. While the grain stocks thus used have been minuscule in the global food picture, they have repeatedly saved lives in suffering societies such as Ethiopia, Sudan, and, most recently, Afghanistan and Iraq.

27. Leisinger et al. 2002; World Bank 2000; see also Gardner and Halweil 2000. A recent report by the World Health Organization estimated that some 3.4 million people, mostly children, die of hunger every year, not counting hundreds of thousands of children who die prematurely of diseases that wouldn't have killed them had they been well fed.

28. E.g., Anonymous 2003f.
29. Pers. comm., 17 August 2003. In the counterintuitive language of economists, the solution for hunger is to increase the demand for food among the poverty-stricken (remember, supply will attempt to keep up with demand—the willingness or ability to *pay* for something).
30. Smil 2000, pp. 251–264.
31. Since 1950, while grain harvests tripled, meat production expanded more than fivefold. Aquaculture, in scarcely twenty years, has grown from a negligible source to account for more than 30 percent of the total fish harvest (Worldwatch Institute 2002; World Resources Institute 1998), most of which also ends up on the tables of the rich.
32. The global birthrate has dropped impressively in the past three decades, from 1.8 percent per year in the mid-1970s to 1.2 percent (United Nations [Population Division] 2003) or 1.3 percent (Population Reference Bureau 2003) now. But one should not be misled by that clear progress. The 1.8 percent was applied to a population of 4 billion, meaning that only slightly more than 70 million people were being added to the population each year.
33. Smil 2000, pp. 182–187.
34. E.g., Smil 2000, pp. 302–303.
35. The leading food exporters are the United States, Canada, Australia, Argentina, Thailand, and members of the European Union. It is ironic that the rich industrial countries that so heavily depend on resources from other regions reverse the flow by supplying basic foods to those regions.
36. But see Smale (1997), who doesn't think the problems of genetic erosion and vulnerability, at least in wheat, are as severe or as traceable to the green revolution as often claimed.
37. Ted Agres, Biodiversity treaty called disastrous, *The Scientist,* 10 September 2003, http://www.the-scientist.com.
38. Yield is production of a given crop per unit area.
39. Worldwatch Institute 2002.
40. Smil 2000, p. 315. Thomas Robert Malthus was the famous British economist and clergyman who warned in 1798 that population growth could outstrip food supply.
41. Falcon 2002; Falcon and Fowler 2002.
42. Shiva 2003, p. 149.
43. Quoted in Hughes 1975, p. 70.
44. For an excellent recent history, see Williams 2003.
45. World Resources Institute 2000; Food and Agriculture Organization of the United Nations (FAO) 2001; Bryant et al. 1997. The situation is complicated by the differing methods of calculating forest cover and loss among various international agencies.
46. Bryant et al. 1997; Worldwatch Institute 2002.

47. World Resources Institute 2000.
48. World Resources Institute 2000.
49. Reuters, U.S. Democrats blast Bush plan to cut land purchases, 13 February 2003.
50. Oldeman 1998; Daily 1995.
51. Smil 2000.
52. Gardner 1996; Imhoff et al. 1998.
53. American Farmland Trust 1997.
54. Kolankiewicz and Beck 2001.
55. See http://www.touregypt.net/fayoum2.htm. The site is about sixty-five miles southwest of Cairo, and the dam blocked a natural canal that connected the lake in the depression to the Nile.
56. See http://geography.about.com/library/weekly/aa012698.htm?once=true&.
57. Eckholm 2003, pp. 1ff.; http://www.chinaonline.com/refer/ministry_profiles/threegorgesdam.asp. More than 15 million people are expected to benefit from the resultant flood control and electricity generation.
58. Gleick 2002.
59. Simon 1998; Gleick 2000.
60. The controlled water supply from irrigation more than doubles crop yields. Some 40 percent of the world's agricultural products are from irrigated land. Postel 1998, 1999; Food and Agriculture Organization of the United Nations (FAO), FAOSTAT Statistics Database, land use and irrigation data collections, http://apps.fao.org; Meinzen-Dick and Rosegrant 2001; Worldwatch Institute 2002.
61. Reisner 1986; Postel et al. 1996.
62. Postel 1998, 1999.
63. Gleick 2000.
64. Associated Press 2003.
65. Opie 1993, pp. 3–4.
66. Glennon 2002, p. 32.
67. Jehl 2002.
68. Postel 1999; Gleick et al. 1999. For an example of struggles over Colorado River water, see Murphy 2003b.
69. Postel 1998, 1999; Meinzen-Dick and Rosegrant 2001; Worldwatch Institute 2002.
70. Postel 1998.
71. Meinzen-Dick and Rosegrant 2001.
72. Anonymous 2003l.
73. Gleick et al. 2002. While in many cases prices for water *should* be higher to reflect all the costs in human effort and environmental decline involved in providing it (in economic terms, water's "social costs"), one legitimate role for government is to subsidize the supply of so vital a substance to those unable to pay their share of those costs.

74. Murphy 2003a; Service 2003.
75. Gleick 2002.
76. Agence France-Presse 2002.
77. Meinzen-Dick and Rosegrant 2001.
78. Gleick 2002.
79. Effluvium from confined animal feeding operations (CAFOs), which often hold tens of thousands of hogs in a concentrated complex of buildings, is pumped into lagoons, from which it may leak or be washed out by storms into nearby streams or offshore. In the latter case, the effects may resemble the Gulf of Mexico dead zone.
80. World Resources Institute 2000.
81. The importance of wise management of increasingly constrained water resources for future food production and human well-being was elucidated in a recent study by the International Food Policy Research Institute; see Rosegrant et al. 2003, pp. 24–36. The analysis showed that failure to address the problem politically was likely to result in higher water prices and increased domestic shortages (and thus less consumption by poorer groups). Significantly reduced grain production because of inefficient irrigation would lead to higher food prices and further deterioration of water-dependent natural ecosystems.
82. Pauly et al. 2002; Pauly and Maclean 2003.
83. Ehrlich et al. 1977. The plight of the whales was a centerpiece of the first United Nations Conference on the Human Environment in 1972, and regulation of whaling ensued, more or less successfully, including bans on hunting of the most endangered species. Following this, some whale species began to show signs of recovery. But by 2003 things seemed to be moving backward. A new study indicated that previous estimates of original unexploited whale populations had been too small, and thus the degree of overharvesting had been underestimated (Roman and Palumbi 2003). Meanwhile, first Japan and Norway and then Iceland had returned to whaling under the supremely phony excuse that it was for "scientific research."
84. World Resources Institute 1998; Food and Agriculture Organization of the United Nations (FAO) 1997.
85. Lubchenco et al. 2003; Pearce 2003b; Leahy 2003.
86. Pauly and Watson 2003.
87. Jackson et al. 2001. Coastal populations of fish, shellfish, sea turtles, and marine mammals have been harvested so intensively that most of them, even where supposedly underfished today, are very small in comparison with prehistoric levels.
88. Thirty square miles of coastal marshes are lost annually in the United States alone. Perhaps 15 to 20 percent of the marine harvest is composed of fishes that depend on those wetlands for part of their life history, representing some 25 to 30 percent of the value of the catch

because of the higher prices commanded by shellfish and a few prized fish species. These are guesstimates by a very knowledgeable fisheries biologist, Andrew A. Rosenberg, Department of Natural Resources, University of New Hampshire (pers. comm., 7 January 2003). Global warming, which is also connected to human population size and growth, is exacerbating the trend of wetlands loss (Ray et al. 1992).

89. The *Exxon Valdez* spilled almost 11 million gallons of oil.

90. Pew Oceans Commission, *America's Living Oceans: Charting a Course for Sea Change* (Pew Oceans Commission, Arlington, VA, May 2003), executive summary, http://www.pewoceans.org/oceans/oceans_overview.asp.

91. Watson and Pauly 2001.

92. Worldwatch Institute 2002.

93. Naylor et al. 2000; for a recent overview, see Naylor et al. 2003.

94. Ellis 2003.

95. Pearce 2003c.

96. For one approach, see Zabel et al. 2003.

97. Especially natural capital in the form of biodiversity (Ehrlich and Ehrlich 1981, 1992; Wilson 2002).

98. Repetto and Holmes 1983; Repetto et al. 1987.

CHAPTER 2: THE COSTS OF SUCCESS

1. Catton 1980, p. 17.

2. Carson 1962; for the book's accuracy and impact, see Ehrlich 1979.

3. Ehrlich et al. 1977, pp. 854ff.

4. E.g., Rudd 1964; Woodwell 1967.

5. Genesis 1:28. God said, "Be fruitful and increase in number: fill the earth and subdue it" (Committee on Bible Translation 1984, pp. 1–2). Our daughter, Lisa, was told by an intelligent but uneducated Latin American–born friend many years ago that the friend was disgusted by her sister, who kept having babies even though she was on welfare. Surprised, because she knew her friend was a fundamentalist Christian, Lisa asked if the sister wasn't just following the biblical injunction. Her friend simply replied, "Ya conquistada"—It's subdued already.

6. Daily 1997; Ehrlich and Ehrlich 1992; Ehrlich and Roughgarden 1987, pp. 519ff.

7. Ehrlich and Ehrlich 1981; Daily 1997; Chapin et al. 2000; Beattie and Ehrlich 2001.

8. Ehrlich and Mooney 1983, p. 252.

9. There is a trend toward such valuation, however (e.g., Daily and Ellison 2002).

10. Social costs are examples of negative externalities.

11. E.g., Tilman et al. 1994; Heywood 1995; Myers 1996; Hughes et al. 1997, 2000; Tilman 2000.

12. E.g., Rolston 1988; Nash 1989. Unfortunately, this ethical view is not

widely enough shared. For example, people are exterminating our closest living relatives on the planet, chimpanzees and bonobos, through a combination of habitat destruction and hunting for "bushmeat" by local human groups. Yet humanity has already learned much about itself by studying these fascinating other apes (Ehrlich 2002; Goodall 1986; Waal 1997), so close to us that Jared Diamond christened human beings the "third chimpanzee" (Diamond 1991). And we may have much more to learn, especially from the bonobos. After all, they solve their disputes not with warfare but usually with mutual genital rubbing (Waal 1997, pp. 108ff.)!

13. Defined as areas still largely capable of supplying their original suite of ecosystem services sustainably.

14. Balmford et al. 2002; the quote is from p. 953. The opportunity costs in the calculation are the value of the next best possible uses of the areas preserved—for instance, the sale price of timber that might be harvested from a reserve.

15. Myers 1979; Ehrlich and Ehrlich 1981.

16. Marshall and Ward 1996; Raup 1991.

17. Myers 1988, 1990.

18. Tilman et al. 1994; Hanski and Ovaskainen 2002.

19. Ehrlich and Daily 1993; Daily and Ehrlich 1995; Ceballos and Ehrlich 2002.

20. This definition is oversimplified but will do for our purposes. For more details, see Ehrlich and Hanski 2004.

21. Hughes et al. 1997, 2000.

22. A serious question has arisen as to how the scarce resources devoted to conservation should be allocated between two important goals of preserving biodiversity. One is preserving hot spots, areas such as the Amazon basin, which is incredibly rich in species; the other is protecting "cool spots," places not incredibly rich in species diversity but with many populations of a relatively few species delivering essential services to humanity (Kareiva and Marvier 2003).

23. For some insight into crooked Florida politics for those who don't remember the 2000 presidential election, see Hiaasen 2001 and Palast 2002.

24. Kiple 1993, p. 962.

25. McCarthy 2003; Pain et al. 2003.

26. Pain et al. 2003.

27. Quoted in Ehrlich and Ehrlich 1981, p. 250.

28. Ehrlich 2000, pp. 171–172.

29. Myers 1996; Ehrlich 2001b; Palumbi 2001b.

30. World Resources Institute 2000. There also are about 1.7 billion domestic sheep and goats and many billions of chickens.

31. Ehrlich and Ehrlich 1981; Daily 1997.

32. Coevolution is the reciprocal evolution of ecologically intimate organisms—for instance, parasites creating selection pressures on hosts, predators on prey, herbivores on plants, and, in each case, vice versa— Ehrlich and Raven 1964.
33. E.g., King 1984; Drake et al. 1989; Simberloff et al. 1997; Baskin 2002; O'Dowd et al. 2003.
34. Baskin 2002.
35. E.g., Palumbi 2001a, 2001b.
36. Intergovernmental Panel on Climate Change (IPCC) 2002; Karl and Trenberth 2003.
37. Sample 2003.
38. World Meteorological Organization, Extreme weather events might increase, press release, 2 July 2003, Geneva.
39. Root et al. 2003; Parmesan and Yohe 2003.
40. Curran et al. 2003.
41. Wolfson and Schneider 2002. These are the conditions prevailing on the moon and presumably on Mars (which is farther from the sun and even colder). Venus, by contrast, is so shrouded in greenhouse gases— mainly $CO_2$—that it is too hot for life as we know it.
42. Intergovernmental Panel on Climate Change (IPCC) 2002.
43. Wolfson and Schneider 2002. A positive feedback occurs when the results of a process themselves enhance the process.
44. These gases remain in the atmosphere for various amounts of time on average, ranging from many centuries for some CFCs and related chemicals to a century or so for $CO_2$ and $N_2O$ and perhaps a decade for $CH_4$.
45. Benedick 1991; Turco 1997.
46. Technically, this process is known as evapotranspiration.
47. Firor and Jacobsen 2002.
48. Root et al. 2003; Parmesan and Yohe 2003.
49. For more on potentially catastrophic nonlinearities in the climate system, see Pearce 2003a.
50. Schneider 1997b, pp. 90—92; Firor and Jacobsen 2002.
51. Harte et al. 1991.
52. Simonich and Hites 1995; McGinn 2002.
53. Colborn et al. 1996; for updates, see http://www.ourstolenfuture.org/.
54. Baker et al. 1996.
55. Goolsby et al. 1997.
56. Harte et al. 1991.
57. Ehrlich et al. 1977, pp. 574—575.
58. Ehrlich et al. 1977, pp. 571ff.
59. Cone 2003.
60. Ehrlich et al. 1977, p. 574.
61. Smil 2000, p. 82.

62. See, most recently, Hileman 2003, which describes recent findings on rising adverse effects of toxic exposures on children in the United States.
63. Worldwatch Institute 2002; World Health Organization (WHO), Air pollution, fact sheet no. 187, September 2000, http://www.who.int/inf-fs/en/fact187.html.
64. Colborn et al. 1996.
65. Daily and Ehrlich 1996a, 1996b.
66. Brasher and Altman 2003.
67. AIDS symptoms usually don't appear until years after HIV exposure. The modes of transmission and the long symptom-free period have led to denial of the problem by both infected individuals and governments, especially in very poor countries where many people are uneducated and health facilities are weak to non-existent.
68. Baranauckas 2002.
69. For some notion of the seriousness of the flu threat, see Webster and Walker 2003 and Webby and Webster 2003.
70. Daily and Ehrlich 1996a; McMichael 2001.
71. Total confirmed infections totaled only somewhat more than 4,000.
72. Ginsburg 2003.
73. Altman 2003.
74. McMichael 2001, pp. 301ff.
75. The SARS episode clearly revealed shortcomings in the global health network, including lack of uniformity in testing procedures, but nevertheless the disease was successfully contained. The question is, will it recur? If it does, will it again be quickly detected and contained? See Altman 2003.
76. With people, the concept of carrying capacity is quite complex—for details, see Daily and Ehrlich 1992 and Ehrlich et al. 1992.
77. Wackernagel et al. 2002.
78. The numbers cited, for example, do not consider a buffer of land devoted to the critical task of biodiversity preservation. If the reserve for conservation of 12 percent of biologically productive land recommended by the Brundtland Report (World Commission on Environment and Development 1987) were included in the figures, overshoot would have begun in the early 1970s and the current overshoot would be some 40 percent (Wackernagel et al. 2002).
79. Borgstrom 1965.
80. Rees 1996; Wackernagel and Rees 1996.
81. Rees 2001, p. 230. If you would like to calculate your footprint, see any of the following Web sites: http://www.lead.org/leadnet/footprint/intro.htm; http://www.redefiningprogress.org/programs/sustainabilityindicators/ef/; http://www.earthday.net/footprint/index.asp (or http://www.myfootprint.org/); http://www.ecologicalfootprint.com/.

82. Rees 2002.
83. Rahnema 2002; Cobb 2002.
84. Stone 2002.
85. Gardner and Halweil 2000.
86. Ehrlich and Ehrlich 1981; Vitousek et al. 1986; Ehrlich et al. 1995; Daily 1995.
87. E.g., Simonich and Hites 1995.
88. E.g., Buchmann and Nabhan 1996; Nabhan and Buchmann 1997; Inouye 2001.
89. Schneider and Londer 1984; Schneider 1989, 1997b.
90. Michener et al. 1997.
91. Shiva 2003, p. 147.
92. Anderson and May 1991.
93. For an in-depth analysis of the connections in complex systems, see Gunderson and Holling 2001.
94. E.g., Vitousek et al. 1996, 1986, 1997; Vitousek and Matson 1993.
95. Holdren and Ehrlich 1974; Holdren 1991; National Academy of Sciences USA 1993; Union of Concerned Scientists 1993.
96. Vitousek et al. 1997, p. 499.

CHAPTER 3: THE TIDE OF POPULATION

1. Osborne 1948, p. 201.
2. This story was first told in Ehrlich 1997.
3. Action Comores, Environmental crisis in the Comores, http://vsb.nott. ac.uk/Action-Comores/achomepage3.html.
4. Anonymous 1997a.
5. Sangonet, Le chef autoproclamé de l'île sécessionniste d'Anjouan (Comores), le colonel Saïd Abeid, renversé par un putsch ce 9 août 2001 (Sangonet, 2003), http://www.sangonet.com/Fich2ActuaInterAfric/ AnjouanPutsch9aout01.html; Central Intelligence Agency (CIA), Comoros, in *The World Factbook 2003* (CIA, Washington, DC, 2003), http:// www.cia.gov/cia/publications/factbook/geos/cn.html. See also (Europa World 2003); Africa Intelligence, Surveys: The Anjouan crisis, *Indian Ocean Newsletter,* http://www.africaintelligence.com/dossiers/aia/dos_ aia_com_anjouan.asp.
6. U.S. Department of State, Bureau of Consular Affairs, Consular information sheet: Comoros, http://travel.state.gov/comoros.html.
7. Central Intelligence Agency (CIA), Comoros, in *The World Factbook 2003* (CIA, Washington, DC, 2003), http://www.cia.gov/cia/publications/ factbook/geos/cn.html.
8. Diamond 1989; Ehrlich 2000, especially pp. 161ff. For an interesting recent examination of this issue, see d'Errico 2003.
9. Ehrlich 2000; for references, see p. 403, note 36.

10. Ehrlich 2000; especially chap. 10.

11. E.g., Smith 1995.

12. Easter Island is a classic example (Diamond 1995). Some other civiliza-
    tions in which population growth probably played a role in generating
    collapse include those of the classic Maya, the Anasazi, and the Greeks
    (Ehrlich and Ehrlich 1996, pp. 84–86).

13. E.g., Tainter 1988, 2000; Webster 2002; Redman and Kinzig 2003.

14. Diamond 1995, 1997.

15. E.g., Davis 2001.

16. United Nations (Population Division) 2001, 2003.

17. Population Reference Bureau 1976, 2002.

18. United Nations (Population Division) 2003.

19. Wackernagel and Rees 1996, p. 15.

20. T. Bearden, Drought in the Northeast, *NewsHour with Jim Lehrer,* 23 April
    2002.

21. Brody 2003.

22. McMichael 2001, pp. 117–118; Blockstein 1998.

23. Population growth of states in the 1990s is from U.S. Census data sum-
    marized in McGeveran 2003.

24. Brown and Halweil 1998.

25. Severe acid rain from this source was reported two decades ago in Harte
    1983. The situation persists: see, e.g., APEC Virtual Center for Environ-
    mental Technology Exchange, Acid rain in China, http://www.apec-vc.
    org.cn/english/dq/ccaid.htm; UNEPnet/Mercure Beijing Earth Sta-
    tion, State of the environment, China '97: Acid rain, http://svri-
    pek.unep.net/soechina/acid/acids1.htm; C. Kirk, Environment report—
    July 5, 2002: Conditions in China, http://www.manythings.org/voa/
    02/020705er_t.htm.

26. Current population statistics in this chapter are from the Population
    Reference Bureau's (PRB's) annual World Population Data Sheet or its
    Web site (http://www.prb.org) unless otherwise cited. The data sheet is
    an invaluable resource and can be purchased from the PRB, 1875 Con-
    necticut Ave., NW, Suite 520, Washington, DC 20009-5728.

27. Yang and Schneider 1997–1998; in typical projections, China will pass
    the United States in $CO_2$ emissions well before 2050—see the table on
    p. 400.

28. For a view we share, see Diamond 1997.

29. The TFR is essentially the lifetime average number of children born
    per woman in a population (technically, TFR is calculated by running
    an imaginary cohort of newborn females through the age-specific fer-
    tility and mortality schedules pertaining for the year in which the esti-
    mate is made, and determining how many children the average woman
    bears in her lifetime). In replacement reproduction, the extra fraction

of a child is to compensate for those newborn infants who do not survive to reproductive age.

30. Ornstein and Ehrlich 1989.
31. Population Reference Bureau 2003.
32. Ehrlich 1968.
33. Vogt 1948; Brown 1954.
34. This ignores the centrally planned economies of the Soviet Union, most of which were industrialized by then and had low fertilities but stagnant economies.
35. For more details, see Ehrlich et al. 1995.
36. Along the way to that understanding, there was considerable controversy over whether family planning programs were of any value in lowering birthrates—a controversy that reached its zenith at the first United Nations World Population Conference in 1974. Motivation was the key issue: why do people choose to have larger or smaller families? The answer was not at all clear at that time, but much has been learned since, especially about the importance of women's schooling and economic opportunities (e.g., Ehrlich et al. 1995).
37. Ehrlich et al. 1995.
38. United Nations Population Fund (UNFPA) 2002.
39. United Nations (Population Division) 2003.
40. U.S. Census Bureau, International Data Base (IDB), Summary demographic data for United States, October 2002 version, http://www.census.gov/cgi-bin/ipc/idbsum?cty=US. In the early 1970s, the U.S. TFR fell as low as 1.7, but then it rose slowly until about 2001. Then it dropped slightly, possibly in response to the economic recession.
41. Ehrlich et al. 1995.
42. World Bank 2000.
43. Ehrlich et al. 1995.
44. Literacy and health data in this and succeeding paragraphs are from World Bank 2000; TFRs are from Population Reference Bureau 2002.
45. One example is Bangladesh, which had a TFR of 3.6 in 2003, reduced from 4.9 since 1990 (Population Reference Bureau 1990, 2003). A family planning success story resulted from recruitment of village women to provide information, advice, and materials to neighboring families, along with basic health care—an echo of China's "barefoot doctors" of the 1970s. Yet female literacy is low—some 27 percent in 1997—and hunger and poverty are still prevalent. Several Southeast Asian nations have reduced their TFRs below 3, including Vietnam, Indonesia (the world's fourth largest nation, with more than 200 million people), and Sri Lanka. Some other Asian countries, including Malaysia, the Philippines, Nepal, and Pakistan, have more slowly

reduced their TFRs to between 3 and 4 but have mixed success in development. Western Asia and northern Africa also present a varied picture: as we indicated, conservative societies, such as in Saudi Arabia and Yemen, have maintained high birthrates despite high incomes and female literacy rates; others have seen declines in average family sizes to levels ranging from 2.5 to 5.

46. Population Reference Bureau 1990, 2003. Perhaps more important, average family size in Brazil, in the same period, dropped from 3.3 to 2.2, and in Mexico, the second largest nation in the region, from 3.8 to 2.8. Except for some Caribbean islands with below-replacement reproduction, Latin American TFRs range between 2 and 4.7.

47. Population Reference Bureau 2003. In the mid-1980s, Kenya was a record-holder, with a TFR of 8.1; by 2003, its TFR had fallen to 4.4.

48. United Nations (Population Division) 2003. Prospects are also discouraging in some countries in western Asia, where the TFR in Yemen is 7.2, in the Palestinian territory 5.9, in Saudi Arabia 5.7, and in pre-war Iraq 5.4, but the total number of people involved is about 100 million, as opposed to nearly 700 million in sub-Saharan Africa. In addition, the wealth of the oil-rich nations of the Middle East helps buffer some of the consequences of rapid population growth there.

49. E.g., Dasgupta 1993, 2000, 2003.

50. Dasgupta 2003, p. 222.

51. Dasgupta 2003, p. 233.

52. Kates and Haarmann 1992.

53. United Nations (Population Division) 2003.

54. United Nations (Population Division) 2003.

55. United Nations (Population Division) 2001; United Nations (Population Division) 2003; Lamptey et al. 2002.

56. United Nations (Population Division) 2003.

57. By 2002, besides more than 20 million deaths from AIDS in the two decades since it was recognized, nearly 40 million more people were infected and likely to die prematurely, and an additional 45 million people were expected to be infected by 2010 (Lamptey et al. 2002; United Nations Joint Programme on HIV/AIDS [UNAIDS] 2002). Unsafe sex and HIV/AIDS were ranked second in the World Health Organization's list of leading risk factors (Agence France-Presse 2002).

58. United Nations (Population Division) 2003.

59. O'Neill and Balk 2001.

60. Recent United Nations projections extend only to 2050.

61. The momentum results from previous higher birthrates that produced ever larger generations of people, who then become parents and grandparents, living alongside their children and grandchildren, before dying

of old age. When a formerly growing population reaches replacement reproduction, it takes roughly a lifetime (seventy or so years) before growth stops. If fertility falls below replacement level, there will still be a lag, although a shorter one, before growth ends and the population starts to shrink slowly.

62. United Nations (Population Division) 2003.
63. E.g., Bruni 2002; Wattenberg 1987.
64. The relationship of population growth and structure to political instability is both important and complex (Goldstone 1991), and we're dealing with only one obvious aspect here.
65. Approximately 90 percent of those on the FBI's most wanted terrorist list in 2001 were males who were twenty-two to thirty-four years old when their first alleged terrorist act took place (Federal Bureau of Investigation, Most wanted terrorists, http://www.fbi.gov/mostwant/terrorists/fugitives.htm).
66. Merari 1990.
67. United Nations (Population Division) 2001.
68. Browne 2002.
69. Ehrlich and Ehrlich 1989.
70. Ehrlich and Holdren 1971.
71. Such as the Competitive Enterprise Institute. For an egregious example, see Eberstadt 1995.
72. United Nations (Population Division) 2002b.
73. Sheehan 2002.
74. Sheehan 2002.
75. Sheehan 2002.
76. Technically, it is described by an equation of degree higher than one. The square example is of degree two.
77. Diamond 1991, pp. 168–169.
78. Stambaugh 1988, p. 337.
79. Carcopino 1940, p. 42.
80. McNeill 1976, pp. 115ff.; Stark 1996, chap. 4.
81. Daily and Ehrlich 1996a; Levin and Anderson 1999; McMichael 2001, chap. 4.
82. E.g., Ehrlich and Ehrlich 1970, pp. 148–150.
83. For a recent report from the frontlines, see Anonymous 2003g.
84. Calhoun 1962.
85. Ehrlich and Freedman 1971.
86. For a fascinating account of how people adapted to the horrors of Nazi extermination camps, see Frankl 1984.
87. For more details, see Ehrlich and Ehrlich 1990.
88. Homer-Dixon 1994; Homer-Dixon and Blitt 1998.
89. Cooley 1984; Kelly and Homer-Dixon 1998; Klare 2001.

90. Howard and Homer-Dixon 1998.
91. E.g., Gizewski and Homer-Dixon 1998; Renner 2002.
92. *New Scientist* 1975.
93. Klare 2001; for fascinating background information on Afghanistan, see Rashid 2001.
94. E.g., Mimouni 1992.
95. E.g., Courbage 1994; Fargues 1997.
96. Population Reference Bureau 2001.
97. Fargues 2000.
98. *Undocumented* is the current politically correct euphemism for *illegal.*
99. Population Reference Bureau 2003.
100. Projected from United States Census Bureau, 2002, http://www.census.gov/.
101. United Nations (Population Division) 2003.
102. For a general discussion, with emphasis on migration from Mexico to the United States, see Ehrlich et al. 1981.
103. Ehrlich et al. 1981.
104. Many migrants to industrialized countries send part of their earnings back home, which compensates in part for the resources or profits that rich countries extract from developing ones. The same is true for urban migrants in developing countries. An African son who moves from his family's poor farm, gets a job in the city, and sends money home may allow his family to have a better diet (which may increase its productivity) and substitute kerosene for firewood, taking some pressure off dwindling local forests. Depending on the son's consumption level and other factors, in many cases migration thus may help to reduce overall environmental pressures.
105. United Nations (Population Division) 2003.
106. Liu et al. 2003.
107. Frank 1999, p. 3.
108. In 2002, some of the nations poised on the edge of population shrinkage because of low birthrates were Finland, Greece, Italy, Portugal, the Czech Republic, Slovakia, Hungary, Poland, and Russia. South Africa, Botswana, and Zimbabwe were, tragically, projected to shrink because of high mortality from AIDS. While Russia's TFR is far below replacement level (1.3, compared with 2.1), breakdowns in public health have led to high death rates: 16 per 1,000, compared with 9 per 1,000 in the United States; life expectancy of sixty-five years, compared with seventy-seven (Population Reference Bureau 2002).
109. This includes the United Nations demographers, whose medium projection included a TFR for Europe in the period 2045–2050 of 1.8; in 2002 it was 1.4. But the projection doesn't assume a rebound above replacement level. United Nations (Population Division) 2003.

CHAPTER 4: THE CONSUMPTION FACTOR

1. Rosenblatt 1999, p. 2.
2. Sabloff 1994.
3. Webster 2002, pp. 234–236.
4. Wilk 1985.
5. Webster 2002; Diamond 2003b.
6. For what follows in this paragraph, we're deeply indebted to Richard D. Hansen (pers. comm., 17 June 2003).
7. Hansen 1995.
8. Schreiner 2002.
9. Hansen 1998.
10. Webster 2002, p. 348.
11. Ehrlich and Ehrlich 1989, 1991b.
12. World Bank 2001.
13. Cross 2000, p. 1. Much of what follows is covered in depth in this interesting book.
14. Cohen 2002, p. 11.
15. For a fine description of the consumer society in the context of its environmental impact, with wonderful examples, see Durning 1992.
16. In technical economic terms, a "negative externality."
17. Frank 1999, p. 3.
18. Liu et al. 2003.
19. World Resources Institute 2003.
20. Kiley 2002.
21. Kiley 2002.
22. The rest was used as fuel for commercial vehicles, trucks, railroads, aircraft, industrial machinery, space heating, power generation, and the military.
23. Friedman 2003a.
24. A *very* crude estimate. Roughly half of the petroleum used in the United States goes into gasoline for motor vehicles, about half of which are private cars. If $110 billion of the roughly $340 billion military budget (including veterans' benefits) is assignable to obtaining the approximately 175 billion gallons of imported petroleum consumed, and the oil used to run automobiles comes from imported oil (as opposed to domestic) in the same ratio as overall consumption (58 percent), that amounts to more than $0.38 per gallon in any use, including, of course, fuel for Hummers.
25. Frank 1999, pp. 1–2.
26. Frank 1999, p. 24.
27. Results of a Zogby International poll of Americans whose yearly incomes exceeded $250,000 or who had a net worth greater than $1 million. Reported in Arthur Spiegelman, The rich are eyeing space tourism, poll says, Reuters (Los Angeles), 20 May 2002.

28. Material in this paragraph is based primarily on Tempest 2002.
29. Pirages and Ehrlich 1972.
30. Myers and Kent 2004. This book is the main source for the material in this paragraph.
31. Purchasing power parity adjusts national currency values to "international dollars." PPP indicates how much the per capita GNP in local currency would purchase as dollars in the United States (http://pacific.commerce.ubc.ca/xr/PPP.html). Depending on the country, that can be between 1.4 and 4.8 times more than international exchange dollars.
32. Hughes et al. 2002.
33. Much of what follows is based on Tucker 2000.
34. Carrere 2001.
35. In 2003, we discovered that large areas of the lowland forest of New Britain had been converted to palm plantations, damaging much of the ecotourism potential of the area.
36. Siscawati 2001.
37. Bishop 2003.
38. For information about environmental impacts on bird fauna, see Lambert and Collar 2002.
39. Bishop 2003.
40. Nobody knows the origin of the name.
41. Information in this paragraph is largely from Samuel Kepuknai, Kiunga, Papua New Guinea (pers. comm., 1 August 2003).
42. Edward Zackery, Port Moresby, Papua New Guinea, pers. comm., 12 August 2003.
43. Vogt 1948.
44. Vogt 1948, p. 284. The American public might be enlightened if the precise impact of their population growth on the demand for tropical products could be easily calculated. Obviously, the 140 million Americans of the World War II era consumed much less from the tropics than did the 285 million Americans in 2000, but the harvesting, shipping, and storage technologies that now bring many tropical products to American markets were also less advanced in 1945, so per capita demand for the products has doubtless increased disproportionately. Population growth and rising per capita affluence have a multiplicative interaction, and they can be further augmented, as in this case, by technological advances. Unfortunately, the role of population growth in both rich and poor societies in generating the consumption that has caused so much tropical deforestation is very complex. Even so, the obvious role of increasing numbers of affluent people in amplifying demand for timber is frequently neglected.

    Since World War II, there has been about a twenty-five-fold increase in transport activity globally (how much of that is carrying tropical goods to rich countries is not known). That consumption-related activity carries with it a substantial environmental burden. As a single example of its scale, it is estimated that a plate of food on an American dinner table has traveled, on average, some 1,500 miles before it makes the trip from plate to mouth (Mander 2003, p. 117). For those fond of tropical fruits, the mileage is doubtless much higher.

45. E.g., see http://www.ourstolenfuture.org/.

46. Rosegrant et al. 2001.

47. Klare 2001; Renner 2002.

48. Renner 2002, p. 6.

49. Klare 2001, p. 196; Jared Diamond, pers. comm., 15 September 2003.

50. Aceh and Lhokseumawe 2002; Perlez 2003.

51. Renner 2002, pp. 40–42.

52. Renner 2002.

53. World Resources Institute 2003, pp. 132–136. See also World Bank 2003 and Anonymous, How banks do well while doing good, editorial, *New York Times,* 18 November 2003.

54. E.g., Rall 2002; note also Rashid 2001, especially the map opposite p. 1, and chap. 12.

55. PakNews.com, Agreement on US $3.2 billion gas pipeline project signed, 28 December 2002, http:www.truthout.org/docs_02/12.30A. afgh.pipe.p.htm.

56. Central Asia Gas Pipeline, Consortium formed to build Central Asia gas pipeline, news release, 27 October 1997, http://www.unocal.com/uclnews/97news/102797a.htm.

57. Rashid 2001, p. 6.

58. BBC News, Afghanistan plans gas pipeline, 13 May 2002, http://news.bbc.co.uk/1/hi/business/1984459.stm.

59. The oil connection, as well as President Bush's lying to get the United States to attack Iraq, was made explicit by Senator Max Cleland (CNN, *NewsNight with Aaron Brown,* 25 September 2002).

60. For a short, not politically correct rant on the role that oil played in creating the modern Middle East, see Day 1998; for a scholarly history, Fromkin 1989 is excellent. The best single book we've found on oil is Daniel Yergin's (1991).

61. At this writing (December 2003), no threatening stock of weapons of mass destruction (WMD) has been found (Power 2003), and the U.S. government has given no coherent reason why, if Iraqis *did* have WMD, they could not have been deterred from using them. After all, the United States deterred the Soviet Union from using tens of thousands of such weapons (and vice versa) for decades, and there was never any sign that Saddam Hussein or his henchmen were suicidal.

62. But soon after the invasion, U.S. and British refiners began to take advantage of the occupation; see O'Brien 2003.

63. Yager and Steinberg 1975; Ehrlich et al. 1977; Yergin 1991.
64. Kleveman 2003.
65. Baer 2003.
66. The Saudi and Iraqi governments badly need oil revenues and would doubtless continue to sell oil to anyone who would buy. But, among other things, their facilities are very vulnerable to acts of terrorism by their own increasingly radicalized populations.
67. David Corn, Bush's *Top Gun* photo-op, *The Nation*, 1 May 2003, http://www.thenation.com/capitalgames/index.mhtml?bid=3&pid=633. Bush obviously enjoyed playing soldier after having worked hard to avoid being a real one. See, e.g., Sugg 2002; for more, see http://www.awolbush.com/.
68. Pratap Chatterjee, The war on terrorism's gravy train, *CorpWatch*, 2 May 2002, http://www.corpwatch.org/issues/PID.jsp?articleid=2471.
69. Halliburton was described by *New York Times* columnist Bob Herbert as "a slithery enterprise with its rapacious tentacles in everybody's pockets. It benefits from doing business with the enemy, from its relationship with the U.S. military when the U.S. is at war with the enemy, and from contracts to help rebuild the defeated enemy" (Herbert 2003a). By May 2003, the Halliburton subsidiary had received nearly $500 million for work related to Iraq, much of it under the "Logistics Civil Augmentation Program, an obscure but lucrative contract to provide logistical support to the army" (letter from Henry A. Waxman, Democrat from California, ranking minority member, House of Representatives Committee on Government Reform, to Les Brownlee, acting secretary of the Army, 29 May 2003). See also Herbert 2003b and Neil Mackay, Carving up the new Iraq, *Glasgow Sunday Herald*, 13 April 2003, http://www.sundayherald.com/33021. As another columnist, Conn Hallinan, put it, "War is bad business? Not for everyone." Conn Hallinan, War is good business, ZNet, 11 January 2003, http://www.zmag.org/content/showarticle.cfm?SectionID=15&ItemID=2851. (Hallinan is provost of the University of California, Santa Cruz, and a columnist for the *San Francisco Examiner*.) The best way to "support our troops" surely is not to get them killed to keep America overconsuming and make more money for giant corporations (Anonymous 2003a). Interestingly, the latter editorial did not mention former secretary of state George Shultz' chairmanship of the advisory board of the Committee for the Liberation of Iraq, a front group for Bush's plans to invade Iraq (Herbert 2003b); see also Kurt Nimmo, The Committee for the Liberation of Iraq: PR spinning the Bush doctrine, *CounterPunch*, 19 November 2002, http://www.globalpolicy.org/ngos/credib/2002/1119bush.htm. That the life of even one American youngster (to say nothing of those of thousands of Iraqis) should be lost in such an enterprise was a disgrace.

70. Herbert 2003b. See also U.S. awards contract to rebuild Iraq's infrastructure, Associated Press, 17 April 2003; And the winner is Bechtel, *New York Times,* 19 April 2003.

71. Krugman 2003; Johnson 2003. Representative Henry Waxman of the House Committee on Government Reform put the situation equally plainly, describing Halliburton's price gouging in transporting gasoline from Kuwait to Baghdad: "There is growing evidence that favored contractors like Halliburton and Bechtel are getting sweetheart deals that are costing the taxpayer a bundle but delivering scant results ... the Administration is shielding Halliburton and Bechtel from any competition by granting them virtual monopolies over basic services." Contracting abuses in Iraq, statement of Rep. Henry A. Waxman to House Committee on Government Reform, 108th Cong., 1st sess., 15 October 2003, http://www.house.gov/reform/min/pdfs_108/pdf_inves/pdf_admin_halliburton_contract_oct_15_state.pdf. On the other hand, conservative columnist David Brooks claims that the corporations that get to rake in war profits are determined by bureaucrats in a well-structured procurement system (Brooks 2003).

72. Much of what follows is based on Ehrlich and Liu 2002.

73. Prestowitz 2003.

74. See http://www.bp.com/centres/energy/oil/reserves.asp.

75. Klare 2002; Baer 2003.

76. Klare 2001, pp. 29ff.

77. As represented by conservative interventionists, who explicitly believe that "At no time in history has the international security order been as conducive to American interests and ideals. The challenge for the coming century is to preserve and enhance this 'American peace.'" This is to be done by building and repositioning U.S. military forces and maintaining "nuclear strategic superiority." Thomas Donnelly, Rebuilding America's defenses: Strategy, forces, and resources for a new century, Project for the New American Century, September 2000, http://www.newamericancentury.org/publicationsreports.htm, p. iv.

78. Much of what follows is based on proclamations in the National Security Strategy: see National Security Council, *The National Security Strategy of the United States of America,* 20 September 2002, http://www.whitehouse.gov/nsc/nss.html; see also http://www.whitehouse.gov/homeland/.

79. E.g., Deffeyes 2001; Monbiot 2003b.

80. "Recessional" (Kipling 1942, p. 892).

81. Daalder and Lindsay 2003. *Preemptive* is actually the wrong term unless there is a clear, immediate threat (there was none from Iraq). *Precautionary* would be more accurate, but *preemptive* is more current.

82. On nuclear agreements, see John P. Holdren, Testimony before Senate Committee on Foreign Relations, 12 September 2002.

83. The Kyoto Protocol is the implementing mechanism for the first phase of compliance with the Framework Convention on Climate Change produced at the Earth Summit in 1992. See Athanasiou and Baer 2002; Dernbach 2002.

84. Linking the U.S. love affair with SUVs and George W. Bush's pressing for war on Iraq, Thomas Friedman wrote that going to war partly for oil would look better if it were accompanied by "a real program for energy conservation." (That seems unlikely, since Bush's friends make money by selling oil, not conserving it.) Friedman concluded: "I have no problem with a war for oil . . . provided we behave in a way that makes clear to the world we are protecting everyone's access to oil at reasonable prices—not simply our right to binge on it" (Friedman 2003b).

85. Quoted in An open letter to the members of Congress, *The Nation,* editorial, 14 October 2002.

86. Richard Neville, American psycho, *Sydney Morning Herald,* 19 May 2001, http://www.richardneville.com/PDFs/ American_Psycho_excerpt.pdf.

87. Nussbaum 2002.

88. E.g., Singer 2002.

CHAPTER 5: TECHNOLOGY MATTERS

1. Basalla 1988, p. 205.

2. Roan 1989 provides a good overview of the ozone discussion that follows.

3. Molina and Rowland 1974.

4. The overall history of this surprise is well told in Roan 1989, an accurate popular book.

5. Farman et al. 1985.

6. TOMS operated by measuring solar ultraviolet radiation "backscattered" from the lower atmosphere through the stratospheric ozone layer. The deep plunge during 1980–1982 was not detected because, although the readings at first were above the 180 "throw-out" value, the data were not examined closely enough to detect the downward trend immediately. American scientists eventually noted some decline, but by then TOMS was beyond its expected useful life, which added uncertainty to interpretation of the data.

7. This reconstruction of the Nimbus-7 story is based on e-mail correspondence with F. Sherwood Rowland, December 1995, and was first published in Ehrlich and Ehrlich 1996, p. 289.

8. Solomon et al. 1986.

9. European Fluorocarbon Technical Committee, HCFCs: Environment, 2001, http://www.fluorocarbons.org/frame.htm?chfamilies/HCFCs/ environ/environ.htm.

10. E.g., Commoner 1971.

11. Allenby and Richards 1994; Gottlieb 1995.
12. World Resources Institute 2003; Allenby and Richards 1994.
13. Perrin 1979.
14. Dower 2003.
15. Success, of course, is narrowly defined here in terms of what people decide they want. By many standards (e.g., environmental impact, comfort, and time to travel short distances) trains would be more successful than airplanes.
16. Falcon and Fowler 2002; Walter Falcon, Stanford University, pers. comm., 17 August 2003.
17. Geller 2003.
18. For instance, was the green revolution a response to increasing population or to advances in technology? Are proliferating freeways a response to population growth, increased affluence, or some combination? Rising congestion, pollution, and greenhouse gas emissions generated by more and more vehicles obviously are all products of interactions between population, affluence, and technology.
19. Ehrlich and Holdren 1971; Holdren and Ehrlich 1974; Ehrlich and Ehrlich 1990; Ehrlich 1995; McDaniel and Borton 2002.
20. Schneider 1997b; Intergovernmental Panel on Climate Change (IPCC) 2001.
21. Per capita energy use is better than per capita gross domestic product (GDP) in gauging environmental impact for a number of reasons. In a service-based economy, GDP may be the same as for one based on heavy industry, but per capita energy use might be considerably less. Also, inefficient energy use is much more environmentally damaging and provides less service per unit employed than efficient use, and energy demand also is affected by factors such as climate or transportation and settlement patterns.
22. Calculated from data in World Bank 2001.
23. The term *commercial energy* refers to that sold in markets. It does not include the gathering and use of fuelwood by poor rural families—which also increased in the past half-century.
24. Worldwatch Institute 2000, 2002.
25. World Bank 2000; Ehrlich et al. 1992.
26. Calculated from data in World Bank 2000.
27. World Bank 2000.
28. For a pioneering analysis, see Holdren 1991.
29. Holdren 1990.
30. Intergovernmental Panel on Climate Change (IPCC) 2001.
31. Holdren 1991; Von Wiezacker et al. 1998.
32. We use the term *engineering efficiency* here to distinguish it from economic efficiency—a policy increases economic efficiency if it produces aggregate net benefits (increases welfare).

33. Von Wiezacker et al. 1998.
34. For insight into the importance of access to petroleum deposits, see Yergin 1991 and Economides and Oligney 2000.
35. Energy Information Service 2002; World Resources Institute 2000.
36. Von Wiezacker et al. 1998; Rosenfeld 1999; Casten 1998.
37. Schneider et al. 2002.
38. With regard to the latter, the barrier to adoption has primarily been the relatively high purchase price of the lightbulbs, even though the cost is soon recovered by reduced power bills and replacement costs.
39. Wind is actually also a form of solar power, since the sun's energy drives the weather system. So is hydropower, since it is solar energy that lifts water from the surface so it can rain and snow into mountain watersheds. So are biomass and fossil fuels, which represent solar energy captured by photosynthesis recently and in the distant past. But we use the term *solar power* here to refer to direct solar energy as captured in solar thermal apparatus and solar photovoltaic cells.
40. Geller 2003, chaps. 3 and 5; Dernbach 2002; see especially chaps. 2, 3, and 28.
41. Bush's EPA even failed to support the administration's most highly touted program of energy conservation, dramatically slashing its budget (Hebert 2003).
42. Von Wiezacker et al. 1998; Geller 2003, chap. 2.
43. Romero 2003.
44. Geller 2003, chap. 1.
45. Announcement from the World Meteorological Organization, July 2003, reported in Anonymous 2003k.
46. Schneider et al. 2002; Athanasiou and Baer 2002; Goulder 2002; Burns 2002; Sawin 2003. Details of the protocol can be found in Grubb et al. 1999. For an interesting but technical analysis of the incentive structure, successes, and failures of international environmental treaties by a first-rate economist, see Barrett 2003.
47. Stokstad 2003; Rosencranz 2002; Anonymous 2003j; Kennedy 2003. The Clinton administration was more interested in energy efficiency but did not press very hard for it and was stymied by a Republican Congress after 1994.
48. Romm 1999.
49. To see that some politicians (or ex-politicians) do their homework, see the excellent article by Wirth et al. 2002.
50. Makhijani and Saleska 1999.
51. Geller 2003; Mock et al. 1997.
52. Ehrlich 1995.
53. E.g., Wyman 1999.
54. Geller 2003, chap. 1.
55. Johansson et al. 1993.

56. Geller 2003, chap. 2. In the United States, development of both wind and solar power has also been impeded by the government's failure to provide appropriate incentives, although subsidies and tax breaks have continued to be lavished on the coal, oil, and gas industries.
57. Worldwatch Institute 2003.
58. Romero 2003.
59. Broder 2002; Oppel et al. 2002; Oppel 2003.
60. Worldwatch Institute 2003.
61. Stephen Schneider, Stanford University, pers. comm., January 2003.
62. Ehrlich and Ehrlich 1991a, p. 60.
63. World Resources Institute 2000.
64. Wright 1999. Figures for vehicle numbers conflict from one source to another according to the way they are categorized. Later editions of the *World Almanac* do not include numbers for vehicles registered in the United States other than passenger cars. Thus, the 76 million trucks (a category that includes sport utility vehicles) counted for 1996 in the 1999 almanac are not seen in later editions.
65. McGeveran 2003.
66. Bernow et al. 2002. Feasible mileage levels for cars and light trucks for 2015 and 2020 are indicated on p. 200.
67. Consumers Union 2002.
68. McGeveran 2003.
69. Sheehan 2001. That it can be accomplished, however, is shown in the success of Portland, Oregon: Jeff Gerritt, Portland shows how to control sprawl: Boundary pushed growth into city, *Detroit Free Press,* 5 May 1999, http://www.freep.com/news/metro/qport5.htm; Northwest Environment Watch, Sprawl and smart growth in metropolitan Portland, 9 May 2002, http://www.northwestwatch.org/press/recent_portsprawl.asp; Northwest Environment Watch, Fueling up: Gasoline consumption in the Pacific Northwest, 23 October 2002, http://www.northwestwatch.org/press/recent_gas.asp; Reid Ewing et al., Measuring sprawl and its impact: The character and consequences of metropolitan expansion (Smart Growth America, Washington, DC, 2002), http://www.smartgrowthamerica.com/sprawlindex/sprawlindex.html.
70. This ratio does not include trucks or SUVs; including them, the ratio is 0.79 motor vehicle per person. A similar proportion in China would increase the numbers to an even more gargantuan level.
71. Data on U.S. automobile registrations are from McGeveran 2003; estimated number of vehicles in China is from World Resources Institute 2000. There were about 133.6 million registered cars in the United States in 2001 and perhaps 3.9 million in China in the late 1990s. To have the same ratio of autos to people, China would need some 598 million.

72. Worldwatch Institute 2003.
73. McGeveran 2003.
74. Organicraze, *Sierra Club Currents* 3, no. 77 (Thursday, 16 October 2003), Currents@sierraclub.org.
75. Freund and Martin 1993; Kay 1997.
76. American Public Transportation Association 2002.
77. Ogden 1999.
78. Ehrlich and Ehrlich 1991a, pp. 61—62; Ogden 1999. See also Romm 2004.
79. Tromp et al. 2003.
80. Dunn 2001.
81. E.g., Smith 1995.
82. Ehrlich et al. 1995.
83. E.g., Glaeser 1987.
84. E.g., New Mexico State University, College of Agriculture and Home Economics, News center, http://spectre.nmsu.edu/media/news2.lasso?i =News599; Peter Walker, Patsy Waterfall, and Vicki Richards, To drip or not to drip, that is the question, *Arizona Water Resource* 8, no. 3 (November—December 1999), http://ag.arizona.edu/AZWATER/awr/dec99/drip.htm.
85. Smil 2000, p. 130.
86. Ehrlich and Ehrlich 1990, p. 97.
87. Daily et al. 2001, 2003. The approach of conservation biologists to the crucial job of preserving humanity's natural capital is gradually getting more realistic. They have also added to their important focus on saving species diversity the equally critical one of conserving populations and thus ecosystem services (e.g., Ceballos and Ehrlich 2002; Hughes et al. 1997, 2000; Kareiva and Marvier 2003; Luck et al. 2003). Those services are crucial for, among other things, supporting agricultural production. And some progress is being made in aligning conservation goals with financial incentives—making protection of Earth's biological capital profitable (Daily and Ellison 2002). An example is Costa Rica's practice of paying farmers to preserve forests on their land, thus monetizing ecosystem services (carbon sequestration, flood control, pollinator protection, etc.) that normally do not enter the financial economy.
88. Ehrlich and Ehrlich 1996, pp. 165—166.
89. Ehrlich et al. 1995.
90. Lubchenco et al. 2003; Pauly and Watson 2003.
91. Countryside biogeography can help, but ultimately the amount of the planet's land area set aside in relatively large tracts to maintain nature also must be increased.
92. To get this point of view, see Hill 2002 or visit the Web site of the Nuclear Energy Institute: http://www.nei.org/. The question of which

energy technologies should substitute for current fossil fuel systems in order to reduce $CO_2$ emissions is now gaining prominent notice in the press; e.g., see Chang 2003.

93. Makhijani and Saleska 1999.
94. E.g., Holdren and Raven 2002.
95. Beck 1999.
96. Bivens 2003.
97. Hirsch et al. 2003.
98. Schwartz 2003. Subsequent news stories indicated that upward of 7,000 more people were killed in Germany.
99. Such as graphite moderation. For more on the active-passive problem, see Garwin and Charpak 2001.
100. A fundamental problem is that, because of the rush to show that nuclear power could be a benefit for humanity, early generations of power reactors were basically scaled-up submarine reactors. They get a lot of power out of a small volume (have a "high power density"), since submarines must be as small as possible to avoid detection. A high power density is accompanied by a relatively high risk of accident, however. Had the reactors been designed for land-based power generation from the ground up, they would be a lot safer. For a basic discussion of how nuclear power can be generated and the problems nuclear technologies can present, see Ehrlich et al. 1977.
101. Holdren and Herrera 1971, chap. 4, especially pp. 84–85.
102. Ehrlich and Ehrlich 1996.
103. E.g., Willrich and Taylor 1974; Holdren 1976.
104. Bennett 2003.
105. Garwin and Charpak 2001. For a technical discussion of both nuclear terrorism and bioterrorism, see Richard Garwin, Nuclear and biological megaterrorism, 21 August 2002, http://www.fas.org/rlg/020821-terrorism.htm. Those who are concerned today about the possession of nuclear weapons by rogue states and groups such as al Qaeda might want to read the warning we and John Holdren gave about proliferation a quarter-century ago in a book on environmental sciences (Ehrlich et al. 1977, pp. 453–456); Holdren was primarily responsible for that section.
106. E.g., Turco et al. 1983; Ehrlich et al. 1983.
107. Federation of American Scientists, Strategic command and control, 5 October 2000, http://www.fas.org/nuke/guide/russia/c3i/. One shouldn't be fooled by the story that Presidents Yeltsin and Clinton had "de-targeted" Russian and U.S. missiles so they are no longer aimed at each other. This is a typical official lie—before launch, the missiles could be almost instantly retargeted (Weinberg 2003).
108. Weinberg 2003.

109. See John P. Holdren, "Beyond the Moscow Treaty," testimony before the Committee on Foreign Relations, United States Senate, Hearings on Treaty on Strategic Offensive Reductions, 12 September 2002.

110. National Transportation Safety Board, Aircraft accident report: Loss of control and impact with Pacific Ocean, Alaska Airlines flight 261, http://www.ntsb.gov/publictn/2002/AAR0201.htm.

111. Wald 2002.

112. Perrow 1999. In the Alaska Airlines example, the failure of a jackscrew caused a critical part, the horizontal tail, to malfunction lethally.

113. Perrow 1999.

114. Lipton et al. 2003. It seems possible that the power failure that afflicted most of Italy a month later had similar roots (Povoledo 2003).

115. Sherman 2003. They are also called "man-portable surface-to-air missiles."

116. Perrow 1999, pp. 355ff.

117. Myers and Kent 2001.

118. Ehrlich and Birks 1990.

119. Struglinzky 2002.

120. Anonymous 2003n; Michael Scherer, The half-life of pork, MotherJones.com, 19 June 2003, http://www.motherjones.com/news/update/2003/25/we_435_01.html.

121. Garwin and Charpak 2001.

122. Dispersion helps too; for example, rooftop solar panels are vastly safer than centralized power plants, especially nuclear power plants; they are also significantly safer than living downstream from large dams or near oil refineries. Terminals for giant liquefied natural gas (LNG) tankers and other large LNG facilities should be sited far from population centers. In addition, the heights of buildings could be limited; super-sized high-rises, as the World Trade Center towers were, can be disasters waiting to happen—by earthquake, fire, accidental or deliberate airplane impact, or terrorist attack by other means. Large refineries, smelters, and chemical plants should not be sited in or near large cities, regardless of labor force considerations.

123. Perrow 1999, p. 354.

124. This aspect of the human predicament was elucidated in Barney 1980.

125. Myers and Kent 2001.

126. Myers and Kent 2001, pp. 22–25.

127. Wright 1999.

128. A classic example is the massive subsidization of sugar growing in Florida wherein U.S. taxpayers, through the machinations of corrupt politicians, pour money into the pockets of rich growers and help destroy the everglades and Florida Bay (Hiaasen 2001, p. 61). Investigative reporter Carl Hiaasen's book and, especially, his wonderful novels about Florida,

arguably the most corrupt state of the United States, offer a hilarious opportunity to savor how political power works for the rich and against the poor and the environment. In the process, Americans are forced to pay at least twice the world market price of sugar. Charles Schumer, now a Democratic senator, called the sugar subsidy "one of the most insidious, inefficient, Byzantine, special-interest Depression-era programs" (Anonymous 2001); what follows is based primarily on this source.

Besides greatly increasing the price of sugar, the subsidy raises the price of corn-based sweeteners, makes every product containing sugar more expensive, costs taxpayers as much as $1.8 billion annually, and hurts the economies of developing nations such as Mexico and the Philippines (and poor farmers in those nations), which would like to sell us sugar at prices far below those charged by the Florida barons but can't because of import restrictions. Subsidies of $1.5 billion have led to a million tons of surplus sugar being stored in government warehouses. Those subsidies were bought by payments of $3.4 million to politicians of both political parties, including George W. Bush, Al Gore, Hillary Clinton, Rick Lazio, and Dick Gephardt. The sugar barons covered all their bases. Republican senator Judd Gregg of New Hampshire wanted to shift the sugar subsidy dollars into the federal Food Stamp Program, but Congress refused. Hillary Clinton refused to support that because she wanted help in shoveling money via a subsidy to New York's dairy farmers. Your tax dollars at work.

The problem extends far beyond the borders of the United States (Anonymous 2003d), as the turmoil at the World Trade Organization's conference on agricultural subsidies at Cancun in September 2003 made abundantly clear. The conference ended early when delegates from the Caribbean region, Asia, and Africa walked out (Becker 2003a). No decisions were made in the face of angry demonstrations by farmers from developing countries and strong insistence by their governments that the rich countries' subsidies were destructive of their agricultural systems and were preventing their entry into the world market.

129. Parry and Small 2002.

CHAPTER 6: BILLIONS, BIRTHRATES, AND POLICIES
 1. Martin Luther King Jr., speech delivered on receiving the Margaret Sanger Award in Human Rights, 1966.
 2. Kelly 2002.
 3. See also Daily and Ehrlich 1992.
 4. Ehrlich et al. 1992.
 5. Remember, though, that going beyond the limited areas that can be set

aside as preserves, scientists called countryside biogeographers are working to make disturbed areas more hospitable to biodiversity; e.g., see Daily et al. 2003.

6. Vitousek et al. 1997, p. 498.
7. Rollin 1995.
8. Daily et al. 1994.
9. To allow a large margin of safety against an unexpected overshoot, 1.5 billion would be more in accordance with the precautionary principle. That would be the number at the turn of the twentieth century, and what is said in the rest of the paragraph would still apply.
10. For details and references on many of the issues discussed in this section, see Ehrlich et al. 1995.
11. Bledsoe et al. 1999.
12. Ehrlich et al. 1995, pp. 74–75.
13. Holl et al. 1993, p. 322.
14. Ehrlich et al. 1995, p. 96.
15. Ehrlich et al. 1995, pp. 87–89.
16. In recent years, new birth control methods have become available. One is simply a new use for an old method—the "morning after" pill. Taken within a few days after sexual contact, it can prevent pregnancy. Another, more controversial one is RU-486 (mifepristone), a pharmaceutical treatment that arrests an early pregnancy and is effective for as long as nine weeks after conception. RU-486 was invented in France and has been in use in Europe and other developed nations since the early 1990s (Lader 1991). But its approval by the U.S. Food and Drug Administration was held up for years by the anti-abortion movement in the United States, and its availability is still hindered by that opposition and by the public's lack of knowledge of its existence.
17. United Nations Population Fund (UNFPA) 2002; Caldwell et al. 2002.
18. Dasgupta 1993.
19. Dasgupta 2003, p. 235.
20. Potts et al. 1977.
21. Potts et al. 1977, p. 89. One estimate cited a range of 390,000 to 860,000 per year around 1970.
22. Brunner 2002, p. 131. See also data from the Centers for Disease Control at http://www.cdc.gov/od/oc/media/pressrel/fs031031.htm.
23. Anonymous 1997b.
24. If we were mosses, the haplophase (in which there is only one copy of each chromosome in the cell, as in human sperm and eggs) would be the large, obvious, dominant "adult" stage, not the diplophase (with at least two copies per cell) as in *Homo sapiens.*
25. Ehrlich et al. 1995.

26. Ehrlich et al. 1995, pp. 113–119.
27. Attané 2002; Population Reference Bureau 2003.
28. United Nations (Population Division) 2002b.
29. Ehrlich et al. 1992.
30. Ehrlich 1968, pp. 136–137.
31. Lawrence Goulder, pers. comm., long ago. A more detailed treatment of this topic can be found in a paper Paul and Gretchen Daily wrote with him: Ehrlich et al. 1992.
32. For insight into the plight of those poor, see Ehrenreich 2001.
33. For a discussion giving historical background, see Tim Flannery's superb book *The Future Eaters* (1994), pp. 363–375.
34. Central Intelligence Agency (CIA), Australia, in *The World Factbook* 2003 (CIA, Washington, DC, 2003), http://www.cia.gov/cia/publications/factbook/geos/as.html#Geo.
35. Recher 1999.
36. Frank Talbot, pers. comm., Sydney, 8 December 2002.
37. Talbot 2000.
38. Unlike the system of scientific support in the United States, which awards competitive grants to scientists employed in universities and research institutions, Australia's government employs scientists directly in CSIRO, which has offices and laboratories in each of the states.
39. Barney Foran and Franzi Poldy, Future dilemmas: Options to 2050 for Australia's population, technology, resources, and environment (CSIRO Sustainable Ecosystems, Canberra, October 2002), http://www.cse.csiro.au/research/Program5/futuredilemmas/.
40. For more insight into Murdoch's power and behavior, see Cockburn 2003.
41. Katharine Betts, pers. comm., 22 September 2003.
42. The insightful headline on this brilliant editorial (*Weekend Australian,* 9–10 November 2002, p. 18) was "Population Debate Is about People."
43. *The Australian,* 29 November 2000, p. 3.
44. Information and quotes are from Dasgupta 2003, pp. 198–199.
45. Fogel 1994, 1999; Maddison 2001.
46. Ehrlich and Ehrlich 1987, pp. 186–187.
47. Parsons 1977. The same problem can be seen by considering Dasgupta 2003, pp. 130–131 and note 32.
48. Dasgupta 2001, pp. 130–131. This was a very rough calculation (and, for example, average world per capita purchasing power parity is now a little more than $7,000), but changing the numbers by even 50 percent changes his conclusion not at all.
49. For many examples, see Ehrlich and Ehrlich 1996.
50. Kelly 2002. Of course, scientists have documented how adaptable we

are. (For a summary, see Ehrlich 2000.) And wiser Australians, led by their ecological community, *are* adapting when they have fewer children and challenge their growth-manic political leaders by pointing out the likely environmental costs of further growth of their overpopulated nation. Indeed, as we have seen, people around the world have been restricting their reproduction "in response to new situations."

51. Michael Millett, We'll be right with 50 million, *Sydney Morning Herald,* 2 November 2002, http://www.smh.com.au/articles/2002/11/01/103 6027035712.html.

52. Charles Birch, pers. comm., November 2002. Birch, among many other accomplishments, was co-author of the book that transformed ecology into a modern science (Andrewartha and Birch 1954), and his ideas remain seminal.

53. Andrew Beattie, pers. comm., November 2002. Dr. Graham Pyke, principal research scientist at the Australian Museum, agreed, noting that population boosters usually overlook resource constraints such as limited fresh water (pers. comm., November 2002).

54. Harry Recher, pers. comm., Sydney, 8 December 2002.

55. See Saunders et al. 1993.

56. Lefroy et al. 1993.

57. Wentworth Group 2002.

58. Millett and Nicholls 2002. Carr is one of the few leading politicians anywhere who understand the human predicament.

59. Bob Carr, pers. comm., 8 December 2002. We highly recommend Carr's book *Thoughtlines* (Carr 2002).

60. Ehrlich 2000, 2002.

CHAPTER 7: CONSUMING LESS

1. Trent Lott, interviewed on NBC's *Meet the Press,* 10 November 2002.

2. Collins 2000; much of what follows is based on this fine book. See also Cohen 2002. The quote by Trent Lott in the epigraph is quite typical; to see how central growth is to government policy, visit the U.S. Department of Commerce's Web site (http://www.commerce.gov/).

3. Collins 2000, p. 39.

4. Cohen 2002.

5. E.g., Tversky and Kahneman 1986; Green and Shapiro 1994.

6. Holdren et al. 1995.

7. John Snow, interviewed on NBC's *Meet the Press,* 11 May 2003.

8. This assumes Snow meant real growth rates, which would be the only meaningful ones. But even if 1–2 percent of that was inflation, preposterous levels of wealth would soon be generated.

9. Fogel 1999, p. 6.

10. Economic journalist Martin Wolf, who emphasizes the connection be-

tween competitive market economies and democracy, claims that zero economic growth would quickly lead to an authoritarian government (Wolf 2003). We can't be sure whether he's right, but we can be certain that, if society survives long enough, we'll sooner or later find out.

11.  Boulding 1966, p. 9.

12.  Perhaps others haven't paid much attention to this not only because they think the end of growth is too far off to worry about but also because they see few questions that interest them professionally in a no-growth situation. But we think that moving away from the temporary (on a historical time scale) growth-and-consumption mania that grips most societies today *will* pose challenges to economists—some pretty interesting ones at that.

13.  For a sample of the discussion of these issues, see Daly 1973, 1991b, 1996; Perrings 1987; and Daly and Cobb 1994. On the related topic of the problems of growth, see Douthwaite 1993.

14.  The consumption factor in GNP includes more than what individuals consume; it also includes the goods and services collectively consumed through local, state, and federal governments.

15.  E.g., Dolan 1969; Weisskopf 1971, chapter on "GNP-Fetishism"; Ehrlich et al. 1977, pp. 844ff.

16.  Dasgupta 2001, p. 29.

17.  Of course, first-rate economists understand it isn't supposed to do these things, but many economists and pundits often speak as if it did.

18.  There are technical issues in the relationship, for example, of NNP to genuine wealth, having to do with the inevitable changes in accounting ("social" or "shadow") prices of capital assets, which we have not gone into. Those interested should consult Dasgupta 2001, pp. 149–151.

19.  There have been attempts to develop other indices of well-being (see Daly and Cobb 1989), such as the United Nations Development Programme's Human Development Index (HDI), but none have really taken hold. GNP is what is reported regularly in the press, especially in business reports.

20.  E.g., Dasgupta 2001, pp. 29–30. This wonderful book is a must for those wishing to consider the role of natural capital in producing human well-being. We've learned a great deal from it and have leaned on it heavily. See also Arrow et al. 2003.

21.  This idea owes much to the thought of Kenneth Boulding (1966).

22.  This definition of overconsumption, living beyond one's means even if those means are not enough to satisfy basic needs sustainably, should not be confused with consuming much more than required for satisfaction of basic needs, which is the meaning we use throughout *Nineveh*. This discussion and what follows are largely based on Arrow et al. 2003.

23.  Technically an externality of rich-nation consumption.

24. Quoted by Peter Raven in *Calypso Log*, June 1989.
25. Davis 2001.
26. From a pioneering study by economists Kirk Hamilton and Michael Clemens (1999).
27. For a technical perspective, see discussions of the difference between engineering resilience and ecosystem resilience, as well as other issues, in Gunderson and Holling 2001.
28. Arrow et al. 2003.
29. Diener and Diener 1995; Diener and Lucas 1998.
30. Easterlin 1973; Myers and Diener 1995.
31. Easterlin 1995; Frank 1999, p. 72.
32. Argyle 2001, p. 139. For a general discussion, see pp. 138–144.
33. Hamilton 2002.
34. For a summary in an evolutionary context, see Ehrlich 2000. Work on this issue stretches at least back to Veblen 1967 (1899).
35. Donald Kennedy, pers. comm., Chocolate Group seminar, Stanford University, 14 January 1999.
36. Townsend 1987.
37. Durning 1992, p. 40. See this excellent source for an in-depth discussion of "the dubious rewards of consumption."
38. The term comes from Schor 1998. See also Howarth 1996.
39. Wilkinson 1997; see especially fig. 5.6.
40. Frank 1999, chap. 4. As we will discuss later, the most serious costs are probably environmental.
41. Frank and Cook 1995.
42. Ehrlich 2000.
43. Green 2003.
44. Ehrlich 2000, pp. 193, 238–239, 330–331.
45. Maschio 2002.
46. For more details written for the layperson, see Ehrlich 2000, pp. 16ff.
47. Boesch and Boesch-Achermann 2000, pp. 202–204.
48. Hrdy and Williams 1983, p. 7.
49. Details and references on the issues in this and the two preceding paragraphs can be found in Ehrlich 2000.
50. Frank 1999, p. 16.
51. The first was Djoser's (2654–2635 BC) Step Pyramid. Construction of true pyramids started under Snefru (Snoferu) (2613–2589 BC).
52. First reports of its building came from the Greek historian-tourist Herodotus (ca. 425 BC) almost 2,000 years after the pyramid's construction, and details of how it was built remain uncertain. Were straight earthen ramps used, or did workers travel upward on a spiral ramp around the growing pyramid, or did they use switchbacks? The leveling was to a precision of close to two inches. The outer limestone cladding

(which made the pyramid smooth but is now mostly worn away) was so well fitted that even today one can't slide paper between the blocks.

53. For an excellent modern discussion of the pyramids, on which we base some of the above, see Lehner 1997.

54. The fascinating story of the resurrection of the lost ancient Egyptian language can be found in Solé and Valbelle 2002.

55. Quoted from Brackman 1980, p. 3, who in turn was quoting Diodorus Siculus, a Greek historian of the first century BC.

56. Frank and Cook 1995.

57. Frank 1999, p. 53.

58. Deffeyes 2001.

59. Parris N. Glendening, address to Society of Environmental Journalists, Baltimore, Maryland, 11 October 2002.

60. E.g., Durning 1992; Stern et al. 1997; Schor 1998; Frank 1999; Cross 2000; Princen et al. 2002.

61. Cross 2000, p. 53.

62. Pincetl 1999.

63. E.g., Ehrlich and Ehrlich 1989.

64. Phillips 2002, p. 76.

65. See Frank 1999, pp. 211ff., for a summary.

66. Frank 1999, pp. 223ff.; Seidman 1997.

67. Frank 1999, pp. 213–226.

68. Pigou 1920.

69. Goulder 1995b; Bovenberg and Goulder 1996; Baumol and Oates 1998; Dasgupta 2001.

70. Goulder 1995a, 1995b.

71. There is an extensive technical economics literature on Pigovian taxes and related topics. For a fine overview, see Dasgupta 2001, especially chaps. 10 and 11.

72. Federal Insurance Contributions Act.

73. E.g., see http://www.cato.org/dailys/6-24-98.html for the Cato Institute feeling good about dumping iron filings in the ocean.

74. This quote and some of the CEO salary numbers are from *The Hightower Lowdown* 5, no. 6 (June 2003); other salary information is from Institute of Management and Administration (IOMA), *Report on Salary Surveys,* June 2003, http://web.lexis-nexis.com/universe/document?_m= 6da287b34898898d12edc3989cac38cd&_docnum=1&wchp=dGLbV tb-lSlAl&_md5=570dc9d6db7d9d09a93d4f365fd100ea.

75. E.g., Ehrenreich 2001.

76. E.g., Kelly 2001.

77. Pearson 1969.

78. Holdren 1991. That gap is growing today, even within the United States, where the top 400 taxpayers received more than 1 percent of total U.S. income (Johnston 2003). This represents a return to previous highs of

wealth concentration of the late Gilded Age (say, 1905–1906; data are scanty) and the late 1920s (better data). The share of wealth held by the top 1 percent of the American population roughly doubled between 1976 and 2000 (Phillips 2002, pp. 121ff.).

79. Nye 2001, pp. 8ff.
80. Daily et al. 1994.
81. Korten 1995, p. 261.

CHAPTER 8: A CULTURE OUT OF STEP

1. Boulding 1966, p. 14.
2. Ehrlich 2000, p. 5.
3. Franklin D. Roosevelt, address to the 77th Congress, January 6, 1941; we are indebted to Peter Raven for supplying us with the text.
4. Hitler 1943 (1925); see, e.g., pp. 344–345 on the vesting of unlimited power and authority in the elected leader of a young movement—like National Socialism. See also Adorno et al. 1950 and Fromm 1995 (1960).
5. For a discussion of how this culture gap evolved, see Ornstein and Ehrlich 1989 and Ehrlich 2000.
6. Ehrlich and Holm 1963, pp. 285ff.; Ehrlich 2000, p. 63. Anthropologists and social scientists often formulate more complex definitions of culture; e.g., Holloway 1969; Waal 1999. They started long ago. Pioneering anthropologist Edward B. Tylor defined it thus: "Culture or Civilization, taken in its wide ethnographic sense, is that complex whole which includes knowledge, belief, art, morals, law, custom, and any other capabilities and habits acquired by man as a member of society" (Tylor 1920 [1871], p. 1). Defining culture as humanity's store of non-genetic information is more general and a lot shorter.
7. E.g., Ornstein and Ehrlich 1989.
8. National Academy of Sciences USA 1993 and Union of Concerned Scientists 1993 are outstanding examples, but there have been literally thousands of books, scientific papers, and popular articles on the topic.
9. We're considering human history here as beginning with the first small-brained upright hominids about 5 million years ago. If we don't consider upright small-brained hominids as "human" but restrict the term to Homo sapiens, then today's kind of power has been around for about 1 percent of our history.
10. E.g., Barnard and Woodburn 1988, pp. 7ff.; Béteille 1994.
11. Summarized and documented in Ehrlich 2000, chap. 10.
12. Saul 1997.
13. Bacevich 2002.
14. Bacevich 2002, pp. 149–157; Mark Shields, Bush's "ouchless" war against Saddam Hussein, 27 August 2002, http://www.cnn.com/2002/ ALLPOLITICS/08/27/column.shields/.
15. C. Suetonius Tranquillus, The Lives of the Twelve Caesars, vol. 5, Project

Gutenberg eBook, 2003, http://www.gutenberg.net/browse/BIBREC/
BR6390.HTM, sec. XVII.

16. The material that follows is based on the introduction to a book Paul
    wrote for his fellow ecologists (Ehrlich 1997).

17. Bishop et al. 1997.

18. Mander 2003, p. 111. Mander started out as an advertising executive.

19. Specter 1994; Kuman 1994; Daily and Ehrlich 1996a, 1996b.

20. Leopold 1966, p. 197.

21. Union of Concerned Scientists 1993.

22. Barney 1980.

23. Barney 1980, p. iii.

24. See, e.g., Representative Henry A. Waxman's presentation of the issue
    at    http://www.house.gov/reform/min/politicsandscience/example_
    wetlands.htm.

25. Clymer 2002.

26. *Lancet* 2002.

27. Letter to EPA assistant administrator Stephen L. Johnson from Jay
    Vroom (president of CropLife America) and Allen James (president of
    RISE), 8 July 2002; letter to EPA administrator Christine Todd Whit-
    man from Representative Henry A. Waxman, ranking minority mem-
    ber of the Committee on Government Reform of the House of
    Representatives, 20 December 2002. See also Wargo 1998.

28. See, e.g., Ehrlich and Ehrlich 1996, chap. 10.

29. E.g., Harte et al. 1991; Simonich and Hites 1995; Colborn et al. 1996.

30. Vidal 2003.

31. Symons 2003.

32. U.S. House of Representatives, Democratic Staff Committee on
    Resources, Weird science: The Interior Department's manipulation of
    science for political purposes, 17 December 2002. See http://
    resourcescommittee.house.gov/resources/democrats/hot2002/weird-
    science.html for a link to the report.

33. Eric V. Schaeffer, Cheney named new EPA chief, TomPaine.common
    sense, 21 May 2003, http://www.tompaine.com/feature2.cfm/ID/7863.

34. Bruce Morton, Contempt citation isn't what it used to be, *CNN,* 7
    August 1998, http://www.cnn.com/ALLPOLITICS/1998/08/10/con-
    tempt.morton/.

35. Symons 2003.

36. Pianin 2003.

37. We are especially indebted to Scott Stephenson for his help on this
    topic. See also Natural Resources Defense Council (NRDC), Rewrit-
    ing the rules, year-end report 2002: The Bush administration's assault
    on the environment, http://www.nrdc.org/legislation/rollbacks/roll
    backsinx.asp#.

38. Jay MacDonald, A Hummer of a tax break for business drivers, 10 October 2003, http://www.bankrate.com/brm/itax/biz_tips/20030403a1.asp.

39. Minnard 2003. Miller is Southwest Director of Defenders of Wildlife.

40. Kolbert 2003. Another atrocity was committed in November 2003. At that time it was announced that the EPA would drop investigations into fifty power plants accused of past violations of the Clean Air Act—a reward for the utility industry, which had contributed heavily to Bush campaigns. Democratic senator Frank Lautenberg of New Jersey stated: "This latest attack on the environment sends a clear message to the president's corporate polluting cronies. . . . Profits are more important than cleaning the air for children who suffer from asthma and seniors with respiratory diseases" (Drew and Oppel 2003).

41. Revkin and Seelye 2003b.

42. Letter to the editor, *New York Times,* 21 June 2003. Whitman ended her EPA career with a pathetic media defense of the bowdlerized report.

43. Thucydides 1910 (ca. 400 BC); see Pericles' "Funeral Oration" (pp. 93–94).

44. See the program's Web site at http://www.leopoldleadership.org/content/index.jsp.

45. For a fine, balanced overview, see Pigliucci 2002.

46. An added complexity in trying to understand social issues and formulate sound policy to deal with them is that non-specialists are apt to think they know the answers of social science ahead of time.

47. Ehrlich and Ehrlich 1996, p. 1.

48. E.g., Brock 2002, pp. 86–87. Much disinformation is targeted at fooling the public into thinking there is no problem of anthropogenic climate change. A recent example is an exercise by the George C. Marshall Institute (whose president, William O'Keefe, was once an executive of the American Petroleum Institute) attempting to discredit the idea that recent global warming is at least partly caused by human activities and to assert that climate scientists are deeply divided on that issue—they are not (Nesmith 2003). For technical details, see Mann et al. 2003.

49. See http://www.luntz.com/. See also http://www.luntzspeak.com/.

50. See Luntz Research Companies, The environment: A cleaner, safer, healthier America, http://www.luntzspeak.com/graphics/LuntzResearch.Memo.pdf; Lee 2003.

51. Ehrlich 2001a.

52. For details on press coverage by a first-rate journalist, see Colin Woodard, The tabloid environmentalist: How a pseudo-scientist duped the big media—big time, TomPaine.common sense, 7 December 2001, http://www.tompaine.com/feature.cfm/ID/4747.

53. E.g., for scientific reviews, see the series in the January 2002 issue of *Scientific American.*

54. Colin Woodard, The shifty environmentalist, TomPaine.common sense, 14 January 2003, http://www.tompaine.com/feature.cfm/ID/7089.

55. Bjorn Lomborg, The truth about the environment, *Economist,* 2 August 2001.

56. Doomsday postponed, *Economist,* 6 September 2001.

57. They attacked even though the committee's members were not a group of environmental scientists: "The panel's ruling—objectively speaking—is incompetent and shameful." The *Economist'*s deputy editor, Clive Crook, said the Danish decision "offers nobody any reason to change their minds on Lomborg's books." Colin Woodard, The shifty environmentalist, TomPaine.common sense, 14 January 2003, http://www.tompaine.com/feature.cfm/ID/7089 (Woodard cites similar statements from other Lomborg fans).

58. The full quote included the following: "The *Economist* staff (even those higher up) who claim to be economists are PPE (Philosophy, Politics, Economics) inspired. The magazine writers write very well indeed (the undergraduate tutorial system from which they have emerged focuses on writing skills), but the economics on which they base their pieces . . . is rarely above the sophomoric. But the unwary would miss that fact because of the self confidence with which the writers draft their pieces (another feature of the British undergraduate education system in the Humanities). You will have noticed, for example, that the *Economist* regards the economics of the natural environment as concerning externalities, which is certainly the beginning of a thought, but the *Economist* firmly believes that it should be the end of the thought process." Partha Dasgupta, e-mail to a set of colleagues, 13 January 2003. This gives the flavor of Dasgupta's remarks, stimulated by the *Economist'*s treatment of Lomborg. Those who want the details can consult his fine book *Human Well-being and the Natural Environment* (Dasgupta 2001).

59. Quoted in Speth 2003, p. 161.

60. Pielke 2003.

61. See, for example, the symposium titled "The Politicization of Science: Learning from the Lomborg Affair" at the 2003 meeting of the American Association for the Advancement of Science, Denver, Colorado, 16 February 2003.

62. See, e.g., Bradotti et al. 1994, p. 143.

63. Except in the former case, perhaps, by tobacco company executives.

64. Sahlins 1968; Diamond 1989.

65. Ehrlich 2000.

66. Diamond 1997.

67. It might, for instance, reinforce urges in the Indian military to launch a nuclear strike at Pakistan should it appear that Islamic extremists might seize control of the Pakistani government and that country's nuclear weapons.
68. Kristof 2003.
69. Lapham 2003; Clarke 2003.
70. The total fertility rate (TFR—roughly, completed family size) in many countries with largely Catholic populations has fallen to record low levels. In 2002, the TFR in the Czech Republic was 1.1, that in Spain 1.2, Austria 1.3, Italy 1.3, Germany 1.3, Poland 1.3, Portugal 1.5, France 1.9, and Puerto Rico 1.9. The rate that will eventually lead to zero population growth is 2.1 or less, and that is about the current rate in the United States (Population Reference Bureau 2002).
71. Maguire 2003. He also pointed out: "The Vatican—newly allied with conservative Muslim nations—blocked reference to contraception and family planning at a U.N. conference in Rio de Janeiro in 1992. This alliance also disrupted proceedings at a 1994 U.N. conference in Cairo, where any reasonable discussion of abortion was impeded."
72. Mydans 2003 and the Population Reference Bureau are the sources of what follows.
73. For a detailed discussion of conscious evolution, see Ornstein and Ehrlich 1989, especially chap. 9.
74. Diamond 1991.
75. On pseudokin, see Ehrlich 2000, p. 193. See the same source for a discussion of which, if any, of our diverse behaviors are in some sense genetically "programmed." Outside of kin recognition and preference and a penchant for group living, most other behaviors can probably be most parsimoniously explained by cultural evolution in a very smart, language-possessing animal who has a need for food, sex, and security, who lives in a vast diversity of habitats, and who has certain constraints on its perceptual systems and on its mental abilities (e.g., limits to the number of relationships or obligations it can keep track of).
76. For an interesting discussion of moral structures in early hunter-gatherers and later civilizations, see Black 1976, 1998.
77. Ornstein and Ehrlich 1989.
78. Ehrlich 2000, especially chap. 1 and pp. 299–300.
79. Flack and de Waal 2000.
80. For example, can humanity find ways to minimize the instability that historically has sometimes been generated by a combination of small-group attitudes, migration of peoples, and the spread of free-market democracy? "Market-dominant minorities," such as the Chinese in Indonesia, Malaysia, the Philippines, and other parts of Southeast Asia and the Indians in East Africa, often can take advantage of the system

and breed great resentment by their economic success. The advent of democracy can transfer power to the majority and lead to its tyranny, often with disastrously vengeful results. The issue of the market-dominant minorities and how their existence can generate murder and mayhem is described in Amy Chua's fine book *World on Fire* (2003).

81. An outstanding example of performing a biological task is ecologist Dan Janzen's "growing" of the Guanacaste Conservation Area—a long crusade to use the area's ecosystem services to finance the regeneration of its original flora and fauna (Daily and Ellison 2002; Janzen 2000).

82. Ehrlich 2000, pp. 325–326 and p. 431, note 117. More than thirty years ago, Paul attempted to achieve a fusion of the preposterous structure of the social sciences in order to get a "behavioral sciences" core course taught in Stanford University's Human Biology Program, but the disciplinary structure prevented it. Interestingly, today distinguished social scientists are very critical of that structure; e.g., see Wallerstein 2003.

83. Schneider 1992; Daily and Ehrlich 1999.

84. Schneider 1988. Schneider is one of the most thoughtful interdisciplinary scientists; see also Schneider 1997a.

85. In the United States, which has the best university system in the world, the parallel with the fate of the medical community is disturbing. A couple of decades ago, physicians had total control of the health-care system and enjoyed high incomes and splendid perks. But they showed no interest in managing the enterprise, in which technological advances were pushing the costs of first-rate treatment through the roof. The government's failure to take appropriate remedial action and the privatization of medical care resulted in the mess we have today, with health maintenance organizations (HMOs) telling doctors how many patients they must see per hour and what procedures and drugs they are allowed to recommend. If members of American university faculties persist in largely ignoring the parallel need to transform the system of higher education, they will not be in much of a position to help heal the disconnect, and, like the doctors, they might end up as largely powerless employees rather than independent professionals.

Interestingly, the business community is providing some clues to methods that both scientists and non-scientists who wish to become moral entrepreneurs (those who wish to create ethical rules for society to follow) might employ in steering society toward sustainability. Business has done it through developments in the relatively new area of marketing. See, e.g., Becker 1963, p. 147. Scientists should not ignore the skills and effectiveness of marketing and public relations simply because they may disapprove of some of the uses to which business puts them.

86. Turco et al. 1983; Ehrlich et al. 1983.

87. E.g., Hertz 2001, chap. 11.

CHAPTER 9: HUMAN BEHAVIOR AT THE MILLENNIUM

1. Boulding 1966, pp. 3—4.
2. The terms *full world* and *empty world* were first used by pioneering "steady-state" economist Herman Daly (1991a). They are, of course, ideas closely related to Boulding's "cowboy" and "spaceship" economies; see Boulding 1966.
3. Vitousek et al. 1986.
4. Worldwatch Institute 2002; World Resources Institute 2000.
5. Spencer 1891 (1860); Carneiro 1970.
6. See Ehrlich 2000, pp. 238ff., for an overview.
7. Hauer 1988.
8. North 1986.
9. Renfrew 1982.
10. Tainter 2000, p. 36.
11. Boulding 1966; quotes in this paragraph are on pp. 11—12.
12. E.g., Kant 1956 (1788), 1996 (1797); Mill 1998 (1863), 2003 (1859).
13. E.g., Rawls 1971.
14. Property rights are a complex issue; see, e.g., Bromley 1991. See also Hanna et al. 1995, 1996; Arrow 1996; and Ostrom and Schlager 1996.
15. E.g., Ehrlich and Ehrlich 1981, p. 258.
16. Recher 2002.
17. A pioneering attempt was Graham Allison's classic study of the Cuban missile crisis (1971). It's not that social scientists haven't tried to find answers; it's just that it's extremely difficult. For instance, in attempting to model group behavior in "rational actor theory," "rational choice theory," and "public choice theory," social scientists early employed an appealing assumption that people could reasonably be viewed as rational utility maximizers. By this is meant that individuals do what they think will provide them with a maximum of satisfaction. But there is increasing evidence that this often is not an adequate description of individual human behavior. A large literature has developed around attempts to discover the degree to which human beings in some sense act "rationally" and have more or less stable preferences, as exemplified by the work of Tversky and Kahneman (1986, 1974); Stigler and Becker (1977); Goetze and Galderisi (1989); Thaler (1992); Coleman (1994); Hines and Thaler (1995); Siegel and Thaler (1997); Gintis (2000); and Bowles (2001). See also Green and Shapiro 1994. Such contradictions as radically different consumption and childbearing choices made by individuals sharing the same information about the environment make development of a coherent theory of behavior extremely difficult.

    Worse yet, it is often virtually impossible to aggregate individual behaviors to determine group preferences (Arrow 1951), although rational choice theorists assume that group behaviors are the collective result of individual choices (with the individuals usually thought to be maximizing utility). And, for many reasons, common interests do not necessarily produce collective actions (Olson 1971 [1965]; Kerr 1996). This is especially a result of the "free rider" problem. Free riders are individuals who gain benefits from collective actions while not paying their share of the costs. For instance, we do not ordinarily donate to gun control groups, but we nonetheless benefit from the small progress they have made in restricting handgun insanity in the United States—in this case, we're free riders. Sorting out motives, such as why people are often willing to bear the costs of free riders, can be difficult (Bandura 1997, pp. 488–489).

18. Levin 1999.
19. Skocpol 1979; Goldstone 1991; Collins 1994; Braithwaite 1994. Similarly, historians can document shifting attitudes over centuries on biological topics such as animal rights, race, the place of women in society, and approaches to conservation, tracing their cultural microevolution (Ehrlich 2000, pp. 228–229), without aggregating the views of individuals. In just such a way, Peter Grant could document genetic microevolution in Galápagos finches (e.g., 1986) without knowing anything of the shifting frequencies of nucleotide sequences that, in aggregate, interacted with environmental change and produced the observed trends.
20. Summarized in Ehrlich 2000 and Ehrlich and Feldman 2003.
21. Daily and Ehrlich 1996b.
22. Sen Gupta 1999.
23. Thinley 1999.
24. E.g., Hiaasen 2001 (see also his wonderful novels); Palast 2002; personal observation.
25. Talbot 2000.
26. E.g., Rogers 1995; Walt 2000.
27. Gladwell 2000; Coleman et al. 1966.
28. Dasgupta 2000, 2003.
29. For a good summary of the distinctions, see Blackmore 1999, pp. 47ff.
30. Mosteller 1981.
31. Betts 1999, p. 10.
32. Kuper 1999.
33. Some analysts think it was because Christians were more compassionate than pagans, which lowered their death rates and increased their numbers (e.g., Stark 1996).
34. Adler and Adler 2000.
35. In the scientific way of orienting to the world, deviance is still both a major factor in the definition of groups and a generator of stickiness, despite the rewards that may eventually accrue to scientific heretics such as Galileo, Darwin, and Einstein (see also Kuhn 1962).

36. Weber 1946, pp. 61ff., 280.
37. E.g., Ehrlich and Ehrlich 1991a, pp. 254–256.
38. Ehrlich 2000, pp. 308ff.
39. E.g., Bentham 1988 (1789); Mill 1998 (1863); Singer 1972, 2002. We don't see any evolutionary basis for ethics—moral lessons can't be derived from the process or results of evolution. We see little evidence for a genetic evolution of particular ethical positions, nor do we see a basis for grounding the selection of behaviors that are ethical in supposed "genetic tendencies" contributing to them. Such a view would suggest a belief in a genetically determined human nature, which to a large degree is illusory (Farber 1994; Ehrlich and Feldman 2003).
40. The picture is not totally dark. Some organizations have been established to encourage discussions of ethics. These include, for example, the Institute for Global Ethics (http://www.globalethics.org), with the broad goal of promoting ethical behavior from the individual to the national level; the Eco-Ethics International Union (http://www.eeiu. org), focusing on ecological (environmental) ethics; the Ethics Resource Center (http://www.ethics.org), which concentrates on institutional ethics (e.g., business ethics, anti-corruption efforts); and those connected with organized religions. The latter include, for example, the World Council of Churches, the American Ethical Union (http://www. aeu.org), and the Unitarian Universalist Association as well as those with specific moral missions, such as opposing abortion, euthanasia, and infanticide (e.g., the Center for Life Principles; see http://www. lifeprinciples.net). But none of these have the global reach and access to the media that is achieved by forums such as the Intergovernmental Panel on Climate Change (IPCC). Biologists themselves could press to add working groups on ethics to the IPCC and to the related Millennium Ecosystem Assessment.
41. Cavalli-Sforza and Feldman 1981; Ehrlich 2000, 2002.
42. The Universal Declaration of Human Rights is available online at http://www.hrweb.org/legal/undocs.html.
43. Becker 1963.
44. Ehrlich 1968; liberals like to dream up rights, assuming people are intrinsically good; conservatives, assuming that people are intrinsically sinful, have long hated the idea of rights except those of God and the aristocracy, and the centuries-old views of Burke (2001 [1789–1790]) and de Maistre (1994 [1797]) are alive and well among neoconservatives today. People are, of course, neither intrinsically good nor intrinsically evil (Ehrlich 2000).
45. E.g., William Kristol on *Nightline,* March 5, 2003.
46. Nye 2001.
47. Mishra 2003.
48. Ehrlich et al. 1977, pp. 454, 914ff. John Holdren and we wrote almost

thirty years ago, " . . . all countries that want nuclear bombs *eventually* will get them, but it is essential to slow the process as much as possible, in order to give the world political community as much time as possible to work out institutions and measures that will make the use of nuclear bombs less likely" (Ehrlich et al. 1977, p. 916).

49. For detailed information on this, see the Nuclear Threat Initiative's Web site, http://www.nti.org/e_research/cnwm/overview/cnwm_home.asp. "A 10 kiloton bomb (roughly the size of that which devastated Hiroshima) detonated by terrorists at Grand Central Station on a typical work day would likely kill some half million people and inflict over a trillion dollars in direct economic damage. America and its way of life would be changed forever" (Bunn et al. 2003, pp. viii–ix). Those interested in their own and society's survival might wish to read the entire report (available online at http://www.nti.org/e_research/cnwm/overview/report.asp) and then discuss it in detail with their congressional representatives.

50. For an overview, see http://www.ucsusa.org/global_security/missile_defense/index.cfm. For the Bush administration's preposterous plan to deploy such a defense in time for the 2004 election, see Coyle 2003. Among other things, Coyle says: "Rumsfeld can either meet a political imperative by October 2004 or build a missile defense system that works. But the technical and operational challenges of an effective missile defense system are such that the Pentagon cannot do both."

51. Weinberg 2003.

52. E.g., Ehrlich and Liu 2002.

53. Anonymous 2002a.

54. Ehrlich et al. 1999.

55. Perrin 1979.

56. Mansfield and Snyder 1995.

57. Singer 1975.

58. E.g., Naess 1973.

59. Stone 1974.

60. E.g., Singer 1993, 2002.

61. Mirrlees 1971 was the seminal paper; it started an entire subject called "public economics." For a less technical discussion, see Dasgupta 1982, especially pp. 207ff. Much of its focus falls, quite naturally, on tax policy (Slemrod 1990) or redistribution through grants (Ballard 1988).

62. Millennium Ecosystem Assessment 2003.

63. Seyfang 2003.

64. E.g., Levin 1999; Carpenter et al. 1999; Gunderson and Holling 2001; Redman and Kinzig 2003.

65. E.g., Tainter 2000.

66. Daniel Esty and Maria Ivanova of the Yale Center for Environmental Law and Policy have proposed the creation of a global environmental

mechanism (GEM) to replace much of today's fragmented and uncoordinated international environmental regime. In their proposal, the GEM would "provide adequate information that can help to track trends, highlight issues, characterize the problems to be addressed, provide analysis and policy options, and facilitate agreement on coordinated intervention. It would provide a 'policy space' for environmental negotiation and bargaining. It should also insure the sustained buildup of capacity at the international, national, and local scales to address the pressing issues of pollution control and natural resource management" (Esty and Ivanova 2003, p. 68). The GEM could work as the main formal coordinating agency in the United Nations with responsibility for environmental affairs. As such, it could be a host agency for the MAHB, much as the World Meteorological Organization sponsors the IPCC, perhaps in partnership with the United Nations Development Programme.

67. Davis 2001.
68. Dasgupta 2002.
69. While social scientists have long been concerned with the use and abuse of power, they have traditionally viewed the exercise of power as socially constrained. That is, social scientists normally evaluate the limitations put on power according to the degree to which people will permit others to control their activities—in other words, as a study of politics. The literature is enormous and diverse—for a few examples, see Weber 1946; Russell 1938; Dahl 1957; Bachrach and Baratz 1962; Lenski 1966; and McNeill 1982.
70. This would immediately raise the question of how to reduce the malignancies in the corporate-government relationship. We will deal with this issue more deeply in the next chapter. Two excellent recent additions to the huge literature on this are Hertz 2001 and Hartmann 2002.
71. For early examples, see Diamond 1997; for a more contemporary one, see Turco et al. 1983 and Ehrlich et al. 1983.
72. Ornstein and Ehrlich 1989.
73. Dernbach 2002; Sitarz 1993.
74. Ehrlich 2001c, pp. 159ff.

CHAPTER 10: SUSTAINABLE GOVERNANCE IN AMERICA
1. Sandel 1996, p. 3.
2. Revkin and Seelye 2003a.
3. Anonymous 2003c.
4. United States Senate, Republican Policy Committee, John Kyl, chairman, The shaky science behind the climate change sense of the Congress resolution, 2 June 2003, http://rpc.senate.gov/~rpc/releases/2003/ev060203.pdf.
5. E.g., see Miura 2003; see also http://web.lexis-nexis.com/universe/

document?_m=c5b86e867ecf9e62d7e048a792e4de00&_
docnum=7&wchp=dGLb.

6. E.g., Stavins 1988.

7. Many of these are discussed in the report of the President's Council on Sustainable Development issued under the Clinton administration (Anderson and Lash 1999).

8. Humanity has struggled with issues related to governance from long before Plato until after Thoreau and right up to today's politicians and political scientists. Governments, whether run by despots or democrats, whether assuming that their power came from God or from their selection by an electorate, are all burdened by that ancient dilemma: power corrupts, and absolute power corrupts absolutely. Thus, people can never afford to lose sight of the need to constrain power.

9. Most people who invoke the name of Adam Smith in support of the idea of unrestrained markets have probably read little of *The Wealth of Nations* (Smith 1976 [1776]) and nothing of his *Theory of Moral Sentiments* (1974 [1759]). As John Ralston Saul put it: "How poor Adam Smith got stuck with disciples like the market economists and the neoconservatives is hard to imagine. He is in profound disagreement with their view of society" (1997, p. 159).

10. "Asymmetric information" in the jargon of economists. Monopolies are also a well-known cause of market failure.

11. For a fine discussion of markets, see McMillan 2002.

12. Ehrlich 2000.

13. Winston Churchill, speech before the House of Commons, 11 November 1947.

14. E.g., Zakaria 2003.

15. On our side in trying to improve governance is that humanity now has a great deal more knowledge of human behavior than it had in the time of Plato (see Ehrlich 2000 for a summary) or even in the times of Machiavelli (1981 [1513]), Hobbes (1997 [1651]), Locke (1988 [1690]), Rousseau (1762), or Churchill some two millennia later. We know, for example, that people were never "solitary" and so never came together to form a social contract, even though too many still, in Hobbes' immortal words, lead lives that are "nasty, brutish, and short" (1997 [1651], p. 70). We are descended from non-human organisms that were highly social for millions of years. We know that people are not intrinsically good or evil—that societies decide, on many different bases, what good and evil are. That's a view, we must admit, that some sophists such as Protagoras already had before 400 BC. As we pointed out earlier, biologists know that there is no genetically programmed "human nature" that explains human violence, reconciliation, honesty, criminality, intelligence, mate choice, or most other interesting behaviors—and genetics certainly

doesn't explain people's choices of governance systems (Ehrlich and Feldman 2003).

16. Many people are ready to follow authoritarian commands, even when the commands involve doing violence to others, and even in situations in which they are not personally threatened (e.g., Milgram 1974; see also Ornstein 1988, pp. 581–584).

17. For a recent view, see Berman 2003.

18. Such as is occurring with the USA Patriot Act. See Tim Grieve, The secret society, 18 April 2003, http://www.salon.com/news/feature/2003/04/18/patriot_act/index.html.

19. Madison 1999 (1787), p. 289.

20. China, which may eventually fractionate into a rich coastal nation and a desperately poor inland one, faces severe problems in this regard. Recently, one official was asked by the central government to investigate corruption in a private clinic in provincial Wuhan (a city of 5 million in the center of the country). He was badly beaten by thugs on the staff of the clinic's owner, in one of a series of such incidents that China's leaders have proven unable to suppress or punish because local officials are beholden to local economic interests (Rosenthal 2003).

21. A persuasive device "intended . . . to induce conviction that a given legal result is just and proper" (Fuller 1967).

22. Quoted in Hessen 1993, p. 563.

23. See differing views in Hessen 1993 and Samuelson and Nordhaus 1989.

24. Korten 1995; Barber 1995; Mander and Goldsmith 1996; Caldwell 1997; Hertz 2001.

25. E.g., Frith and Frith 1999.

26. Ehrlich 2000, p. 311, and references cited there.

27. Committee on Bible Translation 1984, p. 863 (Matthew 7:12).

28. As in the Sullivan principles of social responsibility. The principles deal with equal opportunity, employees' rights of association, adequate compensation, workplace safety, community involvement, and so on. They were originally developed in 1977 by Rev. Leon H. Sullivan as a code of conduct for corporations operating in South Africa; see http://globalsullivanprinciples.org/principles.htm.

29. In *Case of Sutton's Hospital*, 1612, quoted in Evans 1968, p. 128.

30. Thom Hartmann, Now corporations claim the "right to lie," 1 January 2003, http://www.CommonDreams.org/views03/0101-07.htm.

31. For details, see Hartmann 2002, chap. 6.

32. Kennard 2002.

33. Anonymous 2002b.

34. Teather 2003.

35. Anonymous 2003i.

36. Hawken 1993, p. 108.

37. The mission of the Heritage Foundation is to "formulate and promote conservative public policies," and its Web site features an encomium from Rush Limbaugh to the effect that "some of the finest conservative minds in America today" do their work there (http://www.heritage.org/about/). Much more can be gleaned from David Brock's *Blinded by the Right* (2002). Brock once worked at Heritage, and he wrote, among other things, "Heritage is a tax exempt foundation, requiring that it not engage in activities or lobbying benefiting a political party. However, the organization functioned as a de facto arm of the GOP, churning out slick position papers" (pp. 78–79).
38. E.g., Waldmeir 2003.
39. For some examples, see Daily and Ellison 2002, pp. 47ff.
40. E.g., Gelbspan 1997.
41. Buffett 2003; ABC *Nightline,* 21 May 2003.
42. A recent survey found that Americans making more than $70,000 gave 3.3 percent, those making $50,000–$69.999 gave 5.6 percent, and those making $30,000–$49,999 gave 8.9 percent. The issue is complicated by estate taxes and, we suspect, heavy giving to churches by those with less income (Anonymous 2003m).
43. Kelly 2001.
44. Friedman 1970.
45. Ehrlich et al. 1977, p. 879. Corporations live happily with regulations they helped create that say, for instance, they can emit no more than ten tons per day of some toxic substance, because they can then poison us with as much as ten tons with legal impunity. They like the regulations that decree that warnings by the surgeon general must be on all packs of cigarettes. Then they can point to those warnings when people dying of tobacco-related illnesses sue them—the victim was warned and we were obeying government regulations, they say in court. They often use their resources to gain control of those supposed to regulate them, laws or no laws. The salmon aquaculture industry in British Columbia supplies a routine example (Naylor et al. 2003). For more disgusting details, see Hartmann 2002, chap. 10.
46. The giving of unreasonable financial incentives to upper-level managers at the expense of both stockholders and employees at last led the U.S. Securities and Exchange Commission to seek a corporate accounting reform bill, the Sarbanes-Oxley Act of 2002 (Orndorff 2003).
47. Kelly 2001, p. 108.
48. Shiva 2003, p. 152.
49. Mayer 1990, p. 660.
50. Legal transcript of *Mostyn Neil Hamilton v. Mohamed Al Fayed,* 19 November 1999, quoted in Hertz 2001, p. 100.
51. Bill Bilderback, pers. comm., Los Angeles, 4 July 2003.

52. For details on how Exxon Corporation's mismanagement was so extreme as to make it ridiculous to call this an accident, see Palast 2002, pp. 100–105.

53. David Korten suggested this a decade ago (1995, p. 311). We urge you to read the most recent edition of his book (Korten 2001) for a much more detailed discussion of issues related to reining in corporations.

54. Hertz 2001, p. 6.

55. See Korten 2001, pp. 187–188. See also Saul 1997, chap. 4.

56. Korten 1995, p. 317.

57. Kelly 2001.

58. World Resources Institute 2003, chap. 6.

59. See http://www.sierraclubfunds.com. Full disclosure: we just purchased some!

60. Originally a group of propertied white males.

61. Originally members of the House of Representatives and state legislators who, in turn, would select senators and presidential electors.

62. Madison 1999 (1787), pp. 46–51.

63. It worked pretty well originally. It did not, however, prevent otherwise admirable people from doing unadmirable things, as when the founding fathers managed to pass laws that made sure they were first in line to get their government loans repaid with interest after the American Revolution. Morgan 1992, p. 131.

64. The similarity of this neologism to *mediocrity* and the related term *mediocracy,* "rule by the mediocre," is not accidental.

65. Olson 1971 (1965).

66. Becker 2003c; data are from Center for Responsive Politics, Agribusiness: Long-term contribution trends, http://www.opensecrets.org/industries/indus.asp?Ind=A.

67. Arianna Huffington, Hungry lobbyists gnawing away at democracy, 19 August 1999, http://www.ariannaonline.com/columns/files/081999.html.

68. Center for Responsive Politics, Lobbyists database, 2003, http://www.opensecrets.org/lobbyists/index.asp.

69. Kelly 2001, p. 161. Of course, mobilization bias and lobbying can benefit non-governmental organizations such as the Sierra Club that are trying to move society toward sustainability, but often they are outdone by interests with less admirable goals. Members of Congress are heavily pressured by business interests and constituent groups and by the need to be perpetually raising funds for the television commercials that now play a central role in elections—and too many just cave in. One suspects that the average quality of representatives has declined as their power to perform independently has waned, but part of the problem has been the proliferation of topics they need to be informed about.

70. Marsha Kinder, ONEUSC, University of Southern California, The embedded news coverage of the war, 26 May 2003, http://www.usc.edu/programs/oneusc/kinder_embedded.html.
71. John Baker, Effects of the press on Spanish-American relations in 1898, 2001, http://www.humboldt.edu/~jcb10/spanwar.shtml.
72. Stockdale and Stockdale 1990; Jim Stockdale, pers. comm., over the South Pacific, January 1996. The lies put patriotic military people such as Stockdale, who knew that the war was based on a lie, in a terrible psychological position.
73. In the middle of the 2002 congressional election campaign, further evidence of the then nearly comatose state of U.S. investigative reporting appeared. Bob Woodward, who with Carl Bernstein had played a significant role in exposing the Watergate scandal, published a book on the administration's behavior in response to the 9/11 attacks (Woodward 2002). It was a fawning, one-dimensional puff-piece that made Woodward's book indistinguishable from an administration press release. For a more favorable view, see Hitchens 2003; for a more humorous take, see Adams 2003.
74. See, e.g., Wells 2003. For a laundry list of Bush lies, refer to Corn 2003; see also Anonymous 2003b and Conason 2003. For an extremely amusing discussion of the recent orgy of right-wing lying, see Franken 2003. All presidents and administrations lie; the Bush administration has just pressed on to new heights of prevarication, outdoing even the administrations of Lyndon B. Johnson and Richard Nixon.
75. Alterman 2003.
76. When was the last time you heard one of those pundits say something that indicated that he or she was knowledgeable about science and technology?
77. Hindman and Cukier 2003.
78. NOW *with Bill Moyers,* 23 May 2003; see Big media: Overview, http://www.pbs.org/now/politics/bigmedia.html. Even conservatives are disturbed by this trend; e.g., see Safire 2003.
79. Kaplan 1998.
80. Blinder 1997.
81. Zakaria 2003.
82. Zakaria 2003, p. 167.
83. In the 1960s and 1970s, it was not clear whether human use of the atmosphere as a garbage dump was going to lead to warming or cooling, and roughly half of the factors that were driving toward warming were unknown (Ehrlich and Ehrlich 1970, pp. 145ff.; Ehrlich and Ehrlich 1991a, pp. 76ff.).
84. See Daly 1991b, pp. 61ff., for details.
85. Economists have long recognized the shortcomings of the most used

macroeconomic indicators, but no satisfactory replacement has yet been adopted. The FEA could, in theory, change that (Nordhaus and Tobin 1972; Daly and Cobb 1989).

86. Ehrlich 1968, p. 138; Ehrlich and Ehrlich 1970, pp. 288ff.
87. Morgan 1995.
88. E.g., Hertz 2001, pp. 56ff.
89. Wilkinson 1997.
90. Not the Federal Election Commission, which is focused on enforcing campaign finance laws.
91. E.g., see U.S. Senate, Republican Policy Committee, S.J. Res. 18—constitutional amendment allowing Congress and the states to regulate contributions and expenditures in elections, 12 March 1997, http://rpc.senate.gov/~rpc/releases/1997/SJRES18.LO.htm.
92. See http://caselaw.lp.findlaw.com/scripts/getcase.pl?court=US&vol=424&invol=1; Sunstein 2000a, 2000b.
93. E.g., Bork 1997, p. 277.

CHAPTER 11: HEALING A WORLD OF WOUNDS

1. Mander 2003, p. 110.
2. Holling et al. 2002.
3. Brown 2003, p. 18.
4. E.g., Bacevich 2002; Prestowitz 2003.
5. Mander 2003, p. 112.
6. Examples are drawn from Palast 2002 and from conversations with Argentinian and Mexican colleagues.
7. Monbiot 2003c; see also Douthwaite 1993.
8. Becker 2003b.
9. Stern 2002; International Bank for Reconstruction and Development/ World Bank 2000, 2003.
10. Becker 2003c; data on contributions are from the Center for Responsive Politics (http://www.opensecrets.org/).
11. Forero 2003.
12. Palast 2002, p. 111.
13. Palast 2002, p. 112.
14. For example, the Clinton administration (the secretaries of energy and the treasury, and the Federal Energy Regulatory Commission) collaborated in an effort to find a solution before the blackouts occurred. Christopher Edmonds, California blackout? The pols and utilities are full of gas, TheStreet.com, 10 January 2001, http://www.thestreet.com/pf/comment/christopheredmonds/1251217.html. Unfortunately, the federal effort ended when George W. Bush took office as president.
15. Palast 2002, p. 112.
16. Palast 2002, p. 54.

17. Nicanor Apaza, quoted in Rohter 2003.
18. Rohter 2003.
19. There is a giant literature on the problems associated with globalization of corporate power. E.g., see Barnet and Cavanagh 1994; Barber 1995; Korten 1995; Mander and Goldsmith 1996; Steger 2001; Greider 1997; Hertz 2001; Stiglitz 2002. It is countered, of course, by another set expounding the advantages of free trade, e.g., Friedman 1999 and Lindsey 2001.
20. For many details, see Stiglitz 2002. There is increasing news coverage of the slowing of globalization because of its negative effects on the poor; e.g., see Leonhardt 2003; Cowell 2003; and Eviatar 2003.
21. E.g., Pincetl 1999, p. 241.
22. It's a development that deserves additional analysis. In the presence of highly mobile capital, specialization still leads to higher value added from production in each of the countries involved in trade, just as comparative advantage theory states. These gains may not accrue, however, to the *residents* of each country.
23. Hiss 1991.
24. Ostrom 1996.
25. Barnet and Cavanagh 1994, p. 22.
26. Birch and Paul 2003.
27. Ehrenreich 2001.
28. Assuming that minimum-wage workers average approximately $15,000 per year, and using numbers cited in Phillips 2002, p. 129. Amazingly, Ehrenreich's straightforward book was attacked by Republican legislators when the University of North Carolina, Chapel Hill, selected it for its students to read. Among other things, the legislators called *Nickel and Dimed* "intellectual pornography" and "indoctrination" and said that its choice showed an overall "anti-Christian bigotry" on the part of the university! Jane Stancill, Lawmakers bash book choice, *Raleigh News and Observer*, 10 July 2003, http://newsobserver.com/front/story/2682582p-2487126c.html.
29. See, e.g., Saul 1997.
30. Stiglitz 2002, p. 214.
31. E.g., Hertz 2001, pp. 79–81; Hartmann 2002.
32. Anonymous 2003e.
33. Stiglitz 2002, pp. 219ff. For a very readable overview of markets, see McMillan 2002.
34. Swedberg 1994.
35. For interesting material on the role of information (and uncertainty) in markets, see Akerlof 1984, chap. 2.
36. Consult Stiglitz 2002, pp. 229ff., for details, and read between the lines to see why we're not optimistic. Monopoly can also hinder the efficient

functioning of markets, as it classically did in the Soviet Union, where huge state enterprises clogged the system nearly everywhere. But rapid and careless breaking up of those monopolies through privatization in formerly communist nations, without regulatory safeguards in place, often led to a loss of wealth, higher consumer prices, and a lot of people made more miserable. Individuals and societies are at the mercy of the way markets function. Markets can match supplies of gasoline to demands better than an international government could. On the other hand, the failure of the United States government (and many others) to take steps to internalize many of the externalities of gasoline consumption, such as global warming, are one cause of the human predicament.

37. Kelly 2001, p. 76.
38. See Nicholas Stein, Banana peel, *Columbia Journalism Review,* September–October 1998, http://archives.cjr.org/year/98/5/chiquita3.asp.
39. Hertz 2001, pp. 84–85.
40. Korten 1995, pp. 322–324.
41. Monbiot 2003d.
42. For some Utopian ideas, see Monbiot 2003a.
43. Charnovitz 1997.
44. Anderson and Lash 1999, p. 87.
45. As this book went to press, we received a copy of a fine new book by distinguished political scientist Dennis Pirages and a young colleague that gives their take on many of the issues we discuss (Pirages and DeGeest 2003).
46. Also in need of airing is the necessity for ample safety margins against unforeseen consequences, a topic of increasing concern and research among scientists interested in how complex ecological-economic systems work; e.g., see Holling et al. 2002.
47. National Security Council, *The National Security Strategy of the United States of America,* 20 September 2002, http://www.whitehouse.gov/nsc/nss.html.
48. French 2002.
49. Note that the calculations here reflect a percentage of the national budget, not GNP—which is roughly 4.5 times the budget. To view the results of the poll, see http://www.globallearningnj.org/global_ata/Public_Opinion_Poll_Views_on_Foreign_Aid.htm#Questions.
50. Rees 2003.
51. As historian Arthur Schlesinger Jr. put it, "who can doubt that there is an American empire?—an 'informal' empire not colonial in polity, but still richly equipped with imperial paraphernalia: troops, ships, planes, bases, proconsuls, local collaborators, all spread around the luckless planet." Arthur M. Schlesinger Jr., *The Cycles of American History* (Houghton Mifflin, Boston), p. 141. Quoted in Bacevich 2002, p. 30.

Actually, American imperialism extending beyond North America traces to the Spanish-American War and the brutal conquest of the Philippines (Karnow 1989). Rudyard Kipling was one of the cheerleaders of that conquest in his racist poem "The White Man's Burden," urging "the United States, with special reference to the Philippines, to join Britain in the pursuit of the racial responsibilities of empire: 'Your new-caught sullen peoples, half devil and half child'" (Anonymous 2003h). In the poem, Kipling wrote of "The savage wars of peace," one of which may be what the Bush administration thought it was waging in Iraq.

52. Ehrlich 2000, pp. 329–330.
53. CNN, 20 January 2003. A transcript of the speech is available at http://www.stanford.edu/group/King/publications/speeches/address_at_march_on_washington.pdf.

AFTERWORD

1. *The Independent* (London) Online Edition, 30 March 2005; Graham-Rowe and Holmes 2005; Revkin 2005b; Stokstad 2005.
2. *The Independent* (London) Online Edition, 30 March 2005.
3. Mooney 2005.
4. History professor Walter Williams described the run-up to the election as follows: "The extent to which deceptive propaganda had been employed in Bush's first three years to sell major policy proposals makes the Bush administration radically different from any earlier presidency" (Williams 2004). When asked if he viewed the Bush administration as the worst in American history, another historian—one of Stanford University's most distinguished—said he did, and added, "They'll lie about absolutely anything."
5. An outstanding example was *CBS News'* pathetic backing down from a story on the well-documented Vietnam War dodging of George W. Bush (Palast 2005).
6. Priest 2005.
7. This plan is coming closer to fruition; see Anonymous 2005.
8. Frank 2004. Previous administrations may have been more corrupt or jingoistic, but the George W. Bush administration's combination of military aggressiveness, greed, ignorance, megalomania, disregard of civil rights, *and* ability to destroy the world is unique.
9. Rev. Jerry Vines, a former president of the Southern Baptist Convention, the largest Protestant domination. Cited in Moghaddam 2005 and reported in an article in the *Washington Post* (20 June 2002, p. A3), which cited top evangelical Christians such as Rev. Jerry Falwell supporting that view.
10. Tyerman 2004.

11. See also Goodstein 2005.

12. E.g., Danforth 2005.

13. Moyers 2005.

14. Moyers 2005. The extreme religiosity, including support of Creationism (better called "malign design"), of the United States as compared with European nations may trace to the absence of an established church (with political entanglements) and a resultant vigorous competition among denominations. See also Frank 2004 and Lakoff 2004.

15. Scherer 2004.

16. Kennedy 2005.

17. Linzer 2005.

18. Stelzer 2002.

19. Hanley 2005.

20. See, e.g., the Sound Science Initiative of the Union of Concerned Scientists (http://www.ucsusa.org).

    The administration lacked a science advisor; the person who signed up for that position, physicist John Marburger III, was demoted soon after his acceptance of the position of science advisor to being just the director of the Office of Science and Technology Policy (OSTP). Despite suffering further indignities, Marburger did not resign but became a lapdog for the administration, defending its indefensible scientific behavior (Anonymous 2004). He basically sat mute while the Bush administration, for example, continued its efforts to deceive the public about the seriousness of rapid climate change (Hanley 2005, Revkin 2005a).

21. Allen 2005. She was writing about the big lie of the United States having been being founded on Christian principles.

22. Just consider warnings on impending climate threats to global food production (McCarthy 2005) and the prospects of monster flu epidemics (e.g., Hopper 2005).

23. E.g., Rohter 2005; Wu et al. 2005; Revkin 2005c; O'Brien 2005; Beard 2005; Hansen et al. 2005; Root et al. 2005. Sadly, data also suggest that uncertainties are large enough that, if humanity is unlucky, warming of even 11 degrees Celsius is possible (Stainforth et al. 2005)—which would trigger an unbelievable disaster worldwide.

24. Fickling 2003.

25. Pearce 2005a.

26. Browne 2004.

27. E.g., Pandolfi et al. 2005.

28. Graham-Rowe and Holmes 2005.

29. Klein 2005.

30. Technically, upper-middle-income, like Mexico, Malaysia, or Estonia (World Bank 2005).

31. Perkins 2004.
32. Forero 2005.
33. Ehrlich and Gilbert 1973.
34. E.g., Rich 2005b.
35. Lakoff 2004.
36. For a general commentary, see Rich 2005a.
37. Johnston 2005.
38. See pp. 73–75 of this book.
39. E.g., Pearce 2005b.
40. Brady et al. 2003.
41. Diamond 2005.
42. Easterbrook 2005, p. 11.
43. Harris 2004.

# References

Aceh, B., and Lhokseumawe. 2002. A new bid to end violence in Aceh. *The Economist* (21 December): 53.

Acemoglu, D., S. Johnson, and J. A. Robinson. 2002. Reversal of fortune: Geography and institutions in the making of the modern world income distribution. *Quarterly Journal of Economics* 117:1231–1294.

Acemoglu, D., S. Johnson, and J. Robinson. 2003. Disease and development in historical perspective. *Journal of the European Economic Association* 1 (April): 397–405.

Adams, P. 2003. Dumb and dumberer. *The Weekend Australian,* 4–5 October.

Adams, R. M. 1978. Strategies of maximization, stability, and resilience in Mesopotamian Society. *Proceedings of the American Philosophical Society* 122:329–335.

Adler, P. A., and P. Adler, eds. 2000. *Constructions of Deviance: Social Power, Context, and Interaction.* 3rd ed. Wadsworth, Belmont, CA.

Adorno, T. W., E. Frenkel-Brunswick, D. S. Levinson, and R. N. Sanford. 1950. *The Authoritarian Personality.* Harper and Row, New York.

Agence France-Presse. 2002. Agency puts hunger number 1 on list of world's top health risks. *New York Times,* 31 October.

Akerlof, G. A. 1984. *An Economic Theorist's Book of Tales.* Cambridge Univ. Press, Cambridge.

Allen, B. 2005. Our godless constitution. *The Nation,* 21 February.

Allenby, B. R., and D. J. Richards, eds. 1994. *The Greening of Industrial Ecosystems.* National Academy Press, Washington, DC.

Allison, G. 1971. *Essence of Decision: Explaining the Cuban Missile Crisis.* Little, Brown, Boston.

Alterman, E. 2003. *What Liberal Media? The Truth about Bias and the News.* Basic Books, New York.

Altman, L. K. 2003. Outbreak that wasn't: A SARS false alarm. *New York Times,* 9 September.

Altman, L. K., and J. Wilgoren. 2003. Less lethal cousin of smallpox arrives in U.S. *New York Times,* 9 June.

American Farmland Trust. 1997. *Farming on the Edge.* American Farmland Trust, Washington, DC.

American Public Transportation Association. 2002. Use of public transportation by one in ten Americans would lead to cleaner air and reduce U.S. oil dependency by 40 percent. PRNewswire.

Anderson, R. C., and J. Lash. 1999. *Towards a Sustainable America: Advancing Pros-*

*perity, Opportunity, and a Healthy Environment for the 21st Century.* President's Council on Sustainable Development Publications, Washington, DC.

Anderson, R. M., and R. M. May. 1991. *Infectious Diseases of Humans: Dynamics and Control.* Oxford Univ. Press, Oxford.

Andrewartha, H. G., and L. C. Birch. 1954. *The Distribution and Abundance of Animals.* Univ. of Chicago Press, Chicago.

Anonymous. 1997a. Comoros island troops arrest hundreds. *New York Times,* 17 March.

Anonymous. 1997b. Saving women's lives. *Population Reports* 25, ser. L, no. 10 (September). Johns Hopkins School of Public Health, Population Information Program, Center for Communications Programs, Baltimore.

Anonymous. 2001. Sugar subsidy leaves sour taste for taxpayers. *Buffalo* (New York) *News,* 17 December.

Anonymous. 2002a. China has world's tightest Internet censorship, study finds. *New York Times,* 4 December.

Anonymous. 2002b. When Nike speaks. *New York Times,* 10 December.

Anonymous. 2003a. And the winner is Bechtel. *New York Times,* 19 April.

Anonymous. 2003b. Bush the misleader. *The Nation,* 13 October.

Anonymous. 2003c. Emissions omission. *Boston Globe,* 21 June.

Anonymous. 2003d. Farm subsidies aren't long-term solution: The average European dairy farmer collects a subsidy of $2.50 on each cow per day. *Wisconsin State Journal* (Madison), 21 January.

Anonymous. 2003e. The great catfish war. *New York Times,* 22 July.

Anonymous. 2003f. Harvesting poverty: The rigged trade game. *New York Times,* 20 July.

Anonymous. 2003g. HIV/AIDS in Asia. *Science* 301:1650–1663.

Anonymous. 2003h. Kipling, the "white man's burden," and U.S. imperialism. *Monthly Review* (November): 1–11.

Anonymous. 2003i. Live issue—Nike. Nike faces legal challenge to its freedom of speech. *Campaign,* 11 July.

Anonymous. 2003j. The missing energy strategy. *New York Times,* 23 March.

Anonymous. 2003k. Reaping the whirlwind: Extreme weather prompts unprecedented global warming alert. *The Independent* (London), 3 July.

Anonymous. 2003l. Replumbing the planet. *New Scientist,* 7 June.

Anonymous. 2003m. The rich *are* different. *Atlantic Monthly* (October): 48.

Anonymous. 2003n. Senate, House legislation push for nuclear provisions. *Nuclear News,* June.

Anonymous. 2004. The science advisor's rejoinder. *New York Times,* 10 April.

Anonymous. 2005. Bush's ax. *Boston Globe,* 7 May.

Argyle, M. 2001. *The Psychology of Happiness.* Routledge, East Sussex, England.

Arrow, K. 1951. *Social Choice and Individual Values.* Yale Univ. Press, New Haven, CT.

Arrow, K. J. 1996. Foreword. Pp. xiii–xv in S. S. Hanna, C. Folke, and K.-G. Mäler, eds., *Rights to Nature: Ecological, Economic, Cultural, and Political Principles of Institutions for the Environment.* Island Press, Washington, DC.

Arrow, K., P. Dasgupta, L. H. Goulder, G. Daily, P. Ehrlich, G. Heal, S. Levin, K.-G. Mäler, S. H. Schneider, D. Starrett, and B. Walker. 2003. Are we consuming too much? *Journal of Economic Perspectives,* in press.

Associated Press. 2003. Millions face water shortage in North China, officials warn. *New York Times,* 6 June.

Athanasiou, T., and P. Baer. 2002. *Dead Heat: Global Justice and Global Warming.* Seven Stories Press, New York.

Attané, I. 2002. China's family planning policy: An overview of its past and future. *Studies in Family Planning* 33:103–113.

Bacevich, A. J. 2002. *American Empire: The Realities and Consequences of U.S. Diplomacy.* Harvard Univ. Press, Cambridge, MA.

Bachrach, P., and M. S. Baratz. 1962. The two faces of power. *American Political Science Review* 56:947–952.

Baer, R. 2003. *Sleeping with the Devil: How Washington Sold Our Soul for Saudi Crude.* Crown, New York.

Baker, L. W., D. L. Fitzell, J. N. Seiber, T. R. Parker, T. Shibamoto, M. W. Poore, K. E. Longley, R. P. Tomlin, R. Propper, and D. W. Duncan. 1996. Ambient air concentrations of pesticides in California. *Environmental Science and Technology* 30:1365–1368.

Ballard, C. L. 1988. The marginal efficiency cost of redistribution. *American Economic Review* 78:1019–1033.

Balmford, A., A. Bruner, P. Cooper, R. Costanza, S. Farber, R. E. Green, M. Jenkins, P. Jefferiss, V. Jessamy, J. Madden, K. Munro, N. Myers, S. Naeem, J. Paavola, M. Rayment, S. Rosendo, J. Roughgarden, K. Trumper, and R. K. Turner. 2002. Economic reasons for conserving wild nature. *Science* 297:950–953.

Bandura, A. 1997. *Self-Efficacy: The Exercise of Control.* W. H. Freeman, New York.

Baranauckas, C. 2002. UN report finds women make up 50 percent of HIV infections. *New York Times,* 26 November.

Barber, B. R. 1995. *Jihad vs. McWorld.* Ballantine, New York.

Barnard, A., and J. Woodburn. 1988. Property, power, and ideology in hunter-gathering societies: An introduction. Pp. 4–31 in T. Ingold, D. Riches, and J. Woodburn, eds., *Hunters and Gatherers,* vol. 2., *Property, Power, and Ideology.* Berg, Oxford.

Barnet, R. J., and J. Cavanagh. 1994. *Global Dreams: Imperial Corporations and the New World Order.* Simon and Schuster, New York.

Barney, G. O., ed. 1980. *The Global 2000 Report to the President: Entering the Twenty-first Century.* U.S. Government Printing Office, Washington, DC (reprinted by Penguin Books, New York).

Barrett, S. 2003. *Environment and Statecraft: The Strategy of Environmental Treaty-Making.* Oxford Univ. Press, New York.

Basalla, G. 1988. *The Evolution of Technology.* Cambridge Univ. Press, Cambridge.

Baskin, Y. 2002. *A Plague of Rats and Rubbervines: The Growing Threat of Species Invasions.* Island Press, Washington, DC.

Baumol, W., and W. E. Oates. 1998. *The Theory of Environmental Policy.* 2nd ed. Cambridge Univ. Press, Cambridge.

Bazzaz, F., G. Ceballos, R. Dirzo, P. R. Ehrlich, T. Eisner, et al. 1998. Ecological science and the human predicament. *Science* 282:879.

Beard, M. 2005. Climate change wreaking havoc with seasons. *Independent News,* 15 April, http://news.independent.co.uk/low_res/story.jsp?story=629530&host=3&dir=58.

Beattie, A. J., and P. R. Ehrlich. 2001. *Wild Solutions: How Biodiversity Is Money in the Bank.* Yale Univ. Press, New Haven, CT.

Beck, P. W. 1999. Nuclear energy in the twenty-first century: Examination of a contentious subject. In R. Socolow, D. Anderson, and J. Harte, eds., *Annual Review of Energy and the Environment.* Annual Reviews, Palo Alto, CA.

Becker, E. 2003a. Delegates from poorer nations walk out of world trade talks. *New York Times,* 15 September.

Becker, E. 2003b. Western farmers fear Third-World challenge to subsidies. *New York Times,* 9 September.

Becker, E. 2003c. WTO breakdown: Why the walkout. *International Herald Tribune,* 16 September.

Becker, H. S. 1963. *Outsiders: Studies in the Sociology of Deviance.* Free Press, New York.

Benedick, R. E. 1991. *Ozone Diplomacy: New Directions in Safeguarding the Planet.* Harvard Univ. Press, Cambridge, MA.

Bennett, D. 2003. Critical mess: How the neocons are promoting nuclear proliferation. *American Prospect* 14:47−50.

Bentham, J. 1988 (1789). *Introduction to the Principles of Morals and Legislation.* Prometheus Books, Amherst, NY.

Berman, P. 2003. *Terror and Liberalism.* W. W. Norton, New York.

Bernow, S., A. Bailie, W. Dougherty, S. Kartha, and M. Lazarus. 2002. Carbon abatement with economic growth: A national strategy. Pp. 189−218 in S. H. Schneider, A. Rosencranz, and J. O. Niles, eds., *Climate Change Policy: A Survey.* Island Press, Washington, DC.

Béteille, A. 1994. Inequality and equality. Pp. 1010−1039 in T. Ingold, ed., *Companion Encyclopedia of Anthropology.* Routledge, London.

Betts, K. 1999. *The Great Divide: Immigration Politics in Australia.* Duffy & Snellgrove, Sydney, New South Wales, Australia.

Birch, C., and D. Paul. 2003. *Life and Work: Challenging Economic Man.* Univ. of New South Wales Press, Sydney, New South Wales, Australia.

Bishop, D., T. Root, P. R. Ehrlich, and A. H. Ehrlich. 1997. A field trip to a Javanese bird market. Manuscript.

Bishop, K. D. 2003. The decimation of the once glorious Sundaic and New Guinea lowland forests. Manuscript.

Bivens, M. 2003. Nuclear deregulation. *Moscow Times,* 14 July.

Black, D. 1976. *The Behavior of Law.* Academic Press, New York.

Black, D. 1998. *The Social Structure of Right and Wrong.* Rev. ed. Academic Press, London.

Blackmore, S. 1999. *The Meme Machine.* Oxford Univ. Press, Oxford.

Blanko, R. E., J. O. Blomeke, and J. T. Roberts. 1967. Solving the waste disposal problem. *Nucleonics* 25:58.

Bledsoe, C. H., J. B. Casterline, J. A. Johnson-Kuhn, and J. G. Haaga, eds. 1999. *Critical Perspectives on Schooling and Fertility in the Developing World.* National Academy Press, Washington, DC.

Blinder, A. 1997. Is government too political? *Foreign Affairs* 76 (November–December): 115–126.

Blockstein, D. E. 1998. Letter to the editor. *Science* 279:1831.

Boesch, C., and H. Boesch-Achermann. 2000. *The Chimpanzees of the Taï Forest: Behavioural Ecology and Evolution.* Oxford Univ. Press, Oxford.

Borgstrom, G. 1965. *The Hungry Planet.* Macmillan, New York.

Bork, R. H. 1997. *Slouching toward Gomorrah: Modern Liberalism and American Decline.* HarperCollins, New York.

Boulding, K. E. 1966. The economics of the coming Spaceship Earth. Pp. 3–14 in H. Jarrett, ed., *Environmental Quality in a Growing Economy.* Johns Hopkins Univ. Press, Baltimore.

Bovenberg, A. L., and L. H. Goulder. 1996. Optimal environmental taxation in the presence of other taxes: General-equilibrium analyses. *American Economic Review* 86:985–1000.

Bowles, S. 2001. Individual interactions, group conflicts, and the evolution of preferences. In S. Durlauf and P. Young, eds., *Social Dynamics.* MIT Press, Cambridge, MA.

Brackman, A. C. 1980. *The Luck of Nineveh.* Eyre Methuen, London.

Bradotti, R., E. Charkiewicz, S. Häusler, and S. Wieringa. 1994. *Women, the Environment, and Sustainable Development: Towards a Theoretical Synthesis.* Zed Books, London.

Brady, H. E., J. F. Fishkin, and R. C. Luskin. 2003. Informed public opinion about foreign policy: The uses of deliberative polling. *The Brookings Review* 21 (Summer): 16–19.

Braithwaite, J. 1994. A sociology of modeling and the politics of empowerment. *British Journal of Sociology* 45:445–479.

Brasher, K., and L. R. Altman. 2003. Scientists find animal link for SARS virus. *New York Times,* 23 May.

Brecher, J. 1993. Global village or global pillage. *The Nation* (6 December): 685–688.

Brock, D. 2002. *Blinded by the Right: The Conscience of an Ex-conservative.* Three Rivers Press, New York.

Broder, J. M. 2002. California power failures linked to energy companies. *New York Times,* 18 September.

Brody, J. E. 2003. Fighting Lyme disease, with a pinhead as the enemy. *New York Times,* 20 May.

Bromley, D. W. 1991. *Environment and Economy: Property Rights and Public Policy.* Basil Blackwell, Cambridge, MA.

Brooks, D. 2003. Cynics without a cause. *New York Times,* 11 November.

Brown, H. 1954. *The Challenge of Man's Future.* Viking, New York.

Brown, L. R. 2003. A planet under stress: Rising to the challenge. *The Futurist* (November–December): 18–23.

Brown, L. R., and B. Halweil. 1998. China's water shortage could shake world food security—part 1. *World Watch* (July–August).

Browne, A. 2002. Pop the pill and think of England: Who's afraid of declining population? *New Statesman,* November 4.

Browne, A. 2004. On Asia's coasts, progress destroys natural defenses. *Wall Street Journal,* 31 December.

Bruni, F. 2002. Persistent drop in fertility reshapes Europe's future. *New York Times,* 26 December.

Brunner, B., ed. 2002. *Time Almanac 2002, with Information Please.* Family Information Company, Boston.

Bryant, D., D. Nielsen, and L. Tangley. 1997. *The Last Frontier Forests: Ecosystems and Economies on the Edge.* World Resources Institute, Washington, DC.

Buchmann, S. L., and G. P. Nabhan. 1996. *The Forgotten Pollinators.* Island Press, Washington, DC.

Buffett, W. 2003. Dividend voodoo. *Washington Post,* 20 May.

Bunn, M., A. Weir, and J. P. Holdren. 2003. *Controlling Nuclear Warheads and Materials: A Report Card and Action Plan.* Nuclear Threat Initiative and Project on Managing the Atom, Harvard Univ., Washington, DC.

Burke, E. 2001 (1789–1790). *Reflections on the Revolution in France.* Edited by J. C. D. Clark. Stanford Univ. Press, Stanford, CA.

Burns, T. G. 2002. Global climate change: A business perspective. Pp. 275–291 in S. H. Schneider, A. Rosencranz, and J. O. Niles, eds., *Climate Change Policy: A Survey.* Island Press, Washington, DC.

Caldwell, J. C., J. F. Phillips, and Barkat-e-Khuda. 2002. Family planning programs in the twenty-first century. *Studies in Family Planning* 33, special issue (March).

Caldwell, L. K. 1997. Implications of a world economy for environmental policy and law. Pp. 220–237 in P. Dasgupta, K. Mäler, and A. Vercelli, eds., *The Economics of Transnational Commons.* Clarendon Press, Oxford.

Calhoun, J. B. 1962. Population density and social pathology. *Scientific American* 206:139–148.

Carcopino, J. 1940. *Daily Life in Ancient Rome.* Yale Univ. Press, New Haven, CT.

Carneiro, R. L. 1970. A theory of the origin of the state. *Science* 169:733–738.

Carpenter, S. R., D. Ludwig, and W. Brock. 1999. Management of lakes subject to potentially irreversible change. *Ecological Applications* 9:751–771.

Carr, B. 2002. *Thoughtlines: Reflections of a Public Man.* Penguin, Camberwell, Victoria, Australia.

Carrere, R. 2001. Oil palm: The expansion of another destructive monoculture. Pp. 13–19 in World Rainforest Movement, *The Bitter Fruit of Oil Palm: Dispossession and Deforestation.* World Rainforest Movement, Montevideo, Uruguay.

Carson, R. 1962. *Silent Spring.* Houghton Mifflin, Boston.

Casten, T. R. 1998. *Turning Off the Heat: Why Americans Must Double Energy Efficiency to Save Money and Reduce Global Warming.* Prometheus Books, Amherst, NY.

Catton, W. R. 1980. *Overshoot: The Ecological Basis of Revolutionary Change.* Univ. of Illinois Press, Urbana.

Cavalli-Sforza, L. L., and M. W. Feldman. 1981. *Cultural Transmission and Evolution: A Quantitative Approach.* Princeton Univ. Press, Princeton, NJ.

Ceballos, G., and P. R. Ehrlich. 2002. Mammal population losses and the extinction crisis. *Science* 296:904–907.

Chang, K. 2003. As Earth warms, the hottest issue is energy. *New York Times,* 4 November.

Chapin, F. S., E. S. Zavaleta, V. T. Eviner, R. Naylor, P. M. Vitousek, H. L. Reynolds, D. U. Hooper, S. Lavoret, O. Sala, S. E. Hobbie, M. C. Mack, and S. Diaz. 2000. Consequences of changing biodiversity. *Nature* 405:234–242.

Charnovitz, S. 1997. Two centuries of participation: NGOs and international governance. *Michigan Journal of International Law* 18:183–286.

Chua, A. 2003. *World on Fire: How Exporting Free Market Democracy Breeds Ethnic Hatred and Global Instability.* Doubleday, New York.

Clarke, C. 2003. Bush's bizarre science. *Earth Island Journal* 18:36–40.

Cloud, P. 1968. Realities of mineral distribution. *Texas Quarterly* 11:103–126.

Clymer, A. 2002. U.S. revises sex information, and a fight goes on. *New York Times,* 27 December.

Cobb, J. B. Jr. 2002. Introduction to special issue: Population, environment, and poverty. *Population and Environment* 24:3–13.

Cockburn, A. 2003. The London trip of a global tyrant. *The Nation,* 8 December.

Cohen, L. 2002. *A Consumers' Republic: The Politics of Mass Consumption in Postwar America.* Knopf, New York.

Colborn, T., D. Dumanoski, and J. P. Myers. 1996. *Our Stolen Future.* Dutton, New York.

Coleman, J. S. 1994. A rational choice perspective on economic sociology. In N. J. Smelser and R. Swedberg, eds., *The Handbook of Economic Sociology.* Princeton Univ. Press, Princeton, NJ.

Coleman, J. S., E. Katz, and H. Menzel. 1966. *Medical Innovation: A Diffusion Study.* Bobbs-Merrill, New York.

Collins, R. 1994. *Four Sociological Traditions.* Oxford Univ. Press, New York.

Collins, R. M. 2000. *More: The Politics of Economic Growth in Postwar America.* Oxford Univ. Press, New York.

Committee on Bible Translation. 1984. *The Holy Bible: New International Version.* Zondervan, Grand Rapids, MI.

Commoner, B. 1971. *The Closing Circle.* Knopf, New York.

Conason, J. 2003. *Big Lies: The Right Wing Propaganda Machine and How It Distorts the Truth.* St. Martin's Press, New York.

Cone, M. 2003. Warnings on canned tuna urged. *Los Angeles Times,* 4 May.

Consumers Union. 2002. Shades of green. *Consumer Reports,* December.

Cooley, J. 1984. The war over water. *Foreign Policy,* no. 54:3–26.

Corn, D. 2003. *The Lies of George W. Bush: Mastering the Politics of Deception.* Crown, New York.

Cotterell, A., ed. 1980. *The Encyclopedia of Ancient Civilizations.* Mayflower Books, New York.

Courbage, Y. 1994. Demographic change in the Arab world: The impact of migration, education, and taxes in Egypt and Morocco. *Middle East Report* 190, no. 24:19–22.

Cowell, A. 2003. Beside blossoming fields, where poverty grows. *New York Times,* 4 June.

Coyle, P. E. 2003. Is missile defense on target? *Arms Control Today* 33 (October).

Cross, G. 2000. *An All-Consuming Century: Why Commercialism Won in Modern America.* Columbia Univ. Press, New York.

Curran, M. A. J., T. D. van Ommen, V. L. Morgan, K. L. Phillips, and A. S. Palmer. 2003. Ice core evidence for Antarctic sea ice decline since the 1950s. *Science* 302:1203–1206.

Daalder, I. H., and J. M. Lindsay. 2003. *America Unbound: The Bush Revolution in Foreign Policy.* Brookings Institution Press, Washington, DC.

Dahl, R. A. 1957. The concept of power. *Behavioral Science* 2:201–215.

Daily, G. C. 1995. Restoring value to the world's degraded lands. *Science* 269:350–354.

Daily, G. C., ed. 1997. *Nature's Services: Societal Dependence on Natural Ecosystems.* Island Press, Washington, DC.

Daily, G. C., G. Ceballos, J. Pacheco, G. Suzán, and A. Sánchez-Azofeifa. 2003. Countryside biogeography of Neotropical mammals: Conservation opportunities in agricultural landscapes of Costa Rica. *Conservation Biology* 17 (December): 1814–1826.

Daily, G. C., A. H. Ehrlich, and P. R. Ehrlich. 1994. Optimum human population size. *Population and Environment* 15:469–475.

Daily, G. C., and P. R. Ehrlich. 1992. Population, sustainability, and Earth's carrying capacity. *BioScience* 42:761–771.

Daily, G. C., and P. R. Ehrlich. 1995. Population extinction and the biodiversity crisis. Pp. 45–55 in C. A. Perrings et al., eds., *Biodiversity Conservation.* Kluwer Academic, Netherlands.

Daily, G. C., and P. R. Ehrlich. 1996a. Global change and human susceptibility to disease. *Annual Review of Energy and the Environment* 21:125–144.

Daily, G. C., and P. R. Ehrlich. 1996b. Impacts of development and global change on the epidemiological environment. *Environment and Development Economics* 1:309–344.

Daily, G. C., and P. R. Ehrlich. 1999. Managing Earth's ecosystems: An interdisciplinary challenge. *Ecosystems* 2:277–280.

Daily, G. C., P. R. Ehrlich, and A. Sánchez-Azofeifa. 2001. Countryside biogeography: Utilization of human-dominated habitats by the avifauna of southern Costa Rica. *Ecological Applications* 11:1–13.

Daily, G. C., and K. Ellison. 2002. *The New Economy of Nature: The Quest to Make Conservation Profitable.* Island Press, Washington, DC.

Dalley, S. 1997. The hanging gardens of Babylon at Nineveh. Pp. 19–24 in W. Waetzold and H. Hauptmann, eds., *Assyrien im Wandel der Zeiten.* Rencontre Assyriologique Internationale (Heidelberg 1992), Heidelberg.

Daly, H. E., ed. 1973. *Toward a Steady-State Economy.* W. H. Freeman, San Francisco.

Daly, H. E., ed. 1991a. From empty world economics to full world economics: Recognizing an historic turning point in economic development. Pp. 29–38 in R. Goodland, H. E. Daly, S. El Serafy, and B. Von Droste, eds., *Environmentally Sustainable Economic Development: Building on Brundtland.* UNESCO, Paris.

Daly, H. E. 1991b. *Steady-State Economics.* 2nd ed. Island Press, Washington, DC.

Daly, H. 1996. *Beyond Growth: The Economics of Sustainable Development.* Beacon Press, Boston.

Daly, H. E., and J. B. Cobb Jr. 1989. *For the Common Good: Redirecting the Economy toward Community, the Environment, and a Sustainable Future.* Beacon Press, Boston.

Daly, H. E., and J. B. Cobb Jr. 1994. *For the Common Good: Redirecting the Economy toward Community, the Environment, and a Sustainable Future.* 2nd ed. Beacon Press, Boston.

Danforth, J. C. 2005. In the name of politics. *New York Times*, 30 March.

Dasgupta, P. 1982. Utilitarianism, information, and rights. Pp. 199–218 in A. Sen and B. Williams, eds., *Utilitarianism and Beyond.* Cambridge Univ. Press, Cambridge.

Dasgupta, P. 1993. *An Inquiry into Well-being and Destitution.* Oxford Univ. Press, Oxford.

Dasgupta, P. 2000. Population, resources, and poverty: An exploration of reproductive and environmental externalities. *Population and Development Review* 26:643–649.

Dasgupta, P. 2001. *Human Well-being and the Natural Environment.* Oxford Univ. Press, Oxford.

Dasgupta, P. 2002. Is contemporary economic development sustainable? *Ambio* 31:269–271.

Dasgupta, P. 2003. Population, poverty, and the natural environment. Pp. 191–247 in K.-G. Mäler and J. R. Vincent, eds., *Handbook of Environmental Economics*, vol. 1. Elsevier Science, New Amsterdam.

Davis, M. 2001. *Late Victorian Holocausts: El Niño Famines and the Making of the Third World*. Verso, New York.

Day, J. M. 1998. *What Every American Should Know about the Mid East and Oil*. Bridger House, Carson City, NV.

Deffeyes, K. F. 2001. *Hubbert's Peak: The Impending World Oil Shortage*. Princeton Univ. Press, Princeton, NJ.

de Maistre, J. 1994 (1797). *Considerations on France*. Cambridge Univ. Press, Cambridge.

Dernbach, J. C., ed. 2002. *Stumbling toward Sustainability*. Environmental Law Institute, Washington, DC.

d'Errico, F. 2003. The invisible frontier: A multiple species model for the origin of behavioral modernity. *Evolutionary Anthropology* 12:188–202.

Diamond, J. M. 1989. The great leap forward. *Discover* 10:50–60.

Diamond, J. M. 1991. *The Rise and Fall of the Third Chimpanzee*. Radius, London.

Diamond, J. M. 1995. Easter's end. *Discover* (August): 63–69.

Diamond, J. M. 1997. *Guns, Germs, and Steel: The Fates of Human Societies*. W. W. Norton, New York.

Diamond, J. 2003a. The erosion of civilization. *Los Angeles Times*, 15 June.

Diamond, J. 2003b. The last Americans: Environmental collapse and the end of civilization. *Harper's Magazine* (June): 43–51.

Diamond, J. 2005. *Collapse: How Societies Choose to Fail or Succeed*. Viking, New York.

Diener, E., and C. Diener. 1995. The wealth of nations revisited: Income and the quality of life. *Social Indicators Research* 36:275–286.

Diener, E., and R. E. Lucas. 1998. Personality and subjective well-being. In D. Kahneman, E. Diener, and N. Schwartz, eds., *Understanding Well-being: Scientific Perspectives on Enjoyment and Suffering*. Russell Sage, New York.

Dolan, E. G. 1969. *TANSTAAFL: The Economic Strategy for Environmental Crisis*. Holt, Rinehart and Winston, New York.

Douthwaite, R. 1993. *The Growth Illusion*. Council Oaks Books, Tulsa, OK.

Dower, J. W. 2003. The other Japanese occupation. *The Nation,* June.

Drake, J. A., H. A. Mooney, F. di Castri, R. H. Groves, F. J. Kruger, M. Rejmánek, and M. Williamson, eds. 1989. *Biological Invasions: A Global Perspective*. Scientific Committee on Problems of the Environment (SCOPE), New Delhi.

Drew, C., and R. A. Oppel Jr. 2003. Lawyers at EPA say it will drop pollution cases. *New York Times*, 6 November.

Dunn, S. 2001. Hydrogen futures: Toward a sustainable energy system. Worldwatch Paper 157. Worldwatch Institute, Washington, DC.

Durning, A. 1992. *How Much Is Enough?The Consumer Society and the Future of the Earth.* W. W. Norton, New York.

Dyson, F. 1975. The hidden cost of saying no! *Bulletin of the Atomic Scientists* 31:23–27.

Easterbrook, G. 2005. There goes the neighborhood. *New York Times Book Review* (30 January): 10–11.

Easterlin, R. A. 1973. Does money buy happiness? *Public Interest* 30:3–10.

Easterlin, R. A. 1995. Will raising the incomes of all increase the happiness of all? *Journal of Economic Behavior and Organization* 27:35–47.

Easterly, W. 2002. *The Elusive Quest for Growth: Economists' Adventures and Misadventures in the Tropics.* MIT Press, Cambridge, MA.

Eberstadt, N. 1995. Population, food, and income. Pp. 7–48 in R. Baily, ed., *The True State of the Planet.* Free Press, New York.

Eckholm, E. 2003. As dam on Yangtze closes, Chinese tally gain and loss. *New York Times,* 9 June.

Economides, M., and R. Oligney. 2000. *The Color of Oil.* Round Oak, Katy, TX.

Ehrenreich, B. 2001. *Nickel and Dimed: On (Not) Getting By in America.* Henry Holt, New York.

Ehrlich, A. H., and J. W. Birks, eds. 1990. *Hidden Dangers: Environmental Consequences of Preparing for War.* Sierra Club Books, San Francisco.

Ehrlich, A. H., and P. R. Ehrlich. 1987. *Earth.* Franklin Watts, New York.

Ehrlich, P. R. 1968. *The Population Bomb.* Ballantine Books, New York.

Ehrlich, P. R. 1975. The benefits of saying YES! *Bulletin of the Atomic Scientists* 31:49–51.

Ehrlich, P. R. 1979. Paul R. Ehrlich considers *Silent Spring.* (Review.) *Bulletin of the Atomic Scientists* 35:34–36.

Ehrlich, P. R. 1989. Carbon dioxide and the human predicament: An overview. Pp. 5–11 in J. John Cairns and P. F. Zweifel, eds., *On Global Warming: Proceedings of the First Presidential Symposium on World Issues.* Virginia Polytechnic Institute and State Univ., Blacksburg.

Ehrlich, P. R. 1993. The scale of the human enterprise. Pp. 3–8 in D. A. Saunders, R. J. Hobbs, and P. R. Ehrlich, eds., *Nature Conservation 3: Reconstruction of Fragmented Ecosystems.* Surrey Beatty & Sons, Midland, Australia.

Ehrlich, P. R. 1995. The scale of the human enterprise and biodiversity loss. Pp. 214–226 in J. H. Lawton and R. M. May, eds., *Extinction Rates.* Oxford Univ. Press, Oxford.

Ehrlich, P. R. 1997. *A World of Wounds: Ecologists and the Human Dilemma.* Ecology Institute, Oldendorf/Luhe.

Ehrlich, P. R. 2000. *Human Natures: Genes, Cultures, and the Human Prospect.* Island Press, Washington, DC.

Ehrlich, P. R. 2001a. The brownlash rides again. (Review of *The Skeptical*

*Environmentalist: Measuring the Real State of the World* by Bjorn Lomborg, Cambridge Univ. Press, 2001.) *TREE* 17:51.

Ehrlich, P. R. 2001b. Intervening in evolution: Ethics and actions. *Proceedings of the National Academy of Sciences USA* 98:5477–5480.

Ehrlich, P. R. 2001c. Tropical butterflies: A key model group that can be "completed." *Lepidoptera News* 2:1, 10–12.

Ehrlich, P. R. 2002. Human natures, nature conservation, and environmental ethics. *BioScience* 52:31–43.

Ehrlich, P. R., L. Bilderback, and A. H. Ehrlich. 1981. *The Golden Door: International Migration, Mexico, and the United States.* Wideview Books, New York.

Ehrlich, P. R., and G. C. Daily. 1993. Population extinction and saving biodiversity. *Ambio* 22:64–68.

Ehrlich, P. R., G. C. Daily, and L. H. Goulder. 1992. Population growth, economic growth, and market economies. *Contention* 2:17–35.

Ehrlich, P. R., and A. H. Ehrlich. 1970. *Population, Resources, Environment: Issues in Human Ecology.* W. H. Freeman, San Francisco.

Ehrlich, P. R., and A. H. Ehrlich. 1981. *Extinction: The Causes and Consequences of the Disappearance of Species.* Random House, New York.

Ehrlich, P. R., and A. H. Ehrlich. 1989. Too many rich folks. *Populi* 16:20–29.

Ehrlich, P. R., and A. H. Ehrlich. 1990. *The Population Explosion.* Simon and Schuster, New York.

Ehrlich, P. R., and A. H. Ehrlich. 1991a. *Healing the Planet.* Addison-Wesley, Reading, MA.

Ehrlich, P. R., and A. H. Ehrlich. 1991b. The most overpopulated nation. *The NPG Forum* (January): 1–4.

Ehrlich, P. R., and A. H. Ehrlich. 1992. The value of biodiversity. *Ambio* 21:219–226.

Ehrlich, P. R., and A. H. Ehrlich. 1996. *Betrayal of Science and Reason: How Anti-Environmental Rhetoric Threatens Our Future.* Island Press, Washington, DC.

Ehrlich, P. R., A. H. Ehrlich, and G. C. Daily. 1993. Food security, population, and environment. *Population and Development Review* 19:1–32.

Ehrlich, P. R., A. H. Ehrlich, and G. C. Daily. 1995. *The Stork and the Plow: The Equity Answer to the Human Dilemma.* Putnam, New York.

Ehrlich, P. R., A. H. Ehrlich, and J. P. Holdren. 1977. *Ecoscience: Population, Resources, Environment.* W. H. Freeman, San Francisco.

Ehrlich, P. R., and M. W. Feldman. 2003. Genes and cultures: What creates our behavioral phenome? *Current Anthropology* 44:87–107.

Ehrlich, P. R., and J. Freedman. 1971. Population, crowding, and human behavior. *New Scientist and Science Journal* (1 April): 10–14.

Ehrlich, P. R., and L. E. Gilbert. 1973. Population structure and dynamics of the tropical butterfly *Heliconius ethilla. Biotropica* 5:69–82.

Ehrlich, P. R., and I. Hanski, eds. 2004. *On the Wings of Checkerspots: A Model System for Population Biology.* Oxford Univ. Press, Oxford.

Ehrlich, P. R., J. Harte, M. A. Harwell, P. H. Raven, C. Sagan, G. M. Woodwell, et al. 1983. Long-term biological consequences of nuclear war. *Science* 222:1293–1300.

Ehrlich, P. R., and J. P. Holdren. 1969. Population and panaceas: A technological perspective. *BioScience* 19:1065–1071.

Ehrlich, P. R., and J. Holdren. 1971. Impact of population growth. *Science* 171:1212–1217.

Ehrlich, P. R., and R. W. Holm. 1963. *The Process of Evolution.* McGraw-Hill, New York.

Ehrlich, P. R., and J. Liu. 2002. Some roots of terrorism. *Population and Environment* 24:183–192.

Ehrlich, P. R., and H. M. Mooney. 1983. Extinction, substitution, and ecosystem services. *BioScience* 33:248–254.

Ehrlich, P. R., D. D. Murphy, M. C. Singer, and C. B. Sherwood. 1980. Extinction, reduction, stability, and increase: The responses of checkerspot butterfly (*Euphydryas*) populations to the California drought. *Oecologia* 46:101–105.

Ehrlich, P. R., and P. H. Raven. 1964. Butterflies and plants: A study in coevolution. *Evolution* 18:586–608.

Ehrlich, P. R., and J. Roughgarden. 1987. *The Science of Ecology.* Macmillan, New York.

Ehrlich, P. R., G. Wolff, G. C. Daily, J. B. Hughes, S. Daily, M. Dalton, and L. Goulder. 1999. Knowledge and the environment. *Ecological Economics* 30:267–284.

Ellis, R. 2003. *The Empty Ocean.* Island Press, Washington, DC.

Energy Information Service, U.S. Department of Energy. 2002. *Monthly Energy Review* (August).

Esty, D. C., and M. H. Ivanova. 2003. Toward a global environmental mechanism. Pp. 67–82 in J. G. Speth, ed., *Worlds Apart: Globalization and the Environment.* Island Press, Washington, DC.

Europa World. 2003. *Year Book 2003* 1:1221ff.

Evans, B. 1968. *Dictionary of Quotations.* Delacorte Press, New York.

Eviatar, D. 2003. Striking it poor: Oil as a curse. *New York Times,* 7 June.

Falcon, W. 2002. Review of Vaclav Smil, *Feeding the World: A Challenge for the Twenty-first Century.*

Falcon, W., and C. Fowler. 2002. Carving up the commons—emergence of a new international regime for germplasm development and transfer. *Food Policy* 27:197–222.

Farber, P. L. 1994. *The Temptations of Evolutionary Ethics.* Univ. of California Press, Berkeley.

Fargues, P. 1997. From demographic explosion to social rupture. Pp. 75–83 in N. S. Hopkins and S. E. Ibrahim, eds., *Arab Society.* American Univ. in Cairo Press, Cairo.

Fargues, P. 2000. Protracted national conflict and fertility change: Palestinians and Israelis in the twentieth century. *Population and Development Review* 26:441–482.

Farman, J., B. Gardiner, and J. Shanklin. 1985. Large losses of total ozone in Antarctica reveal $ClO_x/NO_x$ interaction. *Nature* 315:207–210.

Feshbach, M., and A. Friendly Jr. 1992. *Ecocide in the USSR.* Basic Books, New York.

Fickling, D. 2003. Islanders consider exodus as sea level rises: Tuvalu leaders look for a new home before waves wash their low-lying country away. *The Guardian,* 19 July.

Firor, J., and J. E. Jacobsen. 2002. *The Crowded Greenhouse: Population, Climate Change, and Creating a Sustainable World.* Yale Univ. Press, New Haven, CT.

Flack, J. C., and F. P. M. de Waal. 2000. "Any animal whatever": Darwinian building blocks of morality in monkeys and apes. Pp. 1–29 in L. D. Katz, ed., *Evolutionary Origins of Morality: Cross-Disciplinary Perspectives.* Imprint Academic, Bowling Green, OH.

Flannery, T. F. 1994. *The Future Eaters: An Ecological History of the Australasian Lands and People.* Grove Press, New York.

Fogel, R. W. 1994. Economic growth, population theory, and physiology: The bearing of long-term processes on the making of economic policy. *American Economic Review* 84:369–395.

Fogel, R. W. 1999. Catching up with the economy. *American Economic Review* 89:1–19.

Food and Agriculture Organization of the United Nations (FAO). 1997. *The State of World Fisheries and Aquaculture.* FAO, Rome.

Food and Agriculture Organization of the United Nations (FAO). 2001. *State of the World's Forests.* FAO, Rome.

Forero, J. 2003. South America pushes trade alliance to counter U.S. *International Herald Tribune,* 16 September.

Forero, J. 2005. U.S. considers toughening stance toward Venezuela. *New York Times,* 26 April.

Frank, R. H. 1999. *Luxury Fever: Why Money Fails to Satisfy in an Era of Excess.* Free Press, New York.

Frank, R. H., and P. J. Cook. 1995. *The Winner-Take-All Society.* Free Press, New York.

Frank, T. 2004. *What's the Matter with Kansas: How Conservatives Won the Heart of America.* Henry Holt, New York.

Franken, A. 2003. *Lies (and the Lying Liars Who Tell Them): A Fair and Balanced Look at the Right.* Dutton, New York.

Frankl, V. E. 1984. *Man's Search for Meaning.* Rev. and updated ed. Washington Square Press, New York.

French, H. 2002. Reshaping global governance. Pp. 175–198 in L. Starke, ed., *State of the World 2002.* W. W. Norton, New York.

Freund, P., and G. Martin. 1993. *The Ecology of the Automobile.* Black Rose Books, New York.

Friedman, M. 1970. The social responsibility of business is to increase its profits. *New York Times Magazine,* 13 September.

Friedman, T. L. 1999. *The Lexus and the Olive Tree: Understanding Globalization.* Farrar, Straus and Giroux, New York.

Friedman, T. L. 2003a. Hummers here, Hummers there. *New York Times,* 25 May.

Friedman, T. L. 2003b. A war for oil? *New York Times,* 5 January.

Frith, C. D., and U. Frith. 1999. Interacting minds—a biological basis. *Science* 286:1692–1695.

Fromkin, D. 1989. *A Peace to End All Peace.* Henry Holt, New York.

Fromm, E. 1995 (1960). *Escape from Freedom.* Henry Holt, New York.

Fuller, L. L. 1967. *Legal Fictions.* Stanford Univ. Press, Stanford, CA.

Gardner, G. 1996. *Shrinking Fields: Crop Loss in a World of Eight Billion.* Worldwatch Paper 131. Worldwatch Institute, Washington, DC.

Gardner, G., and B. Halweil. 2000. *Underfed and Overfed: The Global Epidemic of Malnutrition.* Worldwatch Institute, Washington, DC.

Garwin, R. L., and G. Charpak. 2001. *Megawatts + Megatons: The Future of Nuclear Power and Nuclear Weapons.* Univ. of Chicago Press, Chicago.

Gelbspan, R. 1997. *The Heat Is On: The High Stakes Battle over Earth's Threatened Climate.* Addison-Wesley, Reading, MA.

Geller, H. 2003. *Energy Revolution: Policies for a Sustainable Future.* Island Press, Washington, DC.

Gilmour, D. 2002. *The Long Recessional: The Imperial Life of Rudyard Kipling.* John Murray, London.

Ginsburg, J. 2003. The new polio? *New Scientist,* 7 June.

Gintis, H. 2000. Beyond *Homo economicus*: Evidence from experimental economics. *Ecological Economics* 35:311–322.

Gizewski, P., and T. Homer-Dixon. 1998. The case of Pakistan. Pp. 147–200 in T. Homer-Dixon and J. Blitt, eds., *Ecoviolence: Links among Environment, Population, and Security.* Rowman & Littlefield, Lanham, MD.

Gladwell, M. 2000. *The Tipping Point: How Little Things Can Make a Big Difference.* Little, Brown, Boston.

Glaeser, B., ed. 1987. *The Green Revolution Revisited.* Allen and Unwin, London.

Gleick, P. 2000. *The World's Water, 1998–1999: The Biennial Report on Freshwater Resources.* Island Press, Washington, DC.

Gleick, P., ed. 2002. *The World's Water 2002–2003: The Biennial Report on Freshwater Resources.* Island Press, Washington, DC.

Gleick, P., G. Wolff, E. L. Chalecki, and R. Reyes. 2002. The privatization of water and water systems. In P. Gleick, ed., *The World's Water 2002–2003: The Biennial Report on Freshwater Resources.* Island Press, Washington, DC.

Gleick, P., A. Wong, A. Steding, D. Haasz, R. Wilkinson, M. Fidell, and

S. Gomez. 1999. *Sustainable Use of Water: California Success Stories.* Pacific Institute, Oakland, CA.

Glennon, R. 2002. *Water Follies: Groundwater Pumping and the Fate of America's Fresh Waters.* Island Press, Washington, DC.

Goetze, D., and P. Galderisi. 1989. Explaining collective action with rational models. *Public Choice* 62:25–39.

Goldstone, J. A. 1991. *Revolution and Rebellion in the Early Modern World.* Univ. of California Press, Berkeley.

Goodall, J. 1986. *The Chimpanzees of Gombe: Patterns of Behavior.* Harvard Univ. Press, Cambridge, MA.

Goodstein, L. 2005. Evangelical leaders swing influence behind effort to combat global warming. *New York Times,* 10 March.

Goolsby, D. A., E. M. Thurman, M. L. Pomes, M. T. Meyer, and W. A. Battaglin. 1997. Herbicides and their metabolites in rainfall: Origin, transport, and deposition patterns across the midwestern and northeastern United States, 1990–1991. *Environmental Science and Technology* 31:1325–1333.

Gottlieb, R., ed. 1995. *Reducing Toxics: A New Approach to Policy and Industrial Decisionmaking.* Island Press, Washington, DC.

Goulder, L. H. 1995a. Effects of carbon taxes in an economy with prior tax distortions: An intertemporal general equilibrium analysis. *Journal of Environmental Economics and Management* 29:271–297.

Goulder, L. H. 1995b. Environmental taxation and the double dividend: A reader's guide. *International Tax and Public Finance* 2:157–183.

Goulder, L. H., and B. M. Nadreau. 2002. International approaches to reducing greenhouse gases. Pp. 115–149 in S. H. Schneider, A. Rosencranz, and J. O. Niles, eds., *Climate Change Policy: A Survey.* Island Press, Washington, DC.

Graham-Rowe, D., and B. Holmes. 2005. The world can't go on living beyond its means. *New Scientist* (2 April): 8–11.

Grant, P. R. 1986. *Ecology and Evolution of Darwin's Finches.* Princeton Univ. Press, Princeton, NJ.

Green, D. P., and I. Shapiro. 1994. *Pathologies of Rational Choice Theory: A Critique of Applications in Political Science.* Yale Univ. Press, New Haven, CT.

Green, J. 2003. "Pricey" is understating it. *Los Angeles Times,* 16 July.

Green, M. 1979. *Dreams of Adventure.* Basic Books, New York.

Greider, W. 1997. *One World, Ready or Not: The Manic Logic of Global Capitalism.* Simon and Schuster, New York.

Grubb, M., C. Vrolijk, and D. Brack. 1999. *The Kyoto Protocol: A Guide and Assessment.* Royal Institute of International Affairs, London.

Gunderson, L. H., and C. S. Holling, eds. 2001. *Panarchy: Understanding Transformations in Human and Natural Systems.* Island Press, Washington, DC.

Hamilton, C. 2002. The politics of affluence. *The Australia Institute* 33 (December): 1–2, 4.

Hamilton, K., and M. Clemens. 1999. Genuine savings rates in developing countries. *World Bank Economic Review* 13:333–356.

Hanley, C. J. 2005. U.S. seeks to scuttle conference text linking climate change to disasters. Associated Press, 21 January.

Hanna, S., C. Folke, and K.-G. Mäler. 1995. Property rights and environmental resources. Pp. 15–29 in S. Hanna and M. Munasinghe, eds., *Property Rights and the Environment*. Beijer International Institute of Ecological Economics and the World Bank, Washington, DC.

Hanna, S. S., C. Folke, and K.-G. Mäler, eds. 1996. *Rights to Nature: Ecological, Economic, Cultural, and Political Principles of Institutions for the Environment*. Island Press, Washington, DC.

Hansen, J., L. Nazarenko, R. Ruedy, M. Sato, J. Willis, A. Del Genio, D. Koch, A. Lacis, K. Lo, S. Menon, T. Novakov, J. Perlwitz, G. Russell, G. Schmidt, and N. Tausnev. 2005. Earth's energy imbalance: Confirmation and implications. *Science* 308:1431–1435.

Hansen, R. D. 1995. Early environmental impact: The ecological consequences of incipient Maya settlement. National Geographic Society Report NGS 4984-93. National Geographic Society, Washington, DC.

Hansen, R. D. 1998. Continuity and disjunction: Preclassic antecedents of classic Maya architecture. Pp. 49–122 in S. D. Houston, ed., *Function and Meaning in Classic Maya Architecture*. Dumbarton Oaks, Washington, DC.

Hanski, I., and O. Ovaskainen. 2002. Extinction debt at extinction threshold. *Conservation Biology* 16:666–673.

Harris, S. 2004. *The End of Faith: Religion, Terror, and the Future of Reason*. W. W. Norton, New York.

Harte, J. 1983. An investigation of acid precipitation in Qinghai Province, China. *Atmospheric Environment* 17:403–408.

Harte, J., C. E. Holdren, R. Schneider, and C. Shirley. 1991. *Toxics A to Z: A Guide to Everyday Pollution Hazards*. Univ. of California Press, Berkeley.

Hartmann, T. 2002. *Unequal Protection: The Rise of Corporate Dominance and the Theft of Human Rights*. Rodale Books, New York.

Hauer, C. 1988. The rise of the Israelite monarchy. *American Behavioral Scientist* 31:428–437.

Hawken, P. 1993. *The Ecology of Commerce: A Declaration of Sustainability*. HarperBusiness, New York.

Healy, M. 1991. *The Ancient Assyrians*. Osprey, Botley, Oxford.

Hebert, H. J. 2003. Touted initiative's funds cut: EPA drew from energy program. *Boston Globe*, 30 August.

Herbert, B. 2003a. Dancing with the devil. *New York Times*, 22 May.

Herbert, R. 2003b. Spoils of war. *New York Times*, 10 April.

Hertz, N. 2001. *The Silent Takeover: Global Capitalism and the Death of Democracy*. Free Press, New York.

Hessen, R. 1993. Corporations. Pp. 563–568 in D. R. Henderson, ed., *The Fortune Encyclopedia of Economics.* Warner Books, New York.

Heywood, V. H., ed. 1995. *Global Biodiversity Assessment.* Cambridge Univ. Press, Cambridge.

Hiaasen, C. 2001. *Paradise Screwed.* Berkley Books, New York.

Hileman, B. 2003. Children's health. *Chemical and Engineering News* (7 April): 23–26.

Hill, R. C. 2002. Nuclear power as an energy source. *Science* 298:1553–1554.

Hindman, M., and K. N. Cukier. 2003. More news, less diversity. *New York Times,* 2 June.

Hines, J. R. Jr., and R. H. Thaler. 1995. Anomalies: The flypaper effect. *Journal of Economic Perspectives* 9:217–226.

Hirsch, D., D. Lochbaum, and E. Lyman. 2003. The NRC's dirty little secret. *Bulletin of the Atomic Scientists* 59:44–51.

Hiss, T. 1991. *The Experience of Place: A New Way of Looking at, and Dealing with, Our Radically Changing Cities and Countryside.* Vintage Books, New York.

Hitchens, C. 2003. Aural history. *Atlantic Monthly* (June): 95–103.

Hitler, A. 1943 (1925). *Mein Kampf.* Houghton Mifflin, New York.

Hobbes, T. 1997 (1651). *Leviathan.* W. W. Norton, New York.

Holdren, J. P. 1976. The nuclear controversy and the limitations of decision-making by experts. *Bulletin of the Atomic Scientists* 32:20–22.

Holdren, J. P. 1990. Energy in transition. *Scientific American* 263:156–163.

Holdren, J. P. 1991. Population and the energy problem. *Population and Environment* 12:231–255.

Holdren, J. P., G. C. Daily, and P. R. Ehrlich. 1995. The meaning of sustainability: Biogeophysical aspects. Pp. 3–17 in M. Munasinghe and W. Shearer, eds., *Defining and Measuring Sustainability: The Biogeophysical Foundations.* World Bank, Washington, DC.

Holdren, J. P., and P. R. Ehrlich. 1974. Human population and the global environment. *American Scientist* 62:282–292.

Holdren, J. P., and P. Herrera. 1971. *Energy.* Sierra Club Books, San Francisco.

Holdren, J. P., and P. H. Raven. 2002. Nuclear power as an energy source. *Science* 298:1553–1554.

Holl, K., G. C. Daily, and P. R. Ehrlich. 1993. The fertility plateau in Costa Rica: A review of causes and remedies. *Environmental Conservation* 20:317–323.

Holling, C. S., L. H. Gunderson, and D. Ludwig. 2002. In quest of a theory of adaptive change. Pp. 3–22 in L. H. Gunderson and C. S. Holling, eds., *Panarchy: Understanding Transformations in Human and Natural Systems.* Island Press, Washington, DC.

Holloway, R. L. Jr. 1969. Culture: A human domain. *Current Anthropology* 10:395–412.

Homer-Dixon, T. 1994. Environmental scarcities and violent conflict: Evidence from cases. *International Security* 19:5–40.

Homer-Dixon, T., and J. Blitt, eds. 1998. *Ecoviolence: Links among Environment, Population, and Security*. Rowman & Littlefield, Lanham, MD.

Hopper, L. 2005. Avian flu catastrophe may loom: Disease is just a mutation away from launching a human pandemic. *Houston Chronicle*, 8 May.

Howard, P., and T. Homer-Dixon. 1998. The case of Chiapas. Pp. 19–55 in T. Homer-Dixon and J. Blitt, eds., *Ecoviolence: Links among Environment, Population, and Security*. Rowman & Littlefield, Lanham, MD.

Howarth, R. 1996. Status effects and environmental externalities. *Ecological Economics* 16:25–34.

Hrdy, S. B., and G. C. Williams. 1983. Behavioral biology and the double standard. Pp. 3–17 in S. K. Wasser, ed., *Social Behavior of Female Vertebrates*. Academic Press, New York.

Hughes, J. B., G. C. Daily, and P. R. Ehrlich. 1997. Population diversity: Its extent and extinction. *Science* 278:689–692.

Hughes, J. B., G. C. Daily, and P. R. Ehrlich. 2000. The loss of population diversity and why it matters. Pp. 71–83 in P. H. Raven, ed., *Nature and Human Society: The Quest for a Sustainable World*. National Academy Press, Washington, DC.

Hughes, J. B., G. C. Daily, and P. R. Ehrlich. 2002. Conservation of tropical forest birds in countryside habitats. *Ecology Letters* 5:121–129.

Hughes, J. D. 1975. *Ecology in Ancient Civilizations*. Univ. of New Mexico Press, Albuquerque.

Imhoff, M. L., D. Stutzer, W. T. Lawrence, and C. Elvidge. 1998. Assessing the impact of urban sprawl on soil resources in the United States using nighttime "city lights" satellite images and digital soil maps. In T. D. Sisk, ed., *Perspectives on the Land Use History of North America: A Context for Understanding Our Changing Environment*. U.S. Geological Survey, National Technical Information Service, Springfield, VA.

Inouye, D. W. 2001. Role of pollinators. *Encyclopedia of Biodiversity* 4:723–730.

Intergovernmental Panel on Climate Change (IPCC). 2001. *Climate Change 2001: Synthesis Report*. Cambridge Univ. Press, Cambridge.

Intergovernmental Panel on Climate Change (IPCC). 2002. *Climate Change 2001: Contribution of Working Group I to the Third Assessment Report of the IPCC*. Cambridge Univ. Press, New York.

International Bank for Reconstruction and Development/World Bank. 2000. *World Development Report 2000/2001: Attacking Poverty*. World Bank, Washington, DC.

International Bank for Reconstruction and Development/World Bank. 2003. *Global Economic Prospects and the Developing Countries*. World Bank, Washington, DC.

Jackson, J. B. C., M. X. Kirby, W. H. Berger, K. A. Bjorndal, L. W. Botsford, B. J. Bourque, R. H. Bradbury, R. Cooke, J. Erlandson, J. A. Estes, T. B. Hughes, S. Kidwell, C. B. Lange, H. S. Lenihan, J. M. Pandolfi, C. H. Peterson, R. S. Steneck, M. J. Tegner, and R. R. Warner. 2001. Historical overfishing and the recent collapse of coastal ecosystems. *Science* 293:629–638.

Jacobsen, T., and R. M. Adams. 1958. Salt and silt in ancient Mesopotamian agriculture. *Science* 128:1251–1258.

Janzen, D. H. 2000. Costa Rica's Area de Conservación Guanacaste: A long march to survival through non-damaging biodevelopment. *Biodiversity* 1:7–20.

Jehl, D. 2002. Arkansas rice farmers run dry, and U.S. remedy sets off debate. *New York Times*, 11 November.

Johansson, T. B., H. Kelly, A. K. N. Reddy, and R. H. Williams, eds. 1993. *Renewable Energy: Sources for Fuels and Electricity*. Island Press, Washington, DC.

Johnson, C. 2003. The war business: Squeezing a profit from the wreckage in Iraq. *Harper's Magazine* (November): 53–58.

Johnston, D. C. 2003. Very richest's share of wealth grew even bigger, data show. *New York Times,* 26 June.

Johnston, D. C. 2005. A real killing. *The American Prospect* 16 (May): 37–38.

Kant, I. 1956 (1788). *Critique of Practical Reason.* Bobbs-Merrill, Indianapolis.

Kant, I. 1996 (1797). *The Metaphysics of Morals.* Cambridge Univ. Press, Cambridge.

Kaplan, S. 1998. Payments to the powerful. *Columbia Journalism Review* (September–October).

Kareiva, P., and M. Marvier. 2003. Conserving biodiversity hotspots. *American Scientist* 91:344–351.

Karl, T. R., and K. E. Trenberth. 2003. Modern global climate change. *Science* 302:1719–1723.

Karnow, S. 1989. *In Our Image: America's Empire in the Philippines.* Random House, New York.

Kates, R. F., and V. Haarmann. 1992. Where the poor live. *Environment* 34:4.

Kay, J. H. 1997. *Asphalt Nation: How the Automobile Took Over America and How We Can Take It Back.* Crown, New York.

Kelly, K., and T. Homer-Dixon. 1998. The case of Gaza. Pp. 67–107 in T. Homer-Dixon and J. Blitt, eds., *Ecoviolence: Links among Environment, Population, and Security.* Rowman & Littlefield, Lanham, MD.

Kelly, M. 2001. *The Divine Right of Capital: Dethroning the Corporate Aristocracy.* Berrett-Koehler, San Francisco.

Kelly, P. 2002. Deep green dilemma. *The Weekend Australian,* 9–10 November.

Kennard, J. 2002. Individual rights: Freedom of speech. *California Supreme Court Service,* 3 May.

Kennedy, D. 2003. The policy drought on climate change. *Science* 299:309.

Kennedy, D. 2005. Twilight for the Enlightenment? *Science* 308:165.

Kerr, N. L. 1996. Does my contribution really matter? Efficacy in social dilemmas. Pp. 209–240 in W. Stroebe and M. Hewstone, eds., *European Review of Social Psychology.* Wiley, Chichester.

Kiley, D. 2002. Baby boomers splurge on "road candy," just for fun. *USA Today,* 21 June.

King, C. 1984. *Immigrant Killers: Introduced Predators and the Conservation of Birds in New Zealand.* Oxford Univ. Press, Auckland.

Kiple, K. F., ed. 1993. *The Cambridge World History of Human Disease.* Cambridge Univ. Press, Cambridge.

Kipling, R. 1942. *A Kipling Pageant.* Halcyon House, Garden City, New York.

Klare, M. T. 2001. *Resource Wars: The New Landscape of Global Conflict.* Henry Holt, New York.

Klare, M. T. 2002. Oiling the wheels of war. *The Nation* (7 October): 6–7.

Klein, N. 2005. Allure of the blank slate: From Aceh to Haiti, a predatory form of disaster capitalism is reshaping societies to its own design. *The Guardian,* 18 April.

Kleveman, L. 2003. The new great game: The "war on terror" is being used as an excuse to further U.S. energy interests in the Caspian. *The Guardian,* 20 October.

Kolankiewicz, L., and R. Beck. 2001. *Weighing Sprawl Factors in Large U.S. Cities.* NumbersUSA, Arlington, VA.

Kolbert, E. 2003. Clouding the air. *New Yorker,* 29 September.

Korten, D. C. 1995. *When Corporations Rule the World.* Kumarian Press and Berrett-Koehler, West Hartford, CT, and San Francisco.

Korten, D. C. 2001. *When Corporations Rule the World.* 2nd ed. Kumarian Press and Berrett-Koehler, Bloomfield, CT, and San Francisco.

Kristof, N. D. 2003. Killing them softly. *New York Times,* 23 September.

Krugman, P. 2003. Who's sordid now? *New York Times,* 30 September.

Kuhn, T. S. 1962. *The Structure of Scientific Revolutions.* Univ. of Chicago Press, Chicago.

Kuman, S. 1994. Malaria runs amok in India. *New Scientist* (5 November): 9.

Kuper, A. 1999. *Culture: The Anthropologists' Account.* Harvard Univ. Press, Cambridge, MA.

Lader, L. 1991. *RU 486: The Pill That Could End the Abortion Wars and Why American Women Don't Have It.* Addison-Wesley, Reading, MA.

Lakoff, G. 2004. *Don't Think of an Elephant! Know Your Values and Frame the Debate.* Chelsea Green, White River Junction, VT.

Lambert, F. R., and N. J. Collar. 2002. The future of Sundaic lowland forest birds: Long-term effects of commercial logging and fragmentation. *Forktail* 18:127–146.

Lamptey, P., M. Wigley, D. Carr, and Y. Collymore. 2002. Facing the HIV/AIDS pandemic. *Population Bulletin* 57:1–38.

*Lancet.* 2002. Keeping scientific advice non-partisan. *Lancet* 360:1525.

Landes, D. S. 1999. *The Wealth and Poverty of Nations: Why Some Are So Rich and Some So Poor.* W. W. Norton, New York.

Lapham, L. H. 2003. Shock and awe. *Harper's Magazine* (May): 7–9.

Layard, A. H. 2001 (1882). *Nineveh and Its Remains.* Lyons Press, Guilford, CT.

Leahy, S. 2003. Trawlers threaten ocean's biodiversity. *New Scientist* (30 August): 6.

Lee, J. 2003. A call for softer, greener language. *New York Times,* 2 March.

Lefroy, E., R. Hobbs, and M. Scheltma. 1993. Reconciling agriculture and nature conservation: Toward a restoration strategy for the Western Australia wheatbelt. Pp. 243–257 in D. Saunders, R. Hobbs, and P. Ehrlich, eds., *Reconstruction of Fragmented Ecosystems: Global and Regional Perspectives.* Surrey Beatty & Sons, Chipping Norton, New South Wales, Australia.

Lehner, M. 1997. *The Complete Pyramids: Solving the Ancient Mysteries.* Thames and Hudson, London.

Leick, G. 2001. *Mesopotamia: The Invention of the City.* Penguin, London.

Leisinger, K. M., K. M. Schmitt, and R. Pandya-Lorch. 2002. *Six Billion and Counting: Population and Food Security in the 21st Century.* International Food Policy Research Institute, Washington, DC.

Lenski, G. E. 1966. *Power and Privilege.* Univ. of North Carolina Press, Chapel Hill.

Leonhardt, D. 2003. Globalization hits a political speed bump. *New York Times,* 1 June.

Leopold, A. 1966. *A Sand County Almanac, with Essays from Round River.* Ballantine Books, New York.

Levin, B. R., and R. M. Anderson. 1999. The population biology of anti-infective chemotherapy and the evolution of drug resistance: More questions than answers. Pp. 125–137 in S. C. Stearns, ed., *Evolution in Health and Disease.* Oxford Univ. Press, Oxford.

Levin, S. 1999. *Fragile Dominion.* Perseus Books, Reading, MA.

Lindsey, B. 2001. *Against the Dead Hand: The Uncertain Struggle for Global Capitalism.* Wiley, New York.

Linzer, D. 2005. Search for banned weapons in Iraq ended last month. *Washington Post,* 12 January.

Lipton, E., R. Perez-Pena, and M. L. Wald. 2003. Overseers missed big picture as failures led to blackout. *New York Times,* 13 September.

Liu, J., G. C. Daily, P. R. Ehrlich, and G. W. Luck. 2003. Effects of household dynamics on resource consumption and biodiversity. *Nature* 421:530–533.

Locke, J. 1988 (1690). *Two Treatises of Government.* Cambridge Univ. Press, London.

Lubchenco, J., R. Davis-Born, and B. Simler. 2003. Lessons from the land for protection in the sea. *Open Spaces* 5:10–19.

Luck, G., G. Daily, and P. R. Ehrlich. 2003. Population diversity and ecosystem services. *Trends in Ecology and Evolution* 18:331–336.

Machiavelli, N. 1981 (1513). *The Prince*. Bantam Books, New York.

Maddison, A. 2001. *The World Economy: A Millennial Perspective*. Organization for Economic Cooperation and Development, Development Research Center, Paris.

Madison, J. 1999 (1787). No. 51: The structure of the government must furnish the proper checks and balances between the different departments. Pp. 288–293 in C. Rossiter and C. R. Kesler, eds., *The Federalist Papers*. Penguin Putnam, New York.

Maguire, D. C. 2003. A papacy's 25 years of unfulfilled potential. *Los Angeles Times*, 17 October.

Makhijani, A., and S. Saleska. 1999. *The Nuclear Power Deception*. Apex Press, New York.

Mallett, P. 2003. *Rudyard Kipling: A Literary Life*. Palgrave Macmillan, New York.

Mander, J. 2003. Intrinsic negative effects of economic globalization. Pp. 109–129 in J. G. Speth, ed., *Worlds Apart: Globalization and the Environment*. Island Press, Washington, DC.

Mander, J., and E. Goldsmith, eds. 1996. *The Case against the Global Economy—and for a Turn toward the Local*. Sierra Club Books, San Francisco.

Mann, M. E., C. M. Amman, R. S. Bradlye, K. R. Briffa, T. J. Crowley, M. K. Hughes, P. D. Jones, M. Oppenheimer, T. J. Osborne, J. T. Overpeck, S. Rutherford, K. E. Trenberth, and T. M. L. Wirgley. 2003. On past temperatures and anomalous late-20th-century warmth. *Eos* 84:256–257.

Mansfield, E., and J. Snyder. 1995. Democratization and the danger of war. *International Security* 20:5–16.

Marshall, C. R., and P. D. Ward. 1996. Sudden and gradual molluscan extinctions in the latest Cretaceous of western European Tethys. *Science* 274:1360–1363.

Maschio, T. 2002. The refrigerator and American ideas of "home." *Anthropology News* (May): 8.

Mayer, C. J. 1990. Personalizing the impersonal: Corporations and the Bill of Rights. *Hastings Law Journal* 41:577–667.

McCarthy, M. 2003. Scruffy, seedy, and sorely needed: Why the decline of India's vultures has become a threat to public health. *The Independent (London)*, 4 February.

McCarthy, M. 2005. Climate change poses threat to food supply, scientists say. *The Independent* (London), 27 April.

McDaniel, C. N., and D. N. Borton. 2002. Increased human energy use causes biological diversity loss and undermines prospects for sustainability. *BioScience* 52:929–936.

McGeveran, W. A. Jr., ed. 2003. *The World Almanac and Book of Facts: 2003*. World Almanac Books, New York.

McGinn, A. P. 2002. Reducing our toxic burden. Pp. 75–100 in C. Flavin, ed., *State of the World 2002*. W. W. Norton, New York.

McMichael, A. J. 2001. *Human Frontiers, Environments, and Disease: Past Patterns, Uncertain Futures*. Cambridge Univ. Press, Cambridge.

McMillan, J. 2002. *Reinventing the Bazaar: A Natural History of Markets*. W. W. Norton, New York.

McNeill, W. H. 1976. *Plagues and Peoples*. Doubleday, New York.

McNeill, W. H. 1982. *The Pursuit of Power: Technology, Armed Force, and Society*. Univ. of Chicago Press, Chicago.

Meinzen-Dick, R. S., and M. W. Rosegrant. 2001. *Overcoming Water Scarcity and Quality Constraints*. Focus 9, Brief 1. International Food Policy Research Institute, Washington, DC.

Merari, A. 1990. The readiness to kill and die: Suicidal terrorism in the Middle East. Pp. 192–207 in W. Reich, ed., *Origins of Terrorism: Psychologies, Ideologies, Theologies, States of Mind*. Cambridge Univ. Press, New York.

Michener, W. K., E. R. Blood, K. L. Bildstein, M. M. Brinson, and L. R. Gardner. 1997. Climate change, hurricanes and tropical storms, and rising sea level in coastal wetlands. *Ecological Applications* 7:3.

Milgram, S. 1974. *Obedience to Authority: An Experimental View*. Harper and Row, New York.

Mill, J. S. 1998 (1863). *Utilitarianism*. Oxford Univ. Press, Oxford.

Mill, J. S. 2003 (1859). *On Liberty*. Yale Univ. Press, New Haven, CT.

Millennium Ecosystem Assessment. 2003. *Ecosystems and Human Well-being: A Framework for Assessment*. Island Press, Washington, DC.

Millett, M., and S. Nicholls. 2002. Carr: 50m population is nonsense. *Sydney Morning Herald*, 9 November.

Mimouni, R. 1992. *De la Barbarie en Général et de l'Intégrisme en Particulier*. Les Préaux Clercs, Paris.

Minnard, A. 2003. Reintroduced wolves dying in Southwest. *New York Times*, 4 November.

Mirrlees, J. 1971. An exploration in the theory of optimum income taxation. *Review of Economics Studies* 38:175–208.

Mishra, P. 2003. The other face of fanaticism. *New York Times Magazine* (2 February): 43–46.

Miura, L. 2003. McCain, Lieberman to offer modified amendment on Senate floor. *Climatic Change*, 2 October.

Mock, J. E., J. W. Tester, and P. M. Wright. 1997. Geothermal energy from the earth: Its potential impact as an environmentally sustainable resource.

In R. H. Socolow, D. Anderson, and J. Harte, eds., *Annual Review of Energy and the Environment*. Annual Reviews, Palo Alto, CA.

Moghaddam, F. M. 2005. The staircase to terrorism: A psychological exploration. *American Psychologist* 60:161–169.

Molina, M., and S. Rowland. 1974. Stratospheric sink for chlorofluoro methanes: Chlorine atom catalyzed destruction of ozone. *Nature* 249:810–814.

Monbiot, G. 2003a. *The Age of Consent: A Manifesto for a New World Order*. Flamingo, London.

Monbiot, G. 2003b. Bottom of the barrel: The world is running out of oil—so why do politicians refuse to talk about it? *The Guardian*, 2 December.

Monbiot, G. 2003c. Enslaved by free trade. *New Scientist* (31 May): 25.

Monbiot, G. 2003d. How to stop America. *New Statesman*, 7 June.

Mooney, C. 2005. Some like it hot. *Mother Jones* (May–June): 36.

Morgan, E. S. 1992. *The Birth of the Republic, 1763–89*. 3rd ed. Univ. of Chicago Press, Chicago.

Morgan, G. 1995. Death by congressional ignorance: How the congressional Office of Technology Assessment—small and excellent—was killed in the frenzy of government downsizing. *Pittsburgh Post-Gazette*, 2 August.

Mosteller, F. 1981. Innovation and evaluation. *Science* 211:881–886.

Moyers, B. 2005. Welcome to doomsday. *New York Review of Books* (24 March): 8–10.

Murphy, D. 2003a. California report supports critics of water diversion. *New York Times*, 7 January.

Murphy, D. E. 2003b. In a first, U.S. officials put limits on California's thirst. *New York Times*, 5 January.

Mydans, S. 2003. Resisting birth control, the Philippines grows crowded. *New York Times*, 21 March.

Myers, D. G., and E. Diener. 1995. Who is happy? *Psychological Science* 6:10–19.

Myers, N. 1979. *The Sinking Ark*. Pergamon Press, New York.

Myers, N. 1988. Threatened biotas: "Hot spots" in tropical forests. *The Environmentalist* 8:187–208.

Myers, N. 1990. The biodiversity challenge: expanded hot-spots analysis. *The Environmentalist* 10:243–256.

Myers, N. 1996. The biodiversity crisis and the future of evolution. *The Environmentalist* 16:37–47.

Myers, N., and J. Kent. 2001. *Perverse Subsidies: How Misused Tax Dollars Harm the Environment and the Economy*. Island Press, Washington, DC.

Myers, N., and J. Kent. 2004. *The New Consumers: The Influence of Affluence on the Environment*. Island Press, Washington, DC.

Nabhan, G. P., and S. L. Buchmann. 1997. Services provided by pollinators. Pp.

133–150 in G. Daily, ed., *Nature's Services: Societal Dependence on Natural Ecosystems.* Island Press, Washington, DC.

Naess, A. 1973. The shallow and the deep, long-range ecology movement: A summary. *Inquiry* 16:95–100.

Nagle, D. B., and S. M. Burstein. 2002. *The Ancient World: Readings in Social and Cultural History.* 2nd ed. Prentice-Hall, Upper Saddle River, NJ.

Nash, R. F. 1989. *The Rights of Nature: A History of Environmental Ethics.* Univ. of Wisconsin Press, Madison.

National Academy of Sciences USA. 1993. A joint statement by fifty-eight of the world's scientific academies. *Population Summit of the World's Scientific Academies.* National Academy Press, New Delhi.

Naylor, R., J. Eagle, and W. L. Smith. 2003. A global industry with local impacts: Salmon aquaculture in the Pacific Northwest. *Environment* 45:18–39.

Naylor, R. L., R. J. Goldburg, J. H. Primavera, N. Kautsky, M. C. M. Beveridge, J. Clay, C. Folke, J. Lubchenco, H. Mooney, and M. Troell. 2000. Effect of aquaculture on world fish supplies. *Nature* 405:1017–1024.

Nesmith, J. 2003. Nonprofits push controversial climate study. *Atlanta Journal-Constitution,* 1 June.

Newman, P. G., and J. K. Kenworthy. 1989. *Cities and Automobile Dependence: A Source Book.* Gower Technical, Brookfield, VT.

*New Scientist.* 1975. Is the cod war really a red herring? *New Scientist* (27 November): 500.

Nordhaus, W. D., and J. Tobin. 1972. Is growth obsolete? In National Bureau of Economic Research, *Economic Growth.* Columbia Univ. Press, New York.

North, D. C. 1986. A neoclassical theory of the state. Pp. 248–260 in J. Elster, ed., *Rational Choice.* New York Univ. Press, New York.

Nussbaum, B. 2002. Commentary: Foreign policy: Bush is half right. *Business Week,* 7 October.

Nye, J. S. Jr. 2001. *The Paradox of American Power.* Oxford Univ. Press, New York.

Oak Ridge National Laboratory. 1968. *Nuclear Energy Centers, Industrial and Agro-industrial Complexes.* Summary Report ORNL-4291. Oak Ridge National Laboratory, Oak Ridge, TN.

O'Brien, T. M. 2003. Just what does America want to do with Iraq's oil? *New York Times,* 8 June.

O'Brien, D. 2005. Oceans bearing brunt of climate shift, study finds. *Baltimore Sun,* 13 March.

O'Dowd, D. J., P. T. Green, and P. S. Lake. 2003. Invasional "meltdown" on an oceanic island. *Ecology Letters* 6:812–817.

Ogden, J. 1999. Prospects for building a hydrogen energy infrastructure. In R. Socolow, D. Anderson, and J. Harte, eds., *Annual Review of Energy and the Environment.* Annual Reviews, Palo Alto, CA.

Oldeman, L. R. 1998. *Soil Degradation: A Threat to Food Security?* International Soil Reference and Information Center (ISRIC), Wageningen, Netherlands.

Olson, M. 1971 (1965). *The Logic of Collective Action: Public Goods and the Theory of Groups.* Harvard Univ. Press, Cambridge, MA.

O'Neill, B., and D. Balk. 2001. World population futures. *Population Bulletin* 56:1–40.

Opie, J. 1993. *Ogallala: Water for a Dry Land.* Univ. of Nebraska Press, Lincoln.

Oppel, R. A. Jr. 2003. Panel finds manipulation by energy companies. *New York Times,* 27 March.

Oppel, R. A. Jr., and J. M. Broder. 2002. Seeking huge electricity refund, California is told to pay instead. *New York Times,* 13 December.

Orndorff, M. 2003. Shelby defends provisions of corporate reform law. *Birmingham News,* 10 September.

Ornstein, R. 1988. *Psychology: The Study of Human Experience.* 2nd ed. Harcourt Brace Jovanovich, Orlando, FL.

Ornstein, R., and P. Ehrlich. 1989. *New World/New Mind: Moving toward Conscious Evolution.* Doubleday, New York.

Osborne, F. 1948. *Our Plundered Planet.* Little, Brown, Boston.

Ostrom, E. 1996. Incentives, rules of the game, and development. Pp. 207–234 in World Bank, ed., *Proceedings of the Annual World Bank Conference on Development Economics, 1995.* World Bank, Washington, DC.

Ostrom, E., and E. Schlager. 1996. The formation of property rights. Pp. 127–156 in S. S. Hanna, C. Folke, and K.-G. Mäler, eds., *Rights to Nature: Ecological, Economic, Cultural, and Political Principles of Institutions for the Environment.* Island Press, Washington, DC.

Pain, D. J., A. A. Cunningham, P. F. Donald, J. W. Duckworth, D. C. Houston, T. Katzner, J. Parry-Jones, C. Poole, V. Prakash, P. Round, and R. Timmins. 2003. Causes and effects of temporospatial declines of *Gyps* vultures in Asia. *Conservation Biology* 17:661–671.

Palast, G. 2002. *The Best Democracy Money Can Buy.* Pluto Press, London.

Palast, G. 2005. CBS gets standing Rove-ation at White House: Dan Rather feared the price of "asking questions" before network's purge of investigative reporters. http://www.gregpalast.com/detail.cfm?artid=371&row=1, 11 January.

Palumbi, S. R. 2001a. *The Evolution Explosion: How Humans Cause Rapid Evolutionary Change.* W. W. Norton, New York.

Palumbi, S. R. 2001b. Humans as the world's greatest evolutionary force. *Science* 293:1786–1789.

Pandolfi, J. M., J. B. C. Jackson, N. Baron, R. H. Bradbury, H. M. Guzman, T. P. Hughes, C. V. Kappel, F. Micheli, J. C. Ogden, H. P. Possingham, and E. Sala. 2005. Are U.S. coral reefs on the slippery slope to slime? *Science* 307:1725–1726.

Parmesan, C., and G. Yohe. 2003. A globally coherent fingerprint of climate change impacts across natural systems. *Nature* 421:37–42.

Parry, I. W. H., and K. Small. 2002. *Does Britain or the United States Have the Right Gasoline Tax?* Discussion Paper 02-12. Resources for the Future, Washington, DC.

Parsons, J. 1977. *Population Fallacies.* Elek/Pemberton, London.

Pauly, D., V. Christensen, S. Guénette, T. J. Pitcher, U. R. Sumaila, C. J. Walters, R. Watson, and D. Zeller. 2002. Toward sustainability in world fisheries. *Nature* 418:689–695.

Pauly, D., and J. Maclean. 2003. *In a Perfect Ocean: The State of Fisheries and Ecosystems in the North Atlantic Ocean.* Island Press, Washington, DC.

Pauly, D., and R. Watson. 2003. The last fish. *Scientific American* 289 (July): 43–47.

Pearce, F. 2003a. Doomsday scenario. *New Scientist* (22 November): 40–43.

Pearce, F. 2003b. Europe's deep corals are facing devastation. *New Scientist* (23 June): 5.

Pearce, F. 2003c. Southeast Asia's coral reefs at risk from cyanide fishing. *Boston Globe,* 29 April.

Pearce, F. 2005a. Cities may be abandoned as salt water invades. *New Scientist* (16 April): 9.

Pearce, F. 2005b. Oceans are hiding climate time bomb. *New Scientist* (7 May): 14.

Pearson, L. B. 1969. *Partners in Development.* Praeger, New York.

Perkins, J. 2004. *Confessions of an Economic Hit Man.* Berrett-Koehler, San Francisco.

Perlez, J. 2003. Indonesians bearing burden of campaign against rebels. *New York Times International/Asia Pacific,* 25 May.

Perrin, N. 1979. *Giving Up the Gun: Japan's Reversion to the Sword.* G. K. Hall, Boston.

Perrings, C. 1987. *Economy and Environment: A Theoretical Essay on the Interdependence of Economic and Environmental Systems.* Cambridge Univ. Press, Cambridge.

Perrow, C. 1999. *Normal Accidents: Living with High-Risk Technologies.* Rev. ed. Princeton Univ. Press, Princeton, NJ.

Phillips, K. 2002. *Wealth and Democracy: A Political History of the American Rich.* Random House, New York.

Pianin, E. 2003. EPA eases clean air rule on power plants. *Washington Post,* 28 August.

Pielke, R. Jr. 2003. The skeptical environmentalist. *International Herald Tribune,* 20 January.

Pigliucci, M. 2002. *Denying Evolution: Creationism, Scientism, and the Nature of Science.* Sinauer Associates, Sunderland, MA.

Pigou, A. C. 1920. *The Economics of Welfare.* Macmillan, London.

Pimm, S. L. 2001. *The World according to Pimm.* McGraw-Hill, New York.

Pincetl, S. 1999. *Transforming California: A Political History of Land Use and Development.* Johns Hopkins Univ. Press, Baltimore.

Pirages, D. C., and T. M. DeGeest. 2003. *Ecological Security: An Evolutionary Perspective on Globalization.* Rowman & Littlefield, Lanham, MD.

Pirages, D., and P. R. Ehrlich. 1972. If all Chinese had wheels. *New York Times,* 16 March.

Pirie, N. W. 1966. Leaf protein as human food. *Science* 152:1701–1705.

Pirie, N. W. 1969. *Food Resources, Conventional and Novel.* Penguin, Baltimore.

Population Reference Bureau. 1976. 1976 World population data sheet. Population Reference Bureau, Washington, DC.

Population Reference Bureau. 1990. World population data sheet 1990. Population Reference Bureau, Washington, DC.

Population Reference Bureau. 2001. 2001 World population data sheet. Population Reference Bureau, Washington, DC.

Population Reference Bureau. 2002. 2002 World population data sheet. Population Reference Bureau, Washington, DC.

Population Reference Bureau. 2003. 2003 World population data sheet. Population Reference Bureau, Washington, DC.

Postel, S. 1998. Water for food production: Will there be enough in 2020? *BioScience* 48:629–637.

Postel, S. 1999. *Pillar of Sand: Can the Irrigation Miracle Last?* W. W. Norton, New York.

Postel, S. L., G. C. Daily, and P. R. Ehrlich. 1996. Human appropriation of renewable fresh water. *Science* 271:785–788.

Potts, M., P. Diggory, and J. Peel. 1977. *Abortion.* Cambridge Univ. Press, New York.

Povoledo, E. 2003. Most of Italy is blacked out for several hours. *New York Times,* 28 September.

Power, T. 2003. The vanishing case for war. *New York Review of Books* (4 December): 12–17.

Prestowitz, C. 2003. *Rogue Nation: American Unilateralism and the Failure of Good Intentions.* Basic Books, New York.

Priest, D. 2005. Iraq new terror breeding ground: War created haven, CIA advisers report. *Washington Post,* 14 January.

Princen, T., M. Maniates, and K. Conca. 2002. Confronting consumption. Pp. 1–20 in T. Princen, M. Maniates, and K. Conca, eds., *Confronting Consumption.* MIT Press, Cambridge, MA.

Pritchett, L. 1997. Divergence, big time. *Journal of Economic Perspectives* 11 (Summer): 3–17.

Rahnema, M. 2002. A different look at the "population problem." *Population and Environment* 24:97–104.

Rall, T. 2002. *Gas War: The Truth behind the American Occupation of Afghanistan.* Writers Club Press, New York.

Rashid, A. 2001. *Taliban.* Yale Univ. Press, New Haven, CT.

Raup, D. M. 1991. *Extinction: Bad Genes or Bad Luck?.* W. W. Norton, New York.

Rawls, J. 1971. *A Theory of Justice.* Harvard Univ. Press, Cambridge, MA.

Ray, G. C., B. P. Hayden, A. G. Bulger Jr., and M. G. McCormick-Ray. 1992. Effects of global warming on the biodiversity of coastal-marine zones. Pp. 91–104 in R. L. Peters and T. E. Lovejoy, eds., *Global Warming and Biological Diversity.* Yale Univ. Press, New Haven, CT.

Recher, H. F. 1999. The state of Australia's avifauna: A personal opinion and prediction for the new millennium. *Australian Zoologist* 31:11–27.

Recher, H. F. 2002. What revolution? Pp. 116–129 in D. Lunney and C. R. Dickman, eds., *A Zoological Revolution: Using Native Fauna to Assist in Its Own Survival.* Royal Zoological Society of New South Wales and Australian Museum, Mosman, New South Wales, Australia.

Redman, C. L. 1999. *Human Impact on Ancient Environments.* Univ. of Arizona Press, Tucson.

Redman, C. L., and A. P. Kinzig. 2003. Resilience of past landscapes: Resilience theory, society, and the *longue durée. Conservation Ecology* 7:14.

Rees, M. 2003. *Our Final Hour: How Terror, Error, and Environmental Disaster Threaten Humankind's Future in This Century—on Earth and Beyond.* Basic Books, New York.

Rees, W. E. 1996. Revisiting carrying capacity: Area-based indicators of sustainability. *Population and Environment* 17:195–215.

Rees, W. E. 2001. Ecological footprint, Concept of. Pp. 229–244 in S. A. Levin, ed., *Encyclopedia of Biodiversity,* vol. 2. Academic Press, San Diego.

Rees, W. E. 2002. An ecological economics perspective on sustainability and prospects for ending poverty. *Population and Environment* 24:15–46.

Reisner, M. 1986. *Cadillac Desert: The American West and Its Disappearing Water.* Viking, New York.

Renfrew, A. C. 1982. Polity and power: Interaction, intensification, and exploitation. Pp. 264–290 in C. Renfrew and M. Wagstaff, eds., *An Island Polity: The Archaeology of Exploitation on Melos.* Cambridge Univ. Press, Cambridge.

Renner, M. 2002. *The Anatomy of Resource Wars.* Worldwatch Institute, Washington, DC.

Repetto, R., and T. Holmes. 1983. The role of population in resource depletion in developing countries. *Population and Development Review* 9:609–632.

Repetto, R., M. Wells, C. Beer, and F. Rossini. 1987. *Natural Resource Accounting for Indonesia.* World Resources Institute, Washington, DC.

Revkin, A. C., and K. Q. Seelye. 2003a. Environmental warning is altered in White House: References to emission problems deleted. *New York Times,* 20 June.

Revkin, A. C., and K. Q. Seelye. 2003b. Report by EPA leaves out data on climate change. *New York Times,* 19 June.

Revkin, A. C. 2005a. Bush aide edited climate reports. *New York Times,* 8 June.

Revkin, A. C. 2005b. Report tallies hidden costs of human assault on nature. *New York Times,* 5 April.

Revkin, A. C. 2005c. 2004 was the fourth-warmest year ever recorded. *New York Times,* 10 February.

Rich, F. 2005a. A culture of death, not life. *New York Times,* 10 April.

Rich, F. 2005b. Laura Bush's mission accomplished. *New York Times,* 8 May.

Ricketts, H. 1999. *The Unforgiving Minute: A Life of Rudyard Kipling.* Chatto & Windus, London.

Roaf, M. 1990. *Cultural Atlas of Mesopotamia and the Ancient Near East.* Andromeda Books, Abingdon, England.

Roan, S. 1989. *Ozone Crisis: The 15-Year Evolution of a Sudden Global Emergency.* Wiley, New York.

Rogers, E. M. 1995. *Diffusion of Innovations.* 4th ed. Free Press, New York.

Rohter, L. 2003. Bolivia's poor proclaim abiding distrust of globalization. *New York Times,* 17 October.

Rohter, L. 2005. Antarctic, warming, looks ever more vulnerable. *New York Times,* 25 January.

Rollin, B. E. 1995. *Farm Animal Welfare: Social, Bioethical, and Research Issues.* Iowa State Univ. Press, Ames.

Rolston, H. 1988. *Environmental Ethics: Duties to and Values in the Natural World.* Temple Univ. Press, Philadelphia, PA.

Roman, J., and S. R. Palumbi. 2003. Whales before whaling in the North Atlantic. *Science* 301:508–510.

Romero, S. 2003. Big shortage of natural gas is raising economic worries. *New York Times,* 17 June.

Romm, J. J. 1999. *Cool Companies: How the Best Businesses Boost Profits and Productivity by Cutting Greenhouse Gas Emissions.* Island Press, Washington, DC.

Romm, J. J. 2004. *The Hype about Hydrogen: Fact and Fiction in the Race to Save the Climate.* Island Press, Washington, DC.

Root, T. L., J. T. Price, K. R. Hall, S. H. Schneider, C. Rosenzweig, and A. Pounds. 2003. "Fingerprints" of global warming on wild animals and plants. *Nature* 421:57–60.

Root, T. R., D. P. MacMinowski, M. D. Mastrandrea, and S. H. Schneider. 2005. Human modified temperatures induce species changes: Joint attribution. *Proceedings of the National Academy of Sciences* 102:7465–7469.

Rosa, E. A., R. York, and T. Dietz. 2003. Tracking the anthropogenic drivers of ecological impacts. *Ambio,* in press.

Rosegrant, M. W., X. Cai, and S. Cline. 2003. Will the world run dry? *Environment* 45:24–36.

Rosegrant, M. W., M. S. Paisner, S. Meijer, and J. Witcover. 2001. *2020 Global Food Outlook*. International Food Policy Research Institute, Washington, DC.

Rosenblatt, R., ed. 1999. *Consuming Desires: Consumption, Culture, and the Pursuit of Happiness*. Island Press, Washington, DC.

Rosencranz, A. 2002. U.S. climate policy. Pp. 221–233 in S. H. Schneider, A. Rosencranz, and J. O. Niles, eds., *Climate Change Policy: A Survey*. Island Press, Washington, DC.

Rosenfeld, A. H. 1999. The art of energy efficiency: Protecting the environment with better technology. In R. Socolow, D. Anderson, and J. Harte, eds., *Annual Review of Energy*. Annual Reviews, Palo Alto, CA.

Rosenthal, E. 2003. Chinese official fights corruption, and loses, for now. *New York Times*, 1 January.

Rousseau, J.-J. 1762. *The Social Contract*. J. M. Dent, London.

Roux, G. 1980. *Ancient Iraq*. 2nd ed. Penguin, London.

Rudd, R. L. 1964. *Pesticides and the Living Landscape*. Univ. of Wisconsin Press, Madison.

Russell, B. 1938. *Power: A New Social Analysis*. Allen and Unwin, London.

Sabloff, J. A. 1994. *The New Archaeology and the Ancient Maya*. W. H. Freeman, New York.

Sachs, J. D., and A. M. Warner. 2001. The curse of natural resources. *European Economic Review* 45:827–838.

Safire, W. 2003. The great media gulp. *New York Times*, 22 May.

Sahlins, M. 1968. Notes on the original affluent society. Pp. 85–89 in R. B. Lee and I. Devore, eds., *Man the Hunter*. Aldine, Chicago.

Sample, I. 2003. Not just warmer: It's the hottest for 2,000 years. *The Guardian*, 1 September.

Samuelson, P. A., and W. D. Nordhaus. 1989. *Economics*. 13th ed. McGraw-Hill, New York.

Sandel, M. J. 1996. *Democracy's Discontent: America in Search of a Public Philosophy*. Harvard Univ. Press, Cambridge, MA.

Sapolsky, R. 1997. *The Trouble with Testosterone and Other Essays on the Biology of the Human Predicament*. Scribner, New York.

Saul, J. R. 1997. *The Unconscious Civilization*. Penguin, London.

Saunders, D. A., R. J. Hobbs, and P. R. Ehrlich, eds. 1993. *Reconstruction of Fragmented Ecosystems*. Surrey Beatty & Sons, Chipping Norton, New South Wales, Australia.

Sawin, J. 2003. Charting a new energy future. In Worldwatch Institute, *State of the World 2003*. W. W. Norton, New York.

Scherer, G. 2004. The godly must be crazy: Christian-right views are swaying politicians and threatening the environment. *Grist Magazine*, 27 October.

Schneider, S. H. 1988. The whole earth dialogue. *Issues in Science and Technology* 4:93–99.

Schneider, S. H. 1989. *Global Warming*. Sierra Club Books, San Francisco.

Schneider, S. H. 1992. The role of the university in interdisciplinary global change research: Structural constraints and the potential for change. An editorial. *Climatic Change* 20:vii–x.

Schneider, S. H. 1997a. Defining and teaching environmental literacy. *Trends in Ecology and Evolution* 12:457.

Schneider, S. H. 1997b. *Laboratory Earth: The Planetary Gamble We Can't Afford to Lose*. Basic Books, New York.

Schneider, S. H., and R. Londer. 1984. *The Coevolution of Climate and Life*. Sierra Club Books, San Francisco.

Schneider, S. H., A. Rosencranz, and J. O. Niles, eds. 2002. *Climate Change Policy: A Survey*. Island Press, Washington, DC.

Schor, J. B. 1998. *The Overspent American: Upscaling, Downshifting, and the New Consumer*. Basic Books, New York.

Schreiner, T. P. 2002. Traditional Maya Lime Production: Environmental and Cultural Implications of Native American Technology. Ph.D. diss., Univ. of California, Berkeley.

Schwartz, P. 2003. Nuclear plants in the hotseat. *ENN*, 11 September.

Seidman, L. 1997. *The USA Tax: A Progressive Consumption Tax*. MIT Press, Cambridge, MA.

Sen Gupta, B. 1999. *Bhutan: Towards a Grass-root Participatory Polity*. Konark, New Delhi.

Service, R. 2003. "Combat biology" on the Klamath. *Science* 300:36–39.

Seyfang, G. 2003. Environmental mega-conferences—from Stockholm to Johannesburg and beyond. *Global Environmental Change* 13:223–228.

Sheehan, M. O. 2001. City limits: Putting the brakes on sprawl. Worldwatch Paper 156. Worldwatch Institute, Washington, DC.

Sheehan, M. O. 2002. Where the sidewalks end. *World Watch* (November–December): 20–32.

Sherman, R. 2003. The real terrorist missile threat and what can be done about it. *FAS Public Interest Report* 56:1–8.

Shiva, V. 1999. *Stolen Harvest: The Hijacking of the Global Food Supply*. South End Press, London.

Shiva, V. 2003. The myths of globalization exposed: Advancing toward living democracy. Pp. 141–154 in J. G. Speth, ed., *Worlds Apart: Globalization and the Environment*. Island Press, Washington, DC.

Siegel, J. J., and R. H. Thaler. 1997. Anomalies: The equity premium puzzle. *Journal of Economic Perspectives* 11:191–200.

Simberloff, D., D. C. Schmitz, and T. C. Brown, eds. 1997. *Strangers in Paradise: Impact and Management of Nonindigenous Species in Florida*. Island Press, Washington, DC.

Simon, P. 1998. *Tapped Out: The Coming World Crisis in Water and What We Can Do about It*. Welcome Rain, New York.

Simonich, S., and R. Hites. 1995. Global distribution of persistent organochlorine compounds. *Science* 269:1851–1854.

Singer, P. 1972. Famine, affluence, and morality. *Philosophy and Public Affairs* 1:229–243.

Singer, P. 1975. *Animal Liberation.* New York Review, New York.

Singer, P. 1993. *How Are We to Live? Ethics in an Age of Self-Interest.* Text, Melbourne, Australia.

Singer, P. 2002. *One World: The Ethics of Globalization.* Yale Univ. Press, New Haven, CT.

Siscawati, M. 2001. The case of Indonesia: Under Soeharto's shadow. Pp. 47–60 in World Rainforest Movement, *The Bitter Fruit of Oil Palm: Dispossession and Deforestation.* World Rainforest Movement, Montevideo, Uruguay.

Sitarz, D., ed. 1993. *Agenda 21: The Earth Summit Strategy to Save our Planet.* Earthpress, Boulder, CO.

Skocpol, T. 1979. *States and Social Revolutions: A Comparative Analysis of France, Russia, and China.* Cambridge Univ. Press, Cambridge.

Slemrod, J. 1990. Optimal taxation and optimal tax systems. *Journal of Economic Perspectives* 4:157–178.

Smale, M. 1997. The green revolution and wheat genetic diversity: Some unfounded assumptions. *World Development* 25:1257–1269.

Smil, V. 2000. *Feeding the World: A Challenge for the Twenty-first Century.* MIT Press, Cambridge, MA.

Smith, A. 1974 (1759). *The Theory of Moral Sentiments.* Clarendon Press, Oxford.

Smith, A. 1976 (1776). *An Inquiry into the Nature and Causes of the Wealth of Nations.* Univ. of Chicago Press, Chicago.

Smith, B. D. 1995. *The Emergence of Agriculture.* Scientific American Library, New York.

Solé, R., and D. Valbelle. 2002. *The Rosetta Stone.* Four Walls Eight Windows, New York.

Solomon, S., R. R. Garcia, F. S. Rowland, and D. J. Wuebbles. 1986. On the depletion of Antarctic ozone. *Nature* 321:755–758.

Specter, M. 1994. Russia fights a rising tide of infection. *New York Times,* 2 October.

Spencer, H. 1891 (1860). *Essays: Scientific, Political, and Speculative.* Vol. 1. D. Appleton, New York.

Speth, J. G. 2003. Environment and globalization after Johannesburg. Pp. 155–165 in J. G. Speth, ed., *Worlds Apart: Globalization and the Environment.* Island Press, Washington, DC.

Stainforth, D. A., T. Alna, C. Christensen, M. Collins, N. Faull, D. J. Frame, J. A. Kettleborough, S. Knight, A. Martin, J. M. Murphy, C. Piani, D. Sexton, L. A. Smith, R. A. Spicer, A. J. Thorpe, and M. R. Allen. 2005.

Uncertainty in predictions of the climate response to rising levels of greenhouse gases. *Nature* 433:403–406.

Stambaugh, J. E. 1988. *The Ancient Roman City.* Johns Hopkins Univ. Press, Baltimore.

Stark, R. 1996. *The Rise of Christianity: A Sociologist Reconsiders History.* Princeton Univ. Press, Princeton, NJ.

Starr, C. G. 1991. *A History of the Ancient World.* Oxford Univ. Press, New York.

Stavins, R., ed. 1988. *Project 88: Harnessing Market Forces to Protect Our Environment: Initiatives for the New President.* A Public Policy Study Commissioned by Senator Timothy E. Wirth, Colorado, and Senator John Heinz, Pennsylvania. Washington, DC.

Steger, M. B. 2001. *Globalization: The New Market Ideology.* Rowman & Littlefield, New York.

Stelzer, I. M. 2002. Oil's well that ends well: The key to a sound energy policy is a strong military. *The Weekly Standard* (13 May): 24.

Stern, N. 2002. *Cutting Agricultural Subsidies.* World Bank, Washington, DC.

Stern, P. C., T. Dietz, V. W. Ruttan, R. H. Socolow, and J. L. Sweeney, eds. 1997. *Environmentally Significant Consumption: Research Directions.* National Academy Press, Washington, DC.

Stigler, G., and G. S. Becker. 1977. De gustibus non est disputandum. *American Economic Review* 67:76–90.

Stiglitz, J. 2002. *Globalization and Its Discontents.* W. W. Norton, New York.

Stockdale, J., and S. Stockdale. 1990. *In Love and War.* 2nd ed. Naval Institute Press, Annapolis, MD.

Stokstad, E. 2003. EPA report takes heat for climate change edits. *Science* 300:2013.

Stokstad, E. 2005. Taking the pulse of Earth's life-support systems. *Science* 308:41–43.

Stone, C. D. 1974. *Should Trees Have Standing? Toward Legal Rights for Natural Objects.* W. Kaufmann, Los Altos, CA.

Stone, G. D. 2002. Fallacies in the genetic-modification wars, implications for developing countries, and anthropological perspectives. *Current Anthropology* 43:611–630.

Struglinzky, S. 2002. Senate approves extending nuclear insurance 10 years. *Environment and Energy Daily,* 8 March.

Study of Critical Environmental Problems. 1970. *Man's Impact on the Global Environment.* MIT Press, Cambridge, MA.

Sugg, J. 2002. Roast the chicken hawks. *San Francisco Chronicle,* 8 October.

Sunstein, C. 2000a. Chipping away at Buckley. *American Prospect* (September 25–October 9): 23–24.

Sunstein, C. 2000b. Rescuing politics from money: Round two. *American Prospect* (September 25–October 9): 25.

Swedberg, R. 1994. Markets as social structures. In N. J. Smelser and R. Swedberg, eds., *The Handbook of Economic Sociology.* Princeton Univ. Press, Princeton, NJ.

Symons, J. 2003. How Bush and co. obscure the science. *Washington Post,* 13 July.

Tainter, J. A. 1988. *The Collapse of Complex Societies.* Cambridge Univ. Press, Cambridge.

Tainter, J. A. 2000. Problem solving: Complexity, history, sustainability. *Population and Environment* 22:3–41.

Talbot, F. H. 2000. Will the Great Barrier Reef survive human impact? Pp. 331–348 in E. Wolanski, ed., *Oceanographic Processes of Coral Reefs: Physical and Biological Links in the Great Barrier Reef.* CRC Press, London.

Teather, D. 2003. Media guardian: Nikes loses freedom of speech argument. *The Guardian,* 27 June.

Tempest, R. 2002. Recreation: The king of four-wheeler trails, the Rubicon, is so popular that its future is at risk. *Los Angeles Times,* 5 July.

Thaler, R. H. 1992. *The Winner's Curse.* Free Press, New York.

Thinley, L. J. Y. 1999. Gross national happiness and human development—searching for common ground. Pp. 7–11 in The Centre for Bhutan Studies, *Gross National Happiness.* Centre for Bhutan Studies, Thimphu, Bhutan.

Thucydides. 1910 (ca. 400 BC). *History of the Peloponnesian War.* J. M. Dent, London.

Tilman, D. 2000. Causes, consequences, and ethics of biodiversity. *Nature* 405:208–211.

Tilman, D., R. M. May, C. L. Lehman, and M. A. Nowak. 1994. Habitat destruction and the extinction debt. *Nature* 371:65–66.

Townsend, P. 1987. Deprivation. *Journal of Social Policy* 16:125–146.

Tromp, T. K., R.-L. Shia, M. Allen, J. M. Eiler, and Y. L. Yung. 2003. Potential environmental impact of a hydrogen economy on the stratosphere. *Science* 300:1740–1742.

Tucker, R. P. 2000. *Insatiable Appetite: The United States and the Ecological Degradation of the Tropical World.* Univ. of California Press, Berkeley.

Turco, R. P. 1997. *Earth under Siege: From Air Pollution to Global Change.* Oxford Univ. Press, Oxford.

Turco, R., O. Toon, T. Ackerman, J. Pollack, and C. Sagan. 1983. Nuclear winter: Global consequences of multiple nuclear weapons explosions. *Science* 222:1283–1292.

Tversky, A., and D. Kahneman. 1974. Judgement under uncertainty: Heuristics and biases. *Science* 185:1124–1131.

Tversky, A., and D. Kahneman. 1986. Rational choice and the framing of decisions. *Journal of Business* 59:S251–S278.

Tyerman, C. 2004. *Fighting for Christendom: Holy War and the Crusades.* Oxford Univ. Press, Oxford.

Tylor, E. B. 1920 (1871). *Primitive Culture: Researches into the Development of Mythology, Philosophy, Religion, Language, Art, and Custom.* 6th ed. J. Murray, London.

Union of Concerned Scientists. 1993. *World Scientists' Warning to Humanity.* Union of Concerned Scientists, Cambridge, MA.

United Nations (Population Division). 2001. *World Population Prospects: The 2000 Revision.* United Nations, New York.

United Nations (Population Division). 2002a. *International Migration Report 2002.* ST/ESA/SER.A/220. United Nations Department of Economic and Social Affairs, Population Division, New York.

United Nations (Population Division). 2002b. *World Urbanization Prospects: The 2001 Revision.* ESA/P/WP.173. United Nations, New York.

United Nations (Population Division). 2003. *World Population Prospects, 2002 Revision.* Department of Economic and Social Affairs, United Nations, New York.

United Nations Joint Programme on HIV/AIDS (UNAIDS). 2002. *Report on the Global HIV/AIDS Epidemic—July 2002.* United Nations, New York.

United Nations Population Fund (UNFPA). 2002. *State of the World Population 2002: People, Poverty, and Possibilities.* United Nations, New York.

Veblen, T. 1967 (1899). *The Theory of the Leisure Class.* Penguin, New York.

Vidal, J. 2003. Toxic shocker. *The Guardian,* 28 October.

Vitousek, P. M., C. M. D'Antonio, L. L. Loope, and R. Westbrooks. 1996. Biological invasions as global environmental change. *American Scientist* 84:468–478.

Vitousek, P. M., P. R. Ehrlich, A. H. Ehrlich, and P. A. Matson. 1986. Human appropriation of the products of photosynthesis. *BioScience* 36:368–373.

Vitousek, P. M., and P. A. Matson. 1993. Agriculture, the global nitrogen cycle, and trace gas flux. Pp. 193–208 in R. Oremland, ed., *Biogeochemistry of Global Change: Radiatively Active Trace Gases.* Chapman and Hall, New York.

Vitousek, P. M., H. A. Mooney, J. Lubchenco, and J. M. Melillo. 1997. Human domination of Earth's ecosystems. *Science* 277:494–499.

Vogt, W. 1948. *Road to Survival.* William Sloan, New York.

Von Wiezacker, E., A. Lovins, and L. H. Lovins. 1998. *Factor Four: Doubling Wealth, Halving Resource Use.* Earthscan, London.

Waal, F. de. 1997. *Bonobo: The Forgotten Ape.* Univ. of California Press, Berkeley.

Waal, F. de. 1999. Cultural primatology comes of age. *Nature* 399:635–636.

Wackernagel, M., and W. Rees. 1996. *Our Ecological Footprint: Reducing Human Impact on the Earth.* New Society Publishers, Gabriola Island, British Columbia.

Wackernagel, M., N. B. Schulz, D. Deumling, A. C. Linares, M. Jenkins, V. Kapos, C. Monfreda, J. Loh, N. Myers, R. Norgaard, and J. Randers. 2002. Tracking the ecological overshoot of the human economy. *Proceedings of the National Academy of Sciences USA* 99:9266–9271.

Wald, M. L. 2002. Alaska Airlines crash that killed 88 is tied to long failure to lubricate tail-control part. *New York Times,* 11 December.

Waldmeir, P. 2003. Should companies have a constitutional right to lie? *Financial Times,* 15 September.

Wallerstein, I. 2003. Anthropology, sociology, and other dubious disciplines. *Current Anthropology* 44:453–460.

Walt, S. M. 2000. Fads, fevers, and firestorms. *Foreign Policy* (November–December): 34–42.

Wargo, J. 1998. *Our Children's Toxic Legacy: How Science and Law Fail to Protect Us from Pesticides.* 2nd ed. Yale Univ. Press, New Haven, CT.

Watson, R., and D. Pauly. 2001. Systematic distortions in world fisheries catch trends. *Nature* 414:534–536.

Wattenberg, B. 1987. *The Birth Dearth.* Pharos Books, New York.

Webby, R. J., and R. G. Webster. 2003. Are we ready for pandemic influenza? *Science* 302:1519–1522.

Weber, M. 1946. *From Max Weber: Essays in Sociology.* Oxford Univ. Press, New York.

Webster, D. 2002. *The Fall of the Ancient Maya.* Thames and Hudson, London.

Webster, R. G., and E. J. Walker. 2003. Influenza. *American Scientist* 91:122–129.

Weinberg, S. 2003. Nuclear terror: Ambling toward apocalypse. *FAS Public Interest Report* 56:1–4, 8.

Weisskopf, W. 1971. *Alienation and Economics.* Dutton, New York.

Wells, M. 2003. TV watchdog checks claims of bias on Murdoch channel. *The Guardian,* 8 May.

Wentworth Group. 2002. *Blueprint for a Living Continent.* WWF Australia, Sydney, New South Wales, Australia.

Wilk, R. R. 1985. The ancient Maya and the political present. *Journal of Anthropological Research* 41:307–326.

Wilkinson, R. G. 1997. *Unhealthy Societies: The Afflictions of Inequality.* Routledge, London.

Williams, M. 2003. *Deforesting the Earth: From Prehistory to Global Crisis.* Univ. of Chicago Press, Chicago.

Williams, W. 2004. *Reaganism and the Death of Representative Democracy.* Georgetown Univ. Press, Washington, DC.

Willrich, M., and T. Taylor. 1974. *Nuclear Theft: Risks and Safeguards.* Ballinger, Cambridge, MA.

Wilson, E. O. 2002. *The Future of Life.* Knopf, New York.

Wirth, T. E., C. B. Gray, and J. D. Podesta. 2002. The future of energy policy. *Foreign Affairs* 82:132–155.

Wolf, M. 2003. The morality of the market. *Foreign Policy* (September–October): 47–50.

Wolfson, R., and S. H. Schneider. 2002. Understanding climate science.

Pp. 3–51 in S. H. Schneider, A. Rosencranz, and J.O. Niles, eds., *Climate Change Policy: A Survey*. Island Press, Washington, DC.

Woodward, B. 2002. *Bush at War*. Simon and Schuster, New York.

Woodwell, G. M. 1967. Toxic substances and ecological cycles. *Scientific American* 216:24–31.

World Bank. 2000. *Entering the 21st Century: World Development Report 1999/2000*. Oxford Univ. Press, New York.

World Bank. 2001. *World Development Report 2000/2001: Attacking Poverty*. Oxford Univ. Press, Oxford.

World Bank. 2003. *World Development Report 2004: Making Services Work for Poor People*. Oxford Univ. Press, Oxford.

World Bank. 2005. *World Development Report 2005: A Better Investment Climate for Everyone*. Oxford Univ. Press, New York.

World Bank and International Monetary Fund. 1999. *Comprehensive Development Framework*. World Bank, Washington, DC.

World Commission on Environment and Development. 1987. *Our Common Future*. Oxford Univ. Press, New York.

World Resources Institute. 1998. *World Resources 1998–99*. Oxford Univ. Press, New York.

World Resources Institute. 2000. *World Resources 2000–2001*. World Resources Institute, Washington, DC.

World Resources Institute. 2003. *World Resources 2002–2004*. World Resources Institute, Washington, D.C.

Worldwatch Institute. 2000. *Vital Signs 2000: The Trends That Are Shaping Our Future*. W. W. Norton, New York.

Worldwatch Institute. 2002. *Vital Signs 2002: The Trends That Are Shaping Our Future*. W. W. Norton, New York.

Worldwatch Institute. 2003. *Vital Signs 2003: The Trends That Are Shaping Our Future*. Worldwatch Institute, Washington, DC.

Wright, J. W., ed. 1999. *The New York Times Almanac*. New York Times, New York.

Wu, P., R. Wood, and P. Stott. 2005. Human influences on increasing Arctic river discharges. *Geophysical Research Letters* 32:L02703.

Wyman, C. E. 1999. Biomass ethanol: Technical progress, opportunities, and commercial challenges. In R. Socolow, D. Anderson, and J. Harte, eds., *Annual Review of Energy and the Environment*. Annual Reviews, Palo Alto, CA.

Yacoub, J. 1986. *The Assyrian Question*. Alpha Graphic, Chicago.

Yager, J. A., and E. B. Steinberg. 1975. *Energy and U.S. Foreign Policy*. Ballinger, Cambridge, MA.

Yang, C., and S. H. Schneider. 1997–1998. Global carbon dioxide emissions scenarios: Sensitivity to social and technological factors in three regions. *Mitigation and Adaptation Strategies for Global Change* 2:373–404.

Yergin, D. 1991. *The Prize: The Epic Quest for Oil, Money, and Power.* Simon and Schuster, New York.

Yoffee, N., and G. L. Cowgill, eds. 1988. *The Collapse of Ancient States and Civilizations.* Univ. of Arizona Press, Tucson.

Zabel, R. W., C. J. Harvey, S. L. Katz, T. B. Good, and P. S. Levin. 2003. Ecologically sustainable yield. *American Scientist* 91:150–157.

Zakaria, F. 2003. *The Future of Freedom: Illiberal Democracy at Home and Abroad.* W. W. Norton, New York.

Acknowledgments

So many people have contributed over the past half-century to our understanding of the issues discussed in this book that it would be impossible to thank them all. Those who have been kind enough to read and criticize all or part of the manuscript are Loy Bilderback (Department of History, California State University, Fresno); Gerardo Ceballos (Instituto de Ecología, Universidad Nacional Autónoma de México); Kai M. A. Chan, Gretchen Daily, and Stephen Schneider (Department of Biological Sciences, Stanford University); Lisa Daniel (Bureau of Economic Research, Federal Trade Commission—retired); Timothy Daniel (economist, NERA Economic Consulting); Sir Partha Dasgupta (Faculty of Economics and Politics, Cambridge University); Jared Diamond (Department of Geography, University of California, Los Angeles); Walter Falcon (Institute for International Studies, Stanford University); Lawrence Goulder (Department of Economics, Stanford University); John Holdren (John F. Kennedy School of Government and Department of Earth and Planetary Sciences, Harvard University); Vaclav Smil (Department of Geography, University of Manitoba); Tim Wirth (United Nations Foundation); and Wren Wirth (Winslow Foundation).

Other people have been extremely helpful in sending information or clarifying points in conversation. They include Kenneth Arrow (Department of Economics, Stanford University); Katherine Betts (Swinburne University of Technology, Melbourne); David Bishop (Armidale, New South Wales); Carol Boggs (Center for Conservation Biology, Stanford University); William Chameides (School of Atmospheric and Earth Sciences, Georgia Institute of Technology); Marcus Feldman, Harold Mooney, Scott Stephenson, Shripad Tuljapurkar, and Peter Vitousek (Department of Biological Sciences, Stanford University); Cary Fowler (Center for International Environment and Development Studies, Agricultural University of Norway); Peter Gleick (Pacific Institute for Studies in Development, Environment, and Security); Richard Hansen (Foundation for Anthropological Research and Environmental Studies, University of California, Los Angeles); Thomas Lovejoy (The H. John Heinz III Center for Science, Economics and the Environment); Jane Lubchenco (Department of Zoology, Oregon State University); Sally Mallam and Robert Ornstein (Institute for the Study of Human Knowledge); Pamela Matson (Dean, School of Earth Sciences, Stanford University); Colleen Mitchell (Henry Madden Library, California State University, Fresno); Dennis D. Murphy (Biological Resources Research Center, University of Nevada, Reno); Rosamond Naylor, Terry Root, and David Victor (Institute for International Studies, Stanford University); Peter Raven (director, Missouri Botanical Garden); A. A. Rosenberg (Department of Natural Resources, University of New Hampshire); and Michael Soulé (Wildlands Project).

447

Loy Bilderback, Gretchen Daily, Lisa Daniel, Wally Falcon, and Larry Goulder were especially helpful, reading the manuscript more than once and engaging in many discussions of the topics covered. Although we occasionally have not taken their advice, their input has been invaluable.

We are also grateful to the personnel of Ed Zackery Expeditions, in particular David Bishop, Tom Lovejoy, Terry Root, Steve Schneider, and their honorary leader, Tim Daniel, for sharing with us many insights during explorations of the world of wounds.

John Fay, Ann McMillan, Joan Schwan, and Peggy Vas Dias of Stanford's Center for Conservation Biology were, as always, a tremendous help with the diversity of chores that accompany the creation of a book. Jill Otto and the rest of the staff of the Falconer Biology Library again proved that the proximity of that wonderful and obliging facility is a major benefit to any biologist at Stanford. And Pat Browne and Steve Masley handled photocopying chores perfectly, as is their wont.

One of the pleasures of working on this book has been long nights on the telephone and e-mail with our Island Press editor, Jonathan Cobb. We have remained friends since Jonathan worked closely with Paul on *Human Natures,* and our admiration for his skill, knowledge, patience, and perspicacity has only grown. Paul and Jonathan had dinner together in Washington, DC, the awful night of 9/11 (with Jean Black, Jane Lubchenco, Stuart Pimm, and Susan Solomon)—and their conversations that night and the following day formed part of the genesis of *One with Nineveh.* Pat Harris, who also struggled with Paul's writing in *Human Natures,* copyedited this manuscript with the care, insight, and good humor that made her such a pleasure to interact with before. Anne says that Paul now writes books just to maintain his late-night phone and e-mail contacts with our two favorite editors. As before, it has been wonderful to publish with Island Press, a non-profit company struggling to roll back the tide of environmental destruction.

This will be the last book we'll do with our agent of a quarter-century, Virginia Barber. Ginger has retired from the business and will no longer have to listen to our complaints about other publishers (not to be named). Enjoy your rest, Ginger—we sincerely hope *One with Nineveh* makes you a fortune!

Finally, we once again are deeply in debt to the many people who have supported our work over the years, in particular Peter and Helen Bing, Larry Condon, Stanley and Marion Herzstein, Walter and Karen Loewenstern, the late LuEsther T. Mertz, and Wren Wirth. We only wish LuEsther were still with us—she, among our friends, could have described the present political situation most colorfully.

PAUL R. EHRLICH is Bing Professor of Population Studies, Department of Biological Sciences, Stanford University. An expert in the fields of evolution, ecology, taxonomy, and population biology, Ehrlich has conducted fieldwork from the Arctic and the Antarctic to the tropics, and from high mountains to the ocean floor. Professor Ehrlich has written more than 800 scientific papers and popular articles as well as many books, including *The Population Bomb*, *The Process of Evolution*, *The Machinery of Nature*, *The Science of Ecology*, *New World/New Mind*, *Birds in Jeopardy*, *A World of Wounds*, *Human Natures*, and *Wild Solutions*.

Among his many scientific honors, Ehrlich is a Fellow of the American Association for the Advancement of Science (AAAS) and the American Academy of Arts and Sciences, an honorary member of the British Ecological Society, and a member of the United States National Academy of Sciences and the American Philosophical Society. He was awarded the first AAAS/ Scientific American Prize for Science in the Service of Humanity, and he received the Crafoord Prize in Population Biology and the Conservation of Biological Diversity, an explicit substitute for the Nobel Prize in fields of science for which the latter is not given. Ehrlich has also received a Mac-Arthur Fellowship, the Volvo Environment Prize, the International Center for Tropical Ecology's World Ecology Medal, the International Ecology Institute's ECI Prize, the Dr. A.H. Heineken Prize for Environmental Sciences, and the Blue Planet Prize, and he was the first recipient of the Roger Tory Peterson Memorial Medal.

ANNE H. EHRLICH is Senior Research Associate in the Department of Biological Sciences of Stanford University as well as Policy Coordinator of Stanford's Center for Conservation Biology. She is a Fellow of the American Academy of Arts and Sciences and the Californian Academy of Sciences. Besides having conducted research on butterflies and reef fish, she has worked actively with a number of environmental organizations, including Friends of the Earth and the Sierra Club. She was deeply involved in issues such as the environmental impacts of nuclear war and other problems of population, resources, and the environment. She has served as a government advisor and on boards of directors of several organizations and small foundations.

Anne was co-editor of *Hidden Dangers*, and Anne and Paul together have authored a series of books, including *Ecoscience*, *Extinction*, *Earth*, *The Population Explosion*, *Healing the Planet*, *The Stork and the Plow*, and *Betrayal of Science and Reason*.

Anne and Paul together have jointly received the Sasakawa Environment Prize of the United Nations Environment Programme (UNEP), the Heinz Award in the Environment, the American Humanist Association's Distinguished Service Award, the Nuclear Age Peace Foundation's Distinguished Peace Leadership Award, and the Tyler Prize for Environmental Achievement.

## About the Center for Conservation Biology

In 1984, Paul R. Ehrlich founded Stanford University's Center for Conservation Biology to develop the science of conservation biology and to help devise ways and means to protect Earth's life-support systems.

In pursuit of its mission, the Center for Conservation Biology designs experiments to address specific and general questions in conservation biology. It also conducts research on broad-scale policy issues, including human population growth, overconsumption, environmental deterioration, and ecological economics. Among its major goals are to communicate the results of this scientific and policy research to conservation biologists, reserve managers, planners, non-governmental organizations, decision makers, and the public; to educate students and professionals; and to foster collaboration with other scientists and conservation groups around the world.

The Center for Conservation Biology is part of the Stanford University Department of Biological Sciences and is supported by donations and grants from individuals, private foundations, and corporations.

# Index